S

Historical Foundations
of Music Education
in the United States.

by

Lloyd Frederick Sunderman, *1905 —*

The Scarecrow Press, Inc.
Metuchen, N.J.   1971

Copyright 1971 by Lloyd Frederick Sunderman

ISBN 0-8108-0371-2

Library of Congress Catalog Card Number 75-153812

Preface

It is a grateful hand that has the privilege of making available the contents of this volume. Underwood in his Dedication has said, "Gratitude is but a lame sentiment; thanks, when they are expressed, are often more embarrassing than welcome." Truly, this is not so for this writer, because he is not at all abashed to give credit to the large group of workers who so valiantly aided him in ferreting out the information which made the recording of this story possible.

During the nineteenth century some of the city school board reports were hand-written, incomplete, not indexed, or not paged. This proved to be a severe handicap in locating pertinent information. Also, many of the reports were produced in small quantities or were destroyed by fire, making valuable historical information forever irretrievable.

The following libraries made available their facilities for studying primary and secondary sources of information they possessed: Library of Congress, Washington, D. C.; Eastern Illinois State University, Charleston, Illinois; Minneapolis Public Library, Minneapolis, Minnesota; Minnesota State Historical Library, St. Paul, Minnesota; New York State Public Library, Albany, New York; Oswego Public Library, Oswego, New York; the libraries of Oswego State University of New York, Oswego, New York; Syracuse University, Syracuse, New York; University of Illinois, Urbana, Illinois; University of Minnesota, Minneapolis, Minnesota; Westmar College, Le Mars, Iowa; and University of Toledo, Toledo, Ohio.

Among the primary sources were: New York University, Henry Barnard manuscript letters; reports of the United States Commissioner of Education; State reports; Official State Superintendent of Public Instruction reports; local reports: official City

Superintendent of Public Instruction reports. The secondary sources included: music books and collections; pamphlets; bulletins; books; published articles; theses and dissertations; miscellaneous works.

Many published articles were unsigned, initialed, or signed by city address only. No assumptions have been made as to the exact authorship of such articles. Hundreds of other articles were reviewed, but only those containing pertinent information have been listed.

It is hoped that these pages have brought together much recorded evidence of the historical development of music education in the United States. Although this record is not complete, it should aid the reader in discerning the significant strides music education has made since the signing of the Magna Charta of Music Education in Boston in 1838. The monumental achievements in the early development of music in our public schools were the product of vigorous and intelligent leadership by many men. These were not ordinary men. They were the formulators of concepts for teaching music to children; the experimenters and implementers of refined techniques; the missionaries who championed music as a salubrious experience for children in all American schools.

Lloyd Frederick Sunderman
University of Toledo
Toledo, Ohio

Table of Contents

Page

Preface   iii

Chapter

I: The Beginnings of Singing in America   7

II: The Pestalozzian Concept in American Music
      Education   32

III: The First Champion of American Public School
      Music   39

IV: Lowell Mason: Father of American Music Education   46

V: Boston and the Magna Charta of American Music
      Education   62

VI: The Era of Beginnings--1830-1840.   88

VII: American Music Education--1840-1865.   99

VIII: The Post Civil War Expansion of Music Education   129

IX: Educational Conventions: Their Influence on Early
      American Music Education   179

X: The Advent of Method in Music Education   190

XI: Some Early Concepts of the Educational Values
      of Music Education   202

XII: Supervisional and Instructional Aspects of Early
      Music Education   211

XIII: Early Music Instruction in Higher Education   230

XIV: Early Music Education for the Physically
      Handicapped   251

XV: Post World War I--Music Education's Forward
      Thrust   255

XVI: The Depression Years--Music Education Moves
      Forward   279

v

Chapter		Page
XVII:	After World War II	305
XVIII:	The Professional Musician and the Professional Music Educator	314
XIX:	The Professional Organization of Music Educators	336

Appendices

I:	Some Early Leaders and Educators in American Music Education	363
II:	Some Significant Events in Music Education 1603-1895	365
III:	Cities Which Pioneered in Music Education: A Chronological List by Earliest Dates Known	371
IV:	Some Statistical Evidences of the Growth of American Music Education Before 1890	377

Bibliography	402
Name Index	439
Subject Index	445

I: THE BEGINNINGS OF SINGING IN AMERICA[1]

Music in our public schools is accepted today as normal and customary. Group, choral, and assembly singing are so frequent as to excite little comment and no wonderment. So well developed is the practice of singing that it is difficult now to visualize schools in which music is not offered. But it was not always so. In fact, the development was slow, painful, and prolonged.

Numerous obstacles confronted the progress of early American music education. America has produced a musical heritage which was founded originally on three possible cultures: that of the Indians, the Negroes and, to a lesser degree, the people of the Old World. The culture of the Indians was savage, unmusical, and foreign to the white man's mode of musical expression. The Negro gave us the spiritual, a product of his emotionality and the white man's Christianity. The Englishmen sang their songs of Old England with no apparent attempt to fuse them with the cultural life of the New World. The chorale and the congregational hymn singing popularized by Martin Luther, although manifest in idea and expression through the Ainsworth version of the Psalms, soon became sterile.

Without a significant cultural heritage, early American music was nurtured under unfavorable circumstances. Our forefathers were here for the purpose of creating a "living for life" which was to be politically and religiously dissimilar to their Old World environment. When they arrived, they were primarily concerned with meeting physical requirements. For the first one hundred and fifty years they were occupied almost solely in the struggle for existence. Artistic and leisure-time pleasures were taboo because of religious intolerance.

The earliest of civilized music in America was not an indigenous product but an ecclesiastical gift. The Church became the

7

patron saint of early music education in America. Long before the
Pilgrim fathers landed at Plymouth, the Franciscan Friars had settled in what is now known as Florida, teaching vocal and instrumental
music in their schools. Their first students were the Indians whom
they wished to Christianize and educate. The Franciscans of Florida
are known to have started a school at St. Augustine as early as
1603.

The seventeenth century saw the spread of Franciscan education from the West Indies and Mexico to New Mexico and lower
California in the southwest, and later to Texas and Louisiana in the
south. Of their work in New Mexico, Spell relates that, in 1630,
approximately 60,000 Indians were being educated.[2] In the rebellion
of 1680, many of the Franciscan monasteries were destroyed. With
the rebellion over, the Friars continued their work of evangelization
and education.

The effectiveness of the Franciscan music work was seriously
hampered at the beginning of the eighteenth century. Spain, the
mother country, declining as a world power, was finding it impossible to furnish money to the extent that her New World projects had
demanded during the seventeenth century. But even with ever-dimin-
ishing financial support, the Franciscans forged ahead. They followed the Spaniards into Texas (c. 1679) and extended musical and
educational philosophy wherever they could. By 1727 the work had
spread to Louisiana where the Ursulines had established a school
for girls. Both instrumental and vocal music instruction became a
part of their curriculum.[3]

Engelhardt speaks of the early musical accomplishments of
those Indians and whites who studied with the Franciscans. He points
out that all were taught how to chant the whole service of the
Catholic Church. The performance of the music was done in a
cappella or unaccompanied style.[4]

In the Mississippi Valley the French Catholic missionaries were
brilliantly demonstrating their educational zeal. At Kaskaskia and
Mackinaw, during the eighteenth century, both Indians and Whites
were being taught singing in addition to other subjects. Early
Catholic schools were also located at Detroit, St. Louis, and

Vincennes.

While monastic music education was under the direction of the Franciscans, Ralph Crouch started at Newton, Maryland, what is considered the first Catholic elementary school to be regularly established in the English colonies. Lamek indicates that singing was a part of Crouch's curriculum. A study of early Catholic elementary education reveals the frequency with which music was to be found in their programs of study. [5]

Edwards claims that the first celebration of the mass in New England took place on Holy Cross Island in the St. Croix in July, 1604. In 1611 two French Jesuits arrived at Port Royal, Nova Scotia. One of them, Rev. Peter Biard, traveled through Maine and celebrated mass on the eastern shore of Mount Desert Island about 1613. Bancroft has confirmed the singing propensities of the heathen Indians of Maine during this pre-colonization period. [6]

In 1643 there came to Canada Father Gabrielle Druillettes who taught singing to the Indians. A year after his arrival in Quebec, he left on a winter hunt with the Algonquin Indians. It is related that wherever they went he and his Indian cohorts built chapels, performed mass, sang, and offered prayer.

A mission which had been established in 1646 at Norridgewock, Maine, was happily favored by the arrival of Father Sebastian Rale, who had sailed from La Rochelle for Quebec, July 23, 1689. Father Rale quickly realized the need for communication, and that it could only be obtained by means of a thorough study of the Indian languages used in the area. After five months of assiduous study, he was capable of translating many of the masses and chants into the Indians' native parlance. By 1693 he had formed a choir of forty young Indians at Norridgewock, whose members were

> provided with cassocks and surplices to assist at services and to chant hymns for processions in which great numbers of Indians, many of whom came from long distances, participated. This is believed to have been the first attempt to organize a choir or teach choral singing on Maine soil. [7]

The coming of the English to Jamestown and the Pilgrims to Plymouth introduced a new element. They represented the protestant branch of early religious education. Where the Franciscan

and Catholic education embraced music as an indispensable part
of their liturgical service, the English did not permit music in
any form during their church service.   Music, being overtly joyous
and emotional, was tabooed as wordly and secular.   The early
colonizers were not interested in accepting Old World practices,
musical or other.

The Puritans brought with them a single singing book, primarily a manual of psalmody, known as Ainsworth's version of the
Psalms.   This manual was used until the New England version of
it came into being, under the title The Bay Psalm Book.   This
work was a re-composition of the Psalms, done according to the
convictions of a group of about thirty ministers who had arrived
in the colonies by 1636.   It was through their concerted efforts
that The Bay Psalm Book became a reality.   Some of the more
important men involved in making the translation were Welde and
Eliot of Roxbury, and Mather of Dorchester, Massachusetts.
This work marked the beginning of American produced song books.
Most authorities consider the work the first publication in America.

Although The Bay Psalm Book came into being in 1640, not
every singer and church adopted the new edition at once.   The
church at Plymouth, the first in New England, continued to use
the Ainsworth version until the year 1692.   The Ainsworth edition
was used by Pilgrims and Puritans alike.   The Puritans of Boston
and the Pilgrims of Plymouth were distrustful of music, secular
or sacred.

By 1647 a second edition of The Bay Psalm Book has been
printed in the colonies. [8] After the second edition, which was
somewhat enlarged, the Rev. Henry Dunster, President of Harvard
College, and Richard Lyon were appointed as a committee to bring
about another revision which appeared in 1650. [9]

Prior to 1690 The Bay Psalm Book was very likely the only
book used extensively in New England churches.   For fifty years
after the first edition, very little was done to improve the method
of singing in congregational work.   The number of tunes in the
book rarely exceeded five or six. [10] Records indicate that the book

was not even used in Salem, Massachusetts until 1667.

Other churches, such as the First Church in Ipswich, adopted The Bay Psalm Book about the time that it was in use at Salem. By 1692 the church at Plymouth had adopted it. Many of the churches would keep their congregation after the service to learn the new translations which were different from the Ainsworth edition. During the seventeenth century some churches permitted only the saved to sing, while the whole congregation joined in on the Amen. There were still others who countenanced private singing with the aid of the accompaniment.

Down to the year 1700 many of the church congregations were capable of singing only three or four psalm tunes. There was a definite need to add tunes to the Psalm books to alleviate the monotony of singing so few tunes, and it was this need that directly brought about the printing of new music in America.

The Bay Psalm Book went through many editions and many forms, but without major alteration. The book was published in many countries. In Scotland it passed through twenty-two editions, the last edition coming in 1756. In England it was produced in at least eighteen editions. [11] In America, innumerable editions appeared; twenty-six had been produced by 1744. In Antiquarian Hall at Worcester, Massachusetts, there is a copy of the twenty-seventh edition; the exact date does not appear in the preface, but unquestionably it was completed between 1746 and 1750. [12] The total number of editions produced in America and Europe would in all probability reach seventy or more. The seventieth edition, which, according to some authorities, was the last, appeared in 1773.

Although The Bay Psalm Book dominated in America, there was also the Sternhold and Hopkins edition of Psalmody which had been produced in England in 1549; a second edition appeared in 1553. One of its many editions, produced in Cambridge in 1693, was being used in Ipswich, according to an old record of that city. [13] Hood claims that although it was not very popular it did have some usage until the time of the American Revolution. [14]

From the scanty memoriter or rote singing stage of The Bay
Psalm Book and the Sternhold and Hopkins Psalmody, progress
could be seen by 1712, when the reading and learning aspects of
congregational singing began to appear. Rev. Tufts, pastor of
the Second Church in Newbury, Massachusetts, published in 1712
a Layman's psalm book designed to facilitate the learning of psalm
singing through a new approach. [15] He produced another work about
1712-1714 which was bound up with The Bay Psalm Book. [16] In
addition there was a "Supplement containing other Scripture Songs;
placed in order as in the Bible, " containing fifty-eight pages. His
second work introduced letters which were used on the staff instead
of notes; syllable names were used. In addition, five lines were
used and time was indicated. The music was in three parts and
the style was purely choral, the choral style being the only one
employed during that era.

In 1718 Dr. Cotton Mather published his Psalterium America-
num. This book of psalms was all in blank verse, suited to the
tunes then in common use in the church. In 1721 Rev. Thomas
Walter produced a singing book which was the fourth book published
in America. [17] His work, the first one in America to be printed
with bars, was purely choral in style, had three parts and harmony
which was rich and full, and possessed a degree of correctness.
Before the appearance of Walter's Book, no music had been
published in the colonies except that which had appeared in The Bay
Psalm Book.

In early colonial times, there was little part singing, and,
as previously noted, most of the church congregations used only two,
three, or four tunes. It is hardly possible to appreciate the
limited scope of the colonial church goer's singing experiences.
In many churches, even if some of the members possessed a song
book, they would be musically incapable of reading a line. Most
of the singing was taught by the "lining out" method. The pastor
would sing a phrase or line and the congregation would repeat it
in rote fashion.

Unquestionably the singing of church congregations in the
American colonies up to the middle of the eighteenth century was
most uncultivated and distressing to the human ear.   Rev. Walter
says that it sounded "like five hundred different tunes roared out
at the same time. "   Reverend Symmes states that it "is with great
difficulty that this part of worship is performed, and with indecency
in some congregations for want of skill.   It is to be feared, singing must be wholly omitted in some places, for want of skill, if
this art is not revived. "[18]

Beginning about 1720 there was apparently a movement afoot
which had as its particular design the improvement of church singing.   Some of the men who participated in the reform were:
Mathers, Edwards, Stoddard, Symmes, Dwight, Wise, Walter,
Thacher, and Prince.   They represented a type of progressive
lay musical leadership which was none too prevalent during those
colonial days.   A majority of the population was more interested
in subduing the frontier than in learning how to sing.

There must nevertheless, have been some unspoken interest
hidden beneath the lethargy of the masses, because when the time
came for reform and suggestions were offered, many people opposed
the idea.   Some of the principal objections were that:

1.   It was a new way---an unknown tongue.
2.   It was not so melodious as the usual way.
3.   There were so many tunes, one could never learn
     them.
4.   The new way made disturbance in churches, grieved
     good men, exasperated them and caused them to be
     disorderly.
5.   It was popish.
6.   It would introduce instruments.
7.   The names of the notes were blasphemous.
8.   It was needless, the old way being enough.
9.   It was only a contrivance to get money.
10. It required too much time to learn it, made the young
     disorderly, and kept them from the proper influence
     of the family, etc., etc. [19]

At this point our study of early American music and its
beginnings must be considered in the light of its maternal or
paternal guide, the church.   What may be regarded as native

American music began with the Pilgrims and Puritans. It would
be incorrect to state that no music existed in America before 1620.
Unquestionably the men who came to Virginia in 1607 sang of dear
England. We know very little, however, about the extent of music
skills in Virginia during the early seventeenth century.

A book, Observations Made by the Curious in New England,
produced in London in 1673, stated that "In Boston there are no
musicians by trade." What was true of the period prior to 1673,
however, certainly could not be applied to the period between
1700 and 1775. Although colonial New England may have been
devoid of musical opportunities, such was not the case in colonial
Boston. Seybolt[20] has pointed out that during the colonial period,
music in many forms was being taught professionally by a number
of gentlemen. From Seybolt we learn conclusively that music and
music teaching were common in Boston.

1713

AT THE HOUSE of Mr. George Brownell in Wings-Lane
Boston, is taught Writing, Cyphering, Dancing, Treble
Violin, Flute, Spinnet, &c. Also English and French
Quilting, etc. . . . . [21]

1714

AT THE HOUSE of Mr. James Ivers, formerly call'd the
Bowling Green House in Cambridge-Street Boston, is now
set up a Boarding School, where will be carefully Taught,
Flourishing, Embroidery, and all Sorts of Needle-Work,
also Filigrew, Painting upon Glass, Writing, Arithmetick,
and Singing Psalm Tunes. [22]

1720

THIS is to acquaint all Gentlemen and others, that Edward
Enstone, Dancing Master is removed to a Large House in
King Street Boston, where young Ladies may be accommo-
dated with Boarding, and taught all sorts of Needle-Work
with Musick and Dancing, &c. [23]

1730

WHEREAS JOHN WAGHORNE, now resident in Boston, has
been often requested by some of the principal Gentlemen
of this Town, to instruct their Children in Vocal Psalmody,
with a Promise of Encouragement; and he having now a

suitable House for that Purpose, therefore this is to
inform such Persons who will think proper to send their
Children, that said Waghorne intends to instruct Youth in
the Gamut and Measure of Notes &c. according to the
Method of the famous Dr. Crafts, late Organist and Composer to his Majesty's Chappel, and will attend on Monday,
Wednesday, and Friday, from 4 to 6 o'clock in the afternoon. [24]

1743

MR. PETER PELHAM, Jun. who has been from Boston
for these Nine Years past, under the Tuition of an Accomplish'd Professor of the Art of Musick, is now return'd;
and ready to attend Ladies and Gentlemen as a Tutor in
that Art, on the Harpsicord or Spinnet. And further
offers his Attendance on young Ladies and Gentlemen at
his Father's House (or School in Leveret's Lane near King
Street) on Mondays, Wednesdays and Fridays, from Six to
Eight in the Evening (or to Nine if requisite) in order to
Teach the Rudiments of Psalmody, Hymns, Anthems, &c. [25]

1751

TO BE TAUGHT

BY Messirs Skiner Russell and Moses Deshon, at the
House of the said Deshon's in Dock Square, Psalmody in
the best Manner, where any young Gentlemen and Ladies
may apply for Information on what Condition they are to be
taught, or at Mr. Russel's Shop a little below the Draw-
Bridge, Boston. [26]

1753

NOTICE is hereby given to the Publick, That JOHN RICE,
lately from New-York, and Organist of Trinity-Church in
this Town, proposes to teach young Gentlemen and Ladies,
Vocal and Instrumental Musick, viz. Spinnet, or Harpsicord, Violin, German Flute, &c. and is to be spoke with
at Mrs. Harvey's, behind Capt. Tyng's, in Row's Lane.

Boston, November, 17, 1753. [27]

1768

JACOB BUCKNAM Begs Leave to inform the Public,
That he has just opened a singing School, at a convenient
Chamber in Long-Lane at the House of Mr. John Boice --
where young Gentlemen and Ladies may be taught the Art
of Psalmody at a reasonable Rate. The said School will
be kept every Monday and Wednesday Evening. If any

1768 cont.

Gentlemen will send their Children, it will be gratefully
acknowledged by their Humble Servant.

JACOB BUCKNAM. [28]

1769

JOHN BARRY & WILLIAM BILLINGS

BEGS Leave to inform the Publick, that they propose to
open a Singing School THIS NIGHT, near the Old South
Meeting-House, where any Person inclining to learn to
Sing may be attended upon at said School with Fidelity
and Dispatch. [29]

1770

JAMES JOAN

HEREBY acquaints the Publick, that he has removed into
the House lately occupied by Mr. Wallis, nearly opposite
to Bejamin Hallowell, jun. Esqr's, in Hanover-Street,
where he teaches the Violin, Bass-Viol., and German
Flute; He also teaches the French Language, either
grammatically or methodically with its true accent and
pronunciation, it being his Mother Tongue, which he has
taught for several Years past:

The Manufacture of Violins, Bass-Viols, &c. is still
carried on by him at said Place, in the greatest Perfection,
from two to ten Guineas Price. [30]

1771

DAVID PROPERT
Professor of Musick

TAKES THIS METHOD of acquainting the Ladies and Gentlemen of this Town and Neighbourhood, That he teaches the
Harpsichord, Forte Piano, Guittar, German Flute, &c.
and has imported a Variety of new Musick and Musical
Instruments, among which is a very fine Tone Harpsichord,
and a Forte Piano, all which he disposes of at Mr. Roger's
near Peter Chardon, Esq.; in Cambridge-Street, Boston. [31]

1773

MOSES DESHON

TAKES this Method to acquaint the Publick, That he purposes, on suitable Encouragement, to open a SINGING

<u>1773</u> cont.

> SCHOOL, for the Instruction of Youth in the Art of
> Psalmody, on Tuesday and Friday Evenings, from Six to
> Nine O'Clock in the Evening, at his Auction-Room in Ann-
> Street, if a suitable Number appears. [32]

The above excerpts indicate clearly that the private schools
of colonial Boston offered a wide variety of music for study. The
principal instruments studied were the harpsichord, spinet, flute,
violin, and bass-viol. The colonial Bostonian's singing was confined to special private singing lessons, learning the art of psalmody
and hymnology.

For any individual during the early settlement period to suggest
singing or performing instrumental music during a church service,
or even at a secular meeting of any kind, would have been considered gross heterodoxy. The Puritans of early Boston and the Pilgrims
of Plymouth were very skeptical about the merits and the influences
of music.

The first hundred and fifty years of psalm singing in America
(1620-1770) had dulled the musical sensitivity of the people. The
continued drawling of tunes was enough to disgust even the most
unmusical person. Billings, the untrained musician, had attempted,
through the composition of his fuguing tunes,[33] to arouse the people
to higher levels of music appreciation. The music of the Old
World had become decadent in a narrow religious environment.
Music in the New World was now to become an adulterated indigenous expression of Old World music and New World philosophies of life and thought.

The inception of the practice of "lining out"[34] music in early
times resulted from the scarcity of psalm books, and from recognition that the average layman was illiterate musically. The
dreadful state of singing in the churches was responsible for the
beginning of singing-schools. They started simply as a means of
correcting the singing practices which were prevalent during the
beginnings of our country. The need to eliminate the old "tune for
a psalm idea" was beyond the comprehension of many of those

early consecrated souls, however, for they had come to revere
the tune and a given psalm as much as the words of the scripture
itself.   Any attempt to develop a new style of singing meant to a
vast number of the people secularization of that which was held
sacred.   Some of the questions which were discussed relative to
the improvement were:

> Whether you do believe that the singing in the worship
> of God ought to be done skilfully?

> Whether you do believe that skilfulness in singing may
> ordinarily be gained in the use of outward means, by the
> blessing of God?

> Is it possible for Fathers of forty years old and upward to
> learn to sing by rule?   And ought they to attempt at that
> age to learn?[35]

It was said that the old style of singing was so slow and
drawled out that many of the people would take a breath twice
during the chanting or singing of one word.   A step in the right
direction was the beginning of "singing by note," which all authors
seem to agree started about 1720. [36]   Rev. Thomas Symmes' essay,
defense of singing by note, was entitled The Reasonableness of
Regular Singing, or, Singing by Note.   Symmes was probably one
of the earliest to recommend the opening of singing schools. [37]
In 1727 there appeared another essay by Rev. Chauncery, with
the caption, Regular Singing defended, and proved to be the only
Way of Singing the Songs of the Lord.
    A variety of arrangements as to the style of singing to be
practiced were made after the introduction of the idea of singing
by note.   One of the most interesting of these was that the
congregation was permitted to sing half of the music by note and
the other half by rote.[38]   Often, the congregation's singing was
done alternatively: first one song would be sung by rote and then
one by note.   Many other writers, notably Dwight, Thacher, Dan-
forth, and Mather, began to take up the defense of note singing.
From about 1720 to 1790 the battle for note singing as against the
old "lining out" method was fought vigorously.   In many communities
the struggle was extremely bitter.

By 1742 note singing was accepted at Hanover, Massachusetts.
With the increasing agitation for the note style of music presenta-
tion, singing-schools appeared in scattered sections of New England.
They were started by heretic musicians who had turned against the
prevailing, "accepted" style of singing. In 1720, Dr. Benjamin
Coleman's society opened its first singing school in Brattle Street,
Boston.   One of the earliest in a country town was one opened at
Hadley by John Stickney and his wife.[39]

Thomas Symmes, who spoke and wrote in favor of the movement, had urged in 1720 the immediate establishment of the singing-school.   Again, in 1723, he pleaded,

> Would it not greatly tend to promote singing of psalms if
> singing schools were promoted? Would not this be con-
> forming to scripture pattern? Have we not as much need
> of them as God's people of old? Have we any reason to
> expect to be inspired with the gift of singing, any more
> than that of reading?[40]

The first record of the establishment of a singing-school in
America bears the date 1717;[41] the school was located in Boston.
Other schools were later established by John Sather, at Charlestown, S. C. , in 1730; by James Lyon, in Philadelphia, in 1750; by
the Moravian foundation of Nazareth Hall, in Pennsylvania, after
1759.[42] Josiah Davenport was a teacher of singing in Philadelphia
about 1757, and William Tuckey taught in New York about 1754.[43]
Just as one scientific invention stimulates other new discoveries,
so the stimulation of the singing-school fostered a demand for
choir-singing and musical training in the public schools.

Development of the Singing-School.   The singing-school was
probably the most responsible factor in encouraging the production
of psalm-singers during the middle years of the eighteenth century
(1725-1775).   By 1800 the singing-school and society had found its
way from Maine to the Carolinas and Georgia.   There was no
universal adoption of note singing but prejudice against the singing-
school gradually gave way to a certain degree of toleration.   Many
of the singing-school meetings were often intermittently attended.
If an assembly of singers could get together once a week, it was

something of a victory; poor transportation, inclement weather, lack of finances and materials were among the handicaps they faced.

The movement, nevertheless, was a unifying force, bringing men and women together in a common place to pursue a common interest. The musical literature and tutelage of the singing-school movement received great impetus from the following singing-school missionaries:

Table I

Early Singing-School Teachers

Name	Dates
Bailey, Daniel	c 1725-1799
Lyon, James Rev.	1735-1794
Hopkinson, Francis	1737-1791
Flagg, Josiah	c 1738-1794
Selby, William	1738-1798
Billings, William	1746-1800
Law, Andrew	1748-1821
French, Jacob	1754- ?
Read, Daniel	1757-1836
Swan, Timonthy	1758-1842
Kimbal, Jacob, Jr.	1761-1826
Holyoke, Samuel A.	1762-1820
Holden, Oliver	1765-1834?
Cheney, Moses	1776- ?
Gould, Nathaniel D.	1781-1864
Hastings, Thomas	1787-1872
Mason, Lowell	1792-1872
Webb, George J.	1803-1887
Baker, Benjamin F.	1811-1889
Bradbury, William B.	1816-1868
Woodbury, Isaac B.	1819-1858
Root, George F.	1820-1895
Emerson, Luther O.	1820-1915

From 1720 to approximately 1775, most of the singing-schools scarcely dealt with the theory of music. The principal job was getting people to sing melody correctly, and to approximate the singing of correct rhythm. It is difficult to visualize what happened at these singing-school meetings, but one definite record exists in the diary of Dr. Samuel Sewall. Under the date of March 16, 1721, he notes that in Boston,

> At night Dr. Mather preaches in the School-House to the young musicians, from Rev. 14. 3. -- No man could learn that song. -- House was full and the singing extraordinarily excellent, such as had hardly been heard before in Boston. -- Sung four times out of Tate and Brady.[44]

It is highly probable that Tate and Brady were two English poets who had published a book of Psalms in meter before 1696. The edition employed at the above meeting was probably an English one because no American edition of their work had been produced.[45]

The old-fashioned singing-school was very simple in its organization. In 1798, Andrew Law of Salem, Massachusetts, was holding singing classes at Hartford, Connecticut, meeting his singers three times a week between the hours of 5 and 7 P.M.[46] He was charging a fee of two dollars per quarter for instruction. A Cincinnati, Ohio advertisement, dated Dec. 27, 1800, stated that "Those gentlemen and ladies who feel disposed to Patronize a SINGING SCHOOL will please to convene at the court house to-morrow night, as it is proposed to have singing. They will please bring their books with them." In another place, in 1801, a "Levi McLean advertises his singing school, $1.00 for thirteen nights, or $2.00 per quarter; subscribers to find own wood and candles."[47]

A singing teacher of prominence, who was advertising in 1796-97, was Samuel Holyoke of Salem, Massachusetts. By 1806 he was the operator of two schools, one for vocal and the other for instrumental music. In 1808 his singing classes, as a part of their public program, performed the "Hallelujah Chorus" from Handel's Messiah.

The advent of note singing in the United States was the first great step toward attempting music education for all. And the singing-society merits recognition as the first effective institution to bring such an educational opportunity to the layman. The eighteenth century ushered in a period of musical instruction, in which the factual aspects of the printed music page were to receive intelligent consideration. The singing-society and note-singing brought about a demand for music materials; it was now natural to expect the appearance of those who could create for the market which had been established.

William Billings was our first native, self-taught, composer
to meet the challenge.   In 1770 appeared his first work, <u>The New
England Psalm Singer of the American Chorister.</u> [48]   One of the
best works Billings produced, and which he himself considered
as such, was a collection of tunes entitled the <u>Singing Master's
Assistant,</u> published in 1778.   Although his "fuguing tunes" could
not be considered the finest of musical literature, he did arouse
a response, and helped to popularize more interesting music.   One
of his tunes, "Chester," was called the "Battle Hymn of the
Revolution."   It was the only tune that the Continental pipers
used when on the march.   Billings, a devoted patriot and a friend
of Samuel Adams, experienced great popularity during his time.
He was not a great musician in any exact sense of the word,
consequently, his compositions are considered of value only as
"firsts" of an American non-trained musician who took his profession seriously.

Before Billings, there had appeared two of our earliest
American composers, the Rev. James Lyon and Francis Hopkinson.
The former excelled in sacred composition and the latter in secular.
These men were not professional musicians.   They pursued music
solely as an avocation.

The dark ages of American music education may be considered
as the period prior to 1815.   The advent of note-singing, the singing-school, and the lay singing-society were potent factors, however,
in the improvement of American music education.   The teaching of
singing by note in the singing-school was the average man's
opportunity to learn how to follow notes; the singing-school, a
forerunner of systematized music instruction, was a place where
people came together to learn how to read music by note and
according to rule; and the rise of lay and professional singing-
societies was a major fruition of the progress begun by the singing-
school.

The early singing-school and singing-society are almost
synonymous, though the latter certainly functioned at a higher level

of musical efficiency.   The objectives of the two institutions were
different.   The former was interested in teaching people how to
read music, whereas the latter was primarily concerned with
performance.

The oldest singing-society still in existence is the Stoughton
Musical Society of Stoughton, Massachusetts, organized in 1786.
In addition to Stoughton, it was also active in Canton and Sharon.
The Euterpeiad (Boston, May 21, 1821) gives an account of the
growth of the early singing activities in America.   Directly after
1800, Dartmouth College had a Handel singing society, presenting
oratorio performances and lectures on music.   The Massachusetts
Musical Society, organized in 1807, lasted three years.   In the
Portland Gazette, January 17, 1814, there appeared an official
notice regarding the Handel Society of Maine:

> The members of the Handel Society of Maine are hereby
> notified that their first meeting will be holden in Portland
> on Thursday, the third day of February next at 10 o'clock
> A. M. in the Chamber over the Portland Bank.   A general
> attendance is requested not only for the purpose of musical
> performance, but the choice of officers and the adoption
> of necessary regulations. [49]

Under the date of February 7, 1814, the Portland Gazette
carried an editorial entitled "Handel Society," indicating that

> On Thursday last the Handel Society of Maine held their
> first meeting in Portland for the organization of the
> Society.   We understand it consists of Gentlemen in
> various parts of the District, whose object in associating
> is to promote a taste for correct, refined and Classical
> and Church Musick.
>
> John Merrick of Hallowell was chosen President; John
> Watson of Portland, Secretary; Horatio Southgate, Esq. do.
> Treasurer; Prentiss Mellen, Esq. Vice President of the
> Section in Cumberland; Dr. Samuel Emerson, do. do.
> York; Mr. John Eveleth, Vice-President, do. do. Kenne-
> beck; and Professor Abbott, do. do. Lincoln.
>
> Messrs. Merrick, Mellen, and Southgate were the standing
> Committee to superintend Musical publications proposed
> by any member of the society. [50]

The ambitious program the society outlined is really most
admirable, and its idea of publications was unquestionably one of

the first in early New England choral history. The society did not
exist very long; however, it is known that it continuted as least
down to 1817. Just how long it existed after that the available
records do not accurately indicate. [51]

Coming directly on the heels of the organization of the Handel
Society of Maine was the formulation of the Hancock Musical
Association of Bangor, Maine. Knowledge about its beginning is
vague; some people have suggested 1816. There are no extant
records that reveal exactly how long the organization continued to
function. [52]

One of the greatest choral societies in America was the
Handel and Haydn Society of Boston, founded in 1815. No other
organization can boast a greater musical heritage. Another was
the Musical Fund Society of Philadelphia, founded January 7, 1820.
It was under the auspices of this society that the first performance
of the oratorio, "The Creation," was given in Philadelphia, on
June 10, 1822. [53] The society made three distinct contributions
to the musical life of its city: 1) It stimulated interest in early
choral, chamber-music, and orchestral performances; 2) It brought
to Philadelphia outstanding concert artists; 3) It founded the first
music school in Philadelphia, which also was one of the first in
America for non-commercial purposes.

TABLE II

Some Significant Choral Organizations

Society	Location	When Organized
Orpheus*	Philadelphia, Pa.	1759
St. Cecilia Society	Charleston, S. C.	1762
Handel Society, Dartmouth College	Hanover, N. H.	1780
Stoughton Musical Society	Stoughton, Mass.	1786
Handel and Haydn Society	Boston, Mass.	1815
Sacred Music Society	New York, N. Y.	1823
Musical Institute	New York, N. Y.	1844

*Avowedly the first in America

The importance of these early singing-societies lay in their ability to: 1) Provide an outlet for the development of American singing talent; 2) Set standards of attainment for other musically minded individuals and groups; 3) Bring outstanding choral works before the public; 4) Increase commercial and professional opportunities for concert singers and conductors; 5) Give impetus to the singing-school movement. The singing-society, in promoting opportunities for lay and professional musicians, became also the major agent in creating opportunities for the encouragement of secular song creation.

Although emphasis has been placed here upon sacred music, and rightfully so, secular aspects of music education began to emerge during the period under consideration. It is not possible to say when secular music first appeared in this country, but between 1720 and 1800 some private concerts containing secular music were presented in New England. In 1768 a concert of secular music had been presented in Boston at the Music Hall; after the program a ball was given. This custom was followed by many persons in charge of musicales during the colonial period. Elson relates that by 1798 a secular song book appeared, containing "Sentimental, Convivial, Humorous, Satirical, Pastoral, Hunting, Sea, and Masonic Songs."[54]

For the most part the programs were presentations of individual concert pieces, both instrumental and vocal in character. Closer to the revolutionary period the secular song became patriotic in character. The War of Independence popularized "Yankee Doodle" and the War of 1812 added "The Star Spangled-Banner" to the growing list of patriotic songs.

The history of the church choir in the United States reveals the snail-like progress of its growth prior to the nineteenth century. The choral society and the church choir came into existance during the latter half of the eighteenth century. One of the earliest parish charity schools, organized in New York City in 1709, for many years offered a crude form of choir training. By 1761 boys were used in the singing service of the Old Trinity Church in New York

City. The records of Rowley, Ipswich, Hamilton, and Chebacco,
Massachusetts reveal that, before 1788, churches in those
communities were considering the proper place for the seating of
those members of the congregation "who have learned the art of
singing. "[55] In many churches singers with special ability were
allowed to come to the front of the church and help in leading the
congregational singing. Historically, the earliest vested male
choir was in St. Michael's Church, Charleston, South Carolina,
as early as 1798. [56]

Following the singing-school, the singing-society, the church
choir, and the public concert, another musical hybrid sprang-up,
known as the musical convention. It was created because of the
need of music teachers to exchange ideas about better methods of
presenting the content of their subject. During the first half of
the nineteenth century the music teaching specialist was very rare,
and there was a great need for better preparation of people interested in teaching music.

Superstition hampered the growth of music education from
its very beginnings in America. The protestant church tolerated
music only as an adjunct to the liturgical service. Some people
considered musical experience to be enjoyed only by the worldly
or sinful. But the dawn of the nineteenth century American music
education had come a long way. The increased toleration for note-
singing instead of rote, the creation of the singing-school, the
development of the musical convention, the church choir, and the
appearance of America's first serious composer, Billings, had
created a market for musical merchandise.

Although the manufacture of musical instruments may have pre-
dated 1700, we know that in America their production received more
attention after 1725. A Swede, Gustavus Hesselius, was making
spinets by 1742. Another spinet maker was John Harris of Boston.
The Boston Gazette for February 10, 1770 has an advertisement
commending American spinets as being superior to European makes.[57]
The spinet and harpsichord reigned supreme during the eighteenth
century. A few piano-fortes were to be found in the wealthier

homes by the close of the century.   About this time we find that
Captain Benjamin Davis was operating a store on Great Dock Street
in New York City where he sold

> ruling pens for musick books, harpsichord hammers, with
> a variety of musick and blank music books, charms for
> violins. [58]

The scant available evidence indicates however, that the manufacture of American musical instruments prior to 1825 was
negligible.

Summary

This opening chapter endeavors to trace the significant
happenings in American music education from 1600-1830.   A
chronological treatment of the more significant developments of
this period is as follows: 1)   Early music education was first
offered under the auspices of the Catholic Church;   2)   Early
protestant skepticism about the place and value of music in the
liturgical service retarded musical growth;   3)   The Bay Psalm Book
became the first American produced psalm-singer;   4)   This was
the era of the transition from the "Lining out" to the "note method"
of teaching and reading music;   5)   The professional private music
teacher came on the scene;   6)   The singing-school and the singing-
school teacher made significant contributions to the growth of early
American music;   7)   William Billings, America's first native self-
taught composer, began his creative work in secular and sacred
composition;   8)   The early American singing-society became an
established institution;   9)   There was a growth and a limited
acceptance of secular music and musical composition;   10)   The
American church choir became an experimental reality;   11)   The
musical convention arose as a response to the need for teacher-
training;   12)   The manufacture of musical instruments began to
find its place in American industrial life.

Together these events assured a quickening of the cultural
pulse of the nineteenth century American citizen.   It was musical
achievement upon which future growth was certain to be realized.

Notes

1. Sunderman, Lloyd F. "The Beginning of Singing in
    America," The Journal of Musicology, Vol. III. No. 2
    (Fall, 1941), 101-119. This chapter appeared as an
    article as indicated. Changes have been made where
    evidence warrants. Reprinted with the permission of
    Bennett Shimp, Editor, Journal of Musicology.

2. Lamek, John E. "Music Instruction in Catholic Ele-
    mentary Schools." Unpublished Doctoral Dissertation.
    New York University, 1930. 6-7.

3. Gleeson, W. History of the Catholic Church in California
    (Quotation in Lamek) Ibid. , 29.

4. Engelhardt, Zephrin. Catholic Educational Work in
    California (Quotation in Lamek), Ibid. , 366.

5. Lamek, John E. op. cit. , 9-11.

6. Edwards, George T. Music and Musicians of Maine.
    (Portland, Maine: The Southworth Press, 1928), 4.

7. Ibid. , 6.

8. Hood, George. A History of Music in New England:
    With Biographical Sketches of Reformers and Psalmists.
    (Boston, Mass.: Wilkins, Carter and Co. , 1846), 25.

9. Ibid. , 25-26. The revised edition appeared under the
    title: "The Psalms Hymns and Spiritual Songs of the Old
    and New Testament, faithfully translated Into English
    Metre, For The Use, Edification and Comfort of the
    Saints in public and private, especially in New England. "

10. Grove's Dictionary of Music and Musicians, Pratt, Waldo
    Seldon, Editor. Volume 6 (American Supplement).
    (Philadelphia, Pennsylvania: Theodore Presser Company,
    1920), 125-126. Not until the 9th edition (1698) was
    music added, and then only about twelve tunes.

11. The publisher of the seventeenth and eighteenth editions
    in London was J. H. for T. Longman, at the Ship, in
    Pater Noster Row; the first coming in 1737 and latter in
    1754.

12. Hood, George. op. cit. , 50.

13. Ibid. , 60.

14. Ibid. , 60.

15. "A very plain and easy Introduction to the Art of Singing Psalm Tunes: With the Cantos or Trebles of Twenty-eight Psalm Tunes, contrived in such a manner, as that the Learner may attain the Skill of Singing them, with the greatest ease and Speed imaginable. By Rev. Mr. John Tufts. "

16. "An introduction to the singing of Psalm-Tunes; in a plain and easy method; with a Collection of Tunes in three Parts. By the Reverend Mr. Tufts. "

17. "The Grounds and Rules of Musick explained; Or an Introduction to the Art of Singing by Note: Fitted to the meanest capacities. "

18. Hood, George. op. cit., 85.

19. Ibid., 86-87.

20. Seybolt, Robert F. The Private Schools of Colonial Boston, (Cambridge, Mass.: Harvard University Press, 1935), 12-71.

21. The Boston News Letter, Feb. 23-Mar. 2, 2-9, 9-16, 1713.

22. Ibid., Apr. 12-19, 1714.

23. The Boston Gazette, Sept. 12-19, 19-26, Oct. 3, 1720.

24. Ibid., July 9-16, 16-23, 1739.

25. The Boston Evening Post, May 30, June 6, 13, 20, 27, 1743.

26. The Boston Gazette, or Weekly Journal, Jan. 29, 1750-51.

27. The Boston Evening Post, Nov. 19, 26, Dec. 3, 1753.

28. The Boston Gazette and Country Journal, Feb. 8, 15, 22, 1768.

29. Ibid., Oct. 2, 9, 16, 1769.

30. The Massachusetts Gazette and Boston News-Letter, Sept. 6, 13, 20, 1770.

31. The Massachusetts Gazette and The Boston Weekly News-Letter, Jan. 31, 1771. He was an organist at Trinity Church, Boston.

32. Ibid., Dec. 9, 1773. The Boston Gazette and Country Journal, Dec. 13, 1773.

33. "Fuguing Tunes": Billings' definition was, "Music is said to be fuguing when one part comes in after another."

34. Known as reading "between whiles."

35. Hood, George. op. cit., 88-89.

36. Elson, Louis C. The History of American Music. (New York, N.Y.: The Macmillan Company, 1915), 8-11.

37. Ibid., 9. Elson indicates the existance of a singing-school in Boston as early as 1717.

38. Occurred in Glastonbury, Connecticut, February, 1733.

39. Perkins, Charles C. and John S. Dwight. History of the Handel and Haydn Society, (Boston, Mass.: Alfred Mudge and Sons, 1883-1893.), I: 19-20.

40. Mason, Daniel Gregory. The Art of Music. (New York, N.Y.: National Society of Music,   ), 4: 26.

41. Elson, Louis C. op. cit., 9.

42. Brown, Elmer Ellsworth. The Making of Our Middle Schools. (New York, N.Y.: Longmans, Green, and Co., 1902).

43. Birge, Edward Bailey. History of Public School Music in The United States. (Boston, Mass.: Oliver Ditson Co., 1928), 9.

44. Elson, Louis C. op. cit., 11.

45. Ibid., 11.

46. History of the Handel and Haydn Society, 19-20.

47. Shotwell, John B. A History of the Schools of Cincinnati (Cincinnati, Ohio,: The School Life Company, 1902), 531-2.

48. A copy of this work may be found in the Massachusetts Historical Society Library.

49. Edwards, George T. op. cit., 38-39.

50. Ibid., 38-39.

51. Ibid., 38-39.

52. Ibid., 41.

53. The Musical Fund Society of Philadelphia.   Act of
     Incorporation Approved February 22, 1823.   Amendment
     Thereof Approved April 28, 1857.   And By-Laws as
     Revised and Amended May 7, 1912.   Together With a
     List of Officers and Members, Historical Data, and
     List of Portraits.   September, 1930, 62-66.

54. Elson, Louis C.   The National Music of America.
     (Boston, Mass.:   L. C. Page and Company, 1924), 60.

55. Ibid., 50.

56. Lutkin, Peter C.   Music in The Church.   The Hale
     Lectures.   1908-9: (Milwaukee, Wisc.:   The Young
     Churchmen Company, 1910), 188.

57. De Revere, Mary L.   "Public Interest in Music on the
     Eve of the American Revolution."   Unpublished Master's
     Thesis, Columbia University, 1925), 10.

58. Ibid., 12.

II: THE PESTALOZZIAN CONCEPT IN AMERICAN MUSIC EDUCATION

Almost all of the pre-Civil War vocal school music instruction in the American public school systems was guided and patterned according to Pestalozzian principles of teaching. Pestalozzi, the great Swiss educator, ranks high among the men who inspired and greatly influenced American educators. Indirectly, he was an inspirational popularizer of the values to be derived from the study of vocal music in the public schools.

Johann Heinrich Pestalozzi was born at Zurich, Switzerland in 1746. He was the son of a medical practitioner and his mother was a first cousin of the Austrian General Hötze. At the age of six, after his father died, he was left to his mother's care and it was she who attended to his early educational needs. Of this early period he says:

> I was brought up, by the hand of the best of mothers like a spoilt darling, such that you will not easily find a greater. From one year to another I never left the domestic hearth; in short, all the essential means and inducements to the development of manly vigor, manly experiences, manly ways of thinking, and manly exercises, were just as much wanting to me, as, from the peculiarity and weakness of my temperament, I especially needed them.[1]

Under the close scrutiny of his devoted mother, Pestalozzi undoubtedly saw the world "only within the narrow limits of my mother's parlor...to real human life I was almost as great a stranger, as if I did not live in the world in which I dwelt." Protected from much of life's realism, he cultivated a warmth of understanding in keeping with his affectionate and sympathetic mother's understanding.

Pestalozzi was at times an indifferent scholar, but on other occasions demonstrated brilliance, for example in translating one of the orations of Demosthenes from the original Greek. Although Bodmer, Breitinger, and Steinbruchel were among the more influentia teachers who influenced him, it was the work of Rousseau which enlivened his inquiring mind. The works of Rousseau, particularly Emile, which advocated a type of education for the child, gave Pestalozzi the impetus to challenge the then existing formalistic educational tendencies. Rousseau and his system of liberty were a great contrast to the parlor-cloistered education which Pestalozzi received at his mother's feet, and moved Pestalozzi to endeavor to alleviate the human needs of the impoverished.

After the French had laid waste to the Canton of Unterwalden, many children were left homeless and orphaned by the ruthless destruction. Pestalozzi responded by providing shelter for the orphaned; this incident marked the beginning of his educational experience, although, due to lack of personal and outside funds, the project had to be abandoned.

His work at Unterwalden, although shortlived, was widely publicized. This public notice of his many deeds of self-devotion led to his next educational opportunity. Pestalozzi, still anxious to continue the experiment he had planned for at Unterwalden, had an offer from the Canton of Berne to use the Chateau of Burgdorf.

De Fellenberg, who knew Pestalozzi and his contributions in the field of industrial education, and who early became one of Pestalozzi's strong supporters, was given the estate of Hofwyl by his father. Burgdorf and Hofwyl were only nine miles apart, which made it possible for the two men to exchange educational experiences. The Hofwyl institute, however, lacked the necessary organization to become a complete success, and De Fellenberg was approached by Pestalozzi and accepted the entire management of Burgdorf. Pestalozzi then approached the Bernese government to allow him to use a building called München Buchesé which had been used as a convent, located only a ten-minute walk from Hofwyl. Some time later Pestalozzi accepted an offer from the government of the Canton Waadt (Pays de Vaud) to use the Schloss Yverdon.

Many of Pestalozzi's contributions to educational advancement were made through his writings. In 1780 he produced a paper entitled, "The Evening Hour of a Hermit." In 1781, appeared Leonard and Gertrude the work on which the major part of his philosophy rests. In 1782 appeared Christopher and Alice, a book designed to rectify some public impressions of Leonard and Gertrude and also "to produce a manual of instructions for the use of the universal school of humanity, the parlor. I wish it to be read in every cottage. "[2] These ambitions for the book were not realized, and a second edition was not published until 1824. His A Swiss Journal, which appeared weekly, started in 1782. During the same year he published a discourse On Legislation and Infanticide. Between 1780 and 1790 he produced The Figures to my ABC-Book, although it was not published until 1795. A new edition of the same book, under the title of Fables, appeared in 1805. In 1798 his Researches into the Course of Nature in the Development of the Human Race, appeared and in January, 1801 he began work on a book entitled How Gertrude Teaches Her Children: an Attempt to Give Directions to Mothers How to Instruct their own Children. Beginning with 1780, the next twenty-five years were a great period of creative writing for Pestalozzi.

Many European educators recognized the study of vocal music in schools, and Pestalozzi insisted upon the importance of including music in the course of study. Rote musical instruction was not of interest to him; he felt that, if the study of music were to be effective, pupils must study the science of music. They must appreciate the differences among melody, rhythm, harmony, dynamics, starting with the rudiments and eventually being able to translate notation and musical characters into a familiar language; just as if they were reading the letter characters which are a part of a language.

Pestalozzi cannot be given the credit for starting vocal music instruction anywhere except possibly in the institutions of which he was administrative head, but it was he who insisted on the need to formulate some definite principles basic to instruction. The formulation of such principles was almost entirely the work of Pfeiffer and Nägeli.

The decree of 1735 regarding the regulation of the schools in Berlin provided for instruction in singing and specified the attainments which the instructor should realize in the teaching process.[3] The educational regulations drawn up by Hecker and approved by Frederick the Great in 1763 were modified by an ordinance in 1794. The ordinance of 1794 pointed out that vocal music was one of the most important branches of study.[4] These developments illustrate that instruction in singing during the eighteenth century received consideration in the curriculum of the German schoolmaster's programs.

Hans Georg Nägeli was unquestionably one of the most important European names connected with the art of teaching vocal music to children in public and private schools. He was born at Wetzekon, a village in the Canton of Zurich, Switzerland, and his early education was received at home. After a rudimentary education, he went to Zurich in 1786 to pursue further schooling. Due to homesickness he returned home shortly after his arrival in Zurich and took up serious study of music. By 1790, he returned to Zurich where after a time we find him in a music store, operating a circulating music library. In 1800 he started publishing a periodical which was mainly devoted to his profession.

In 1794 his song "Life let us cherish" appeared and had widespread popularity in Europe. He was one of the early founders of the Swiss musical league; some claim him to be its originator. He travelled about giving music instruction to various musical societies in nearby Cantons.

In 1810, an outstanding musical work was published which Nägeli had produced in cooperation with M. T. Pfeiffer. It was entitled The Theory of Instruction in Singing, on Pestalozzian Principles (Die Gesangbildunslehre nach Pestalozzischen Grundsätzen).[5] The work was a product of musical knowledge and principles combined with Pestalozzian educational objectives and methods of application. This work started a new era in the methods

of musical instruction for school children.   It was practical appli-
cations of this work which William C. Woodbridge saw being used
during his first extended visit to Europe (1825-1829).   This work
was the foundation method for teaching vocal music as employed
by The Boston Academy of Music, by Lowell Mason, and by a
host of other music instructors during the nineteenth and twentieth
centuries in the United States.   Nägeli died in Zurich, December
26, 1836.   His name is remembered primarily because of his
association with Pestalozzi.

One of the earliest and probably the first authoritative
representative of Pestalozzianism in the New World was Joseph N.
Naef.   He was one of Pestalozzi's teachers who came to America
and taught in a private school in Philadelphia between 1806 and
1809. [6]   After spending some time in the east, he wandered westward, settling at New Harmony, Indiana and established a colony
based upon the philsophy of Pestalozzi.   Little was ever heard of
Naef's work in the middle west.

William Channing Woodbridge was probably the first American
to really study European forms of education, particularly those of
Germany and Switzerland.   His trips to Europe in 1820 and 1825-
1829 were spent in a study of educational methods and especially
those of Pestalozzi.   Upon his return to America he expended unbounded enthusiasm in promoting Pestalozzi's philosophy of
education.   Two of Woodbridge's textbooks on geography, published
in 1824 and 1833, were patterned according to Pestalozzian principles.   He first induced Elam Ives of Philadelphia to teach vocal
classes of children according to these principles.   Later, Lowell
Mason was introduced to the same methods by Woodbridge, and
used them after his initial skepticism as to their possibilities had
been overcome by Woodbridge.   Mason became the first great
missionary of music education in America, and was the popularizer
of the art of teaching vocal music according to the Pestalozzian
method.

Rev. Calvin E. Stowe, D.D., a professor of Biblical literature
in Lane Seminary, Cincinnati, Ohio, made a trip to Europe in 1832.

Reporting on his European tour to the General Assembly of Ohio, in 1839 in a document entitled Report on Elementary Public Instruction in Europe, he devoted a special section to schools in Prussia and Würtemburg. He reported that children aged eight to ten and from ten to twelve were receiving singing instruction by note and were being taught the science of vocal and instrumental music. [7] In all probability Rev. Stowe had first witnessed the instruction of vocal music as a science in the Prussian school systems. [8]

In one of Stowe's lectures he recounts that

> On my arrival in Berlin, my first inquiry was for schools. I visited three. The structures of their school-houses very nearly resembles the public school houses of Cincinnati.
>
> Music is scientifically taught in all schools. Their musicians are in the habit of using notes on all occasions. Even the trumpeters on military parade have their notes which they contrive to carry with them. [9]

Notes

1. American Journal of Education, III: No. IX (June, 1857), 401-402.

2. Raumer, Carl. "Life and Educational System of Pestalozzi," American Journal of Education, 4: No. X (September, 1857), 65.

3. "Public Instruction in Prussia," American Journal of Education; No. XXI (June, 1860), 403-404.

4. Ibid., 404-405.

5. American Journal of Education. VII: No. XVIII (September, 1859), 300.

6. Cubberly, Elwood P. Public Education in the United States. (New York, N. Y.: Houghton Mifflin Co., 1919), 272.

7. American Journal of Education, Part III. Course of Instruction. 8: No. XXI (June, 1860), 371, 377.

8. Journal of Proceedings of the Seventeenth Annual Meeting of the Music Supervisors National Conference Held at Cincinnati, Ohio. April 7-11, 1924. Address of Welcome, Dr. Randall J. Condon, Superintendent of Cincinnati Public Schools. 46-55.

9. "Professor Stowe's Lectures," The Common School
    Advocate, Cincinnati, Ohio. 4: (April, 1837), 26-27.

III: THE FIRST CHAMPION OF
      AMERICAN PUBLIC SCHOOL MUSIC[1]

Massachusetts contributed three men--William Channing Woodbridge, Lowell Mason, and Horace Mann--who were greatly responsible for laying a solid foundation of American music education.
Woodbridge, the protagonist of school music, so convincingly influenced Lowell Mason, the teacher and missionary enthusiast, that
the momentum of their idea was primarily responsible for the
phenomenal nineteenth century growth of vocal music instruction in
our public schools. Horace Mann, the great champion of the
American public school, lent his enthusiasm to the idea and, through
his influential position as Secretary of the Massachusetts Board of
Education, lectured and traveled, and wrote extensively in his
twelve Annual Reports about the merits and the advisability of
introducing music into the school curriculum. His work was of
inestimable value to the early cause of school music.

Woodbridge was the first among these giants because of his
intimate association with the cause. He was the first influential
outspoken champion of vocal music in American public schools.
Although not a teacher himself, he was the first important interpreter in America of the Pestalozzian principles of teaching music
to school children.

Woodbridge was born in Medford, Massachusetts on December
18, 1794. He was the son of Reverend William Woodbridge, who
made a very definite contribution to the cause of female education
in Connecticut. His mother, who died when William was fourteen
years of age, was the daughter of Dr. W. E. Channing, a minister
of Boston.

In 1798, when he was four years of age, his parents moved
from Medford, Massachusetts to Middletown, Connecticut. It is
reported that his father was actively interested in common school

education and he is supposed to have organized the first Association
of Teachers in the United States.   In 1801 the family moved to
Norwich; from there they moved to Newark, New Jersey where the
father was the head of a female seminary.   During this time young
William's education was making rapid progress: by 1804 he was
studying the Greek Testament; in 1806 he had undertaken the study
of mathematics and chemistry.

At age thirteen and one half, he entered Yale College (June,
1808).   Very little is known of his college activities.   He was
always in frail health, having what medical science pronounced as
"latent scrofula."   His participation in amusements was doubtlessly
curtailed by his physical condition.   He graduated from Yale College
in September, 1811 when he was less than seventeen years of age.
The winter after his graduation he was in Philadelphia pursuing
his own studies.   His private journal relates something about his
work and thinking during this period.

> The study of the Bible in the original language, enters
> into my plan of study.   My own inclination is to pursue
> a course of Biblical criticism, Ecclesiastical History,
> and Doctrinal Theology, as my great object; but to connect
> it with a revival of my collegiate studies particularly the
> mathematics and philosophy. [2]

In July, 1812 he took over the direction of Burlington
Academy in New Jersey.   Of its successes and failures we know
very little.   This position he retained until 1814, when he moved
to New Haven, Connecticut, pursuing the studies of anatomy,
chemistry, philosophy, and other subjects which were attracting
his attention at this period.   The desire for personal educational
improvement was a dominant force in Woodbridge's life.

In addition to his secular interests, Woodbridge was possessed
of a religious fervor which later comforted him during the many
hours of physical distress.   On April 2, 1815 after making a public
profession of his faith in Jesus Christ, he united with the church
at Yale College.   From the time of his profession of faith to
January 11, 1817 he remained a student in the theological course
under the tutelage of Dr. Dwight.   In July, 1817 he became a

divinity student at the Theological Seminary at Princeton, New
Jersey. It is suggested that at this period of his life he seriously
considered becoming a foreign missionary. He left Princeton because he was called to join Messrs. Gallaudet and Le Clerc of
Hartford, Connecticut to conduct the American Asylum for the Deaf
and Dumb, which was just beginning its great work. Woodbridge
found in the asylum work an opportunity for satisfying his missionary desires, for he stated on August 30, 1817 that

> This is missionary ground. It is carrying the gospel of
> those who can not otherwise obtain it; yet compared with
> the opening among the heathen, the asylum offers a very
> limited field.   This is an immediate, certain field of use-
> fulness. A mission is distant and uncertain. [3]

The duties at the asylum were particulary arduous. In
addition to his regular position, he added other work such as
preaching engagements and appearing as a speaker and advocate
of various movements connected with education.

In October, 1820 he sailed for southern Europe for the purpose of restoring his health. This first trip to Europe lasted for
eight months. He spent some time in Palermo, Naples, Leghorn,
Rome, and in other cities of Italy. Returning to Hartford, July 4,
1821 Woodbridge found that he had not only regained his health but
had acquired a store of geographical knowledge. [4] Three years
later, a large work, The Universal Geography was ready for the
press. Prior to 1824, very little had been done to organize the
teaching of geography. A few teachers used Morse, still others
used Nathaniel Dwight's System of Geography in which the information
was arranged in the form of questions and answers. Woodbridge's
Geography began the evolution of a new school of instruction in this
area of learning.

At the same time Woodbridge was working on his system of
teaching, Mrs. Emma Willard of the Troy Female Seminary was
also working on a new system. When the works of these two
people were revealed, however, it was found that both plans were
almost identical in organization.   The two systems were merged
and the Woodbridge and Willard's Geographies soon produced a

revolution in the art of teaching geography. The strain of work
brought about another break in the condition of Woodbridge's health.
In the autumn of 1825 he was again off to southern Europe.   When
travel and rest had restored his health somewhat, he sought southern France and Italy, and at the invitation of M. de Fellenberg
spent three months at Hofwyl.   While there he functioned in the
capacity of visiting teacher.   Overwork again taxed his health and
in January of 1827 he left for Paris where he worked on a new
edition of his large geography.   In October, 1827, he was in Rome,
but he travelled slowly, stopping on his way at Lyons, where he
spent some time in a hospital.   In July, 1828 he went back to
Hofwyl, Switzerland, to study the educational system of Pestalozzi
and remained there until May, 1829.   Before his departure for
Paris in August, he visited educational institutions of southern
Germany, and had seen the educational efforts of Jacatot in
Brussels.

      Upon his return to America in the autumn of 1829, Wood-
bridge worked with unbounded enthusiasm in promoting Pestalozzi's
philosophy of education, and communicated this knowledge to such
men as Rev. Gallaudet, Hon. Henry L. Ellsworth, Dr. John L.
Comstock, and teachers connected with the American Asylum.
His long stay in Europe had sold him upon certain features of
mass education which this country had never before emphasized.
Dr. Henry Barnard felt that as

> soon as I met him, in the spring of 1830, I am inclined to
> the opinion that he was not wholly without the hope of en-
> listing the friends of education at the asylum and elsewhere,
> in a scheme to establish a school for teachers in Hartford;
> and perhaps of finding among the men of wealth in that
> city a second Fellenberg.   But his ill health was an insur-
> mountable barrier to any decisive results, as well as to
> that speedy return to Europe, which he had been meditat-
> ing. [5]

      A writer in the New York Express summed up Woodbridge's
significant contributions to the cause of education in America.

      1.   The conventions of teachers and others, in counties of
           larger districts, owed their plans and first impulses,
           in a great measure to Mr. Woodbridge, as did the

innumerable lyceums and other popular literary societies.

2. He was one of the first to foresee popular opportunities to act in Massachusetts for the advantageous distribution of the money appropriated to the schools, and the most energetic in taking measures for that purpose.

3. He wrote the first letter on popular education in music, and excited and aided Messrs. Mason & Son to attempt the introduction of that important science and art on modern principles. [6]

4. Mr. Woodbridge moved the first resolution ever offered, recommending the study of the Bible as a classic.

5. The first Literary Convention in New York placed him at the head of a committee on that subject; and he not only drew up, but gratuitously published and widely circulated the report, which embraces, in a most distinct and forcible manner, the grand arguments in favor of that object, in a style which no man can read without admiration.

6. He was one of the earliest writers in favor of the introduction of the study of physiology into our schools.

7. He was an active member of the American Lyceum.

8. He was originator and conductor of the American School Society, an organization interested in elementary education.

9. He was one of the charter members of the Boston Phrenological Society.

10. He was a member of the Geographical Societies of Paris, Berlin, and Frankfort.

11. He maintained a regular correspondence with many of the great educational, scientific, literary, and philanthropic men and women of Europe. [7]

Among the significant "firsts" in American public school music education, William Channing Woodbridge ranks as the very first person in America to advocate teaching the Pestalozzian principles of music education. He was possibly the first person to be sensitive to the merits of public school music for American school children. On August 24, 1830 he delivered at the first

meeting of the American Institute of Instruction an address "On
Vocal Music as a Branch of Common Education." He first
championed American public school music. His influence for the
cause was felt through the American Annals of Education and
Instruction, an educational journal which he owned and edited. It
was his enthusiasm which interested early school music leaders
such as Lowell Mason, Elam Ives, and George James Webb.

Pestalozzianism had so affected American music education,
however, that at the close of the nineteenth century it had a
strangle hold upon educational practice. It would be but a slight
exaggeration to state that prior to 1914, school music instruction
was characterized by the scientific approach. The prolonged
acceptance of educational formalism was undoubtedly responsible
for the longevity of the scientific music teaching era.

Pestalozzi had picked up a humanitarian challenge when
others were wallowing in unreality and inhumanity. Philsophically,
he saw the inspirational benefits to be derived from a singing
childhood, but he weakened the power of music by intellectualizing
it. Music became subject matter; it was something to be studied.
Since that curriculum contained only the studied subjects, evaluated
by their mind training efficacies, music became intellectually
enslaved instead of being emotionally liberated for enjoyment.
Music entered the curricula because it was a mind-trainer. No
less a personage than the former President Eliot of Harvard said:
"Music is the best mind-trainer on the list."

Notes

1. Sunderman, Lloyd F. "The First Champion of American
   Public School Music," The Journal of Musicology. 3:
   (Winter, 1941). 173-178. Chapter appeared as article
   indicated above. Corrections and changes have been
   made. Reprinted with the permission of Bennett Shimp,
   Editor, Journal of Musicology.

2. Alcott, W. A. "William Channing Woodbridge," The
   American Journal of Education, 5: (June, 1858). 51-52.

3. Ibid., 51-53.

4. Ibid., 55.

5. Stowe, Calvin E. "Course of Instruction in the Primary
    Schools of Germany, " The American Journal of Education,
    8: (June, 1860).   371, 377.

6. Italics are the writer's.

7. Alcott, op. cit., 62-64.

IV: LOWELL MASON: FATHER OF AMERICAN MUSIC EDUCATION[1]

Lowell Mason has been variously termed (1) the first to advocate the cause of American public school music, (2) the first teacher of school music in the United States, and (3) the Father of Public School Music. All of these statements about Mason contain elements of truth, but they might be challenged as blanket coverage of his intrinsic significance to the history of music in the public schools in America. While he may have advocated the cause, he certainly was not the first person to conceive the idea that music could be successfully taught to children in public schools, and though he was the first official teacher of music in Boston, it must not be deduced that this was the first city in America to offer public school music to children.[2] New York, Ohio, Pennsylvania and Connecticut were states in which pioneer experimentation in teaching school music had previously taken place.

Mason's real significance lies not so much in the above contributions as in the fact that he was the first official supervisor of vocal music in the public schools of Boston.

Lowell Mason was born in Medfield, Massachusetts, January 8, 1792. His father was variously occupied as a manufacturer of straw hats and occasionally as a mechanic. Though the family was respected and of average financial circumstances, the young Lowell had very limited educational opportunities and it was necessary for him to help provide for his own musical education. During the first twenty years of his life he found the time to learn to play various musical instruments. It is known that he was proficient at playing the piano, organ, violoncello, clarinet, and flute. At one time he led the Medfield City Band. One of his early music teachers and guides was Amos Albee, author of the Norfolk Collec-

46

tion of Church Music.

As early as sixteen he was already teaching singing in schools, indicating that through a self-imposed musical education he had attained a measure of musical stature. He was also directing the parish choir and in 1812, with the assistance of Amos Albee, he wrote an anthem for the ordination of Dr. Ranger of Dover, Massachusetts. With the support of the community and the enthusiasm of his family, Mason was encouraged to pursue his musical interests.

When he was twenty years of age Mason moved to Savannah, Georgia. By this time he had developed his musical efficiency to such a point that he was giving solo performances both in singing and on the violoncello. Even with a full-time position as a clerk in a Savannah bank, he found time to complete the organization of a band, direct choirs, guide the destinies of vocal and instrumental groups, and become superintendent of the large Sunday School of the First Presbyterian Church of that city.

In Savannah, he met S. Jubal Howe, W. M. Goodrich, and Colonel Newhall. They urged Mason, who had been exceedingly desirous of publishing his collection of church music, to go to Boston and present his work to the Handel and Haydn Society of that city. Being convinced that such a step was logical, he and Howe went there. When they arrived, Colonel Newhall, who had previously returned to Boston, introduced Mason to Dr. Jackson of the Handel and Haydn Society. Dr. Jackson was favorably impressed by the proposed work. The book was to carry the title, The Boston Handel and Haydn Society Collection of Church Music, Harmonized for Three and Four Voices, with Figured Bass, for Organ and Pianoforte. Dr. Jackson stated:

> I have been highly gratified with the examination of the manuscript of the Handel and Haydn's Society Collection of Music. The selection of tunes is judicious; it contains all the old approved English melodies that have long been in use in the church, together with many compositions from modern English authors. The whole are harmonized with great accuracy, truth, and judgment, according to the acknowledged principles of musical science. I consider the book as a valuable acquisition to the church, as well

> as to every lover of devotional music. It is much the
> best book I have seen published in this country, and I
> do not hesitate to give it my most decided approbation. [4]

President Winchester of the Handel and Haydn Society was
pleased with Mason's work. An agreement was made which allowed
the society to publish the work in its own name. Mason himself
has given his reasons for withholding his name:

> I was then a bank officer in Savannah, and did not wish
> to be known as a musical man, as I had not the least
> thought of ever making music a profession. The clause
> in the contract which gave the Society the right to dispose
> of and sell the property was also inserted at my suggestion,
> because I had more confidence in Mr. Winchester for this
> purpose than in myself, and besides my residence in
> Savannah rendered it proper and even necessary. [5]

It is related by S. Jubal Howe that "Mason probably put $500
into his pocket, and went back to Savannah, where he was still
clerk in a bank, feeling rich. "[6]

In correspondence dated March 14, 1869, Mason related that
some of his early arrangements of musical works had been published
in a volume called the Old Colony Collection. He stated:

> The first music that I ever furnished to the Society will
> be found at page 128 in the second volume of that collection.
> I put the English words to the "Kyrie" of Mozart, and
> sent them to a poor musical friend in Waltham, advising
> him to offer them to the Handel and Haydn Society, and
> perhaps he might obtain some little remuneration. He did
> so, and I believe was rewarded, etc. The next thing was
> the very popular "Gloria" by Mozart, page 133. This was
> about 1820. [7]

In 1826 the first contract which Mason had with the Handel
and Haydn Society had expired. Under the first contract the society
had cleared $2,516.66, but with the issuance of the second, the
total was raised to $5,058.84. The success of the Society's
publications undoubtedly encouraged them to undertake the publication
of additional church music collections.

The members of the Society felt that if Mason were in Boston,
instead of Savannah, he and the organization might more effectively
work together. President Winchester and other interested individuals
had agreed to guarantee Mason an annual salary of $2,000 for two

years. It was through the influence of these men that Mason
received an appointment to take charge of the music in the Hanover
Street, [8] Green Street, and Park Street Churches, [9] remaining at
one place for six months and then going to another. Becoming
dissatisfied with this plan, a new arrangement was made whereby
Mason was to permanently take over the music work at the Bowdoin
Street Church. [10] This made it necessary to withdraw the guarantee, but they procured a position for him as a teller in the American Bank. [11] As a bank teller and church organist Mason found
little time for aiding the society in publishing choral collections.

On September 3, 1827, at the annual meeting of the Handel
and Haydn Society, Mason was elected president. He retained
this position through the season of 1831. [12] As president of the
Society, he made some sweeping innovations which were designed
to improve the quality of its performances. Directly after his
election he secured the cooperation of the board of trustees in
permitting the use of a room furnished with a piano, where it
would be possible for him to instruct the members of the society
who needed vocal training. His particular capacity for leadership,
hard work, and his singular ability to understand those people
with whom he worked were major assets contributing to his
success.

On July 4, 1831, shortly before the end of his term as president of the Society, Mason directed the first performance of the
"original hymn" "America" in Park Street Church, Boston, Massachusetts. The author, Samuel Francis Smith who was a student
at Andover Seminary, had found the tune for his words in a German
songbook. This book had been given to him by Mason, who had
received it in turn from William Channing Woodbridge. This
particular period of Mason's life, his association with William
Woodbridge, marks the beginning of a change of focus for him
in the field of music.

The Beginning of the Public School Music Era. Woodbridge
told Mason about the music teaching he had seen in Germany. At
first, Woodbridge did not find it easy to convince Mason of the

merits of the so-called Pestalozzian plan as outlined by Pfeiffer
and Nägeli, but Mason's interest increased as he heard more about
it and he became interested in its manifold educational possibilities.
The end-result was, of course, that Mason became the first important American musician-educator working in the interest of school
music.   He advanced the thesis that as many children as could
read, could sing.   This was quite an advanced educational concept
for this period and not at all in keeping with conventional contemporary methods of education.

Mason and Woodbridge gave many public demonstrations of
the feasibility of teaching juveniles or adults the art of singing
according to the scientific method, the one which Pfeiffer and
Nägeli (See p. 35) had constructed and based on the Pestalozzian
approach.   Mason was now joined in his efforts by George James
Webb of England, who had settled in Boston about 1830.   Webb's
musicianship, culture, ability to perform on the organ, ability to
teach voice, and his personal charm made him an outstanding
asset to the cause which Mason and Woodbridge were so intensely
interested in seeing consummated.

In 1833 the Boston Academy of Music[13] was established by
Mason, Webb, Woodbridge, Samuel Eliot who was Mayor of Boston
(Father of Charles Eliot, later President of Harvard University)
and other interested citizens.   It became the first significant
academy for the instruction of vocal music in the United States.
Its chief concern was the establishment of "vocal music and
juvenile classes," adult vocal classes, classes for the instruction
of the methods of teaching music, the sponsoring of scientific
lectures, popularizing concerts, the publishing of circulars and
essays, and "to introduce vocal music into the schools."[14]   This
resumé indicates the ambitious character of its program.   The
directors of the Boston Academy had addressed themselves to the
task of propagandizing the efficacy of vocal music teaching in the
American church and public school.

Mason and European Pedagogy.   In 1837 he visited Europe to
investigate the methods of conducting vocal music in schools as

employed in various countries.   He visited London, Hamburg,
Berlin, Dresden, Frankfort, Karlsruhe, Stuttgart, Freiburg, and
other notable centers of music.   While in Europe he heard the
London Philbarmonic Society, the pianists Moscheles, Thalberg,
and Benedict, the singers Grisi, Pasta, Schroeder-Devrient, Balfe,
Signora Eckerlin, and the harpist, Labarre. [15]

In addition to the places mentioned, Mason visited the northern
parts of Switzerland, becoming acquainted with Kübler, Gersbach,
Fellenberg, and many others. [16]

This European trip had made it possible for him to study
at first hand the Prussian and Pestalozzian systems of teaching
school music.   It had served to crystallize for him a practical
method of teaching vocal music to school children and upon his
return he devoted his energy to the cause of introducing vocal
music into the schools.

The seeds of public school music education were germinated
at the Boston Academy of Music. [17]   It was through the direct
efforts of Mason and the Academy that the Boston public schools
gave music formal recognition in 1838.   From January to August
of that year he taught music gratuitously in some of the grammar
schools of Boston.   During this same period of time a group of one
hundred and thirty-four music teachers, representing ten different
states assembled at the academy.   The people who came to these
meetings were taught church music, its importance and literature;
congregational singing and how it should be handled; and methods of
drilling singers.   Juvenile singing class demostrations were presented before these groups.   An outgrowth of these meetings were
the musical conventions which Mason and other singing teachers
conducted throughout the New England states.

Mason's gratuitous teaching[18] in the city schools ended in
August of 1838 with his appointment as superintendent of music.
As superintendent of music he received $130 per year for each of
the schools he supervised.   Of this amount the assistant teacher
who did the actual teaching received $80 per annum; $20 was for
the rental of a piano which Mason furnished each of the schools,

and the remaining $30 was his part for his superintendency of the music work.   Besides the schools for which he received a stipend for his supervisory work, he gave instruction in a number of others, the group lessons probably lasting a half hour were given twice per week.   This work Mason pursued for a period of years.[19]

At the time of Mason's appointment, the Boston School Board, through its intermediary, the Music Committee, permitted him to do all the hiring and firing of his assistants.   Such a system has its disadvantages for it leaves the administrator open to much criticism about the way he handles his job.   It is not to be implied that he resorted to questionable practices, but certainly the lee-way that he possessed was responsible for some criticisim that eventually was heaped upon him.   The attacks upon his success with vocal teaching were mild compared to those that were inveighed against his financial bargainings.   Then too, it was charged that he was showing religious favoritism in the selection of those who became his assistants.   The result of the wholesale criticism was his dismissal from office in 1845 as superintendent of vocal music in Boston.

Historically there is disagreement as to how long Mason served as superintendent of music in the Boston public school system.   Hillbrand found the last year to be 1841.[20]   Grove's Dictionary also states that he remained in charge until 1841, and adds that he was succeeded by B. F. Baker.[21]   The report of the Boston School Committee for 1858 makes the facts still more confusing.   The Rev. Charles Brooks, chairman of the Music Committee, said in his report, dated February 2, 1848, that:

> Up to this time, musical instruction has been given in the following manner: The teacher gathers into one room as many pupils as can conveniently sit within it, and then, with the aid of a pianoforte, he instructs his audience for half an hour.   Each school has two such lessons per week, and for these services the Superintendent receives One Hundred and Thirty Dollars per annum for each school so taught; he providing the piano-fortes and keeping them in tune.   The schools in which music is now taught are twenty in number.   Mr. B. F. Baker is the superintendent of ten, and Mr. Lowell Mason the superintendent of the remaining ten.   The whole cost, therefore, to the City, is Twenty-

Six Hundred Dollars per annum. The Superintendents cannot teach, in person, all the schools under their several
charges. Mr. Baker instructs seven of his ten, confiding
the remaining three to teachers whom he hires. Mr. Mason instructs constantly but two schools, confiding the remainder to hired teachers. The teachers whom the Superintendents have hired have, so far as your Committee knows,
given entire satisfaction. "[22]

Birge states that Mason was retired by action of the school
board in 1850. [23]   Amid all the conflicting data, information
recently found establishes the date of his dismissal as 1845.
Dr. Flueckiger, [24] has made a notable contribution to the gathering
of evidence which establishes the date suggested. Reasons for
Mason's dismissal are not clear and even he, apparently, was not
aware of the cause of such action (see note no. 23). There is
unanimous agreement that B. F. Baker succeeded Mason. During
Mason's term of office as superintendent of music, he had A. N.
Johnson, G. F. Root, A. J. Drake, and J. A. Johnson as his assistants.

After Mason's relations were severed with the Boston Schools,
he launched a campaign of writing, lecturing, and teaching that
made him the outstanding nineteenth-century popularizer of music
education. Besides being connected with the Boston Academy of
Music, and the National Music Convention of Boston, an outgrowth
of Academy work, [25] he launched the Normal Institute, which, as
early as 1851, held meetings in New York City. This latter
organization was the precursor of the present summer school or
summer camp. The institutes lasted from six weeks to three
months, their term being held during the late summer and early
fall. Their curricula included voice, piano, church music and its
literature, theory, and the pedagogy of school music teaching.
Students were drawn to these popular programs from many sections
of the country.

Mason was a particularly effective and stimulating teacher.
Horace Mann once remarked that it was worth a young teacher's
time to walk ten miles to hear one of Mason's lectures. [26]   He
gave great impetus to the Massachusetts Teachers' Institutes,

appearing as lecturer and teacher.   He traveled as far as Rochester,
New York, giving lectures and demonstrations in the interest
of school music.

Mason was America's first important public school music
educator. In order to appreciate the role he played in championing
the cause of school music, it is well to summarize some of his
contributions: 1) It is quite possible that Mason gave to America
the first revision of the science of vocal music instruction according to Pestalozzian principles; 2) He was a profilic compiler of
psalm, hymn, and school music song book collections; 3) As a
teacher he had few peers; 4) As an organizer and instructor he
was prominent in educational conventions and vocal institutes
(George H. Martin said of his institute work, that "In the long list
of institute instructors, the names of Agassiz, Guyot, and Lowell
Mason stand preeminent";[27] 5) He became the first authorized
and financially remunerated superintendent of music in the Boston
Public Schools; 6) He was the father of the systematized study
of the rudiments of music in American public schools; 7) He was
the champion of the improved American singing schools; 8) He was
the great systematizer of late eighteenth and early nineteenth
century music pedagogy; 9) He established a precedent for the
type of song material to be included in nineteenth century church
and school song books.

Summary

Mason was attracted the public schools because the great
opportunities for expressing his sensitivities for music. He believed that the universality of music could be achieved through the
improvement of church music, the introduction of vocal music into
the public school curriculum, and by creating a widespread juvenile
and adult appreciation.

He believed ardently in music. In it he saw many values:
it united man with his Maker; it brought about the harmonious
integration of human personality; it aided social development; it
united the home, church, school, and society; it was a character
builder; it had therapeutic value. He was convinced that few persons

lack the capacity for the enjoyment of music. Mason believed that although mankind possesses this capacity, it does not spring into action of its own accord, but needs to be unfolded through education and the careful attention of the music specialist. He further believed that good music in the home is a potent force for creating desirable attitudes on the part of children; feelings demand as much education as the mind; and a habit acquired in activity would influence other habits. These are an essence of Mason's thoughts regarding the values to be derived from music.

Mason was the preceptor of music education. He was convinced that music would make a contribution to the happiness of children who were still reeling from the impact of the Monitorial system of education. His mission brough a new joy to the class-room. His life spanned a gamut of musical achievement in education which probably will never be experienced by many other men. He was among the pioneers. It was not easy for him to start a great educational movement, yet he succeeded where others would have failed because they lacked what he was in full possession of -- a genius for organization and an ability to teach.

Mason's music publications produced up to 1854:[28]

Juvenile or School Books

Juvenile Psalmist, Boston, 1829.
Juvenile Lyre, (The first book of School Songs published in this country), Boston, 1830.
Manual of Instruction in the Elements of Vocal Music, Boston, 1834.
Juvenile Singing School, Boston, 1835.
Sabbath School Songs, Boston, 1836.
Sabbath School Harp, Boston, 1837.
Juvenile Songster, London, 1838.
Juvenile Music for Sabbath Schools, Boston, 1839.
Boston School Song Book, Boston, 1840.
Little Songs for Little Singers, Boston, 1840.
American Sabbath School Singing Book, Philadelphia, 1843.
Song Book of the School Room, Boston, 1845.
Primary School Song Book, Boston, 1846.
The Normal Singer, (four-part songs,) New York, 1856.

Glee Books, etc.

†The Musical Library, etc., Boston, 1835.
†The Boston Glee Book, Boston, 1838.
†The Odeon, Boston, 1839.
The Gentlemen's Glee Book, Boston, 1842.
†The Vocalist, Boston, 1844.
†The Glee Hive, Boston, 1851.

Sacred and Church Music Books.

The Boston Handel and Haydn Collection of Church Music,
    Boston, 1822.
The Choir, or Union Collection, Boston, 1833.
The Boston Academy Collection, Boston, 1836.
Lyra Sacra, Boston, 1837.
Occasional Psalmody, Boston, 1837.
Songs of Asaph, Boston, 1838.
Boston Anthem Book, Boston, 1839.
The Seraph, Boston, 1838.
The Modern Psalmist, Boston, 1839.
The Carmina Sacra, Boston, 1841.
The Boston Academy Collection of Choruses, Boston, 1844.
†The Psaltery, Boston, 1845.
The National Psalmist, Boston, 1848.
†Cantica Laudis, Boston, 1850.
†The Boston Chorus Books, Boston, 1851.
The New Carmina Sacra, Boston, 1852.
The Home Book of Psalmody, London, 1852.
The Hallelujah, New York, 1854.

†Published in connection with George James Webb.

Many smaller works and single pieces are not included in the
above list.

Notes

1. Sunderman, Lloyd F. "Lowell Mason, Father of
    American Music Education," Journal of Musicology.
    Vol. IV: No. 1 (November, 1944). 27, 53-54.
    Chapter appeared as article indicated above. Correc-
    tions and changes have been made. Reprinted with
    the permission of Bennett Shimp, Editor, Journal of
    Musicology.

2. In his History of Public School Music in the United
    States, Birge says: "During the four generations since
    1838, when public school music was first introduced,
    nearly the whole of our educational history has been
    in the making." p. 1. (Italics are the writer's.)

3. This was the first Sunday School superintendency in that city.

4. History of the Handel and Haydn Society of Boston, Mass. Vol. I. From The Foundation of the Society Through Its 75th. Season, 1815-1890. 80-82.

5. Ibid., 82-83.

6. Ibid.

7. Ibid.

8. Dr. Lyman Beecher, minister.

9. Dr. Lyman Beecher, minister.

10. Flueckiger, S. T. "Lowell Mason's Contribution to the Early History of Music Education in the United States." Doctoral Dissertation, Ohio State University, 1936. Mason was to receive $2,000 a year for his work. This plan, whereby Mason divided his musical energies among three choirs, did not prove satisfactory to him, so he decided to remain [only] with Lyman Beecher's Hanover Street Church ... Since this church did not pay $2,000 for his services ... Mason spent a part of his time as teller in the American Bank." 120-121.

11. History of the Handel and Haydn Society of Boston, Mass. Vol I., Ibid., 91-92.

12. Ibid.,: Appendix, : 12-13.

13. Elson, Louis C. The History of American Music, 79.

14. Ryan, Thomas. Recollections of an Old Musician, 43-44.

15. Mason, Daniel G. "An Unpublished Journal of Dr. Lowell Mason," The New Music Review and Church Music Review, 10-16-18. December, 1910. (See also January, 1911.)

16. "Educational Labors of Lowell Mason," The American Journal of Education, 4:145. September, 1857.

17. Sunderman, Lloyd F. "Sign Posts in the History of American Music Education," Education, 62: 529-536; 543-546. See this discussion regarding, "Boston, The

Hub of American Music Education, " and Some Nineteenth Century Interpreters of American Music Education. " It must be recognized that Woodbridge as
editor of the American Annals of Education could and
did cooperatively champion the cause of early public
school music. See also: Flueckiger, Samuel L.
"Lowell Mason's Contributions to the Early History
of Music Education in the United States, " Chapter VII.
Doctoral Dissertation, Ohio State University, 1936.

18.   Mason provided the books and equipment at his own
      expense.

19.   Flueckiger, Samuel L.   "Why Lowell Mason Left the
      Boston Schools, " Music Educators Journal, 22:
      (February, 1936).   20-23.

20.   Hillbrand, E. K.   "How Music Found its Way into
      American Public Schools, " The Etude, 42: (March,
      1924).   163-164.

21.   Grove's Dictionary, American Supplement, 6: 285-286.

22.   Annual Reports of the School Committee of the City of
      Boston, 1858.   (The Italics are the writer's), 55.

23.   Birge, Edward B.   History of Public School Music in
      The United States, 55.

24.   Flueckiger, Samuel L.   "Lowell Mason's contributions
      to the Early History of Music Education in the United
      States, " Doctoral Dissertation, Chapter VIII.   :   154-
      168.   Excellent evidence regarding dismissal.   Dr. H.
      G. Good, Ohio State University, under the date of
      July 6, 1942 has aided this writer in supporting the
      date of 1845 by submitting the following evidence:
      "In the American Journal of Music and Musical Visitor
      (Boston) November 30, 1845, a correspondent inquiries
      why Mason has been dismissed.   The (Boston) Mercan-
      tile Journal, October 11, 1845, announces that Mason
      has been displaced, another (Baker) appointed, says it
      caused some excitement.   The (Boston) Daily Atlas,
      October 13, 1845, referring to the Mercantile Journal
      article above, attacks the Journal's explanation.
      Journal replies October 14.   Lowell Mason published
      a letter of inquiry why he has been

      unexpectedly, and as I think, very unjustly, deprived
      of the office of master of music of the grammar
      schools, and office which I have held ever since the
      introduction of music into the schools, and so far as

I know to the entire satisfaction of the Committee; and having no charge made against me, or any satisfactory reason assigned as the cause of my removal, nor any opportunity of justifying myself, or of presenting my claims to the office; I take the liberty to address you, respectfully requesting you take such measures as you think proper to cause such an investigation of the circumstances as will place the matter in a proper light before the public, enable me to met the charges, if there are any, and save my professional character from essential injury.

With sentiments of great respect,
Lowell Mason

Letter dated September 29, published in Journal, October 14, 1845.

25. The National Music Convention became the American Music Convention.

26. Mann had said: "I have never before seen anything that came nearer to my beau ideal of teaching."

27. Martin, George H. The Evolution of the Massachusetts Public School System, 173-174.

28. "List of Publications by Lowell Mason." The American Journal of Education, 4: (September, 1857), 148.

Selected Readings on Lowell Mason

1. Baldwin, Sister Mary F. "Lowell Mason's Philosophy of Music Education," Unpublished Master's Thesis. Catholic University of America, Washington, D. C. 1937. 34

2. "Educational Labors of Lowell Mason," Barnard's American Journal of Education. 4: (September, 1857). 140-148.

3. Flueckiger, Samuel L. "Lowell Mason's Contribution to the History of Music Education in the United States." Unpublished doctoral dissertation. Ohio State University, 1936. 325.

4. Flueckiger, Samuel L. "Why Lowell Mason Left The Boston Schools," Music Educators' Journal. 22: (February, 1936), 20-23.

5.   Hadden, J. Cuthbert. "Lowell Mason, American
      Educator and Musical Pioneer, " Etude. (March, 1910).
      28, 165.

6.   Hadden, J. Cuthbert. "Lowell Mason, and Psalmody
      Reform, " The Choir Herald. (November, 1912), 16,
      21-23.

7.   Johnson, James C. "The Introduction of the Study of
      Music Into the Public Schools of Boston and of America, '
      The Bostonian. 1: (March, 1895), 622-632.

8.   Kinnear, William B. "Lowell Mason, Some Teaching
      Peculiarities, " Musical Courier. 103: (July, 1931),
      5.

9.   "List of Publications by Lowell Mason, " The American
      Journal of Education. 4: (September, 1857), 148.

10.   "Lowell Mason, " Dwight's Journal of Music. (August,
      1854).   5, 139.

11.   Mason, Lowell. "Church Music, " The North Ameri-
      can Review, N. S.   15: (1827), 244-246.

12.   Mason, Lowell. How Shall I Teach Music. (Boston,
      Mass.: Oliver Ditson Company, 1875), 32.

13.   Mathews, W. S. B. "Lowell Mason, a Father in Ameri-
      can Music, " The Musician. 16: (November, 1911).
      721-722.

14.   Mathews, W. S. B. "The Lowell Mason Centennial, "
      Music. 1: (February, 1892).   400-408.

15.   Metcalf, Frank J. "Lowell Mason, " The Choir Leader.
      23: (March, 1916), 3-4, 29-30.

16.   Mowery, William A. "Reminiscences of Lowell
      Mason, " Education. 13: (February, 1893), 335-338.

17.   Ross, James H. "Lowell Mason, American Musician, "
      Education. 14: (March, 1894), 411-416.

18.   Smith, S. F. "Recollections of Lowell Mason, " New
      England Magazine. 11: (1895), 648-650.

19.   Thayer, A. W. "Lowell Mason, " Dwight's Journal of
      Education. 39: (December, 1879), 186-187; 195-196.

20. "The Death of Dr. Lowell Mason," Dwight's Journal
of Music. 32: (August, 1872), 295-296.

21. "The Lowell Mason House at Medfield, Mass.,"
The Libretto. 4: (November, 1928), 1.

V.   BOSTON AND THE MAGNA CHARTA OF MUSIC EDUCATION[1]

Boston was the first large city to introduce music into the regular curriculum.   Experiments in teaching vocal music to Boston school children are known to have taken place as early as 1824, for in that year, N. D. Gould was conducting special vocal music classes for some children in the city schools. [2] Little is known of his work; it is but a record in the historical picture of school music teaching in Boston.   Probably the best known of the early attempts to start vocal music in the schools were those sponsored under the leadership of William C. Woodbridge, Lowell Mason, and George J. Webb.

As early as 1830, a statement was expressed to the effect that if a course of music instruction were to be made practicable, two things were essential: "1)   The immediate necessity of securing a number of tunes which were suitable to the abilities, maintaining at the same time a moral and spiritual purpose and 2)   a simple course of instruction. "[3]

Those who advocated the introduction of vocal music in Boston were persistent.   In 1831 one year after Woodbridge's speech before the American Institute of Instruction, a report was submitted by G. H. Snelling, recommending that the following resolution receive serious consideration:

> Resolved.   That one school from each district be selected for the introduction of systematic instruction in vocal music, under the direction of a committee to consist of one from each district and two from the Standing Committee. [4]

The resolution met little opposition and was adopted on January 17, 1832.

In that same year Elam Ives published The American Elementary Singing Book, a first book for the study of music along Pestalozzian principles of teaching vocal music.   The comments appearing in print emphasized an indebtedness:

"to Mr. Ives for the first introduction of this method of
instruction into the United States, by his own rewarded
efforts in 1830, and for the perseverance and success
with which he had continued to labor in the cause, in the
instruction of classes by the preparation of these books...
The value of this system of instruction has been fully
tested in the United States within the two years past by
Mr. Ives, in Hartford and in Philadelphia, and by
Mr. Lowell Mason, in Boston."[5]

Although some of the plans were carried out, realization
of its many aims was never fully attained. Enough was accomplished, however, to project the possibilities of vocal music instruction
in the primary public schools of Boston, and this can be recognized
as the first systematized effort toward the recognition of music
as a branch of elementary school instruction.

Concerted efforts to introduce vocal music into the Boston
public schools came with the formation of the Boston Academy of
Music. A group of people interest in music resolved to establish
an organization that would be actively interested in popularizing the
Swiss and German methods of teaching vocal music in the United
States. They recognized the need for employing competent teachers
familiar with the European methods of instruction. After many
informal discussions, a meeting was held on January 8, 1833, which
culminated in the formation of the Academy. The first professors
of the Academy were Lowell Mason, George James Webb and the
following officers:

Jacob Abbott..........	President
David Greene..........	Vice-president
Geo. Wm. Gordan.....	Recording secretary
Wm. C. Woodbridge...	Corresponding secretary
J. A. Palmer..........	Treasurer

Counsellors

Daniel Noyes	Geo. H. Snelling
Bela Hunting	Benj. Perkins
H. M. Willis	Moses Grant
Wm. J. Hubbard	George E. Mead
J. S. Withington	

A concise declaration of the purposes of the Boston Academy
of Music was stated in The American Annals of Education . . . 1838:

The Boston Academy of Music consists of a number of the
friends of vocal music (as taught on the improved Pestalozzian plan, introduced into this country some few years
since, by Rev. William C. Woodbridge, the former editor
of the journal), associated for the purpose of extending,
by such means as they can, what they deem so valuable
and important a science. [6]

The formation of the Academy in 1833 was one of the most
ambitious of all early music endeavors of the first half of the
nineteenth century.   Those involved stated that it was their desire

1) To establish schools of vocal music and juvenile
    classes.

2) To establish similar classes for adults.

3) To form a class for instruction in the methods of
    teaching music.

4) To form an association of choristers and leading
    members of choirs for the purpose of improvement in
    church music.

5) To establish a course of popular lectures on the nature
    and object of church music.

6) To have scientific lectures.

7) To give exhibition concerts.

8) To introduce vocal music into the schools. [7]

The Academy did realize some of these ambitions to a rather
marked degree.   The vigor with which the officers, professors and
counsellors pursued their objectives was bound to produce results.
Their task was to prove the value of teaching music to children in
the public schools of Boston and America.   They firmly believed
that the educational cause of music would be enhanced by their
efforts.

The first annual report of the Boston Academy of Music
records an account of the introduction of vocal music in America
according to the Pestalozzian principles.   When William C. Woodbridge returned from Europe in 1829, he brought with him representative works of European educators.   Among these works were
those of Nägeli, Pfeiffer, and Kübler on elementary instruction.

Also included were the music cards for class instruction, and the "juvenile" music of Nägeli and Pfeiffer. This first report corroborates evidence found elsewhere that Elam Ives of Hartford, Connecticut, was the sole person under whom the first classes in music teaching according to Pestalozzian principles were conducted in this country.

Among the first steps taken by The Boston Academy of Music was to get Lowell Mason to relinquish a "lucrative situation" and devote his whole time to the cause of vocal music instruction. Mason needed assistance in the pursuit of his work and George James Webb, organist at Boston's St. Paul's Church, was appointed as associate professor of music.

The Boston Academy of Music was housed in some good rooms under the Bowdoin Street Church, but before long additional space was required: the Juvenile class formed under Mason's direction had grown to 400 students and Webb had responsibility for about 100 students. The chapel of the Old South Church in Boston was obtained for two afternoons each week to meet the expanded requirements.

The pupils were required to be seven years of age and had to remain in the classes for a period of one year. Mason did not wait for a year to pass, however, before he presented his charges in concert. The Academy developed the idea of an extensive advertising campaign which would focus public attention on the merits of music education. It was agreed that this could best be done by giving public concerts. Two juvenile concerts were given with remarkable success in the spring of 1833. The pupils who were presented at these concerts were exclusively trained by Mason.

Outside of Boston, Webb formed a juvenile school at Cambridgeport, Massachusetts; Mason started others at Salen and Lynn with about 150 pupils in each town; and in Salem there was an adult class with the same number of students.

The Early Adoption of Vocal Music as a Part of The Regular Course of Instruction in Schools. George Wm. Gordon, Secretary of the Academy, stated in August, 1833 that

It appears from the report of the committee on this
subject, (introduction of vocal music as a part of the
regular course of instruction in schools) that the plan
was first adopted in the Mount Vernon School and the
Monitorial Schools of Mr. Fowle, both for females, had
Mr. Thayer's school for boys, in Chauncey Place, in
each of which there were 100 pupils, who received
instructions twice a week in vocal music.   Instruction
is also given by the professors of the Academy in the
Asylum for the Blind, in the schools of Mr. Hayward
and Miss Raymond, Chestnut St., in Miss Spooner's
school in Montgomery Place, and in the Academy at
Cambridgeport.   The whole number of the pupils under
the care of the Academy exceeds 1500.   In all these
classes and schools deep interest is felt in the subject,
and in the mode of instruction; and surprise is often
expressed, even by those who are familiar with the
ordinary musical instruction, at the simple illustration
of subjects which they had never attempted to understand,
and at the exhibition of important principles to which
they were entire strangers. 8

In the following letters the evidence of the success of the
music program is corroborated:

In reply to inquiries as to the result of the experiment
I have made upon the practicability and utility of teaching
vocal music to large numbers of children, I would remark,
that the experiment has succeeded beyond my expectation.
More than a hundred of my pupils, between the ages of
four and eighteen, have been under the care of Mr. Mason
more than a year.   I intended the exercise rather as a
pastime than a serious study; but, with only two short
lessons a week, the children have acquired no inconsider-
able knowledge of the elements of music.   Before any
experiments were made in this country, I had proofs
enough of the practicability of making simple melody a
part of popular education, and I consider this question
as demonstrated beyond doubt in my school.   Of its
utility as we use it, I have as little doubt.   It is never
allowed to interfere with or supersede the common
branches of study, and I often use it to call attention,
restore order, or promote the innocent recreation of the
pupils.   I consider music one of the arts of peace which
all may cultivate sufficiently to feel its influence upon
their manners and dispositions, and in introducing it
into our schools we are sowing seeds, which if they do
not keep out the tares entirely, will essentially modify
them. 9

William B. Fowle

Monitorial School, Temple Avenue
May 1, 1834.

From E. A. Andrews, teacher of the Mount Vernon Female School,
Masonic Temple, Boston:

> The following, so far as I have observed, have been the
> principal effects of the introduction of music into the Mount
> Vernon School, as a general school exercise.
>
> It has furnished an agreeable variety in our employments.
> It is an exercise so different in its nature from all the
> ordinary employments in the school, that it is generally
> anticipated as a desirable relaxation from our usual
> avocations.
>
> The study of the principles of musical science has appeared
> to afford as salutary a discipline of the mind, as the other
> studies usually pursued in school for this purpose, and I
> have not observed any one successful in becoming acquainted
> with these principles, without a corresponding success in
> other branches.
>
> It has afforded an agreeable amusement during our
> recesses.
>
> It has enabled a large part of the school to join with
> pleasure in the singing of a hymn at the devotional exercises
> at the opening and close of the school.
>
> By singing frequently such words as contain useful senti-
> ments, they occur to the mind in those moments when
> it is not occupied with regular trains of thought, and,
> in this way, useful associations occupy the place of such
> as are useless or pernicious.
>
> By commencing very early in life, most of the difficulties
> which are experienced at a later period in acquiring the
> art are avoided. The propensity to imitation is then
> strongest, and that timidity, which at a subsequent period
> prevents the pupil from making a full attempt to imitate
> musical sounds, is by children scarcely felt. Among the
> younger members of the Mount Vernon School I have not
> observed a single instance of failure in learning to sing,
> while many continually occur among the older members
> who cannot overcome their timidity so far as to attempt
> fearlessly to imitate the sounds which they hear.
>
> From what I have noticed in the Mount Vernon School, and
> in other classes under the direction of the professors of
> the Academy, I am satisfied that the general introduction

of music into schools will be attended with complete
success, if competent instructors are employed for
this purpose. [10]

E. A. Andrews.

Boston, May 8, 1834.

The second annual report of the Boston Academy of Music
bears evidence of the random manner in which music was taught.
The report also pointed out that there was a crying need for suitable elementary singing books. The 1834 report of the academy
shows that in Boston, Salem, Lynn, and Cambridge, during the
year 1833-34, nearly 1200 students varying in age from five to
six upwards were taught music by professors of the academy. [11]
Adult classes totaling about 500 students were receiving instruction
in Boston, Salem, and Harvard University. If we total the number
in the juvenile classes with those of the adult division, we have
1, 700 studying music under the direction of the professors from
the Academy. The Academy report of 1834 vividly indicated that
the professors "have been employed during the past year to give
instruction in music to the pupils of the nine schools (Boston)
including several of the largest and best conducted private schools
in the city, together with one in Cambridgeport and one in Charlestown; embracing about 530 pupils. "[12]

The grand total of students being taught vocal music by members of the Academy for the year 1834 amounted to 2, 200. Two
public concerts were given during the year by the juvenile classes.
The performance of the various groups convinced those who witnessed them that juveniles were capable of: 1) Learning songs by note;
2) Learning the elementary principles or rudiments of music;
3) Reading music with ease and accuracy; 4) Singing intelligently
and independently.

In 1834 The Boston Academy of Music was calling for the
development of qualified teachers who would have a competent
knowledge of music and an acquaintance with various methods of
teaching this science.

The report of that year stressed the need for seeking out promising teaching candidates who, with proper training, would qualify as teachers of the various methods of teaching vocal music. [13]

Both the successful and unsuccessful attempts to offer a vocal music program in a limited number of Boston schools served to focus community attention upon the need for offering this kind of activity in all of its schools. It was generally felt that even though the experiments were successful only in a limited way, the program should be expanded to include all school children. The events leading to the official adoption of vocal music by the Boston school committee are worthy of detailed study. [14] A meeting of the Committee on August 10, 1836, marked the beginning of administrative action for officially introducing vocal music into the public schools. A petition which had been started by a group of interested citizens pleaded that vocal music be introduced into the schools. A select committee was again appointed by the Committee, chosen upon the basis of competence to judge the merits of such a weighty proposition. After long and careful deliberation, a favorable report was submitted August 24, 1837, which stated:

> After mature deliberation and a careful scrutiny of arguments and evidence, the Committee are unanimously of the opinion that it is expedient to comply with the request of the petitioners. They are well aware that the cause which they support can find no favor from a board like this, except so far as it reaches the convictions through the doors, not of the fancy, but of the understanding.... And in regarding the effect of vocal music, as a branch of popular instruction, in our Public Schools, there are some practical considerations, which in the opinion of your Committee, are deserving of particular attention. [15]

Some of the considerations were: 1) A definite relation exists between good reading and good modulation and articulation, the latter coming from the learning of good singing habits; 2) There is need in the school curriculum for a subject which "without being idleness shall yet give rest." The implication here seems to be that a pleasant type of activity which is restful is needed for complete life enjoyment; 3) Due to a regulation of the school commit-

tee which indicated that all schools in Boston must start the day
with exercises which are "becoming, " devotionally, it was suggested
by the committee that no possible subject could be more effective
in achieving such a state of reverence.

There were many cautions and objections raised against the
introduction of vocal music in the Boston Public Schools. Some
of them were   1) An individual must have a musical ear or else
music instruction will be in vain;   2) The amount of time proposed
for the instruction of the vocal music would be inadequate to the
end proposed; and   3) If vocal music were allowed to enter the
curriculum it may lead to the incorporation and acceptance of
other subjects which the populace frowned upon (dancing was one
of the topics suggested).

Finally, the reporting committee asked the board of education
of the Boston Public Schools to adopt the following resolutions:

> Resolved, - That, in the opinion of the School Committee
> it is expedient to try the experiment of introducing vocal
> music, by public authority, as part of the system of public
> instruction into the Public Schools of the City.

> Resolved, - That, the experiment be tried in the four
> following schools, the Hancock School for girls in Hanover
> street, the Eliot School for Boys in North Bennet Street,
> the Johnson School for girls in Washington Street, and
> the Hawes school for boys and girls, at South Boston.

> Resolved, - That this experiment be given in charge to
> the Boston Academy of Music, under the direction of this
> Board; and that a committee of five be appointed from
> this Board to confer with the Academy, arrange all
> necessary details of the plan, oversee its operation, and
> make quarterly report thereof to this Board.

> Resolved, - That the experiment be commenced as soon
> as practicable after the passing of these resolutions, and
> be continued and extended as the Board may hereafter
> determine.

> Resolved, - That these resolutions be transmitted to the
> City Council, and that they be respectfully requested to
> make such appropriation as may be necessary to carry
> this plan into effect. [16]

On September 19, 1837 the resolutions were passed by the
school board of Boston, but due to a lack of funds, nothing
happened in an official way providing for the employment of a
superintendent or director of music.

At the quarterly meeting of the board of education held in
November, 1837 additional resolutions were added to the previous
ones. They were as follows:

> Resolved, - That in the opinion of the School Committee,
> it is expedient that the experiment be tried of introducing
> instruction in vocal music, by public authority, as part
> of the system of public instruction into the Public Schools
> of this City.

> Resolved, - That the experiment be tried in the Hawes
> School in South Boston, under the direction of the Sub-
> Committee of that school and the Committee on Music,
> already appointed by this Board. [17]

Although funds were not forthcoming, instruction in vocal
music did commence in January, 1838 at the Hawes Schools for
boys and girls at South Boston, Massachusetts. The teacher for
this experiment was Lowell Mason, who offered his services on a
gratuitous basis for a period extending from January to August,
1838.

On August 7, 1838, the sub-committee reported the following
to the board of education:

> The Committee on the introduction of music respectfully
> report, that they visited the Hawes School at South Boston,
> on the sixth day of August, inst., and heard the musical
> exercises of the scholars with great satisfaction. The
> success of the experiment thus far has more than fulfilled
> the sanguine expectations which at first were entertained
> in regard to it. The Committee will add, on the authority
> of the masters of the Hawes School, that the scholars are
> further advanced in their other studies at the end of this,
> than of any other previous year. [18]

Final Vote - The Magna Charta of Music Education.

Then followed the final disposition of the question of the
advisability and feasability of introducing music into the public
schools. The final vote came on August 28, 1838. The vote of

the school committee of Boston, at this time has been regarded
as an approval to what has been called the Magna Charta of music
education in the United States. [19]

The resolutions which were submitted along with the vote
stated:

> Resolved, - That the Committee on Music be instructed to
> contract with a teacher of vocal music in the several
> Public Schools of the city, at an expense of not more than
> one hundred and twenty dollars per annum for each school,
> excepting the Lyman and Smith Schools, the teachers in
> which shall not receive more than the sum of sixty dollars
> per annum.
>
> Resolved, - That the instruction in vocal music shall
> commence in the several Public Schools, whenever the
> Sub-Committee respectfully shall determine, and shall
> be carried into effect under the following regulations:
>
> 1) Not more than two hours in the week shall be devoted
> to this exercise,
>
> 2) The instruction shall be given at stated and fixed times
> throughout the city, and until other wise ordered, in
> accordance with the following schedule...,
>
> 3) During the time the school is under the instruction of
> the teacher of vocal music, the discipline of the school
> shall continue under the charge of the regular master or
> masters, who shall be present while the instruction is
> given, and shall organize the scholars for that purpose,
> in such arrangement as the teacher in music may
> desire. [20]

With the Magna Charta of music education being officially
signed in Boston, August 28, 1838, music instruction marched
forward with tremendous impetus. To appreciate the results that
were being obtained in the local schools, one must read the Tenth
Annual Report of the Boston Academy of Music. [21] The report
dated July, 1842 included twenty-one testimonial letters, all of
which, with one exception, were from principals of Boston grammar
schools. Four of these testimonial documents appear below:

Boston, May 20, 1841.

> It is now nearly three years since vocal music was intro-
> duced into this school. It was then considered as an
> experiment, and it has succeeded beyond the expectations

of the most sanguine.   Mr. Mason's instruction is upon
the inductive method, and he succeeds in imparting a
thorough knowledge of the rudiments to his pupils.   We
are fully satisfied that children may obtain a practical
knowledge of the elements of music in our Common Schools,
without deteriment to their progress in other studies.   It
affords a pleasant variety, relieving the mind rather than
tasking it; and its effect upon the pupils, both in a moral
and disciplinary point of view, is highly beneficial.

William D. Swan,
Principal of the Mayhew Grammar School.

Aaron D. Capen,
Principal of the Writing Department.

Bowdoin School, June 16, 1841.

TO LOWELL MASON, Esq. :

Dear Sir, -- Nearly three years ago, vocal music was
introduced into this school under your instruction.   The
result has exceeded our expectations; for you have been
successful in imparting to a large portion of our pupils
a practical knowledge of the elements of the science, and
taught them to sing a great variety of songs, in a manner
very creditable to yourself, and highly gratifying to those
who have witnessed the exercise; and this has been
accomplished without apparent injury to their other studies.
We are confident that music may be usefully taught in our
Common Schools, provided the teacher comes to the task
with a competent knowledge of the subject, and determination to command the attention and respect of his pupils.

Yours, respectfully,

Abraham Andrews,
Principal of Grammar Department.

James Robinson,
Principal of Writing Department.

Boston, July 8, 1841.

LOWELL MASON, Esq. :

Dear Sir, -- I am very willing to record my entire
change of opinion with regard to instruction in music
in our public schools.   Till I had witnessed the experiment, I believed it impossible to interest scholars generally in the study, or to introduce it without many disadvantages. The experience of the past three years,
however, has shown me that nothing but constant and
persevering effort is wanting, to make this study as

interesting to pupils generally, as any other. I have not
found that instruction in this department has interfered in
the least degree with the other pursuits of the schoolroom;
on the contrary, I am satisfied that it is a help, instead
of a hindrance, affording the children another and a strong
bond of attachment to their school.

Respectfully yours,

Henry Williams, Jr.
Principal of the Grammar Department in the Winthrop School.

Eliot School, Boston, July 13, 1841.

LOWELL MASON, Esq.:

Dear Sir, -- The science of music, properly taught, is
an excellent mental exercise, while the practice is essential
to develop and strengthen the vocal powers. We believe
the pupils, since its introduction into our public schools,
have found it a valuable aid in acquiring the mechanical
part of reading. Of its moral effect upon the young, we
can no longer doubt. Nor can there be any doubt that
these schoolroom songs will exert a permanent influence
on the character, if he was versed in human nature, who
said, 'Let me make the ballads of a country, and I care
not who makes the law.' We hope soon to find it a study
in every school in the Union.

Very respectfully,

David B. Tower,
Levi Conant.

During these embryonic beginnings there were educational
leaders who indicated skepticism concerning the advisability of
permitting the introduction of vocal music in the public school
curriculum. A Bostonian who had written an article for the
Boston Medical and Surgical Journal (November 22, 1838) incorporated some of the reasons why he felt that music should become a
part of the school curriculum. He felt that as he was a member
of the medical profession, he should take a stand in the defense of
the introduction of music into the public schools "in its hygienic
relations to a numerous class of the community, and eventually
to all."[22]

After three years, music instruction in the city schools was beginning to speak for itself. A report of the school committee during 1841 spoke most enthusiastically of the results being obtained. The writer of the report has summarized some of the observations made by the committee: 1) Discounting the possibility of becoming proficient performers of music, it has been found that "a very great proportion" of the young persons who experience musical instruction in the schools may benefit tremendously from the experience; 2) After three years experience, it can be stated that the results have answered and met the expectations of the friends and proponents of music; 3) The incorporation of vocal music instruction has in no way affected the morale and discipline of the schools; 4) The introduction of vocal music has in no way harmed the other subjects of the curriculum; 5) The singing of songs, and especially the singing of boys and girls together has been a uniting force for school relations between the sexes.[23]

The amount of time devoted each week was two lessons, each of a half hour duration which was given in all the grammar schools of the city. There were about 3,000 boys and girls receiving instruction in vocal music according to the scientific method (Pestalozzian).

Music in Massachusetts. What effect did the successful introduction of vocal music in Boston have upon music teaching in the state? During the period when the Boston School Committee was establishing vocal music upon an effectual basis, there were other towns and cities in the state offering vocal music.

Many writers admit that prior to 1840 vocal music in the public schools of America was rare but they imply that even though vocal music was introduced into the schools of Boston in 1838, no other city was to be found having music in its school curriculum until 1843. Other evidence seems to contradict this, however. Horace Mann, the editor of the Common School Journal, stated in 1840 that efforts were being made to introduce music into the public school curricula.[24] Music had been introduced in the West School for Girls at Salem in 1841.[25] The Northampton paper

reported in 1840 that singing was in the curriculum in the boys'
high school of that city.   Colonel Barr, who introduced music in
the high school, taught approximately one hundred and fifty boys.
The Northampton paper reports approvingly as follows:

> The readiness with which they read the notes on the black-
> board, give them the proper tones, and then transform
> them into some simple, but cheerful melody, cannot but
> gratify the dullest eye and please the most obtuse ear....
> Northampton should be proud of this excellent school.
> It is not surpassed by any private seminary in
> Massachusetts, and it is infinitely ahead of the great
> majority of the academies in this country. [26]

Not alone do we find evidence that music was being taught
to boys in a high school during the school year of 1839-40 at
Northampton, but we know that Lowell was also offering vocal
music in many of its schools during the year 1841-42. [27]   A report
from Lowell in 1842 relates

> In this City, besides the High School, there are now 8
> Grammar Schools, with 1366 scholars......687 males
> and 679 females; and 26 Primary Schools, kept by 30
> females, with 1, 892 scholars... 955 males and 937
> females: making in all 3, 458 scholars. [28]

Mann in 1844, related the extent to which vocal music was
being taught in the state.   His survey revealed "There are about
five hundred schools in the State where Vocal Music is now practiced.
Half a dozen years ago the number was probably less than one
hundred. "[29]

The five hundred schools were scattered in 117 towns and
cities throughout the state.   This encouraging report came but six
years after the official recognition of music in Boston.

Succeeding reports by the Boston Music Committee for 1848,
1856, 1863, 1864, and 1865 indicate at least a favorable report on
the status of music instruction in the city schools.   In 1848 the
Committee spoke of a "conviction of the utility of this branch of
instruction, if for no farther use, at least as an auxiliary to the
moral training in the Schools, is too deeply seated to be easily
moved. "[30]   Later in 1857 the Boston School Board urged the following: that   1)   There should be no change in the time devoted to

music; 2) It is not claimed that a pupil at the time of leaving
the grammar school will be an accomplished musician (Musicians
cannot be made in a few months; learning to sing requires time
and perseverance); 3) The primary schools should open and
close with singing and the songs should be devotional in character
(The same procedure should be followed for the grammar schools,
with additional time for studying the rudiments of music); 4)
Students in the Girls' High and Normal School should receive such
music instruction as to qualify them to teach vocal music in the
public schools. 5) In the future employment of teachers, their
ability to teach vocal music should be one requirement. "[31]

A year later the Committee on Music formulated rules govern-
ing the

> general supervision over this department of Public
> Instruction in all the schools. They shall appoint, and
> nominate to the Board for confirmation, suitably qualified
> persons as Teachers of Music; they shall make examinations
> of each Grammar School in music; at least once in six
> months, and submit a written report thereupon semi-
> annually, at the quarterly meeting in March and in
> September. [32]

The School Committee of Boston was encouraged to find that
many of the teachers were capable of instructing their pupils in
the art of singing--their estimation being over fifty per cent of the
staff. Many teachers believed in the healthy influence of music
upon school discipline. They found that disciplinary difficulties
decreased or increased in proportion to the presence or absence
of music. [33]

The Board of Education was intensely interested in knowing
the methods employed in the teaching of vocal music in the United
States. A questionnaire was sent to various school superintendents
and music committees and was designed to evoke answers to the
following questions:

> 1) How much time is devoted to the teaching of music
>   in your public schools, and to what extent is it taught?

> 2) What system, if more than one has been tried, has
>   proved the best in practical results, as tested in your
>   schools.

3) What text-book or books have been adopted as the manuals for teaching?

4) Upon what plan, as regards the teachers, is the instruction given? Has every school a teacher, or are more than one taught by the same? The amount of salary, etc.

5) How many classes in the Public Schools enjoy the benefit of the instruction in music?

6) Does singing form a part of the daily exercises in the schools, and how much?

7) Has any attempt ever been made to teach music in the primary schools, and with what success?

8) Has the introduction of music into the schools been opposed, or does it meet with general favor?[34]

Results from the questionnaire revealed that whenever music as a branch of common school education had been fairly tried, the general populace was in favor of the practice.[35]

Annual Music Festivals. The schools of Boston annually presented music festivals depicting their musical achievements. For many years prior to 1858 the custom had been observed without interruption--with one exception in 1847.[36] In 1858 the committee on rules and regulations submitted the following resolution which was subsequently adopted:

> Ordered, That for this year, the usual School Festival in Faneuil Hall be suspended, and that in place thereof there be held at the Music-Hall, at 4 P.M., on the day of the annual exhibition of the Grammar Schools, a Musical Exhibition of the pupils of the Public Schools, in connection with the introduction of the medal scholars to the Mayor, the presentation of bouquets, speeches, addresses, &c., and that a committee of five be appointed to act with the Committee on Music as a joint special committee, to make all necessary arrangements.[37]

The annual exhibition and music festival which had often received much public approbation had aroused adverse comment in 1858. The critics suggested the following reasons for their displeasure: 1) The time spent in preparation may seriously interrupt the regular course of study, and the children lose a part of the benefit which the public schools are meant to afford;

2) The exhibition of children may implant or nourish a love of display, or awaken unpleasant feelings of mortification and jealousy; 3) The expense which is incurred; 4) The exhibition cannot properly be taken as a test of improvement in the studies of the year. [38]

Music in the Primary Grades.   Developing concurrently with introduction of vocal instruction in the grammar schools was pressure for the adoption of school music into the Primary Schools of Boston.   In 1832 after careful consideration, vocal music was introduced into many Primary Schools of the city. [39]   There was some definite action as the result of the voted action concerning primary school music, because in 1840 the standing committee was authorized to furnish the primary school teachers with instruction in vocal music without expense.   Conferences were held with the primary teachers and two meetings had brought together about "two-thirds of the teachers. "[40]

Systematic supervision of primary school music was realized very slowly in Boston.   A committee of three was appointed in 1857 by the School Board to report on the condition of music teaching in the schools.

Their exhaustive study of the many problems confronting the overall music program of the city resulted in the following resoltuion concerning public schools:

> The Exhibitions of the Grammar Schools shall be conducted in such manner as shall best present the actual condition of each school in the prominent branches of study, and shall not exceed two hours in length.   On the first five days of the week previous to the Exhibition, the parents and friends of the children shall be invited to witness the usual exercises of the school, and on the last day of that week the several Grammar Schools shall be closed... in the afternoon of the day,.... of the Annual Exhibitions of the Grammar Schools. "[41]

> In regard to the time and hours already devoted to the music lesson, they would recommend no change.   In their estimation, if the pupils will give undivided attention, or at least apply themselves as diligently as they do under the eye of the teacher in the prosecution of any of the ordinary studies, the two half-hours each week will be ample, not only for the acquirement of the simpler

elements, but good progress can be made towards a
musical education. That a pupil will at the time of his
leaving the Grammar School be an accomplished musician,
is by no means claimed. It is an error to suppose that
music can be taught in a few months. No one can learn
to sing correctly or with facility, except by active, persevering and long-continued effort. A child might as well
be expected to talk or read, after a few lessons in each.
This is not expected nor practicable; but when we take
into account the fact that the average time spent by the
pupils in our public schools is eight years, and that there
are eighty lessons in music each year, the question of
time is in a great measure disposed of.

They would also recommend that each session of the
Primary Schools open and close with singing, and would
suggest that the opening exercise of the morning, and the
closing song of the afternoon session be of a devotional
character. That in the Grammar Schools the morning
session be opened, and the afternoon session be closed,
with appropriate singing, and that musical notation and
the singing of the scale, with exercises in reading simple
music, be practiced twice a week in the two lower classes,
under the instruction of the assistant teachers; and that
the pupils receive credits for attention and proficiency in
this department, and also be examined as in other
branches taught in the schools.

That the first and second classes assemble twice a week,
under the charge of the music teacher of the school, as
at present, and in addition to and in connection with their
vocal exercises, take up the review of what they have already gone over, and proceed as far as the theory of
musical composition and harmony. And in addition, it
shall be the duty of the teacher, for the time being, for
the Girls' High and Normal School, to give such instruction
to the pupils of that institution as shall qualify them to
teach vocal music in our public schools. [42]

The Committee on Music in 1862 and 1863, began exerting

pressure for a systematic introduction of vocal music into the

primary schools of the city. They believed that "the time will

come when every teacher in the Primary Schools will be capable

of teaching singing as well as reading. But such is not the case

now, and it is not likely to be for a considerable period in the

future. "[43]

This hopeful prophecy of 1863 had not been fully realized,

because the supervisor could scarcely trust the music program at the primary school level to the regular classroom teacher.

The Boston School Committee on Music in its report of
September 8, 1863 indicated a growing concern for a systematized
supervisory program of school music at the primary level.   It is
apparent from their statement that in the experimental classes and
schools, that the "Committee have, during the past year, had
opportunity... by personal and critical inspection of several schools
where a well-considered plan of teaching classes of children from
five to seven or eight years of age was being tried as an experiment. [44]

A perusal of the report indicates the conviction of the
committee as to the salutary benefits to be derived from the
study of music at the primary level.   The committee stated
further that to effectually and efficiently accomplish this object,
a special instructor in music for the primary school department
was required--one with experience in that direction, and with a
special aptitude for teaching young children. [45]

All of the above evidence indicates that prior to 1864 primary
music had been taught but had not received direct supervision.
There was need for a concerted plan of action.

J. Baxter Upham, Chairman of the Committee on Music in
a report dated March 8, 1864, related the great need for a primary
supervisor of music in the Boston Schools.   The report also stated
that "1) present requirements, in regard to musical instruction
in this grade of schools, have practically become a dead letter;
and 2) If Music, as a branch of study, is ever to attain to the
excellence which has justly given eclat to our school system, in
most of its departments, it should begin where all other elementary
teaching does--in the Primary Schools. "   Concluding the report,
the Committee issued the following order: "That the Committee
on Music be authorized to nominate to this Board of confirmation,
in addition to the teachers of music in the Grammar Schools, a
suitably qualified person as instructor in music in the Primary
Schools, with a salary not exceeding twelve hundred dollars per
annum. " [46]

A culmination to the above directive was the employment of
Luther Whiting Mason in July, 1864 as special primary school
music instructor. He was the first man to devote all his time
to the supervision and instruction of primary school music in the
city schools. After one year's work, Mason's salary was increased
from $1,200 to $1,800 per annum. He became one of the leaders
of primary and elementary school music in America. [47]

Upham, chairman of the Boston Committee on Music, indicated in an address delivered before the American Institute of
Instruction at its meeting in Lewiston, Maine, August, 1872, the
methods of teaching primary music in the schools of Boston.
Upham stated that before singing, children should be trained to:
"1) Maintain good body position,   2) Use the breath properly,
3) Learn a good quality of utterance,   4) Learn good articulation,
5) Learn to interpret music intelligently,   6) Learn the correct
sounds of the vowels. " Instruction for the first, second, and third
years followed this plan: "1) During the first year a study of
musical notation was started,   2) The second year pupils are
given instruction in note and rest values, quadruple and sextuple
time, beating time, study of accent, chromatics, scales, etc.
3) The third year pupils add the study of intervals of the major
diatonic scales. " [48]

Some additional recommendations were: "1) Rote-singing
should be the first consideration,   2) All first rote-singing experiences should be conducted by the special music teacher,   3) A
correct tonal model should be set up from the start,   4) The child
should be taught to discriminate good singing tone,   5) A study
should be made of motives, sections, and phrases. " [49]

Upham's careful analysis of the primary school music program as conducted in Boston in 1872 serves as an adequate statement of the objectives of nineteenth century primary school music.

Massachusetts the Pioneer in Music Education. Massachusetts
contributed more to the cause of early music education than did
any other single state prior to 1860. It is quite possible that the
schools of Massachusetts were the first public schools to experience

the benefits of vocal music training. While the teaching techniques of the early period were most rudimentary, the early music instructors, in keeping with their period, sought to formalize methods of instruction.

From 1824 to 1838, we find incessant agitation for the incorporation of music into the Boston Public Schools' course of study. Elam Ives was the first to experiment with the teaching of vocal music according to the Pestalozzian principles. The earliest places of vocal teaching were Hartford, Philadelphia, Cambridgeport, Salem, Lynn, and Boston.

The first great leadership to influence all American public school music during the nineteenth century was that of Lowell Mason, a native of Massachusetts. He directed the experimental attempts of introducing music into many of the Boston Schools during the school years 1832 and 1833. Boston was the proving grounds of American music education. The great trio of early music teachers was Elam Ives, George J. Webb, and Lowell Mason.

Not only does Boston represent the earliest place for the advocation of systematic music education in public schools, but the city also claims early musical institutions as the Handel and Haydn Society and the Boston Academy of Music. The former organization affected the cultural life of its citizens while the latter from 1833 became the seat of the Pestalozzian movement of vocal music teaching in the United States. The Academy was the first significant conservatory of music. The lay cultural opportunity in musical art began in Boston and its musical leaders were Lowell Mason and George J. Webb. This institution became a hub for fostering early juvenile, adult and lay singing in this country.

Training Music Teachers. The great surge forward in early Massachusetts and American music education emphasized the need of preparing the itinerant singing-school teacher who was technically speaking, musically illiterate. The Boston Academy of Music was instrumental in bringing the teacher-training issue to a focus. The

first <u>Convention of Vocal Teachers</u> of any consequence met in
Boston in 1836.

This activity started a movement to make vocal music an
official part of the regular course of study in Boston Public Schools.
The official beginning and un-interrupted future of vocal music
teaching in the Boston Public Schools came with the School Committee's sanction, voted August 28, 1838.   This vote of approval has
been called the Magna Charta of music education in America.
Mason was the first official teacher of vocal music in the Boston
Schools.   He must be recognized as the pedagogical father of
American public school music methods.

So much enthusiasm for music has been instilled in the
educational leaders of Massachusetts by 1844, that Horace Mann
stated there were over 500 schools offering music in the state.

Vocal music instruction at the primary level was advocated
very early at Boston.   It is believed that although children were
receiving musical opportunities in some sections of the United
States prior to 1840, pressure for supervised and systematized
primary school music did not come until the period 1855-1865.

The three important centers of supervised primary vocal
music during this period were Cincinnati, Chicago, and Boston.
Luther Whiting Mason was probably America's first authorized
supervisor of primary school music.   After teaching experience
in Louisville, Kentucky, he removed to Cincinnati in 1857, where
he made notable success of primary school music.   In 1864 he was
called to Boston to become its first supervisor of primary school
music.

Notes

1.   Sunderman, Lloyd F.   "Boston and The Magna Charta
     of Music Education", <u>Education.</u>   Vol. 69:   No. 7
     (March, 1949):   425-4<u>37.   Re</u>printed from <u>Education</u> by
     permission of the Bobbs-Merrill Company, <u>Inc.</u>,
     Indianapolis, Indiana.

2.   Hillbrand, E. K.   "How Music Found Its Way Into Ameri-
     can Public Schools, " <u>The Etude.</u>   42:   (March, 1924),
     163.

3.   The American Annals of Education and Instruction, 1832.
     398-400.

4.   Annual Report of the School Committee of The City of
     Boston, 1858.   46.

5.   American Annals of Education and Instruction, 1832.
     398-400.   Italics are the writers.

6.   "Boston Academy of Music," American Annals of Education
     For The Year, 1838.   8: (January, 1838), 44.

7.   Ryan, Thomas.   Recollections of an Old Musician.   (New
     York, N. Y.) E. P. Dutton and Co., 1899), 43-44.

8.   "Boston Academy of Music, First Annual Report," The
     American Annals of Education and Instruction, 3: (August,
     1833), 373-374.

9.   The American Annals of Education and Instruction For
     1834, by William C. Woodbridge, 4: 330-331.

10. Ibid., 330-331.

11. Ibid., "Boston Academy of Music," 4: (July, 1834), 327.

12. Ibid., 327.

13. Ibid., 329.

14. Second Annual Report of the State Commissioner of
     Common Schools to the General Assembly of Ohio, for
     the Year Ending, 1855, 92.

15. Annual Report of the School Committee of the City of
     Boston, 1858- .   47.

16. Ibid., 51.

17. Ibid., 52.

18. Ibid., 52.

19. Ibid., 53.   A statement made by the Boston Academy of
     Music in a report of July, 1839.   Annual Report of the
     School Committee of the City of Boston, 1858.   53.

20. Ibid., 53.

21. "Music in Schools," The Common School Journal.   4:
     (September, 1842), 258-260.

22. The American Annals of Education For The Year, 1838. (Edited by William A. Alcott). 8: 32-34, 44-45.

23. "Singing in Common Schools," The Common School Journal. 3: (June, 1841), 189-190.

24. "Public Singing in Schools," The Common School Journal. 3: (March, 1840), 82-83.

25. Butler, Vera M. "Education as revealed by New England Newspapers." Unpublished Doctoral Dissertation, Temple University, Philadelphia, Pa., 1935. 220-224.

26. "Public Singing in Schools," The Common School Journal. 2: (March, 1840), 82-83.

27. The Annual Report of the School Committee of the City of Lowell, Mass. 1842. 7.

28. Ibid., 4-5.

29. Eighth Annual Report of the Secretary of the Massachusetts Board of Education, 1844. 117.

30. The Report of the Annual Examination of the Public Schools of the City of Boston, 1848. 32.

31. Annual Report of the School Committee of the City of Boston, 1858. 58-61.

32. Ibid., 118.

33. Ibid., 64-65.

34. Ibid., 66-67.

35. Ibid., 68.

36. Ibid., 69.

37. Annual Report of the School Committee of the City of Boston, 1863. 147-155.

38. Annals of the Boston Primary School Committee. From its First Establishment in 1818 to its Dissolution in 1855. 181.

39. Wightman, Joseph M. Annals of the Boston Primary School Committee, from its First Establishment in 1818, to its Dissolution in 1855. (Boston, Mass.: George C. Rand and Avery, 1860). 191.

40.   Ibid., 191.

41.   Annual Report of the School Committee of the City of Boston, 1858.   87.

42.   Ibid., 58.

43.   Seventh Semi Annual Report, Boston Superintendent's Reports, 1862-1863.   143.

44.   Annual Report of the School Committee on Music, the City of Boston, 1864.   37-39.

45.   Ibid., 190-192.

46.   Ibid., 14-15; 189-192.

47.   Annual Report of the School Committee of the City of Boston, 1865.   201.

48.   Upham, Baxter J.   "Vocal Music as a Branch of Education in our Common Schools," Proceedings of the American Institute of Instruction, 1872.   161-185.

49.   Ibid., 161-185.

VI: THE ERA OF BEGINNINGS--1830-1840. [1]

In the history of American school music the decade 1830-
1840 may be considered a period of preparation. Very significant
at the opening of this decade was an epoch making speech by
William Channing Woodbridge, "On Vocal Music as a Branch of
Common Education, " delivered before the American Institute of
Instruction on August 24, 1830. This speech stirred the imagina-
tions of early educational statesmen to the possibilities of vocal
music as a legitimate subject of study and probably did more than
any other utterance prior to the Civil War to articulate and
champion the cause of school music. It was so effective that
scattered instances of school music teaching were reported almost
immediately in New York, Ohio, Pennsylvania, and Connecticut.
While these do not prove universal acceptance of the idea of
public school music, they do indicate its growth and promise.

During the 1830's numerous instances of the rising interest
in school music in New York State are to be found. In 1831 a
proposal was made that music be included in the curriculum of the
schools of Palmyra. [2] It is possible that music instruction was
being offered in some of the schools of New York City as early
as 1829. [3]

Woodbridge again and again used his pen and his voice to
advocate the cause of vocal music instruction. His vigorous
advocacy of school music according to Pestalozzian principles was
not exceeded by any other man in America. At the third annual
meeting of The American Lyceum, which was held in New York,
May 3, 4, and 6, 1833, two speeches were given in the interest
of the introduction of vocal music into the curriculum of the public
schools; Woodbridge and Lowell Mason were the speakers. Woodbridge again delivered "On Vocal Music, As a Branch of Common
Education. " At this meeting a committee was appointed to consider

88

and evaluate his speech.   The committee reported that it was able
to concur with the opinions set forth. [4]

   Earlier, an institution established as the Utica Gymnasium,
at Utica, New York had on its first faculty an Ebenezer Leach,
teacher of Music. [5]   The extent and character of this music which
he taught was not specifically described.   Unquestionably it was of
the applied variety, with additional opportunities for chapel hymn
singing and a possible touch of the science of music.   The first
official adoption and acceptance of music, which was to be taught
as all other subjects, did not come to Utica until 1845. [6]

   At the 1837 New York State Education Convention held at
Utica, delegates to the convention heard a lecture "On Vocal Music
as a Branch of Common School Education, " delivered by Professor
S. N. Sweet. [7]

   Actual music teaching in the public schools of New York State
began very early, at least by 1835 and probably much earlier.
Darius E. Jones, working for The Public School Society of the
City of New York, commenced a course of music lessons in School
No. 10 during 1836.   A Public School Society Report stated that
the total amount of time devoted to music instruction was approximately twenty hours, spread over a period of about six
months.   Only two objections were raised against the introduction
of vocal music: (1) It was expensive;   (2) it would encroach
upon regular school time.   Several music teachers had indicated
a willingness to teach vocal music for a trial period of six months
or a year on a gratuitous basis.   Some regular classroom teachers
had expressed a willingness to teach vocal music.   The committee
offered a resolution which suggested that the schools be at liberty
to have vocal music taught provided it would be done without expense and would not encroach upon regular school time.   The very
appropriate resolution which was passed by the committee concerned
with the adoption of vocal music was laid upon the table and remained
there for some years.   The committee stated that in some of
the primary schools of the Public School Society of New York,
music had been taught by rote, yet, in spite of the attendant

disadvantages of non-supervision, the method was tolerated and continued. [8]

A historical review of early school music teaching in the Buffalo Public Schools states that music was introducted as early as 1837. Two years later Superintendent O. G. Steele stated that vocal music was receiving some attention in several schools. The classroom teachers, however, were teaching the music. [9]

The development of music education in the north-eastern part of the United States was attended by a like activity in the territory between New England and Ohio. Only four years after Woodbridge made his speech "On Vocal Music as a Branch of Common Education," it is recorded in the American Annals of Education and Instruction for 1834 that a society had been formed in Cincinnati under the name Eclectic Academy of Music. The specific aims of the Academy were "to promote the cause of the introduction of vocal music as a branch of school education," and "to foster an improvement of church music." [10]

The trustees of the Academy pointed out that the introduction of school music into the public schools of European centers and its successful inception in Boston and Philadelphia, had shown the practicability of such instruction as a part of common school education. (The Boston Academy of Music reported in its third annual report [1835] that letters from Georgia, South Carolina, Virginia, Illinois, Missouri, Tennessee, Ohio, Maryland, New York, Connecticut, Vermont, New Hampshire, Maine, and Massachusetts were inquiring how to go about the business of introducing music as a branch of common education.) [11]

The formation of the Eclectic Academy in Cincinnati occurred before the idea of music supported by public funds had been accepted in Boston in 1838. The prior existence of the movement in Cincinnati is evidenced by the following excerpt from the American Annals of Education and Instruction for 1835 under the heading, "The Pestalozzian System of Music": "This system has made its way into Kentucky, as well as Ohio. The recent examinations of two schools at Lexington, of 100 scholars each, are spoken of as affording good evidence of the excellence of this system. "[12]

Musical academies which advocated the introduction and the furtherance of the cause of music education existed in Ohio. The Convention of Teachers held in 1835 at Carthage, Ohio, formulated the following resolution: "Resolved, that Vocal Music should be made a part of common elementary education for boys and girls. "[13]

At the fourth annual meeting of the Western Literary Institute and College of Professional Teachers, held in Cincinnati, October, 1834, Professor Nixon of Cincinnati delivered an address "On the Influence of Music. " Nixon said in part that music had power to sway the passions of the human heart and that the universality of music was unquestioned. Recognizing the power of music, he thought it reasonable to question its effects upon mankind. Music soothes the sorrows of the afflicted and draws forth sympathy; an afflicted mankind is greatly cheered by the power of music, he maintained. If the uses of music are employed in perverted ways, the human heart may be stimulated to conquest. Music is capable of refining the coarser nature of man. Music is particularly conducive to a healthful condition of the body. All singing should be in proportion to the strength, age, and healthful condition of the participant. [14]

Later, at the 1836 meeting in Cincinnati of the same organization, a committee was appointed to report at the next annual meeting on vocal music as a branch of common school education. At the 1836 meeting there were 222 members attending the Institute. They came not only from Ohio, but from many of the western and southwestern states. [15]

It requires no stretch of the imagination to visualize the possibilities of such institutes for influencing the cause of music education in America. The appointment of the 1836 committee to survey the potentialities and the advisability of considering music as a branch of common education bore fruit by indirectly influencing other educational conventions. The Convention of the Friends of Common Schools, held at Marietta, Ohio, November 7-8, 1836,

also appointed a committee to report on the introduction of vocal
music into common schools.   As a result, a resolution was adopted
to the effect that the members of the Convention were of the
opinion that the introduction of vocal music into the common
schools would be intellectually, morally, and socially beneficial
to the pupils. [16]

T. B. Mason, Professor in the Eclectic Academy of Music
and Professor of Music in Cincinnati College, made a report on
vocal music which was delivered at the 1838 meeting of the
Western College of Teachers.   It was his conviction "that all mankind possesses the constitutional endowment requisite for the study
of vocal music; that vocal music must be incorporated into our
systems of common education; that appropriate means ought to be
speedily devised for the accomplishment of so desirable an
object. "[17]

Woodbridge was one of the first American educators who
went to Europe to study its educational systems.   A few years
later Professor Stowe of Ohio made a similar trip and later
reported to the legislature of his state what he had seen and
studied in his educational tour.   The fact that Stowe's report
was made to the legislature indicates the significance attached
to his European visit.   He pointed out the wide disparity between
the European and American systems of education.

Pennsylvania also contributed greatly to the development of
music education during the period 1830-1840.   One of the early
nineteenth century writers of singing books in America was Elam
Ives of Philadelphia.   Woodbridge stated that it was Ives whom he
first approached to undertake an experiment of teaching children
vocal music according to the Pestalozzian principles.   His first
classes were taught in Philadelphia and Hartford.   These early
experiments took place in 1830-1831.   The people receiving this
instruction were mostly children, organized into choir groups.

In 1831 Ives published two singing books:

The American Infant School Singing Book, designed as the
first book for the study of Music.   By E. Ives, Jr.

Principal of the Philadelphia Musical Seminary, Hartford.
H. and F. J. Huntington, 1831, pp. 108. 18 mo.

A Manual of Instruction in the Art of Singing, Prepared
for the American Sunday School Union.   By E. Ives, Jr.
Philadelphia, 1831. 8 vo. pp. 40.

Undoubtedly these books were among the first of their kind in
America, constructed according to the "principles of the inductive
system of music originally devised and published by Pfeiffer and
Nägeli, under the direction of Pestalozzi. "[18] Whether or not the
avowed adoption of Pestalozzian principles effected any significant
changes in actual methodology is difficult to determine.

In 1836 the community Shrewsbury, Pennsylvania, was
operating one common school which contained 23 male and 12
female students.   The school year was approximately three months
long.   The course of study included reading, writing, arithmetic,
and sacred music. [19] It is not at all surprising to find the teaching of sacred music, because many of the early teachers of
Pennsylvania were graduates of teacher-training institutions of
Europe; their preparation included the study of the rudiments of
music and the singing of sacred songs.   A report on the condition
of the schools of Lancaster in 1840 shows that the school system
was divided into three divisions: namely, primary, secondary,
and high.   In the primary schools the pupils learned to "repeat
tables, to sing, and read easy lessons. "[20] In one of the schools
oral instruction was being offered.   A further view of the singing
taught in Lancaster is furnished by a letter from Dr. A. D. Bache,
dated December 1, 1841.   His letter reveals that he had observed
with great pleasure, in one of the schools, that musical notation,
as well as the practice of vocal music, was taught, and that the
teacher gave oral instruction in musical notation, using the ledger
lines permanently traced on the blackboard for the purpose.   He
described the curriculum thusly:

> The high school is divided into a male and female depart-
> ment, both under the superintendence of the same instruct-
> or, and the former under his immediate charge...   In the
> male department, bookkeeping, history, natural philosophy,
> geometry and some of the other branches of mathematics,

and music, are taught. [21]

One of the educational periodicals which became a potent force for the cause of education in the state was the Pennsylvania School Journal, published at Lancaster and edited by Thomas H. Burrowes. Frequently during the early 1840's it carried articles under the title of "Music." It is reasonable to believe that they had some definite relationship to the development of a sympathetic attitude which was created for music in the state.

James Mulhern has analyzed the offering in music and in other practical arts in Pennsylvania during the period 1750-1900 (See Tables 1 and 2). His findings indicate that secondary school music was offered prior to and during the period 1830-1840.

Table 1. [22]

Per Cent Institutions Offering Certain Studies

Practical and Fine Arts	1750-1829 (47 Schools)	1750-1889 (163 Schools)	1830-1889 (116 Schools)
Music...................	4	17	22
Drawing................	4	17	22
Mechanics.............	4	5	6

Table 2. [23]

Per Cent of High Schools Offering Certain Subjects

Subjects	1836-1875 (48 Schools)	1836-1900 (140 Schools)	1876-1900 (92 Schools)
Mechanical Drawing.....	2	6	9
Drawing................	33	36	38
Manual Training........	0	3	5
Music..................	12	14	15

Though Pennsylvania was intensely interested in education during the period, the development of school music instruction in the state was very slow. Connecticut, unlike Pennsylvania, made an auspicious attempt to stimulate interest in music instruction. In 1837 the General Assembly of Connecticut passed a resolution providing for the collection of pertinent educational data. Beginning in 1838 detailed questionnaires were sent to the schools of the state.   These circulars of inquiry devoted space to the subject of music teaching.   The eight questions on music were directed to the teachers in charge of the regular classroom.   They were: "Can you sing by note?   Can you play any instrument?   Do you teach or cause singing in school, either by rote or by note?   Do you use singing as a relieving exercise for ill humor or weariness in schools?   Do you use any instrument, or have any used, as an accompaniment to singing?   Do you teach to use the proper musical voice in singing?   Do you do so from ear, or from knowledge of the physiology of the vocal organs?   How many of your pupils prove, on trial, unable to understand music, or acquire even a moderate degree of proficiency in the practice?"[24]

The means for obtaining information were not limited to the questionnaire, as six other points of attack were suggested: 1) By personal inspection and inquiry,   2)   By official returns from school visitors,   3)   By the annual reports of school visitors to their respective societies,   4)   By replies to circulars and letters of inquiry,   5)   By statements and discussions, in county convent- ions, and local school meetings,   6)   By reports from voluntary associations for the improvement of common schools. [25]

The importance of the music questionnaire lies in the fact that it was unquestionably one of the earliest of its kind.   The general findings induced the legislature "to provide for the better supervision of the common schools. "

This survey was aimed at securing both subjective and objective data regarding music instruction.   Although the results are not of special value, it is interesting to find such an early example of a survey of the status of music in the schools of a particular state.   The study brought the status of music education or to the immediate attention of educational leaders, teachers, and laymen.

The Connecticut Common School returns for 1839-1840 indicated that singing had been generally incorporated into the schools of Charlestown.   The account showed that the music (singing) lessons were proving that "no better way could a portion of the school hours be occupied."[26] Henry Barnard in 1841 reported that "Vocal music has been introduced to some extent with the happiest results."[27]

Under the leadership of Barnard (1811-1900) as the first Secretary of the Connecticut State Board of Education, many significant educational reforms were instituted. Barnard remained in office from 1839-1842 at which date his position was abolished.

The precise importance of Woodbridge's remarks to the first meeting of the American Institute of Instruction can never be fully determined, but it is clear that his personality and enthusiasm for public school music profoundly affected the whole period from 1830 to 1840. Though not a musician, he secured the services of Ives, Mason, Webb, and others in helping him experiment with Pestalozzian principles of teaching vocal music in public schools. In the wake of all this enthusiasm many actual programs of school music were developed. Books containing school songs began to be published. Communities in Massachusetts, New York, Pennsylvania, and Ohio, began to experiment with music as a part of the regular school curriculum. The first convention of vocal teachers in America met in Boston in 1836. The Magna Charta of school music was signed in August, 1838, when the Boston School Committee authorized the teaching of music under the direction of Lowell Mason. It was a period when a majority of teachers' conventions were discussing the merits of vocal music as a branch of common education. By the close of the period (1840) the idea of popular school music education in America had germinated to such an extent that the educational forces were becoming sensitive to the merits of school music as a cultural necessity.

Notes

1. Sunderman, Lloyd F. "The Era of Beginnings in American Music Education, 1830-1840," Journal of Research in Music Education. IV: No. 1 (Spring, 1956), 33-39. Chapter appeared as article indicated above. Reprinted with the permission of the Journal of Research in Music Education, Allen P. Britton, (Chairman) Editorial Commit-

tee.

2.   "Music in Common Schools, " The American Annals of
     Education and Instruction. 1: (July, 1831), 330.

3.   "Instruction in the City of New York, " The American
     Annals of Education and Instruction. II: (July, 1832),
     411-412.

4.   "Proceedings of the American Lyceum, " The American
     Annals of Education and Instruction. III: (August, 1833),
     352.

5.   Annual Report of the Utica Public Schools. (Utica, 1876),
     15.

6.   Annual Report of the Superintendent of Schools. (City of
     Utica, 1878), 30-31.

7.   "State Education Convention, " The American Annals of
     Education and Instruction. VII: (July, 1837), 329.

8.   Bourne, William O. History of the Public School Society
     of the City of New York With Portraits of the Presidents
     of the Society. (New York, N. Y. : Wm. Wood and Co. ,
     1870), 632-636.

9.   "A Century of Music in Buffalo Schools, " Music Educators
     Journal. 23: (March, 1937), 26.

10. "Eclectic Academy of Music in Cincinnati, " The American
     Annals of Education and Instruction. 4: (June, 1834),
     289.

11. Elson, Louis C. The History of American Music.
     (New York: The Macmillan Company, 1915), 73-93.

12. "Pestalozzian System of Music, " The American Annals of
     Education and Instruction. V: (April, 1835), 188.

13. "Convention of Teachers at Carthage, " The American
     Annals of Education and Instruction. V: (June, 1835),
     281-282.

14. Professor Nixon, "On the Influence of Music, " The
     American Annals of Education and Instruction. V:
     (November, 1835), 507-510.

15. "Western Literary Institute, " The American Annals of
     Education and Instruction. VII: (January, 1837), 40.

16.   "Common School Convention, At Marietta, " The Ameri-
       can Annals of Education.   VIII: (April, 1838), 181.

17.   "Intelligence from Ohio, " American Annals of Education.
       VIII: (April, 1838), 181.

18.   "Editorial, " The American Annals of Education and
       Instruction.   I: (March, 1832), 136.

19.   Statement of the Operations of the Pennsylvania School
       System, 1836, in All the Accepting Districts Which Have
       Paid Their State Appropriations and Have Reported up to
       February 14, 1837.   28.

20.   Bache, A. D.   "Public Schools of Lancaster, " The
       Connecticut Common School Journal.   V: (June, 1841),
       162-165.

21.   Ibid.

22.   Mulhern, James.   "A History of Secondary Education in
       Pennsylvania. " (Unpublished doctoral dissertation,
       University of Pennsylvania, 1933).   328-329.

23.   Ibid. , 542-543.

24.   "Mr. Barnard's Labors in Connecticut from 1838-1842, "
       Barnard's American Journal of Education.   I: (1856),
       695.

25.   "Mr. Barnard's Labors in Connecticut from 1838-1842, "
       Ibid. , 697.

26.   "Singing, " The Connecticut Common School Journal.   II:
       (March, 1840), 161.

27.   "Third Annual Report of the Secretary of the Board of
       Commissioners of Common Schools, " The Connecticut
       Common School Journal.   III: (May, 1841), 254.

VII. AMERICAN MUSIC EDUCATION--1840-1865.

The period from 1830-1840 was a great epoch in the development of vocal music instruction in American public schools. By the close of this period there was a more receptive attitude toward vocal music instruction. William C. Woodbridge, Elam Ives, Horace Mann, William B. Fowles, Lowell Mason, Joseph Harrington Jr., T. B. Mason, George J. Webb, and Samuel A. Eliot were among the distinguished protagonists of the cause. These men developed a philosophy of teaching and methods of instruction which brought about greater popularization of school music. They were its first effective missionaries. So effective was their work that during the next twenty-five years vocal music became a topic of popular discussion in all educational circles. They were not alone in working for the cause of music education, being ably assisted by a succeeding generation of distinguished school music educators.

Some of the men who were working during this period of significant adoptions (1840-1865) were: William C. Webster, G. V. Vining, Everett Baker, all of Buffalo, New York; Alexander D. Bache, Philadelphia, Pennsylvania; N. Gilbert, F. Lombard, C. Plagge, J. L. Slayton, William Tillinghast, all of Chicago, Illinois; William F. Colburn, Charles Aiken, Luther W. Mason, of Cincinnati, Ohio; Silas Bingham, J. H. Clark, J. F. Hanks, of Cleveland, Ohio; W. C. Van Meter, Mr. Whipple, Charles Godfrey, of Louisville, Kentucky; and Jason White, Charles M. Clarke, and Seth Sumner of Providence, Rhode Island.

It is difficult to give an accurate picture of the spread of public school music. The evidence is often incomplete and the efforts were scattered and somewhat random. Perhaps the best impression of the growth of public school music in the quarter of a century following 1840 can be secured by examining its development in the various states. Materials were available regarding

99

the introduction of school music in Pennsylvania, Ohio, Illinois, and New York. The states will be discussed in the order indicated, because of a desire to treat all sources chronologically. There will be additional discussions of the introduction of public school music in the East--Rhode Island, District of Columbia, Maryland, New Jersey, Connecticut; in the South--Kentucky, Louisiana, Tennessee; in the Middle West--Wisconsin, Missouri, Michigan, Indiana, Iowa; and in the Far West--California.

Pennsylvania

The school music experiments in Pennsylvania during the period 1830-1840 were to some degree responsible for the wide-spread growth that followed. Sources of information relative to the school conditions in the many states were quite often never recorded in permanent report form. Many of the reports were handwritten, particularly those from the smaller communities.

An outstanding personage of influence during this period was Dr. Alexander D. Bache. Upon his return from Europe in 1839 he wrote extensively and became a strong advocate of the Pesta-lozzian system of teaching music. His reports of 1840 and 1841 were cited in the previous chapter (see p. 93). Pertinent to the state of music education at this time he found that primary school children in Lancaster, Pennsylvania, were experiencing singing and musical notation as a part of their regular curriculum. [1] He found also that in the high school--which was the third level of instruction, coming after the primary and secondary divisions--male students, at least, were being taught music. [2]

It is not surprising to find Bache, who was President of Girard College for Orphans, and Acting Principal of the Central High School for Boys in Philadelphia, advocating in 1840, the employment of a professor of vocal and instrumental music. [3] An 1846 report of the names of the professors and teachers, their salaries and attendance records for the high school which was located at Penn Square, Philadelphia, however, reveals no establishment of the position of vocal instructor. [4]

A special committee report on the reduction of studies in
the public schools of Philadelphia, dated 1861, shows that music
was not included among the branches regularly taught. [5] In 1864
the controllers of public schools of Philadelphia stated that vocal
music when taught was given at the expense of the pupils.   No
appropriation had been made for music teachers.   From the 1864
report it is apparent that consideration was being given to the
advisability of employing music instructors in the grammar schools. [6]

Ohio

During the period under consideration, there was rapid
growth in the development of public school music in Ohio. [7]   At
the Cincinnati meeting of the Music Supervisors' National Conference
in 1924, [8] Walter H. Aiken, director of music in the public schools
of Cincinnati, relates the one circumstance which led to the introduction of music in Cincinnati.   On April 5, 1842 upon the occasion
of the meeting of the Temperance Societies of Cincinnati and nearby
towns, a parade was held in the city.   At Vine and Fourth Street,
which was along the march of the great procession, the marchers
were greeted by juvenile singers from the city Sabbath Schools.
They were singing songs in keeping with the occasion.   Some of
the children participating in the singing had been trained by Charles
Aiken, who in 1842 had established a singing class in the basement
of the Sixth Presbyterian Church. [9]

Aiken employed the methods of Lowell Mason.   His fame in
connection with Ohio music education rests upon three considerations:
1) he was the second music teacher in the Cincinnati Public Schools;
2) he was Ohio's first important teacher of public school music;
3) he did much by force of personality to bring to the attention of
the public some of the values to be derived from the study of
vocal music.

G. F. Junkermann contends that vocal music teaching in the
public schools of Cincinnati started in 1842 under the direction of
William F. Colburn.   From the first introduction of school music
instruction in the city, the movable "do" system was employed in
the teaching of reading songs.   Movable "do" means that when the

key name changes, the new key name is called "do." (Illustration:
In changing from the key of C, "C" is "do," to the key of G,
"G" becomes "do").

Other early teachers of music in the school system, were:
Elisha Locke, Luther Whiting Mason, E. Pease, and Joseph P.
Powell. Junkermann states that Colburn, the first music teacher,
was superintendent of music during 1844, 1845, and 1848. Other
superintendents of music for the city during the nineteenth century
were Charles Aiken, 1848-1879, and G. F. Junkermann, 1879-
1900. [10]

Walter H. Aiken, [11] Supervisor of Music in the city during
the period 1900-1920, relates (through evidence furnished by his
father Charles Aiken) what happened during the eventful year of
1842. Charles Aiken was induced to teach a singing class in the
basement of the Sixth Presbyterian Church, (later known as the
Vine Street Congregational Church). It was here that he taught the
Temperance songs. Throughout that year and the next Aiken, on a
gratuitous basis continued to instruct children in singing in the basement of the same church. In addition to the youth group, there
were adults who received instruction in vocal music.

One of the members of his class was William Colburn, who
later became the first music teacher in the city. From 1844 to
1845, Colburn taught gratuitously in the public schools of the city.
He did so with the approval of the Board of Education--the
stipulation being that there should be no cost for the instruction.
During the school year 1844-1845 there were four schools and
3,726 children in daily attendance in the Cincinnati system.

The Trustees of the school system for that year afford us
with extremely significant evaluations. They stated that

> The result has been in every way satisfactory and has
> been the means in some measure of including the Board
> as well as the public to come to the conclusion that
> music ought to be introduced into the schools as a regular
> branch of instruction. In whatever light we view it,
> whether as a means of social enjoyment, or moral in-
> fluence, or intellectual improvement, it seems to have a
> happy effect upon the pupils. The Board has accordingly
> appointed a committee to report a plan by which hereafter,
> music may be regularly taught; this committee will probably

report at an early session of the new Board, and we trust
that our successors may enjoy the privilege of adopting a
plan by which music may be regularly taught to all the
youth in our schools whose parents desire it. [12]

Evidently satisfaction with the vocal examinations of 1845 resulted
in the appointment of Colburn for the ensuring year at the munifi-
cent salary of $45 per month, and having as his assistant a Miss
Thatcher who was to receive $12 per month.

During the period 1842-1846, Charles Aiken was still maintaining his singing school at the Vine Street Congregational Church.
(Formerly Sixth Presbyterian Church). While attending Lane
Seminary (Cincinnati) from which he graduated in 1847, Aiken came
in contact with Calvin E. Stowe and through him he learned about
school music as employed in many European schools. Aiken's music
program was based on the principles of Hullah of London, Silcher of
Germany, and Wilhelm of Paris. With these he fused some of the
Pestalozzian techniques which were basic to the system employed
by Lowell Mason.

Music was introduced into the primary grades on an experimental basis as early as 1853. The period 1857-1863 saw increased activity in the lower grades, with Luther Whiting Mason
being responsible for the systematization of the methods of
instruction. Mason left Cincinnati in 1864 to assume administration
of the primary music program which he was to organize in the
Boston Public Schools. Cincinnati was one of the earliest cities
in America to offer music in the primary grades. To give music
instruction to school children of this grade level was an unprece-
dented act for a middle western board of education prior to 1865.

Cincinnati was not alone in fostering vocal music instruction
for children in Ohio. As early as 1840 Jarvis H. Danks submitted
a petition to the city council of Cleveland, asking for the privilege
of teaching vocal music at a very small salary. The council
frowned upon the idea, one member of the group comparing the
subject of vocal music with the teach of dancing in the schools. [13]

This early effort eventually bore fruit. Lowell Mason of
Boston was asked to come to Cleveland and talk on "Music as a
Branch of Common School Education. " When he came, he spoke

on "Music Taught to Youth on the Pestalozzian System of Instruction. "[14] Many demonstrations on how to teach vocal music were
given with classes of children from the public schools. It was not
until 1846 that Silas Bingham was employed by the common council
to teach music. Subsequently, J. H. Clark, and J. F. Hanks were
employed. Music was being taught in all senior schools but
primary school music was unknown in 1846. By 1851 music was
taught in all the schools. Bingham was reemployed a year later,
remaining until 1858, when a financial crisis caused the release
of all special teachers.

Zanesville might lay claim to the honor of being the first
city in Ohio to have music as a part of its course of study.
During 1842 the boys and girls of the city were separated into
schools for each sex. A special teacher who taught writing and
music was employed to serve both schools, although the city had
not graded its school system. In addition to teaching the two subjects, the music instructor was superintendent of the girls' school.

Music instruction was introduced into other cities in Ohio
at various dates. In 1844 it was offered in the high school at
Oberlin. Five years later singing was practiced under the direction
of a music teacher. That same year James Turpin became the
music instructor for the Dayton Public Schools. Columbus saw to
it that music was included into its school curriculum by 1851, with
the special music teacher being appointed in 1854. E. D. Kingsley,
the superintendent of schools in 1857, indicated that in addition to
the ordinary studies there was a teacher of music. [15] Ripley had a
very pretentious music program in 1853, prescribing vocal and
instrumental music as part of the course of a four year high school
program; extra fees were to be charged those wishing instrumental
instruction. D. Parson, superintendent of the Wellesville Public
Schools for 1854, stated that a thorough course of instruction was
being offered in vocal and instrumental music with forty pupils
studying piano or guitar. [16] Marietta was offering vocal music to
the high school students during the year 1855, while the Chillicothe
public schools were offering vocal music only during the first year

of the grammar department. [17]   In 1858 Toledo was giving music
instruction under the tutelage of a special teacher.   Newark made
such instruction possible in 1861, the teacher being also required
to teach German.

The spread of school music teaching in Ohio was rapid.
Beginning in 1844 with the first teaching of school music in
Cincinnati, it was but a short time until a number of cities
representing all sections of the state were offering music instruction. The music programs for the various primary, intermediate,
grammar, and high school departments included vocal and instrumental instruction. (Before 1865 instrumental instruction implied
instruction in piano and guitar).

Illinois

The data shows that there was a very significant westward
movement of the teaching of music in the schools after 1840.
Simultaneous with the growth of school music in Ohio, there
appeared a noteworthy development in Chicago and later during
the period there was activity in other Illinois cities.

Pressure for the inclusion of vocal music as a part of the
school curriculum started very early in the history of the Chicago
Public Schools. In 1841 a meeting of the inspectors and trustees
of the common schools of the city was held for the purpose of
considering the propriety of introducing music into the schools.
After due deliberation it was unanimously voted to employ a music
teacher. The first teacher, N. Gilbert, was appointed at a salary
of $16 a month. [18] His efforts apparently met with some success
because in September he was appointed for another six months at
the rate of $400 per annum, payable when the taxes are collected.
This encouraging beginning was too good to last because at the end
of the six months, music instruction was discontinued.

Due to the inadequacy of school funds, nothing further was
done about music teaching until the second quarter of 1846--a lapse
of three years--when permission was granted to teach "Music in
the Schools for a small remuneration afforded him by the scholars,
or as many of them as can or will pay. "[19] The Board of School

Inspectors reported "that the scholars are very fond of this new
exercise, and that it is believed to exert a most beneficial influence upon their taste and feelings." In December of that year
the inspectors recommended the employment of a permanent music
teacher, "to devote his whole attention to the several schools of
our City," remarking that "Mr. Whitman has for some months
past been giving lessons in Music to a large number of scholars
in the several districts, and the effect has been of the most
salutary character."

Earlier that year the School Inspectors had granted the
Choral Union Musical Society the use of a recitation room in
one of the school buildings. In lieu of payment for use of the
room, the Society was to give a concert under the supervision
of the school authorities to raise funds for the purchase of books.

In March 1847 the Committee on Schools of the Common
Council considered the advisability of making vocal music one of
the branches of common education. They reported that it would
approve such action if the school fund warranted such financial
outlay, which it did not at that time. In November the School
Inspectors were authorized to employ a music teacher for one year,
appropriating $250 from the School Fund for that purpose. Frank
Lombard was appointed to teach vocal music in January, 1848.

In April 1850 the School Inspectors adopted the following
resolution:

> RESOLVED, That instruction in the elementary principles
> of Vocal Music is desirable in all our public schools, and
> that an appropriation of money should be made for the
> purpose of employing a competent Teacher of Music, at
> as early a day as the finances of the City will permit.

From this resolution it would appear that regular music
teaching in the public schools again had lapsed for a time. The
records show that Mr. Whitman "was permitted, during the year
1850, to give instruction in music free of charge." In July, however, the Common Council ordered that a $400 appropriation be
made for the teaching of vocal music "in the several schools."
It is not clear whether Frank Lombard continued teaching through

all of this period. The records also show that S. P. Warner taught music in 1850.

In December of that year, the Board of School Inspectors invited the School Trustees and other interested parties to witness a demonstration of music teaching in the various schools of the city, the term for which the music teachers were employed being near its close. Later that month Mr. Lombard was elected to take charge of music in the four schools for six months.

The time devoted to music in the schools is indicated in a resolution passed at that time:

> RESOLVED, That the time to be occupied in teaching Music shall be half an hour in the lower room of each school, and three quarters of an hour in the upper room of each school, and that the rudiments of Music be taught in both departments of each school.

It is apparent that the music work of the city schools was being systematically organized.

In 1851 the board of education indicated that music in the public schools of the city was proving to be of such value to the school system that a recommendation was made that the music supervisor be employed for another year. Music teachers employed in Chicago during the decade 1850-1860 were as follows: Frank Lombard 1850-1853; Christopher Plagge 1853-1854; J. L. Slayton 1854-1856; William Tillinghast 1856-1860. Tillinghast was the first supervisor of music in Chicago to receive $1,000 per annum.

In April 1852 Lombard's salary was increased from $400 to $500 because of his added duties in the two new school buildings. He continued in charge of vocal instruction until the end of 1853, when he resigned. Several teachers followed him in the interval ending the middle of October 1860, after which it was voted "inexpedient to appoint a Teacher of Music at the present time."

Superintendent W. H. Wells reported in 1857 that lessons in vocal music were being given once a week in all the schools. [20] The primary school lessons were devoted to the singing of rote songs, the singing by rote of scale exercises, and the giving by dictation of many scale exercises. A major immediate objective

was to get children to sing pitches correctly. Sight reading was
the ultimate objective. In the high school the music lessons were
forty-five minutes long, in the grammar schools, forty, -- and
in the primary schools, thirty.

As early as 1861 the Chicago Superintendent of Instruction,
lamenting the lack of a music teacher in the public schools, asked
if in the employment of the regular in-service school teachers,
consideration should not be given to their musical preparation:

> It is now more than one year since the Board dispensed
> with the services of a teacher of music in the public
> schools. I am not aware that any member of the Board
> expected or desired this arrangement to be permanent,
> and I cannot refrain from expressing the conviction that
> the interests of the schools are suffering seriously from
> the lack of a uniform and efficient system of instruction
> in this important branch. It is true that many of the
> teachers are able to conduct exercises in singing very
> successfully, and, in some of the divisions, the singing
> was never better than at the present time; but it is
> obvious that, in most of the schools, these results cannot
> be expected, without the constant aid of a professional
> teacher of music. . . .
>
> More than one-third of the teachers are now able to
> instruct their pupils in the elements of music, and the
> number might easily be increased to two-thirds, if other
> teachers would make some special effort to qualify them-
> selves. Though there is no reason to expect that we shall,
> for many years to come, be able to sustain this branch
> satisfactorily, without the aid of a music teacher, it is
> highly important that each teacher should be able to
> cooperate with the special teacher, and conduct the sing-
> ing exercises in his absence. Has not the time already
> arrived, when, in selecting teachers for the schools, the
> musical qualifications of the candidates should be taken
> into consideration. [21]

Not until November 1863 was the teaching of music resumed,
however--this time with two instructors, one for the high school
and one for the grammar and primary schools. The salary of
the latter, Orlando Blackman, was fixed at $1,400 before the end
of his first year. It is to be assumed, however, that only about
one-third of this was paid from the school fund, since, when he
was appointed, the Board of Inspectors was to pay "$450 per annum
toward (italics added) his salary. "

Charles Ansorge, the high school music teacher, resigned in January 1865 (or the fall of 1864), to be succeeded in October by Edward E. Whittemore. While the Board had appropriated only $50 a year toward Ansorge's salary when he was hired, it appropriated $600 for the employment of his successor, whose services were limited to three days a week.

Not alone was it difficult to secure funds in order to pay for a teacher of music, but it was likewise hard to procure books and other teaching material. In 1860 the singing book employed in the grammar school was Lowell Mason's Normal Singer, while the primary school used Bradbury's School Melodist. [22] Prior to 1866 the teacher of music furnished graded musical exercises at his personal expense.

To Blackman is attributed the idea of instructing the regular primary teachers in the mechanics of teaching music. According to the report of the Committee on Music: "In March, 1864, Mr. Blackman asked the Board for permission to instruct the Primary Teachers in singing, and also to arrange work for them to give to their pupils. This permission was granted. A Graded Course in singing was then arranged for the Primary Schools. This course, improved in many particulars, is now in use, and seems to be successful. "

In his report to the superintendent of public schools for the year 1865-1866, Blackman stated that the plan of music supervision as effected by him during the year was as follows: 1) That the upper divisions of the Grammar Department were under the direct teaching of music teachers; 2) Graded exercises for the lower primary grades had been set up for the teacher instructing that level; 3) That all teachers of primary grades and lower divisions of grammar grades were to receive music instruction from music teachers one hour each month; 4) All pupils from the lowest to the highest grades were to be taught to read music and to beat time; 5) Music teachers were to visit lower grades and instruct the pupils. [23]

As early as 1859, primary school music had received some
attention in the city schools however. The lessons were chiefly
the learning of songs and hymns taught by rote. [24] Chicago, like
Boston, taught scientific school music, which implied a study of
the theoretical knowledge of music, the singing of scale exercises,
and an early introduction to sight reading.

Chicago retains a place of great significance in the development of early school music in the United States. All available
evidence seems to indicate that it was the earliest mid-western
city to experiment with school music. But it was not the only
city in Illinois to show interest in music before 1865. There is
some evidence of the spread of music teaching in other cities in
the state during this early period. In 1856 it was reported that
a teacher was employed to teach vocal music in Joliet at an annual
salary of $600. He was required to teach music ten hours per
week. [25]

In 1859, The Illinois Teacher reported that music instruction
had been introduced in Jacksonville. Instruction was to be given
in a convenient church building, the teachers being secured for the
purpose of offering music to the children of the city. "Free
tickets to the course are given out in the Sabbath Schools and by
three gentlemen well known in the town, so that every one may
receive the benefit. "[26] Instruction was to be given two times per
week, the meeting hour being "half-past four in the afternoon. "
Another article raised the question of the advisability of continuing
music instruction in public schools without the aid of instruments.
"All teachers of singing are accustomed to avail themselves more
or less of instrumental assistance in imparting instruction. "[27]
It was suggested that where a schoolroom could not afford the
assistance of a music teacher, the piano forte would act as a
guide, for its pitch would be an unfaltering help toward good performance. [28]

The discussion dealing with the need of musical instruments
as aids in music teaching gives an example of what school music
did in America to stimulate the music industry. With the inception

of school music teaching, there were demands for the manufacture
of musical instruments, the publication of music books, the training
of music teachers, and the development of all forms of physical
equipment needed in creating good school music opportunities for
American children.

In 1862 Mrs. M. D. Cooke offered the first vocal music
lessons in Galesburg and thereby became one of the earliest women
teachers of music in American schools. She was allowed to occupy
a room in the Colton Building, teaching only one half hour each
day. One year later she was given full time in one room; however,
by 1865 the Galesburg School Board had taken away the room priv-
lege which she had been granted. [29]

New York

New York State in 1812 had created a state officer for the
coordination and supervision of education in its schools. Many
educational sources were gathered through his contact with the
public schools of the state. Between 1821-1854 the state officer
was the Secretary of State, who was acting Superintendent of
Common Schools. Reports of educational activities for each year
were published and undoubtedly sent to all those educators who
contributed information to make them possible. Many of the
yearly reports carried articles discussing the benefits to be derived from vocal music study. Undoubtedly these articles did
much to stimulate interest in public school music. The agitation
was particularly vigorous after 1840. A glimpse of the status of
school music teaching in the state during 1843, 1844, and 1845
is revealed in the records.

During the year 1843, there were 10,220 pupils engaged during
the winter term in the study and practice of vocal music. The 1844
tabulation showed that the total number had increased to 47,618,
and in 1845 to 71,890 pupils. The figures for the summer term
were as follows: (1843) 17,632; (1844) 43,243; and (1845)
77,925. [30]

Upon many occasions the deputy county superintendents of
schools of New York State when submitting their school returns to

the state superintendent of common schools included some comments regarding vocal music instruction in their counties.   O. W. Randall, deputy superintendent of the Western Division of Oswego County, stated in 1842 that vocal music had been introduced into some of the schools of his county. [31]

Alexander Fonda, reporting for Schenectady County during the same year, said that he had witnessed for the first time in his county the attempt to introduce vocal music.   Pupils attending the summer school session at No. 16, located at Duanesburgh, and under the direction of Jane Coley, were receiving instruction in singing.   The results were most satisfactory.   The voices had been blended together making a most delightful experience for the pupils. [32]

Schools in the southern district of Alleghany County reported introductions of vocal music in 1844. [33]   In the towns of Bolivar and Wirt, pleasing results had followed the introduction of vocal music; previous disciplinary problems had been lessened.   During 1844 vocal music had been deemphasized in Albany, Dutchess (Southern District), Genesee, Green, Livingston, Monroe, Oswego, Putman, St. Lawrence, Schoharie, and Wyoming Counties.   David Nay, superintendent of the common schools of Genesee County, announced that in the winter of 1842 only one school in the county was receiving vocal music.   By 1844 he claimed that sixty pupils were participating in this form of instruction during the winter schools and 463 during the summer schools.   In Livingston County, Ira Patchin, the superintendent, reported 1,915 pupils receiving instruction in 1844 against 486 in 1843. [34]

Turning from state and county reports, many cities were offering vocal music during this period of rapid growth which came after 1843.   The Buffalo Public Schools offered vocal music during this same period.   In 1843 S. Caldwell, the superintendent, pointed out that the council had hired F. Hazelton as a vocal teacher for a period of six months.   He was required to teach vocal music one-half hour twice a week in each school. [35]

Superintendent Steele in 1845 and Superintendent Daniel Bowen in 1846 pointed out that very happy results were being obtained from the study of music. The latter superintendent reported in 1849 that music was being taught in all the city schools. Two years later, William C. Webster was appointed supervisor of music and he remained with the schools until 1855. Mr. G. V. Vining was appointed in 1856. This was during the same year that the state superintendent of public instruction reported that the Buffalo City Superintendent's office reported that one singing master was receiving $1,000 per year for instructional services.[36] The method of teaching music during this period was comparable to the practices found in other sections of the United States. In 1858 it was reported that the method of instruction was to write "simple exercises on the blackboard and to devote a large portion of the hour to drilling the whole school in the rudiments of music."[37] The boys and girls were learning to know the meanings of the lines, spaces, sharps, note values, etc.

No appropriation was made in 1859 for a music teacher. In 1860, the superintendent reported that music was lacking in the curriculum. However, by 1862 music instruction was in full swing again. The superintendent this time indicated that at no time in the history of the schools had music been given more serious attention by the students.[38]

Everett L. Baker, who began work in February, 1863 became one of New York State's outstanding missionaries of early music education. He was identified with the teaching of music in Buffalo for many years.

Undoubtedly one of the most significant early introductions of vocal music into the curriculum of American public schools occurred in the city of Rochester. This took place but four years after the first official introduction in Boston, and all evidence points unequivocally to the fact that it was among the earliest and most permanent introductions into the elementary schools of New York State.

The earliest available Report of the Superintendent of Common Schools, of the City of Rochester, [39] states the "Instruction in vocal music, which should be the last thing dispensed with, and which has for the last two years been introduced with great pleasure and profit -- is, for want of funds, necessarily suspended for the present."[40] This statement made by I. F. Mack, the superintendent in 1844, is evidence substantiating the fact that music was introduced in 1842.

Apparently the interim that existed in music teaching from 1844 on was not long. The Superintendent reported that he was suggesting the "propriety" of making provision for the introduction of music into their schools again, at least on the weekly basis. In 1847 some 1, 987 students were studying vocal music. The salutary benefits derived from vocal music were said to be a more cheerful disposition, a more courteous manner, and greater proficiency in their studies. Daniel Holbrook, the teacher of music, restated that vocal music was taught in all of the schools of the city beginning in 1846. A portion of the schools offered music in 1847; however, no instruction in vocal music was given in 1848. Holbrook championed the idea of vocal music by recommending that it become a weekly exercise and that competent teachers be employed.

In 1852 the superintendent announced that B. W. Durfee and James Murray were teaching music. A year later William Tillinghast of early institute fame was teaching in the city schools.

In 1856 children in the primary department were receiving fifteen minute lessons per day; the second intermediate department devoted the same amount of time in the mornings to Oral Instruction and Singing, and a like period in the afternoon to Gymnastics and Singing; the first intermediate class devoted ten minutes in the afternoon to Elementary Sounds or Singing. Rochester children had received vocal music lessons in the primary and intermediate departments from 1842 to 1862 with but short intervals when no instruction was given due to the lack of funds or when no satisfactory teacher was available.

The official introduction of vocal music into the public
schools of Utica came in 1845. The teacher of vocal music was
a Mr. Edson. He was employed to teach music in all of the
schools with the exception of the Minden and Colored school. He
gave one lesson each week in each of the schools, receiving fifty
cents per lesson.[41] Vocal music was introduced into the Advanced
school during 1846, being a part of the course of study of the
four-year program in the English department.[42]

Syracuse reported in 1852 that vocal music was receiving
some attention under the direction of Mr. Allen. In addition to
vocal training some song books were furnished. The results were
happy, and music was said to improve school cheerfulness, good
social relationships, and a healthy condition for good morals.[43]
Edward Smith, in his History of the Schools of Syracuse, states
that music was introduced into its schools during 1852.[44] George
L. Farnham, clerk and city superintendent of schools, stated in
1859 that it might be possible to hire a music teacher to teach
music in the schools during the coming year, indicating that the
cost would be nominal and the results beneficial.[45] In 1860, the
superintendent reported that "of late, (they) have employed in the
Primary Departments only such teachers as can sing sufficiently
well to take charge of this most delightful exercise. The result
of the plan is, that the practice of vocal music is generally introduced, and there is scarcely a school now in the city where the
school exercises for the day are not begun and ended with singing,
with occasional songs interspersed throughout the day."[46]

New York City reported in 1854, that its course of instruction
included vocal music wherever practicable in the primary and
grammar schools.[47] According to Palmer, singing had been a
part of the school program for several years prior to 1854. Some
school departments were fortunate enough to have the use of
pianos.[48] A year later the superintendent of New York City stated
that in the grammar schools the sciences of music and drawing were
being cultivated with regularity.[49]

The city superintendent of Brooklyn for 1856 pointed out that music was a part of their course of studies. [50]

Music was not a part of the grammar school's outline of studies. Ten years later the superintendent reported that the number of music teachers in the employ of the city was five. [51] In 1868 the city was spending over $7,000 for musical instruction. [52]

Academy education played a dominant role in early New York State education. In 1862 an academy located at West Winfield was offering vocal music to 112 pupils. [53] The Mexico Academy, Mexico, which was established in 1826, had on its faculty during the school year 1863, a music teacher whose salary was derived from fees obtained from the students. [54] Kesseville Academy, an Essex County institution with its location in Clinton County, was offering vocal music during the same period. [55] At this time there was but one academy in Oneida County. Instruction in music was a part of the academy curriculum. There was no mention made as to the location of this particular educational institution. [56]

Rhode Island

Although Cubberly has stated that music was introduced prior to 1848 into the curriculum of the primary and intermediate schools of Providence, Rhode Island, records show that music instruction in the public schools of the city became a reality by 1844, when it was introduced "as an important branch of learning."[57] The first teachers of music in the schools were Jason White, Charles M. Clarke, Seth Sumner and Charlotte O. Doyle. During June, 1846, a report to the city council of Providence on the re-organization of the public schools under Rule and Regulations states the following:

> Primary Schools: Vocal Music. The teachers are required to make vocal music one of the exercises of these schools. The above requirement for these schools was also imposed upon the teachers instructing in the Intermediate, Grammar, High School, and Colored Schools. [58]

In order to positively substantiate the date 1844, the Annual Report of The School Committee of the City of Providence, under the date of June, 1863, said in part

> The steady improvement in Music is among the pleasant
> facts of the later years of our school history. At the
> time of its introduction in 1844, many seriously questioned
> its utility. An apprehension, such as naturally connects
> itself with any untried experiment, was felt that it might
> withdraw interest from other studies, and prove an injury
> to the work of the school-room. [59]

In some communities there was a struggle to bring about the
introduction of vocal music as a part of the school curriculum while
in others there was much apprehension as to the advisability of
introducing music into the curriculum. In Providence, the idea
of incorporating vocal music as a part of the school offerings
was not a protracted one. From the beginnings in 1844, the music
program marched progressively forward. The early method of
teaching music was "more a recitation than a positive study, and
singing by rote was the prevaling practice. " The rote teaching
method did not last more than a decade. In 1856 the superintendent
of the Providence Public Schools, Daniel Leach, reported that
Professor Greene had examined all of the Grammar Schools in
music and he found that there had been a marked improvement in
the subject.

It was reported in 1863 that during the past eight years,
music had been pursued as a science in the Intermediate, Grammar
and High Schools. The boys and girls graduating from the Grammar
and High Schools had developed the ability of "reading at sight, any
tunes commonly sung in public worship on the Sabbath. "[60]

During the year 1866, some of the schools were under the
direction of Walter S. Meade. Other music teachers down to 1875
included, Henry Carter and Benjamin W. Wood.

Washington, D. C.
and
Baltimore, Maryland

In 1845, Washington, D. C. and Baltimore were taking active
measures to make vocal music available to their school children.
The public school trustees of Washington stated in 1845 that they
had authorized the employment of J. H. Hewitt, who was probably
the first official music teacher in the District of Columbia. [61] The

board of trustees stated later in that year that "it was highly
expedient and necessary that Vocal Music be introduced at once
into all the public schools, [and] that the Board of Alderman and
Board of Common Council be requested to make an appropriation
for vocal music instruction. "[62]   A year later the trustees announced
that vocal music was being successfully taught in the city. [63]

New Jersey

School children in Boston had been experiencing music
instruction for a full decade when Jersey City's School No. 1,
which was opened in 1848, included music instruction in its
program of studies. [64]   Before the close of the Civil War other
towns in the state were offering music.   Phillipsburg was able
to report in 1864 that singing had been introduced into one of its
schools.   The superintendent stated that he would recommend its
introduction into all schools of his system where this would be
practicable. [65]

Connecticut

Prior to 1865 there were very few records indicating the
actual teaching of vocal music in the public schools of Connecticut.
In 1857 the superintendent of Hartford said that instruction in music
was being advocated for the high school.   The rules and regulations
of the public schools specified for district schools that a portion
of the time should be devoted to singing. [66]   In 1861 Middletown
set forth a set of rules specifying that vocal music should be
taught to the pupils in the junior and senior grades. [67]

Kentucky

Educational opportunities in the South prior to the Civil War
were very limited.   Free education was but a kind of gesture in
many communities.   Some cities in the South offered free education, but such opportunities were widely scattered and but a few
school systems were offering music.   Caroline Bourgard states
that the minutes of the Louisville, Kentucky, Board of Education
for 1844 passed a resolution recommending that the council appoint

a teacher of vocal music for the city schools at a salary of $350
per year.   Just how long the teacher of music received a stipend
for his services cannot be determined, because the minutes of the
Board of Education for 1846 note that thanks had been given to
W. C. Van Meter for his gratuitous teaching of vocal music.   It
was recommended that the council remit to him the tax imposed
upon all public concerts and that he be appointed for the remainder
of the year at $200. [68]

In 1852 Luther Whiting Mason suggested to the board of
education that he be allowed to teach music at the nominal fee of
$50 per month, for which he would offer two half-hour lessons per
week in each of the six grammar schools.   Mason and William
Fallen were employed for a period of three months to teach vocal
music in each of the referred to schools.   A public examination of
their work took place in 1853 with enthusiastic approval of the
given performances. [69]   There was a succession of music teachers
and events in the Louisville attempt to introduce music.   In 1857
the first introduction to music in the Girls' High School proved to
be unsuccessful; however, a year later a Mr. Whipple succeeded
in achieving the task.   Although Charles Godfrey was appointed
vocal music teacher in 1859 at a salary of $750 per annum, the
teaching of vocal music was abolished and resumed again in 1861.
Mr. Whipple was reappointed music teacher in 1861, and remained
there for "ten or twelve years, " having at times as many as three
music assistants.

Louisiana

An early account of the history of the schools of New Orleans,
Louisiana stated that the schools of the second municipality were
opened in 1842.   Prior to their opening, no schoolhouse had been
established, but within the short space of a year the school enrollment had exceeded 800 pupils.   In 1845 there were 2, 000 pupils
in eleven schools which included the high, intermediate, and primary
grades.   The buildings were so constructed as to make possible
the conversion of the three rooms of each floor into one big rehearsal

room for the purpose of conducting vocal music. [70] Another early
reference stated that music was being offered at St. Tammany
during the school year 1859. [71]

Tennessee was another southern state to offer vocal music
prior to the Civil War.   Memphis was doing so in 1858.   The
instruction was being given only in the senior department of the
female schools, however. [72]

The fact that the schools of the South were slow to recognize
public school music as a part of regular course of instruction
does not in any way diminish the significance of the early introductions in Louisville and New Orleans.   These cities included music
in the school curriculum but six years after its first official introduction in Boston.   These early experiments in the South did not
compare in number with those occurring in the Middle West during
the period 1840-1865.   Records show that there were introductions
in Wisconsin, Missouri, Michigan, Indiana, and Iowa.

Wisconsin

Two years after Wisconsin was admitted to the Union in 1848,
the village of Southport was opening its school each morning with
scripture and vocal music.   During the same year the primary
department of the Geneva Public Schools, containing eighty scholars,
was offering juvenile music under the direction of H. B. Coe, sixty
scholars were regularly receiving music in the higher department. [73]
The Milwaukee Board of School Commissioners in 1864 announced
that in all departments singing was a daily exercise. [74]

Missouri

Very few references relative to early music education in
Missouri were available.   It is believed that instruction in vocal
music started in St. Louis in 1852.   In 1854, John H. Tice,
Superintendent of Schools, reported that vocal music as one of
the regular studies had been started two years previously. [75] Ira
Divoll, Superintendent in 1858, reported that vocal music was not
being taught by the special music teacher in the intermediate and
primary schools.   Only in the normal, high, and grammar schools

was it being taught, and that but once each week. [76]

Michigan

Vocal music had found its way into the public schools of
Detroit by 1853, but only in a "very limited way." In spite of
the seemingly tardy introduction, Michigan has reason to be proud
if we compare it with other mid-western states. [77]

Before 1860 there were other schools in Michigan offering
vocal music. Adrian secondary school departments included vocal
music in its course of regular study in 1859. In the Union School
at Ann Arbor a music room was located in the basement of the
school building, while in the grammar school they were offering
instrumental music. The Battle Creek Union School vocal music
was taught in the fourth class of the primary department during
1859. In the first and second primary and intermediate departments of the Flint Union School singing was being taught to boys
and girls. During the same year the Kalamazoo Union School had
"one or two" music rooms. Instrumental music was offered to
both resident and non-resident students. The high school offered
music in addition to those subjects which prepared students for
"the higher walks of knowledge." The Lansing Second Ward Union
Schools were offering vocal music in the primary, intermediate,
and higher departments. At Monroe, the Union School offered
vocal music in only the grammar department. [78]

Indiana

Terre Haute, Indiana was probably one of the earlier cities
in that state to start agitation for the introduction of vocal music
as a part of its course of studies. The idea of having a singing
school under the direction of the school trustees was proposed in
1853. The proposal did not materialize and the teaching of vocal
music in the public schools was deferred. At a meeting held in
June, 1854 a committee was appointed by the board of education
to notify the music teacher to discontinue "the use of the Seminary"
for singing school purposes. [79] Without other evidence, it is

obvious that the trustees were asking for an action which recognized
that singing was being taught sometime during 1853.

Iowa

There are few evidences of early school music in Iowa before
1865.   The Dubuque County Superintendent stated in 1861 that it
would be his pleasure to see vocal music introduced into all the
Dubuque County Schools and Institutes.   It was desired that music
should be a part of the daily exercises, but the learning of music
should be only by ear.   He said that scientific music should only
be taught by scientific masters. [80]

California

Undoubtedly the pioneer state of public school music in the
far-West was California.   Though far removed from Boston,
California in 1851 drafted a bill on educational organization which
provided for music instruction in the high schools. [81]   Frances
Dickey reported that music was introduced into the San Francisco
Public Schools during the same year. [82]   With the exception of
Miss Dickey's reference regarding San Francisco, California was
merely recommending vocal music as a subject for study in the
high schools.

The foundations of modern music education were established
during the period 1830-1840.   The meritorious efforts in Boston and
in Massachusetts by various school boards, laymen, amateur and
professional musicians were in a great measure responsible for the
rapid and rather widespread acceptance of school music during the
period 1840-1865.   It has been shown that European education had
a direct influence upon the American school musician and public
school administrators.   A chronological recapitulation of the early
adoptions reveals that in the Far West, California had introduced school
music by 1851; in the East: Rhode Island, Washington, D. C., Maryland, New Jersey, and Connecticut by 1857; in the South: Kentucky,
Louisiana, and Tennessee by 1857; and in the Middle West:
Wisconsin, Missouri, Michigan, Indiana, and Iowa by 1861.

Thus, prior to 1865 the European philosophy of vocal music instruction had become known from the Atlantic to the Pacific coast.

From 1838, the year of the Magna Charta of American School music, down to 1865, there was a wide-spread interest and acceptance of school music. During the period from 1840 to 1865, public school music had become a part of school programs. These things grew out of the movement: 1) An appearance of a host of singing and school music instructors; 2) An almost fanatical devotion to the study of the rudiments of music; 3) A formalization of instruction to attain perfections in learning the intellectual-scientific aspects of vocal music study; 4) A development of song and note teaching materials to aid music study; 5) Consideration given by some school systems to the music qualifications of the regular classroom teacher; 6) The incorporation of music into required courses of study; 7) Fostering of the cause of school music by teachers' conventions; 8) The establishment of school music teaching classes for the in-service teacher; 9) An attainment of an important instructional status by the salaried-school music educator and supervisor.

Notes

1. Bache, A. D. "Public Schools of Lancaster," The Connecticut Common School Journal. 5: (June, 1841), 162-165.

2. Ibid., 162-165.

3. Bache, Alexander D. "Report of the Organization of a High School for Girls, and Seminary for Female Teachers," The Connecticut Common School Journal. Vol. III: (November, 1840), 162.

4. Twenty-Ninth Annual Report of the Controllers of the Public Schools of the City and County of Philadelphia, (1847). 17.

5. Report of the Special Committee on Reduction of Studies in the Public Schools of the First District of Pennsylvania, (1861), 9-10.

6.   Forty-Sixth Annual Report of the Controllers of Public
     Schools of the First School District of Pennsylvania,
     (1864), 37.

7.   Cubberley, Ellwood P.   Public Education in the United
     States.   (Boston, Mass.:   Houghton Mifflin Company,
     1919), 125, 171, 274.

8.   Aiken, Walter H.   "Music in the Cincinnati Schools, "
     Journal of Proceedings of the Seventeenth Annual Meeting
     of the Music Supervisors' National Conference, Tulsa.
     1924.   (Tulsa, Oklahoma.:   Board of Education, 1924),
     46-55.

9.   Ibid., 46-55.

10. Shotwell, John B.   A History of the Schools of Cincinnati,
     (Cincinnati, Ohio: The School Life Company, 1902).
     531-532.

11. Aiken, Walter H.   Ibid., 46-55.

12. Ibid., 46-55.

13. Raison, Malissa.   "A Study of the Status of Public School
     Music in Ohio. "   Unpublished Master's Thesis, Ohio
     Wesleyan University, 1930.   9.

14. Ibid., 9-10.

15. "Educational Items, " The Ohio Journal of Education.
     (January, 1857), VI: 25.

16. "Notices of Colleges, Schools, Etc. , " The Ohio Journal of
     Education.   III: (March, 1854).   94-95.

17. Second Annual Report of the State Commissioner of
     Common School to the General Assembly of Ohio, (1855).
     127-128.

18. Twenty-Fifth Annual Report of the Board of Education of
     The City of Chicago, 1879.   70.

19. The source for this and the data which follow is, except
     where noted, "Historical Sketches of the Public School
     System of the City of Chicago, " Department of Public
     Instruction, City of Chicago.   Twenty-Fifth Annual Report
     of the Board of Education, for the Year Ending July 31,
     1879 (Chicago: Clark & Edwards, Printers, 1880), 70-73,
     and "Report of the Committee on Music, " Department of
     Public Instruction, City of Chicago.   Fifteenth Annual
     Report of the Board of Education, for the Year Ending

July 3, 1869 (Chicago: Church, Goodman and Donnelley, Printers, 1869), 118-121, 123-124, 143, 169.

20.   Fourth Annual Report of the Superintendent of the Public Schools of the City of Chicago, for the Year Ending February 1, 1858 (Chicago: Chicago Daily Press, Printers, 1858), 41.

21.   Department of Public Instruction, City of Chicago. Eighth Annual Report of the Board of Education, for the Year Ending December 31, 1861. (Chicago: Chicago Times Book and Job Printing Establishment, 1862), 22-23.

22.   Department of Public Instruction, City of Chicago, Sixth Annual Report of the Board of Education, for the Year Ending February 1, 1860. (Chicago: Press and Tribune, Printers, 1860), 91.

23.   Department of Public Instruction, City of Chicago, Twelfth Annual Report of the Board of Education, from September 1, 1865 to August 31, 1866. (Chicago: Rounds and James, Printers, 1866), 88-89.

24.   Fifth Annual Report of the Superintendent of the Public Schools of the City of Chicago, 1859. 46.

25.   "Editorial, " The Illinois Teacher. II: (April, 1856), 92.

26.   "Music in Jacksonville, " The Illinois Teacher. V: (1859), 243.

27.   "Musical Instruments in School, " The Illinois Teacher, V: (1859), 273-274.

28.   Ibid. , 273-274.

29.   Steele, William L. Galesburg Public Schools - Their History and Work. (Galesburg, Illinois. : Board of Education, 1911), 51-52.

30.   Annual Report of the Superintendent of Common Schools of the State of New York, 1845. 12 Also: Annual Report of the Superintendent of Common Schools for 1846. Journal of the Rhode Island Institute of Instruction, 1: (March, 1846), 99.

31.   Annual Report of the Superintendent of Common Schools of the State of New York, (1843). 306.

32.   Annual Report of the Superintendent of Common Schools of the State of New York, (1843). 331.

33. Annual Report of the Superintendent of Common Schools of the State of New York, (1845). 76.

34. Ibid., 208.

35. "A Century of Music in Buffalo Schools," Music Educators Journal. 23: (March, 1937), 26-27. (Editorial)

36. Second Annual Report of the Superintendent of Public Instruction of the State of New York, 1856. 146.

37. "A Century of Music in Buffalo Schools," Music Educators Journal. Ibid., 78.

38. Ibid., 78.

39. Annual Report of the State Superintendent of Common Schools of the State of New York, 1845. 211.

40. Ibid., 211.

41. Annual Report of the Superintendent of Schools of the City Utica, 1869. 15-16.

42. Ibid., 23.

43. Fourth Annual Report of the Board of Education of the City of Syracuse, 1852. 8.

44. Smith, Edward. A History of the Schools of Syracuse From Its Early Settlement to January 1, 1893. (Syracuse, New York: C. W. Bardeen, 1893.), 77.

45. Eleventh Annual Report of the Superintendent of Schools of the City of Syracuse, 1859. 32.

46. Twelfth Annual Report of the Superintendent of the City of Syracuse, 1860. 28-29.

47. Report of the Superintendent of Public Instruction of the State of New York, 1854. 115-116.

48. Palmer, A. Emerson. The New York Public School Being A History of Free Education in the City of New York. (New York, N. Y.: The Macmillan Company, 1905), 148-149.

49. Second Annual Report of the Superintendent of Public Instruction of the State of New York, 1856. 130.

50. First Annual Report of the City Superintendent of Brooklyn, 1856. 12-13.

51. Thirteenth Annual Report of the Superintendent of the State of New York, 1867. 188.

52. Fifteenth Annual Report of the Superintendent of the State of New York, 1869. 208.

53. Ninth Annual Report of the Superintendent of Public Instruction of the State of New York, 1863. 232.

54. Tenth Annual Report of the Superintendent of Public Instruction of the State of New York, 1864. 209.

55. Eleventh Annual Report of the Superintendent of Public Instruction of the State of New York, 1865. 178.

56. Ibid., 250.

57. Stockwell, Thomas B. A History of the Public Education in Rhode Island, (Providence, R.I.: Providence Press Company, 1876), 203.

58. Report of the City Council of Providence, June 1, 1846. 19, 20, 22.

59. Annual Report of the School Committee of the City of Providence, 1863. 15.

60. Ibid., 15.

61. First Annual Report of the Trustees of the Public Schools. (Washington, D.C., 1845). 16.

62. Annual Report of the Board of Trustees of Public Schools, Baltimore, 1846. 7, 28, 29.

63. Ibid., 7.

64. Harney, Julia C. "The Evolution of Public Education in Jersey City." Unpublished Doctoral Dissertation, New York University, 1931. 229.

65. Annual Report of the Superintendent of the Public Schools of New Jersey, 1864. 179.

66. Report of the Superintendent of Common Schools, Hartford, 1857. 118.

67. Report of the Superintendent of Common Schools, of Connecticut, 1862. 99.

68. Bourgard, Caroline B. "Early Music in the Louisville Public Schools," School Music. XV: (November-

December, 1914) 32, 34.

69. Ibid., 32, 34.

70. "New Orleans, Louisiana." Journal of the Rhode Island
    Institute of Instruction, 1845-1846). I: 236-237.

71. Report of the Superintendent of Instruction of Louisiana,
    1860. 68.

72. Seventh Annual Report of the Superintendent, Memphis,
    1858-1859. 12.

73. Inauguration of Hon. John H. Lathrop, LL.D. Chancellor
    of the University of Wisconsin, (1850). 186, 188.

74. Annual Report of the Board of School Commissioners.
    (Milwaukee, 1864). 17.

75. First Annual Report of St. Louis Public Schools, 1854.
    1, 4.

76. Fourth Annual Report of the Superintendent, St. Louis,
    1858. 48.

77. Annual Report of the Superintendent of Public Instruction,
    Michigan, 1853. 146-147.

78. Twenty-Third Annual Report of the Superintendent of
    Public Instruction, Michigan, (1859). 236, 241, 253,
    276-79, 286, 289-290, 294.

79. Twelfth Annual Report, Terre Haute, 1875. 38.

80. Report of the Secretary of the Board of Education, Iowa,
    1861. 37-38.

81. Report of the Superintendent of Public Instruction,
    California, 1851. 8.

82. Dickey, Frances M. "The Early History of Public
    School Music in the United States," School Music. 15:
    (May, 1914): 5, 16, 19, 23.

VIII.   THE POST-CIVIL WAR EXPANSION
        OF MUSIC EDUCATION

With the close of the Civil War, the social, moral, political, and economic structure of both the North and South was in need of rehabilitation.   American education had suffered a severe set-back.   Musical progress had been retarded in the Northern states during the period from 1860 to 1875.   In the South the birth of public school music education, whose embryonic development had taken place during the period 1845-1860, was severely retarded until near the close of the nineteenth century.   Many of the schools in the smaller communities which had been closed during the war period were extremely slow in re-opening their doors.   Some took a year or two, while others needed more than five years.   In spite of the curtailment of education during the period of civil strife, some communities managed to find a place for music in their curricula.   The East was probably less affected by the conflict than any other section.   At least it showed signs of educational rehabilitation and growth sooner than the South.   Attemps to introduce and stimulate the growth of public school music in the East greatly outnumbered those in the South, Middle West, and Far West.   The tremendous agitation for school music in the United States between 1830-1865, (which was centered in the East) did much to maintain the status quo of school music education.   It had proved to a host of educators in this section that school music was an indispensable subject in the curriculum.

During the period following the Civil War an increasing number of cities in the East appeared to be expressing their faith in school music by requesting that music be retained or added to courses of study.   For a quarter of a century following the close of the War, many states were showing an added interest in music: Rhode Island, Maryland, New York, Connecticut,

District of Columbia, Pennsylvania, New Hampshire, New Jersey, Delaware, and Vermont.

Reports of the Providence, Rhode Island, School Committee indicate that during the period 1844-1865 there had been a steady improvement in the development of a good music program for their city schools. [1] The school committee reported in 1875 that "The progress in Music since its introduction into our schools in 1846....."[2] this statement shows how inaccuracies creep into reports as the time factor separates the original facts. In the school committee report of 1876, under a review entitled "Outline of Events From 1791 to 1876," the statement "in 1844, music was introduced," corroborates the information found in the earlier report. [3]

The salary of the music supervisors of Providence in 1848 was reported as follows: "...the committee have employed a teacher of vocal music to give instruction in the high school, the grammar and intermediate schools. This instruction has been given, under a special contract, at the rate of $540 per annum. "[4]

By 1867, it had become the custom in Providence to submit questions to the boy or girl who was to become a candidate for admission to the Providence High School. Those that were examined in 1867 were asked the following questions: 1) What is a Diatonic Scale? 2) What is a semitone? 3) In what order do the tones and semitones occur in the Diatonic Scale? 4) Why is a scale of eight notes, starting with Do, called the natural scale? 5) What are the names of the notes in the natural scale, between which the semitones occur? 6) If we commence on Sol, what numbers are Mi, Fa, and Ti, Do? 7) How then do we get the semitones between 7 and 8? 8) What sign is used to denote that the 7th is to be raised a semitone? 9) What is the name of the 7th note in the scale of Sol? 10) What is Chromatic Scale? N. B. The average per cent of correct answers given to the above questions, by 100 pupils, was a fraction over eighty. "[5]

The city school Committee had authorized music as a part of the Evening School Course of study in 1873. The collection of songs,

known as the Evening Chimes was adopted in six of the elementary
Evening Schools of the city. [6] The collection was selected by the
principal of the Harrison Street School.

Although Providence was to spearhead the development of
music education in Rhode Island, there were additional early evidences of music instruction being taught in the state. Among these
were significant activities in Newport, Bristol, Burrillville, Exeter,
Hopkinton, Portsmouth, Warren, and Warwick.

Under the heading of Music and Calisthenics, the report of
the School Committee of Newport for 1865 stated that the above
mentioned exercises "which are prescribed by the Regulations
adopted last autumn, are introduced and performed with a good
deal of zeal in the various grades of schools.... The superintendent of schools hopes that in a short time a regular supervisor
of music will be employed for all of their schools. "[7]   From
facts in the same report it was discerned that music was not
being supervised systematically in all the city schools. The
superintendent, however, had a sympathetic attitude toward music.
By 1867, Frederick W. Tilton, stated his pleasure at finding
singing a regular study in nearly all of the schools under his jurisdiction. [8]   The mode of instruction was entirely rote, with apparently no attempt being made to teach the science of music. The
School Committee for 1869 announced that "A very successful
trial for more than a year has, without doubt, given this branch
of [instruction a] permanent place in our regular course of study. "[9]
Music instruction was under the direction of Mr. Reid and Mr.
French. Sight-singing or sight-reading, it was reported, had
attained a degree of proficiency by this period. [10]

Rogers High School in Newport had music instructors on its
staff from its beginnings in 1873. The music instructors were
James F. O. Smith, 1873-1874; and J. L. Frank, who began his
work in 1874, and was still serving in 1883. [11]   In the upper
classes of the city schools, music readers had been introduced as
regular text books in music by 1872-73. [12]   Music readers were
not required in the primary grades. It was claimed that in the

primary schools music charts were better than books; in each
room a set of charts was a part of standard schoolroom equipment.   For the school year 1872-73, a Mr. Smith was offering
music below the First Grammar level for one half-hour each week;
in grades higher than the First Grammar, and in the high school
proper, one hour each week was devoted to music instruction. [13]
The school report for 1876-77, stated "that there were three
primary grades, two intermediate, and four grammar, making
with the school school, 10 grades.   In the various grades music
instruction was to be given at all grade levels. "[14]

Apparently in October 1874, the school committee of Bristol
decided that greater emphasis should be given to the teaching of
singing in its public schools. [15]   Professor A. Jantz of Providence
had been employed for the purpose of conducting the musical
activities proposed by the school committee.   His work apparently
progressed with assuring success.

William Fitz, superintendent of the Burrillville Public Schools,
related in 1875 that more music was being incorporated into their
public schools, an end toward which every one should strive.   The
city did not employ a music teacher in 1875, but the superintendent was pondering if it was not most desirable to expect of future
teachers an ability to teach music. [16]

Willet H. Arnold, superintendent of the Exeter Public Schools,
stated that as early as 1875 they were offering music in many of
their schools. [17]   G. A. Thomas, superintendent of the school in
1882, said that more attention was being extended to music because
singing effected a salutary effect upon student happiness and morale.
Music was being included as a part of some of the Hopkinton
schools course of studies; we are certain that the boys and girls
of Hopkinton were not experiencing daily vocal lessons or singing
experiences, in 1875. [18]

Not all communities were staunch advocates of popular vocal
music instruction.   J. Coggeshall, Clerk of the Portsmouth Public
School system in 1881, stated that they would not whole-heartedly
recommend spending time in teaching the art and science of music.

It was suggested that each school have a suitable instrument and some juvenile music for the purpose of cultivating the voice because it is an aid to better classroom morale. [19]

During 1875, the city of Warren secured the services of Professor Jantz as instructor of music at an annual stipend of $300. [20] He was expected to teach in the rural districts, for which his travelling expense was to be provided. Evidently the music teacher could not be maintained, because in 1881 W. N. Ackley, the superintendent of the Warren Public schools, indicated that no regular instructor of music had been employed to lay "out the work, give special drill in the science and thus incite the pupils to more earnest effort in the important branch. "[21] Ackley pointed out that he was eagerly awaiting the time when a special teacher would be appointed again for the purpose of providing music instruction.

As early as 1868, the public schools of Warwick were finding that among the schools making a more general advancement were those in which singing was encouraged. They felt that no additional proof was needed beyond pupil satisfactions. [22]

Between 1844 and 1875 vocal music was introduced into Newport, Warwick, Bristol, and Burrillville, Exeter, Hopkinton, Portsmouth, and Warren. In some cities all music instruction was by rote, while in others, the science of music was taught. The great growth in music instruction in Rhode Island came after 1865.

Prior to 1865 public school music education in Maryland was negligible. The first annual report of the Maryland State Superintendent of Instruction for 1865-1866, reported that 40, 390 were studying spelling; 35, 010, reading; 28, 729, writing; 25, 310, arithmetic; but in vocal music there were only 30. [23] Of the thousands of boys and girls pursuing academic study, the number receiving vocal instruction was insignificant. Progress in teaching vocal music in the state made great strides by the time of the second report in 1867; the total number receiving vocal instruction had grown to 1, 000. [24]

Primary music education in Baltimore was making great
progress by 1872. In the primary grades singing was taught by
note. It was being recommended that the study of the rudiments
of music should begin in these grades, and should not be deferred,
because primary school children were capable of learning notation.[25]
Baltimore had four teachers of music on a city staff of 614.[26] In
1874 the United States Commissioner of Education reported that
vocal music had long been an important study in the city, dating
from 1843 (officially 1844).[27] By 1875 music had become a subject
of instruction in the primary, grammar, and high school departments of the city. The supervisory staff had been increased to
five music teachers. The secondary school statistics for Maryland
during the year 1877 show that 19 of the 38 schools reporting were
offering music, whereas, eighteen offered instrumental instruction.[28]
Data concerning the growth of school music in Maryland shows that
Baltimore had committed itself to the teaching of the rudiments of
music reading in the primary grades.

The development of school music in New York State after
1865 continued to show progress. The reports of the city and
state superintendents of instruction reveal the development of vocal
music during this period. Though there were hundreds of these
records available, there were few that made a reference to music.
One of the exceptions was a report by the superintendent of schools
of Oswego, New York who stated in 1866 that they had decided to
introduce vocal music, employing Miss S. C. Bancroft at a salary
of $375 per year. Her successor was Edward Trowbridge, a
graduate of Oswego Normal School.[29] In spite of many discourage-
ments, the 1866 examinations in singing were an improvement over
the previous year.[30] Music was not included in the high school
curriculum. By 1869 there were signs of an awakened enthusiasm
under the leadership of J. B. McLean, the new supervisor of
music.[31] By combining certain classes into one, he made it
possible for himself to teach one lesson a week in all the grades,
except the high school.[32]

During 1870, there were 209 students studying vocal music at the Free Academy in Albany. The work for the year was progressing satisfactorily under the direction of T. S. Lloyd. Reports for the same year indicated that Lloyd was making a heroic attempt to teach the scientific or theoretical knowledge about music. [33] Three years later the school music committee provided for the employment of Herbert Green, who was to teach vocal music in the primary department. [34] Later, in 1877, the committee on music and drawing for the Albany schools recommended that the board of education require that music be taught in the primary and intermediate departments. [35] It should be noted here that the state of music education had progressed to the point that committees were now recommending that music be "required."

Music instruction in the city Syracuse was being given as early as 1852. Their Superintendent of Public Schools in 1872 stated that a teacher of music was employed during the year. E. F. Ballou, the special teacher of music, was receiving $1,300 per year, while the music teacher in the high school, Rev. Charles F. Soldan, classified as teacher of German and vocal music, received $900 per year. [36] The music department's objectives for 1873 were 1) to instruct pupils in the rudiments and science of music and 2) to give as thorough an examination of the pupils at the completion of each grade as is required of any other study at that time. Ballou reported in 1875 that a systematized course of vocal instruction, designed for the development of the voice, had been introduced with salutary results. [37] Although music study had been offered sporadically in the high school, even as late as 1887 it was not a part of the regular high school curriculum. [38]

The academy movement which was tremendously popular during the first half of the nineteenth century found great favor in New York State. It is reported that there were more incorporated academies in New York State than in any other state of the Union. [39] Some academies offered music instruction. Ives Seminary, a college preparatory academy located at Antwerp, was offering music instruction in 1877. [40]

Pre-Civil War development of school music in New York
City has already been discussed at length in the previous chapter.
Following the war period, however, more attention was being
given to its development in the city's primary music program.
In 1877 the special music teachers in the primary schools were
giving such lessons as the individual special teacher deemed advis-
able. "In some schools only the definitions of musical terms are
taught, while in others the singing of the scale and a few exercises
on the staff comprise the instruction. "[41] The superintendent reporting on the subject of vocal music in 1884 pointed out that true
pitch, good tone quality, and the observance of rhythmic problems
were essentials to the success of the work. It was suggested that
grade charts and blackboards were to be preferred in the lower
grades. Only in the higher grades could books be used to advantage. [42]

During the school year 1879 the Warsaw Union School was
offering music instruction to its boys and girls under the direction
of Mrs. Horace Howe, teacher of vocal music, and Miss Gertrude
Doolittle, instrumental instructor. [43]

The growth of school music after 1865 in New York State
was steady, meeting with continued success in Syracuse, New York,
Buffalo, and Albany. The practice of offering music in the high
school varied from city to city. Primary music instruction was
almost entirely a study of the science of music.

As time elapsed the superintendents of Buffalo came to evaluate
more critically the music program in their school system. From
available evidence it appears that in many of the larger cities,
particularly during this period, school administrators were unusually
sympathetic to the cause of early music education. This was true
of the Buffalo, Boston, Cleveland, St. Louis, Louisville, and
Cincinnati school systems.

In 1870 Superintendent Thomas Lothrop of Buffalo was pleading
for more music teachers. He found that it was impossible to
develop an effective music program under the leadership of one
music teacher. Lothrop was asking for music education for all the

children when he stated in a report that "the present system of
instruction in music... fails to accomplish the desired object... that
is to impart an elementary knowledge of the science to all the
pupils from the first to the tenth grade." Lothrop urged organization and systematization of the music work in the schools. He
hoped for "such familiarity with music that they can read it as
readily as the letters of the alphabet."[44] In the history of Buffalo,
Dr. Lothrop stands out as a great administrative champion of
school music.

It is quite likely that down to 1873, no general music textbook
adoption had been made in the Buffalo Public Schools. In that year,
Mr. Baker, the supervisor of music in the city, was sent to New
Haven, Connecticut, to evaluate the work of Mr. Benjamin Jepson.
Upon the basis of a recommendation made by Baker, Jepson's
Music Readers were adopted as a basic text in the elementary
schools of Buffalo. With a music textbook which tended to hold in
common the objectives of their elementary music program, the
following statement indicates the results of their adoption: "The
result has been that the elements of music are studied systematically,
with an interest never felt before, and the learning is rapid. The
teachers in the schools are now able to make the music lesson
continuous and persistent, and generally do so with interest and
fidelity."[45]

The science of music rudiments captivated and permeated the
music philosophy in Buffalo down to the close of the nineteenth
century. In 1886, Mr. Baker was annually preparing a "Manual of
Elementary music," which contained "not only progressive lessons
in the elementary principles of music illustrations and characters
and signs employed in musical notation, but also pages with staff
lines for transcriptions of songs, part exercises, scale forms,
etc."[46]

In 1896, Buffalo had three teachers of music who were
receiving annual salaries of $1,600, $1,550, and $1,200 respective-
ly. The city had among its ordinances the following one concerning certain musical instruments, their performance, and activities

in public places.

No person or persons shall, without permission of the
mayor, play upon any hand-organ, barrel-organ, barrel-
accordion, barrel-piano, hurdy-gurdy, or other musical
or wind instrument, upon any street, sidewalk, crosswalk,
dock, wharf or any public ground within the city; nor take
any part in or accompany any procession or company
wherein such instruments or any of them shall be played,
or such singing, shouting or other such noise shall take
place.   This section shall not apply to military companies
belonging to the National Guard, nor to regularly chartered
civic or religious societies or orders, nor to funeral
processions. [47]

Early Music Education in New York State

Date	Community	
1827	Utica	
1827	New York City	
1830	New York City	Some of the Infant Schools as early as 1830 had a semblance of music in the form of an opening exercise.
1831	Palmyra	
1835	Cazenovia	Cazenovia Seminary had a teacher of music.
1836	New York City	School No. 10 experiments with music.
1837	Buffalo	
1842	Rochester	
1842	Oswego County	
1842	Duanesburg	
1842	Genesee County	
1843	Albany County	
1843	Essex	
1843	Willsborough	
1843	Schroon	
1843	Schoharie, Washington, and Yates County	
1844	Bolivar	
1844	Wirt	
1844	Allegany, Delaware, Dutchess, Greene, Livingston, Putnam, St. Lawrence, and Schoharie County Superintendents reported the teaching of vocal music in schools of their districts during this year.	
1844	City and County of New York	Vocal music in practically all schools.
1845	Utica	
1850	Brooklyn	
1852	Syracuse	
1862	West Winfield	
1863	Fulton County	In some schools of the county.
1863	Mexico	
1864	Oneida County	
1864	Williamsburgh	
1864	Brooklyn	Had five teachers of music.

Early Music Education in New York State, cont.

Date	Community
1866	Troy High School
1866	Oswego Public Schools
1869	Antwerp Public Schools
1870	Albany Public Schools
1879	Warsaw Public Schools
1880	Hudson Public Schools

Early Champions of Music Education in New York State

Date	Community	Teacher	
1827	Utica Gymnasium Utica, N. Y.	Ebenezer Leach	
1835	Cazenovia Seminary Cazenovia, N. Y.	Eliza Chandler	
1836	New York City School No. 10	Darius E. Jones	
1842	Duanesburg Summer School No. 16	Jane Coley	(An elementary school teacher who offered music instruction).
1843	Buffalo Public Schools Buffalo, N. Y.	F. Hazelton	
1845	Utica Gymnasium	Mr. Edson	
1847	Utica Gymnasium	A. S. Palmer	
1851	Syracuse Public Schools	Mr. Allen	
1851	Buffalo Public Schools	C. Webster (Mr.)	
1856	Buffalo Public Schools	G. V. Vining	(Was teaching in 1871).
1863-86	Buffalo Public Schools	Everett L. Baker	(A meritorious service record. Undoubtedly one of the earliest music educators to have such a record of continous service).
1865-79	Utica Public Schools	Solon U. Cookinham	
1866	Oswego Public Schools Oswego, N. Y.	Miss S. C. Bancroft	
1866	Troy High School	Mr. T. J. Guy	
1867	Oswego Public Schools	Edward Trowbridge	
1870	Albany Free Academy	Thomas Spencer Lloyd	
1872	Syracuse Public Schools	E. F. Ballou	
1875	Albany Public Schools	Herbert Green	

Early Champions of Music Education in New York State, cont.

Date	Community	Teacher
1879	Warsaw Union School Warsaw, N. Y.	Mrs. Horace Howe
1880	Hudson Public Schools	Professor Comba
1884	Troy Orphan Asylum	George F. Greene

Vocal music was not widely taught in the schools of Connecticut prior to the Civil War. Beginning with Meriden in 1866, and during the next six years, vocal music was being taught in Windon, Canterbury, Manchester, New London, Norwalk, and Wallingford. In 1866 Meriden and Windon were offering considerable practice in singing. [48] The Windon school visitors urged that if music instruction did not seem practicable during school hours, arrangements should be made to conduct singing classes outside of the school day. In 1868 C. P. Grosvenor, the acting school visitor for Canterbury, said: "Music is both a science and an art. Why then should it not be taught in our schools? If the town would employ a competent teacher of vocal music, who should spend two or three hours a week in each school, the money required could not be used in any other way with so great advantage to the schools. "[49] Canterbury during the following year had introduced singing into some of its schools because Grosvenor had found that the singing experience had added much to the worthwhileness of the schools and he foresaw the day when vocal music would be introduced into all of them. [50]

The school visitors of various towns in Connecticut reported a wide variance in administrative policy regarding the instruction of vocal music. East Hartford had made no provision for vocal music instruction, whereas, Manchester had for several years allowed its regular grade teachers to teach singing. This practice by no means included all its school children, nor did it coordinate the music work, but the advisability of introducing music into all the schools was being considered. [51]

New London, Norwalk, and Wallingford reported the enlivening and salutary effects that music instruction had upon the minds of the children. [52] Reverend S. B. Grant, acting school visitor of New London, stated in 1868 that he would recommend that vocal music be introduced into all the schools. He suggested a union of several districts, making possible the employment of a full-time music teacher at a "trivial" expense to each benefiting school. [53]

The experiment of offering a systematic course of instruction for training primary children's voices had been established in New

Haven by 1871.   Children from five to eight years of age were being taught numerals and syllables.   They had developed their music
reading skills to compare favorably with the recall of words in a
reading lesson. [54]

These excerpts from school visitor reports indicate the widespread concern in Connecticut for the introduction of vocal music
instruction after 1865.   Schools were insisting that their children
in the primary grades be required to learn the factual knowledge
of music.

Beginning with introduction of vocal music in the public schools
of Washington, D. C. in 1845, its growth had been steady and
educationally worthwhile.   The music program had been expanded
to include both white and colored children.   The first report of the
city superintendent in 1869   stated that two music teachers were
being employed. [55]   J. Ormond Wilson   said in 1871 that Daniel
and McFarland, the vocal teachers, had under their jurisdiction
123 schools serving 8,290 pupils.   Wilson stated that Daniel had,
more than fifteen years before, introduced music into the public
schools. [56]   Other evidence indicates that music instruction had
started in 1845 instead of 1855, as intimated by Wilson.   By 1873
the direction of vocal music in the District of Columbia was under
one superintendent of music with two assistant teachers. [57]   A year
later the superintendent of Colored Schools stated that John Esputa
was the teacher of music for these schools. [58]   He made excellent
progress during the first year of his service.   His associate teacher
was Henry F. Grant. [59]

A widely scattered sampling of music education in Pennsylvania
during the period 1865-1890 shows that the growth was slow, except
in Philadelphia, Pittsburgh, Allegheny, Harrisburg, Lancaster, Erie,
Norristown, and Carlisle.   The reasons for the rise and growth
of music in these cities may be traced to the pauper school movement in the state.   In 1821 the counties in which Harrisburg, Pittsburgh, Carlisle, and Lancaster are located were allowed to create
their own schools for the education of poor children.   Philadelphia
had done so in 1818. [60]   This meant that these cities were to tax

themselves in order to provide educational opportunities for poor
children.   They were among the earliest in the state to start
taxation for education. [61]   The school music movement needed
funds to make such instruction possible.

The Pittsburgh Schools introduced music as early as 1844,
although their superintendent reported in 1869 that music was not
taught regularly in all its schools.   D. C. Holmes, principal of
the Franklin School, and Samuel F. Patterson, principal of the
Lawrence School, said that they had offered music two years
prior to 1869. [62]   At the Minersville and Oakland Schools, principals
James L. Harrison and Joseph P. Andrews said that music was
taught in their schools.   Philotus Dean, principal of Pittsburgh
Central High School, reported that vocal music was taught once a
week under the direction of four music teachers. [63]   The superintendent of music in Pittsburgh was paid $1, 200 during the school
year 1876-77.   Other music supervisor salaries during the same
year for the following cities were: Allegheny, $1, 000; Erie,
$1, 000; Harrisburg, $700; Lancaster, $1, 000; Norristown, $300,
and Titusville, $380.   Other cities in the state were having special
teachers of music, but only those communities who reported salaries
to the United States Commissioner of Education have been included
here. [64]

The board of public education of Philadelphia for 1870 admitted
that the city had been very slow to discern the benefits to be
derived from music instruction, stating that music had been introduced only two years before.   That music had been included into
the course of instruction by 1870, did not necessarily mean, however, that the formidable opposition to vocal music had entirely
disappeared.   The board indicated only that almost all opposition
had been overcome. [65]

Among other cities of the state, Alleghany reported that by
1874 vocal music had made great strides in its public schools.
The Superintendent reported that year that many students were
receiving instruction with the employment of two music teachers,
each class in the city was receiving one lesson per week. [66]

Before 1880 vocal music had become a permanent educational feature of school curricula in the state.   Opposition to school music in Pennsylvania was not always apparent.   In spite of the difficult financial times which the country was experiencing, some encouraging results had been obtained because there were "286 more public schools, 333 more of them graded, 331 more with uniform text books, 1,532 more in which drawing is taught, <u>494 more in which vocal music forms a study.</u>"[67]

During the school year 1870-1871, the public schools of Perth Amboy, New Jersey were beginning to add music instruction to their programs of study.   Music was to be taught in the grammar department, but not in the primary or intermediate divisions.[68] Henry Farmer, superintendent in 1874, reported that singing was offered in the intermediate department.[69]   The State Superintendent's report for 1873 revealed that singing was not being taught in all of the Plainfield schools during the previous school year.[70]   By 1882 music was required in each of the four years of the Jersey City High School.[71]

After the Civil War, only a few evidences of school music teaching were available in New Hampshire, Delaware, and Vermont. Amos Hadley, the first superintendent of public instruction in New Hampshire, announced that before 1870 music was among the neglected branches of study in his state.   The superintendent for 1878 said that among the improvements since 1871, there was increasing acceptance of singing as one of the common branches of education. Early in the history of New Hampshire there is a record of a schoolmaster in the town of Portsmouth who in 1861 was "to act as a court messenger, to serve summonses, to lead the choir on Sundays, to ring the bell for public worship, to dig the graves, to take charge of the school, and to perform other occasional duties."[72] The schools of Bristol in 1888 were earnestly advocating that a provision be made whereby each department of the schools would have at least a thirty-minute vocal music lesson each day.[73] Under the direction of Mary F. Duxbury the schools of Dover were securing excellent results.[74]

Delaware was also beginning to champion vocal music, because in 1871 Wilmington was offering music taught by J. N. Clemmer, "who had received from each scholar one cent a week as compensation. The board has not yet decided to place vocal music upon the list of regular studies, and has made no provision for it other than having permitted Mr. Clemmer to teach in this way the past few months."[75] By 1875 it was reported that progress had been made in the teaching of vocal and instrumental music in its schools.[76] The exact nature of instrumental instruction was not definitely stated. In 1875 Delaware recorded seven secondary schools receiving vocal and eight receiving instrumental instruction.[77]

The superintendent of Newbury, Vermont recommended singing as a delightful school exercise, but he did not indicate whether or not Newbury was offering such instruction.[78] In 1877 the United States Commissioner of Education published a report concerning the status of secondary music instruction in Vermont. Of the state's thirty reporting schools, nineteen were offering vocal and twenty-five, instrumental music. In 1876 Burlington was paying its music teacher $600 per year.[79] The Vermont state course of study outlined in an 1882 report, made no mention of music.[80]

The preceding pages have disclosed some of the more significant school music developments in the eastern United States after 1865. In some instances the growth was rapid and widespread. Simultaneous with the development of public school music in the eastern states, there appeared many significant, yet scattered embryonic beginnings in the South. Previously it was stated that Kentucky, Louisiana, and Tennessee were probably among the earliest to offer school music. Between 1865-1890 there were promising beginnings in South Carolina, Alabama, Georgia, Arkansas, Florida, Virginia, and Texas.

It has been seen that music was taught in Louisville, Kentucky, in 1844 but it was not until 1866 that vocal music was considered as a regular branch of instruction. During that year vocal teachers were spending most of their time instructing in the grammar and intermediate departments, the primary departments receiving very

little attention.   Although the regular teachers of the primary departments were doing their own teaching of music, their incompe-
tency often hindered the music program.   It was suggested that a
competent teacher be employed to assist the regular teachers at a
salary of $700 per annum.   It was thought that this teacher could
then help with the supervisory music work of the primary department. [81]   During the year 1875 there were four music teachers
employed in the public schools of the city. [82]   The special teacher
of music was receiving a salary of $1,025 per year.   The superin-
tendent of the Louisville Schools stated that the employment of the
music teachers did not continue beyond 1878. [83]

In 1868 the present school system of South Carolina was
established.   One year later Frank Carter, School Commissioner
of Kershaw County, stated that they were urging the teachers in
the schools of his county to include singing as part of the curriculum. [84]   It was not until 1881 that vocal music was a daily
exercise in the Central School at Charleston. [85]   The available
evidence regarding the introduction of vocal music into the state
schools is very meagre.   Not alone was this true of this state,
but characteristic of much of the South.

The state board of education of Louisiana for 1870 advised
that vocal music was to be taught wherever practicable. [86]   The
permissive character of this suggestion was epoch making for a
southern state and most unusual for any state in the Union prior
to 1875.   Some of the schools of Louisiana were carrying out the
suggestion.   In the Girls' High School of the Second, Third, and
Fifth Districts of New Orleans, music was offered during the senior
year of the three year course. [87]   In 1875 New Orleans was employing five teachers of music. [88]   Few communities in Louisiana were
troubling themselves about the introduction of vocal music before
1870.   The United States Commissioner of Education in 1877 reported
that of the ten secondary schools reporting to his office, eight
were offering vocal and instrumental music. [89]

Tennessee, like Louisiana, was slow in its adoption of singing
as a part of the regular public school curriculum.   Nashville was

among the earliest cities in the state to do so.   During the school
year 1870 the course of study for Nashville incorporated singing
in the first and second grade. [90]   Five years later Knoxville offered
music and drawing, and the superintendent pointed out that a special
teacher of music was badly needed. [91]

The Nashville course of study for 1877 indicated that vocal
music was being given in the primary, intermediate, grammar,
and high school departments. [92]   A noteworthy step in Tennessee
education can be found in Leon Trousdale's report as state superintendent of schools for 1880, when he noted that vocal music was
now included in the Graded Course of Study for Country Schools.
The permissive character stated, vocal music, if taught, could be
offered in the primary, intermediate, and grammar grades.   Vocal
music was now a part of the course of study for Tennessee Public
Schools, according to section 31 of their school law. [93]

During this period, school board reports for cities in Alabama
were difficult to obtain.   As early as 1873, the United States
Commissioner of Education reported that in the city of Montgomery
"Neither Latin, Greek, German, nor French is taught in the public
schools and drawing is only in its elements; but vocal music is
attended to in all. "[94]   Vocal music was being taught to some extent in Opelika and Selma.   According to the secondary school
music statistics for 1875, (See Tables 1-3.) one boys' school and
one girls' school were offering vocal and instrumental music; two
schools were offering vocal and instrumental music for both girls
and boys. [95]

Vocal music was being taught in all the schools of Atlanta
during 1873, and the 1, 080 children enrolled in the public schools
of Columbus, Georgia, were receiving vocal and instrumental
instruction. [96]   The United States Commissioner of Education
reported in 1877 that of 105 secondary schools in Georgia, forty-one
were offering vocal music, while instrumental instruction was being
given in fifty-one. [97]

Significant educational progress began to appear in Florida
after 1880. [98]   Of the seven secondary schools reporting to the

United States Commissioner of Education, four were providing vocal and instrumental music. [99] It is difficult to ascertain whether or not all of the secondary schools of the state reported.

Oscar H. Cooper, state superintendent of instruction in Texas, reported in 1888 that the introduction of vocal music had only recently been included in school curriculums in his state. During the same year Fort Worth was successfully teaching notation through all the schools. In Orange, C. F. Johnston, superintendent of public schools, was likewise advocating that "graded singing should become a part of the course of study." [100]

During the post-Civil War period, experimentations in school music teaching appeared in numerous southern states. Educators in Tennessee and Viriginia were making permissive provisions for school music in graded and ungraded schools. The citations tend to indicate that the period from 1870 to 1880 was one of considerable concern for public school music in the South. The superintendent of schools of the state of Virginia stated in 1888 that vocal music was to be taught in the country schools which were graded and had one teacher. [101]

The major problems at the close of the Civil War were those of social and economic reconstruction. Educational development in all sections of the United States was arrested during the period 1860-1875. This postponement of educational growth did much to throttle the spread and development of school music in the Middle West. There is much evidence that school music was firmly established prior to 1860, and the teaching of music, though probably curtailed in some localities, did continue to be effective. One significant observation to be made is that during the period of arrested development, there was a limited number of new adoptions of school music in this region. The subsequent discussion will trace the progress of this growth in the Middle West during the period prior to 1890.

TABLE 1[102]

Secondary Schools for Boys Reporting
Vocal and Instrumental Music Instruction
to
United States Commissioner of Education in 1875

A. -- Number of schools in which vocal music is taught.
B. -- Number of schools in which instrumental music is taught.

State	A	B
Alabama	1	1
California	2	2
Connecticut	6	7
Delaware	1	1
Georgia	1	0
Illinois	3	3
Indiana	1	1
Kentucky	-	-
Louisiana	5	3
Maine	-	1
Maryland	6	6
Massachusetts	5	5
Minnesota	1	1
Mississippi	1	1
Missouri	2	1
New Hampshire	1	1
New Jersey	3	6
New York	22	24
North Carolina	3	-
Ohio	2	4
Oregon	2	2
Pennsylvania	12	10
South Carolina	-	-
Tennessee	1	-
Texas	1	1
Vermont	3	3
Virginia	3	3
West Virginia	-	-
Wisconsin	1	1
District of Columbia	1	-
Indian Territory	-	-
New Mexico	1	1
TOTAL	91	89

TABLE 2[103]

Secondary Schools for Girls Reporting
Vocal and Instrumental Music Instruction to
United States Commissioner of Education in 1875

A. -- Number of Schools in which vocal music is taught.
B. -- Number of Schools in which instrumental music is taught.

State	A	B
Alabama	1	1
California	12	12
Connecticut	11	12
Delaware	1	1
Florida	2	2
Georgia	3	3
Illinois	8	8
Indiana	1	3
Iowa	1	1
Kansas	1	1
Kentucky	12	11
Louisiana	6	6
Maine	4	4
Maryland	11	11
Massachusetts	13	14
Michigan	2	2
Minnesota	2	3
Mississippi	3	2
Missouri	3	3
Nebraska	1	1
New Hampshire	2	3
New Jersey	10	10
New York	54	58
North Carolina	3	4
Ohio	6	7
Pennsylvania	24	21
Rhode Island	2	2
South Carolina	3	4
Tennessee	13	13
Texas	4	4
Vermont	3	4
Virginia	8	10
West Virginia	3	3
Wisconsin	5	5
District of Columbia	10	19
Colorado	2	2
Indian Territory	1	1
New Mexico	1	1
Washington	1	1
Total	259	273

TABLE 3[103]

Secondary Schools for Boys and Girls Reporting
Vocal and Instrumental Music Instruction to
United States Commissioner of Education in 1875

A. -- Number of Schools in which vocal music is taught.
B. -- Number of Schools in which instrumental music is taught.

State	A	B
Alabama	2	2
Arkansas	3	3
California	6	4
Connecticut	10	12
Delaware	4	5
Florida	1	-
Georgia	6	7
Illinois	13	14
Indiana	6	5
Iowa	15	19
Kansas	2	1
Kentucky	18	19
Louisiana	1	1
Maine	14	13
Maryland	4	4
Massachusetts	16	11
Michigan	1	1
Minnesota	6	5
Mississippi	3	6
Missouri	8	9
New Hampshire	18	16
New Jersey	20	20
New York	79	90
North Carolina	7	8
Ohio	20	18
Oregon	2	2
Pennsylvania	26	27
Rhode Island	1	0
South Carolina	2	1
Tennessee	25	24
Texas	4	5
Vermont	12	18
West Virginia	2	2
Wisconsin	5	4
District of Columbia	2	2
New Mexico	-	-
Utah	6	3
Washington	1	1
Total	372	383

During the Civil War, money was spent for music instruction
in the schools of Terre Haute, Indiana.   In 1863 the school trustees
hired Warren Davis to teach music at a salary of $8.00 per month;
he was the first school music teacher in that city.   Two years
later the trustees elected another music teacher for one month;
he was to receive $50.   No available record indicates whether the
position was filled or not.   In 1867 M. S. Tinker was selected to
teach music for a period of three months.   His work for the short
period was so successful that he was asked to continue during the
ensuing school year.   The period 1867 was characterized by <u>two
or three teachers in the music department of the city.</u>   Early in
1868 the superintendent of public schools was instructed to employ
W. H. Paige, who remained for more than five years, retiring at
the close of the 1872-73 school year.   He was succeeded by Mrs.
Anna L. Gould.   According to a report of the superintendent for
1873, vocal music had become one of the regular exercises of the
schools. [104]   From the time that music was accepted as a regular
part of the course of study, it was taught as a science, lessons
were assigned, songs were learned, and examinations were given.

During 1879 George B. Loomis, Superintendent of Music of
Indianapolis, pointed out in a report to Superintendent H. S. Tarbell
that he had been in the employ of the schools since 1866.   Loomis
had not taught public school music in any other public school system
before coming to Indianapolis.   During the school year 1878-1879 he
was receiving, as special teacher of music, $1,150 per year. [105]

Music was introduced into other cities in Indiana during this
same period.   In 1869 E. S. Clark, superintendent of the Aurora
Public Schools, appointed one special music teacher. [106]   In 1883
J. N. Study, superintendent of public schools, Greencastle, was
enthusiastic about the marked progress music study had made during
his administration, although at one time he had expressed skepticism
regarding the advisability of such a program. [107]

Twenty-four years after its introduction into the Chicago
public school system, music teaching was yielding highly satisfying
results.   The Committee on Music was proud to find that even

children of seven years were capable of singing simple songs and
that but few were found incapable of learning to sing. The superintendent was advocating additional time for music instruction. [108]

In 1867 a division of labor was affected, Whittemore taking
entire charge of music in the grammar schools and Blackman
taking over the normal, high, and primary schools. Whittemore
had instituted a graded music course, starting the first year with
material of grades III and IV. The two higher classes reviewed
the material of grade IV and studied the grade III music; the two
lower classes began with grade IV music. The following year
Whittemore added music of grades I and II. Fifteen or twenty
minutes a day were devoted to this study. From then on, the
schools worked upon a systematic course of instruction. Marked
progress resulted, and the Committee on Music reported in 1869
that "such music as the pupils of the Grammar Department were
obliged to study before singing one year ago, they are now able to
sing at sight. " Sight reading was a new adventure for the music
department, introduced by Whittemore during the last term of 1869.

Continuing its report, the Committee said: "We notice that
many of the assistant teachers are fast becoming competent to
conduct the music exercise. In fact, quite a large number have
had good success during the past year. The final examination
consisted of the reading of music at sight prepared by Messrs.
Palmer, Blackman, Murray and Higgins. Most of the classes
examined did themselves great credit, and in all the result was
very satisfactory. During the examination the scholars were intensely interested, which speaks well for those engaged in the work. "

From the individual scores of the pupils in this examination
the average score of each school was obtained. It was found that
of the nineteen schools eleven averaged about 90% in sight reading, six about 80%, and two above 70%. Three schools tied for
top place, 99. 2%. Historically, significance must be attached to
this attempt on the part of music instructors to evaluate the quality
and quantity of music instruction. Chicago was among the first
cities to statistically report school achievement in music.

The superintendent's report on music was enthusiastic: "Our schools have done nobly during the past year in this department of study. A Graded Course of Study in Music has been most successfully carried forward by the music teachers. The examinations held during the last week of the year... were very satisfactory. But little time has been devoted to the work of instruction in music each day. It has not interfered at all with other work. The relief afforded by the pleasant exercises has rather improved than detracted from the quality of other study... With the increase of our schools in number it seems desirable that the number of music teachers should be increased."

The examination given that year to candidates seeking admission to the high school included five questions on music: 1) Give three varieties of measure; the length of the dotted quarter note in each variety; and the department to which the dot belongs. 2) Write the scales of C, D, E, B-flat and A-flat in double measure, writing under each note the name of its pitch. 3) Give the names of the pitches in the scale of A, between which the half steps occur. 4) Define syncopation and illustrate it in triple measure in the key of G. 5) Write four measures of quadruple measure, using three kinds of dotted notes.

A supplementary report of the Committee on Music for 1871 delineates the strides made in the teaching of music in the Chicago Public Schools. The report indicated: 1) That music had become a definite part of the school curriculum; 2) That there had been a definite attempt to teach and demonstrate the need for a technical study of music; 3) That music work included the singing of two and three-part songs; 4) That persistent efforts had been made to get the pupils to create an artistic performance, to recognize the value of good tone quality, and to be cognizant that such tonal beauties are "conducive to throat protection;" 5) That music was recognized as a potent factor in the educational life of Chicago school children. [109]

Increased emphasis on musical theory, choral and individual singing is indicated in the report on music for 1873-74. Individual

instruction had become a popular goal, as it was felt that individual
singing offered the student the greatest goal.   Notable is the fact
that the music festival had been tried, the proceeds being used for
the repair and purchase of musical instruments. [110]

In 1875 it was reported that "class instruction is given
entirely by the regular teachers, the Special Teacher of Music
furnishing the teachers with the exercises to be used in their
respective grades and supervising the works of the teachers."
Whittemore declined re-election in June 1875 because of ill health,
and Blackman took entire charge of music instruction.

Whereas music had been a required subject ever since its
introduction into the public schools with regularly employed teachers,
it became elective in 1875. [111]   Apparently this change was not for
the better, judging from the annual report of 1877-78: "The progress made in Vocal Music during the year has been greater than
in either of the two preceding years, and in some cases it has
risen to the standard attained before the study became optional
(italics added).   If all pupils whose parents do not request that
they be excused were to attend the classes in vocal music, a
higher degree of excellence would be attained.   That music is
popular is attested by the fact that 85 percent of the children in
the schools joined the singing classes, though under the rule they
might have refused to do so. [112]   One of the first courses of study
prepared as a guide for music work in the city schools was adopted
on February 7, 1884.   This was an epoch-making achievement in
curriculum construction.   In the course we find stated objectives,
grade by grade and department by department. [113]

It is not the purpose here to continue the story of Chicago's
significant contributions to American public school music.   In trac-
ing the more outstanding developments throughout the "first generation" of school music in Chicago, one can see the germs of much
of today's philosophy and practice.   For the convenience of the
interested reader or researcher a table of music teachers (or
supervisors, in the case of Blackman and Whittemore, from 1864
on) through 1875 can be found in the notes.   (See note no. 114).

It is significant to note that only four years after Lowell
Mason succeeded in getting the Boston schools to include music
in their curriculum, the Chicago public schools followed suit.
Earlier than most cities, Chicago took into serious consideration
the musical qualifications of its elementary school teachers--and
this during the Civil War period.   Quality instruction was their
major consideration.

In Chapter VII it was stated that Galesburg was offering
music as early as 1862.   It was not, however, until 1870 that
music was made a regular study in the city schools. [115]   During
same year the superintendent of the Springfield Public Schools
stated that children in the city schools were receiving vocal music
instruction. [116]   The Lake View Township High School, Cook County,
reported in 1876 that 99 students were studying vocal music in the
school.   The teacher was O. H. Merwin. [117]

Five years after Kansas was admitted to the Union in 1861,
P. McVicar, State Superintendent of Public Instruction, recorded
that "of the 36, 944 male and female white and 2, 505 blacks who
were in schools, 1, 276 were receiving vocal instruction during
1866-67. "[118]

In 1871 H. D. McCarty, State Superintendent of Public
Instruction of Kansas, recommended in the course of study, that
those pupils in the First Reader classification should have singing
three or four times a day, with three to five minutes devoted each
time to the activity. [119]   Two years later McCarty stated that the
course of study recommended for the district schools of the state
called for daily practice in singing of from five to ten minutes. [120]
In 1875 the State Superintendent announced that music was being
taught in many of the better class common schools.   Even in the
secondary schools, vocal and instrumental music was a part of
instruction.

During the 1870 school year, W. C. Rote, Superintendent of
Schools at Lawrence, stated that the adoption of music by the department of public instruction should be regarded as an advanced
step which characterized general education in the United States. [121]

It was not until 1878 that its schools were offering instruction in
music by a special teacher. [122]

At the opening of the Civil War the available educational records
indicate that vocal music was not part of the curricula of schools
in Iowa.   It was not until 1871 that W. E. Crosby, Superintendent
of Davenport Schools, stated that vocal music had been offered for
the first time.   Before coming to the city, Crosby had been for
nine years principal in a city school system (he did not say where)
where 1,600 children had successfully studied the rudiments of
music.   He said that, if vocal music were properly taught in the
Davenport Public Schools, it would rapidly become one of the
permanent branches of common education.   In Davenport one lesson
a week was given in each of the rooms of the intermediate, grammar, and high school departments.   Primary music was to be taught
by the regular classroom teachers and the special teacher of music
was to instruct the primary teachers how to teach the subject. [123]

Secondary school statistics for Iowa in 1877 revealed that of
thirty-nine schools in the State, twenty-three were offering vocal
and instrumental music. [124]   These statistics represent a survey of
music teaching on the basis of reports to the United States Commissioner of Education.

Prior to 1890 there were probably a dozen school systems in
Iowa offering systematized vocal music instruction.   Less than
fifty-per cent of this group had no special music teacher.   The
board of education of Oskaloosa said that it was one of the first,
if not the first, city in the State to adopt music and place it under
the direction of a special teacher.   Available source information
did not reveal the date of its first introduction. [125]   In 1890 the
Sioux City Superintendent of Schools stated that vocal music was
being successfully taught. [126]

There are scattered references to the early teaching of vocal
music in Wisconsin prior to 1865.   The development of vocal music
in the state during the post Civil-War period was slow and uncertain.
Milwaukee was one of the earliest cities in the state to offer classroom music instruction; during the period 1864-1872 it was taught

by individual classroom teachers. Its board of commissioners
recommended that instruction should be given in music, drawing
and gymnastics, appropriating $1,500 in 1872 for the purpose of
employing three music teachers at salaries of $500 each. [127]

The Wisconsin State Superintendent of Public Schools reported
for 1878, that H. S. Baker, the superintendent of Pierce County,
had stated that some of the teachers in his area were giving
instruction in the rudiments of music. Two years later, J. J.
Fruit, the superintendent at La Crosse, reported that vocal music
was being introduced into the grammar and intermediate departments, the plan being solely experimental in nature. The board of
education had, after employing a music teacher for a trial period
of three months, re-employed the teacher for the school year 1880-
1881. [128]

The school music history of Minnesota begins after the Civil
War; how soon after is not definitely established. The Minneapolis
course of study for 1871 indicated that music was being offered in
grades 1-9 inclusive. Some music was given throughout the three
years of the high school course. [129] The course of study for 1888
stated that O. E. McFadon was the superintendent of music; his
assistant was Stiles Raymond. In the state some teaching of school
music had made progress, because a report in 1885 stated that at
least eleven cities were offering music under the direction of the
classroom or special music teacher. [130]

Prior to 1890, public school music was introduced more
successfully in Ohio than in any other Middle Western State. However, every city that introduced the subject did not necessarily
experience success. A report for the Columbus Public Schools in
1872, said that "music has been included in the course of study
for several years, but so unsatisfactory have been the results that
the subject was in danger of being stricken out."[131] The commissioner of the common schools of Ohio reported upon several
occasions the various branches of study taught in his state. During
the thirty-one year period, 1855-1886, progress may be ascertained
from the number of pupils being taught vocal music. For this span

of time growth comparisons become worthwhile. The following shows the growth in the number of pupils enrolled; 1855--23, 360; 1856--26, 070; 1880--151, 407; 1881--154, 684; 1886--203, 724. The 1886 report also said that "out of 88 counties in the state 2 reported no vocal music. "[132]

A study of the Cleveland City school reports recorded the vicissitudes of its early music teaching. For instance, during 1867-68 there was but one teacher of music, while a year later there was no such teacher. Because the Board found it difficult to secure someone with competency in this area, action "deemed it much wiser to leave the instruction in music to be given by the teachers of the several schools, rather than make the experiment of employing a special teacher who did not give promise of being entirely successful. "[133]

The Cleveland Superintendent of Schools, Andrew J. Rickoff, stated that the wisdom of allowing one, two, or three special teachers to go into the schoolroom and teach a twenty or thirty minute lesson once each week "could never be attended with results adequate to the importance of the study. The pupil felt no responsibility to the teacher, and the teacher could not feel any great degree of responsibility for the advancement of the pupil. "[134] Among hardships were the attitudes of the schoolroom teachers who did not know how to teach a vocal lesson. Many of the regular teachers manifested no interest toward the subject, while others even demonstrated their dislike for the music master. Some schools petitioned that they should be relieved of the duty of teaching such a subject.

The Regular Teacher as a Music Teacher. N. Coe Stewart has been credited with the idea of requiring the regular teachers in Cleveland to teach their music lessons. The Superintendent of Schools in 1869 reported that

> the Board of Education, after due deliberation, quite unanimously adopted the recommendation (instruction of all classes by their regular teachers). It was then determined to secure the services of a music master, whose duty it should be to give instruction to the teachers; to teach the High Schools and highest grades in the Grammar Schools; to direct the work in all the rest of the classes....

A man was required who could command the respect of the
teachers and pupils alike, and who would impart interest
and enthusiasm to all. I am gratified to say that the requirement was fulfilled. 135

This plan interpreted by Superintendent Rickoff was meeting with

some success from both the teacher and the pupil.   The salary of

the new special music teacher Stewart was $1, 800 per year. [136]

Naturally no plan such as the one described above could succeed

unless the music teacher was instructing the regular grade teachers

this was the part he played.

The Superintendent of Schools reported in 1870 a great success

story for the teaching of music in his city. It indicated the remark

able progress being made by the new supervisory plan, whereby

grade teachers were receiving instruction by Stewart.   Rickoff re-

lates:

> The success of the whole scheme depended upon the
> selection of a teacher, and we were in no haste to imperil
> it by choosing one who could not comprehend or carry it
> to a successful issue. About the time mentioned, Stewart
> was finally persuaded to take hold of the work, and at once
> entered upon the discharge of his duties. He had to organ-
> ize and direct the teaching of eight thousand pupils, to see
> that every one was regularly and systematically taught by
> one hundred and sixty different teachers, some of whom
> could not sing, most of whom knew nothing of music as a
> science, and among whom, it is safe to say, not more than
> ten had ever given a lesson in music before. During school
> hours he had to teach at the High Schools and in the higher
> classes of the Grammar Schools. Out of school hours, at
> regular meetings, and as opportunity occurred, he had to
> teach the teachers.
>
> The task assigned Mr. Stewart was not an easy one; but
> we believe that we only pronounce the judgment of the Board
> of Education, and of all concerned in the management of
> the schools, including those keenest of observers -- the
> teachers themselves -- when we say that the work of the
> year has been a gratifying success. 137

Thus during the period 1845-1870, Cleveland had established for

itself a music supervisory program which incorporated the high,

elementary, and primary school levels. In addition, the regular

classroom teacher had become a part of an intensified attempt to

broaden the base of music teaching in the elementary schools.

Early Music Books Published in Ohio

Pease, E.   The Youth's Musical Lamp, and American School Song
Book: (Cincinnati, Ohio.:   Moore, Anderson, Wilstach and Keys,
1854).   160.
>   Clear and scientific notation, arranged according to the
>   improved German method of instruction.   Contains the
>   elements of the science of music, and a great number of
>   tunes on an improved system of numberal notation.   Every
>   attempt to facilitate the cultivation of the science, as well
>   as the art of music in our schools, should receive en-
>   couragement according to its merits.   We commend the
>   effort of Mr. Pease to all who are interested in vocal
>   music.   41

Gibson,   Prairie Vocalist.   Cincinnati.
>   Prof. G. has long been, and still is favorably known, as
>   a successful teacher of vocal and instrumental music in
>   Boston, has composed and compiled numerous treatises
>   on music ... is now preparing a work on vocal music,
>   especially adapted to the wants of the youth in our schools.
>   Shall his efforts for the accomplishments of an end so
>   desirable be seconded by the teachers of the State?   42

Suffern, J. William.   The Galaxy: A New and Brilliant Collection
of Music For Choirs, Conventions Singing Classes and Musical
Societies, (Cleveland, Ohio.: S. Brainard's Sons, 1877).   304.
>   The Galaxy has been prepared in answer to numerous re-
>   quests from Teachers, Choristers, and Leaders of Musical
>   Societies in various parts of the country, for a larger and
>   more elaborate work than the "Singing School and Convention
>   Book; and in the compilation we have endeavored to meet
>   these varied wants as fully as possible.   The Galaxy is
>   divided into five departments: ELEMENTARY, EAST PART
>   SONG, GLEE AND CHORUS, METRICAL, AND ANTHEM. "

Root, Geo. F.   The Glory: A Collection of New Music For Singing
Classes, Musical Conventions and Choirs.   (Cincinnati, Ohio.:
John Church and Co.,   )   400

Before 1885 at least six cities offered music instruction which
was taught entirely by a special music teacher.   But in Michigan,
as in other states, the school music program met opposition.   However, the pleasure that singing brought to school children soon
started to weaken the objections of the opposition.   Although music
was taught in Adrian as early as 1859, sixteen years later the
laity were still questioning the advisability of retaining the music
teacher.   The board of education believed that public sentiment was
growing in favor of a music teacher and that the position would
eventually justify the faith the school administration had invested

in the music program. [138]   In 1875 the superintendent in Pontiac
stated that the schools of that community were sadly in need of
proper instruction in music. [139]   Joseph C. Jones the superintendent
revealed that no systematic instruction was being given at that time.

In 1875 the Michigan Superintendents' Association recommended
for general adoption a course of study for the primary and grammar
departments.   The course recommended that music be given throughout all departments. [140]   Ten years later the Grand Rapids primary
and grammar departments, which included the first eight grades,
had outlined a definite course of study for music. [141]

In the west those states admitted to the Union prior to 1890
were California, Colorado, Montana, Nevada, Oregon, and Washington.   A study of the development of public school music within these
states during the period 1865-1890 provided little evidence of the
introduction of school music.   However, some information was
obtainable for Nevada, California, Colorado, Utah, and Washington.
The materials provided merely suggestions as to the presence of
music instruction.

In Nevada the first annual report of the superintendent of
public instruction for 1865 referred to music in a discussion on
What course of instruction should be adopted in our Industrial
Colleges?   Under the heading of instruction we find

> For moral culture, religious instruction, moral philosophy,
> music (especially vocal, in parts) social gatherings, re-
> unions, at least for some classes, each week, when they
> should meet the professors and their families, having some
> object to bring them together, such as microscopic examin-
> ations, or the magic lantern, music, or portfolios of en-
> gravings, &c., to examine. [142]

This statement which was made one year after Nevada was admitted
to the Union (1864) indicates that vocal music was to be studied outside of school hours.

Among the earliest of the western states to be admitted to the
Union, California was a leader of the school music movement.   It
was stated in the previous chapter (that San Francisco was offering
music instruction in its schools in 1851.   Superintendent Pelton
said in 1867 that he was among the first to advocate the introduction

of music into the schools of the city.   During the latter year, the
budget for music was $3, 600.   There is some evidence that during
the preceding eight years it had been even more. [143]   Deputy
Superintendent Swett related in 1871 that Luther Whiting Mason of
Boston came to California.   In 1873 the pursuit of music in the
city was proving "quite satisfactory.   The instruction in this branch
is so systematically given in the primary grades and lower grammar-
grades that most pupils have a fair knowledge of music when they
graduate from the grammar-schools. "[144]   In 1874 Oakland reported
that vocal music was being taught in all the grades by the regular
grade teachers. [145]   In 1873 the Sacramento Board of Education was
asking for the restoration of music instruction which had been
dropped. [146]

The United States Commissioner of Education revealed that
in 1877 two secondary schools in Colorado reported offerings in
vocal and instrumental music. [147]   In 1881 music was included in
the state course of study for ungraded schools, which embraced
seven years' work, in the graded course of study music was
offered during each of the eight grades. [148]

During this period there was little evidence to report from
Utah.   The 1878-1879 Territorial School Report for Utah Territory
said that a class singing twice a week was a feature of the primary
department of Brigham Young Academy at Provo. [149]

Four years before Washington was admitted to the Union
(1889), the Seattle Superintendent indicated that the rudiments of
music should be taught in his school system.   He strongly urged
that action be taken to secure musical opportunities for the children
of his city. [150]   In 1887 the State Superintendent of Instruction of
the State of Washington advocated that vocal music be inserted in
the state list of studies. [151]

The development of school music in the West was slow compared to the rise and growth in other sections of the United States.
In 1876 a commission of French school leaders and teachers under
the leadership of M. Ferdinand Buisson was sent to America to
investigate our public school system.   In their 700 page report some

attention was given to the question of music instruction in elementary and secondary schools.   The significance of the commission's
report justifies the inclusion of an excerpt on "Singing and Music. "

> Many European countries have long since introduced sing-
> ing and music into elementary education; for example,
> Austria, Germany, Sweden, Switzerland, and even England,
> which places to-day the instruction in singing within the
> reach of everybody, young children not excepted.   But it
> is in the United States that the most persevering and
> systematic efforts have been made to render music, and
> especially vocal music, popular through the school.   Sing-
> ing is obligatory in all the grades of primary schools in
> the large eastern cities; it is especially well organized in
> the schools of Boston, New York, Philadelphia, Washington,
> Cincinnati, St. Louis, Cleveland, Milwaukee, and San
> Francisco.   Even in the South, where education is still in
> its rudiments, singing is often found on the programme of
> city schools e. g. , at Nashville, Louisville, Shelbyville,
> ...Moreover, in places where singing is an optional
> branch of study, it makes rapid progress from year to
> year. "[152]

The foreign recognition of what American educators were
attempting to do for the musical life of the boys and girls of the
United States was indeed a signal achievement; this was but forty
years after some of the early introductions of music into American
public schools.

Other evidences of the growth of school music are to be
found in the United States Commissioner of Education Report for
1878.   Commissioner John Eaton listed over 825 schools offering
vocal or instrumental music, or both, among 1227 secondary schools
in the country. [153]

In 1886, ten years after the French Commission's study,
there appeared a significant survey entitled, The Study of Music in
Public Schools.   John Eaton, United States Commissioner of
Education, appointed Theodore Presser, Charles W. Laudon, H. E.
Holt, N. C. Stewart, George F. Bristow, and Luther W. Mason to
assist the Commissioner's Office in preparing papers for the
stimulation and improvement of music instruction in American
schools. [154]   The findings were a veritable repository of school
music information, showing fifty-years' progress achieved by American public school music.

The study dealt only with public school music instruction. Questionnaires sent to school administrators contained many questions concerned with methods of instruction, materials and physical equipment, and the instructional personnel. The results revealed that of the 343 (sic 344) replies, 247 (sic 248) cities were offering vocal music instruction. By 1880 the population of the United States had reached 50, 155, 783. [155]   The 343 reporting cities represented a total school population of 7, 933, 193, or approximately twelve per cent of the total school population based on the 1880 census; the school population for the cities was 1, 209, 677.

The study further showed: 1) Seventy-two per cent of the reporting cities were offering vocal music instruction. 2) There was a great need for a more uniform nomenclature to be used in describing methods of music instruction. 3) There were varying practices as to the methods of instruction. 4) Over fifty-per cent of the schools were teaching music through the cooperative efforts of the regular and special music teacher. 5) Less than eight per cent of the schools allowed only the special teacher to teach music. 6) Sixty-four per cent were using the movable do system of teaching music notation. 7) The prevailing length of the instructional period was from one to two hours per week. 8) Pianos and organs were the principal instruments used for accompanying the music lesson.

Prior to 1890 there were significant evidences of the popularization of the special music teacher movement. Numerous school systems pointed with pride to their claim to the employment of a special music teacher or supervisor. Not alone did the salaried music teacher become a reality, but there had dawned a new era when there was a systematized methodical approach to teaching music. Children were to study music as a science. One characteristic difference between the period 1840-1865 and the period 1865-1890 was the decided growth in the interest in primary school music. Early school music so often emphasized music instruction for grammar and high school grades. Sight-reading of music was an ever sought objective. School board regulations, rules, and courses of study began to require music instruction for children at all grade levels. The development of formalized drill techniques often hampered music instruction at the expense of enjoyment. We must not gather the impression that all school leaders, finances permitting, would have offered music instruction. Music was viewed with skepticism by many educators. The era 1865–1890 saw the incipiency of increased emphasis upon the regular teacher being required to teach daily music lessons.

This study has indicated the rise and growth of public school music in all sections of the United States during the period 1865–1890. Though progressing at varying tempos, the values to be derived from the study of music had sufficiently rooted themselves in educational thought so as to insure the remarkable development that followed in the twentieth century.

Notes

1. Annual Report of the School Committee of the City, Providence, 1863. 15.

2. Annual Report of the School Committee of the City, Providence, 1875. 14.

3. Annual Report of the School Committee of the City, Providence, 1876. 80–81.

4. Reports and Documents Relating to the Public Schools of Rhode Island, for 1848. By Henry Barnard Commissioner of Public Schools. Published by Order of the General Assembly, Providence, 1849. 76–77.

5. Annual Report of the School Committee of the City of Providence. June, 1867. (Providence: Providence Press Company, City Printers, 1867), 54–58.

6. Annual Report of the School Committee of the City of Providence, July, 1873. (Providence: Hammond, Angell and Co., Printers to the City, 1873), 63.

7. Annual Report of the School Committee of the City of Newport, R.I., For The Year, 1865–66. 14.

8. Twenty-Third Annual Report of Public Schools in Rhode Island, Made To The General Assembly at The January Session. A.D. 1868. (Providence: Providence Company State Printers, 1868), 113.

9. Annual Report of the School Committttee of the City of Newport, R. I. , Together with the Annual Report of the Superintendent of Public Schools, 1869-1870. 36.

10. Eleventh Annual Report of the Board of Education Together With The Thirty-Sixth Annual Report of the Commissioner of Public Schools, of Rhode Island, January, 1881. (Providence: E. L. Freeman and Co. , Printers to the State, 1881), 94.

11. Annual School Report of 1882-1883.

12. Annual Report of the School Committee of the City of Newport, R. I. , Together With the Eighth Annual Report of the Superintendent of Public Schools, 1872-73. (Newport: Mercury Job Office. J. P. Sanborn, Proprietor, 1873), 44.

13. Ibid. , 44.

14. Annual Report of the School Committee of the City of Newport, R. I. , Together With the Report of Head Master of the Rogers High School, and Twelfth Annual Report of the Superintendent of Public Schools, 1876-77. (Newport: Davis and Pitman, Printers, News Office, 1877), 75-83.

15. Fifth Annual Report of the Board of Education, Together With The Thirteenth Annual Report of the Commissioner of Public Schools, of Rhode Island, January 1875. (Providence: Providence Press Company, Printers To The State, 1875), 140.

16. Ibid.

17. Ibid.

18. Fifth Annual Report of Rhode Island, Ibid. , 143.

19. Eleventh Annual Report of The Board of Education To-gether With The Thirty-Sixth Annual Report Of The Commissioner of Public Schools, Of Rhode Island, January, 1881. (Providence: E. L. Freeman and Co. , Printers To The State, 1881), 97.

20. Fifth Annual Report of Rhode Island, Ibid.

21. Eleventh Annual Report of Rhode Island, Ibid.

22. Twenty-Third Annual Report On Public Schools in Rhode Island, Made to The General Assembly at The January Session, A. D. 1868. (Providence: Providence Press Company, State Printers, 1868), 168.

23. First Annual Report of the State Superintendent of Public Instruction, Maryland, 1866. 6-7.

24. Second Annual Report of the State Superintendent of Public Instruction, Maryland, 1867. 6.

25. Report of the United States Commissioner of Education, Washington, D. C., 1872. 151.

26. Report of the State Board of Education of the Public Schools, Maryland, 1872. 40.

27. Report of the United States Commissioner of Education, Washington, D. C., 1874. 170.

28. Report of the United States Commissioner of Education, Washington, D. C., 1877. lxxvii-lxxix.

29. Thirteenth and Fourteenth Annual Reports of the Board of Education, (City of Oswego, 1866/67), 17-18.

30. Fifteenth Annual Report of the Board of Education, (City of Oswego, 1868), 21.

31. Sixteenth Annual Report of the Board of Education, (City of Oswego, 1869), 23.

32. Seventeenth Annual Report of the Board of Education, (City of Oswego, 1870), 16.

33. Fourth Annual Report of the Board of Public Instruction, (City of Albany, 1870), 95.

34. Proceedings of the Board of Public Instruction, (City of Albany, 1873), 456.

35. Proceedings of the Board of Public Instruction, (City of Albany, 1877), 131-133.

36. Twenty-Fourth Annual Report of the Board of Education, (City of Syracuse, 1872), 33-35, 47-48, 145.

37. Twenty-Seventh Annual Report of the Board of Education, (City of Syracuse, 1875), 25.

38. Thirty-Ninth Annual Report of the Board of Education, (City of Syracuse, 1887), 33-46.

39. Ellwood P. Cubberley, Public Education in the United States, (New York: Houghton Mifflin Company, 1919), 184-189.

40. Twenty-Fourth Annual Report of the Superintendent of Public Instruction, (State of New York, 1878), 285.

41. Thirty-Sixth Annual Report of the Board of Education, (City and County of New York, 1877), 165.

42. Forty-Third Annual Report of the Board of Education, (City of New York, 1884), 171-2.

43. Catalogue of the Officers and Students, (Warsaw Union Schools, 1879-80), 4.

44. "A Century of Music in Buffalo Schools, " Music Educators Journal. 23: (March, 1937), 26.

45. Ibid., 26.

46. Ibid., 26.

47. The Charter of the City of Buffalo, compiled by Mark S. Hubbell, City Clerk, Assisted by John J. Hynes, Counselor-at-law. (Buffalo, N. Y., 1896), 425.

48. Annual Report of the Board of Education, (State of Connecticut, 1866), 221-222.

49. Annual Report of the Board of Education, (State of Connecticut, 1868), lv.

50. Annual Report of the Board of Education, (State of Connecticut, 1869), 149.

51. Annual Report of the Board of Education, (State of Connecticut, 1872), 188, 205.

52. Annual Report of the Board of Education, (State of Connecticut, 1872), 232, 238, 253.

53. Annual Report of the Board of Education, (State of Connecticut, 1868), lxxxiii.

54. Annual Report of the Board of Education, (State of Connecticut, 1871), 119.

55. First Annual Report of the Superintendent of Public Schools, (Washington, D. C., 1869), 48.

56. Annual Report of the Superintendent of Public Schools, (Washington, D. C., 1870-1871), 42.

57. Report of the United States Commissioner of Education, (Washington, D. C., 1873), 436.

58. First Report of the Board of Trustees of the Public Schools. (District of Columbia, 1874-75), 310.

59. Ibid., 310.

60. Cubberley, Ibid., 141.

61. Ibid., 140-145.

62. Second Annual Report of the Superintendent of Public Schools. (Pittsburgh, 1870), 39, 46.

63. Ibid., 72.

64. Report of the United States Commissioner of Education. (Washington, D. C., 1877), 342.

65. Report of the United States Commissioner of Education. (Washington, D. C., 1871), 536-537.

66. First Annual Report of the Superintendent of Public School (Allegheny, 1874), 25.

67. Report of the United States Commissioner of Education. (Washington, D. C., 1877), xxv.

68. Report of the State Superintendent of Public Instruction. (New Jersey, 1871), Appendix, 6-8.

69. Report of the State Superintendent of Public Instruction. (New Jersey, 1874), Appendix, 11.

70. Report of the State Superintendent of Public Instruction. (New Jersey, 1873), Appendix, 21.

71. Annual Report of the Board of Directors of Education. (Jersey City, 1883), 109.

72. George G. Bush, History of Education in New Hampshire. Bureau of Education, Circular of Information, No. 3, (Washington, D. C., 1898), 27, 30, 55.

73. Forty-Third Annual Report of the Superintendent of Public Instruction. (New Hampshire, 1889), 23.

74. Ibid., 59.

75. Report of the United States Commissioner of Education. (Washington, D. C., 1872), 55.

76. Report of the United States Commissioner of Education.
     (Washington, D. C. , 1875), 62.

77. Report of the United States Commissioner of Education.
     (Washington, D. C. , 1878), lxxviii-lxxix.

78. Annual Report of the Superintendent of Common Schools.
     (Town of Newbury, 1860-61), 15.

79. Report of the United States Commissioner of Education.
     (Washington, D. C. , 1877), 342-343.

80. Twenty-Seventh Report of the Vermont State Superintendent
     of Education. (1882), 56-57.

81. Annual Report of the Board of Trustees of the Public
     Schools. (Louisville, 1866-67), 17-18.

82. Annual Report of the Superintendent of Public Instruction.
     (Kentucky, 1876), Appendix, 1.

83. Report of the United States Commissioner of Education.
     (Washington, 1878), 83.

84. Report of the State Superintendent of Education. (South
     Carolina, 1869-1870), 76-77.

85. Education in Charleston, S. C. , The Disabilities of the
     Unaided South in Public School Facilities. (1881), 32.

86. Annual Report of the State Superintendent of Public
     Education. (Louisiana, 1870), 153-154.

87. Annual Report of the State Superintendent of Public
     Education. (Louisiana, 1870), 369-370.

88. Annual Report of the State Superintendent of Public
     Education. (Louisiana, 1875), 11.

89. Report of the United States Commissioner of Education.
     (Washington, D. C. , 1877), lxxviii-lxxix.

90. Annual Report of the Superintendent of Public Schools.
     (Nashville, 1871), 42.

91. Annual Report of the City Schools. (Knoxville, 1876), 12.

92. Annual Report of the Superintendent of the City of Nash-
     ville. (Nashville, 1877-78), 50.

93. Annual Report of the State Superintendent of Schools for
     Tennessee. (1880), 25-26.

94. Report of the United States Commissioner of Education.
     (Washington, D. C., 1873), 5.

95. Report of the United States Commissioner of Education.
     (Washington, D. C., 1875), lxvii, lxx, lxxii.

96. Report of the United States Commissioner of Education.
     (Washington, D. C., 1873), 71.

97. Report of the United States Commissioner of Education.
     (Washington, D. C., 1877), lxxviii-lxxix.

98. Cubberley, 250.

99. Report of the United States Commissioner of Education.
     (Washington, D. C., 1877), lxxvii-lxxix.

100. Sixth Biennial Report of the Superintendent of Public
     Instruction. (Texas, 1887/1888), 288.

101. Eighteenth Annual Report of the Superintendent of Public
     Instruction. (Virginia, 1888), 26-30.

102. Report of the United States Commissioner. (1875), lxvi,
     lxx, lxxi-lxxii.

103. Ibid., lxvii.

104. Twelfth Annual Report of the Public Schools. (Terre
     Haute, 1875), 38-40.

105. Eighteenth Annual Report of the Public Schools.
     (Indianapolis, 1879), 108-115.

106. Twenty-Sixth Report of the Superintendent of Public
     Instruction. (Indiana, 1878), 369.

107. Biennial Report of the Public Schools. (Greencastle,
     1882/1883, 30.

108. Department of Public Instruction, City of Chicago, Four-
     teenth Annual Report of the Board of Education, for the
     Year Ending July 3, 1868. (Chicago: Church, Goodman
     and Donnelley, Printers, 1868), 196.

109. Department of Public Instruction, City of Chicago, Seven-
     teenth Annual Report of the Board of Education, for the
     Year Ending June 30, 1871. (Chicago: Spalding and
     La Monte, Printers, 1871), 64-67.

110. Department of Public Instruction, City of Chicago. Twen-
     tieth Annual Report of the Board of Education, for the Yea
     Ending June 26, 1874. (Chicago: Bryant Walker & Co.,

Printers, 1874), 199-201.

111.   Department of Public Instruction, City of Chicago, Twenty-first Annual Report of the Board of Education, for the Year Ending June 25, 1875. (Chicago: Fish & Kissell, Printers, 1875), 22.

112.   Department of Public Instruction, City of Chicago, Twenty-fourth Annual Report of the Board of Education, for the Year Ending July 31, 1878. (Chicago: Hazlitt & Reed, Printers, 1879), 29.

113.   Department of Public Instruction, City of Chicago, Thirty-first Annual Report of the Board of Education, for the Year Ending June 30, 1885. (Chicago: George K. Hazlitt & Co., Printers, 1886), 29-30, 67, and Thirty-second Annual Report of the Board of Education, for the Year Ending June 30, 1886. (Chicago: George K. Hazlitt & Co., Printers, 1887), 15-17.

114.

Teacher	Entered Service	Left Service
N. Gilbert	1842	1843
Mr. Whitman (not regularly employed)	1846	?
Frank Lombard	1848	1853
Mr. Whitman (not regularly employed)	1850	1850
S. P. Warner	1850	1850
Christopher Plagge	1854	1854
J. L. Slayton	1854	1856
William Tillinghast	1856	1860
Charles Ansorge	1863	1865
Orlando Blackman	1863	1875
Edward E. Whittemore	1865	1875

115.   William L. Steele, Galesburg Public Schools: Their History and Work. (Galesburg: Board of Education, 1911), 51-52.

116.   Twelfth Annual Report of the Superintendent of Public Schools. (Springfield, 1870), 90.

117.   Eleventh Biennial Report of the Superintendent of Public Instruction. (Illinois, 1875-1876), 157.

118.   Seventh Annual Report of the Superintendent of Public Instruction. (Kansas, 1868), 2.

119.   Eleventh Annual Report of the Department of Public Instruction of the State of Kansas. (1871), 6, 8.

120.   Classifications and Course of Study Recommended for the
        District Schools of Kansas.   (1873), 18.

121.   Fourth Annual Report of the Board of Education.   (Law-
        rence, Kansas, 1871), 13.

122.   Report of the United States Commissioner of Education.
        (Washington, D. C., 1878), 77.

123.   Fifteenth Biennial Report of the Superintendent of Public
        Instruction.   (Iowa, 1872), 135-136.

124.   Report of the United States Commissioner of Education.
        (Washington, D. C., 1877), lxxviii-lxxix.

125.   Annual Report of the Board of Education.   (Oskaloosa,
        1890), 7.

126.   Report of the Public Schools.   (Sioux City, 1890-1891),
        11.

127.   Annual Report of the Board of School Commissioners.
        (Milwaukee, 1872), 56.

128.   Annual Report of the State Superintendent.   (Wisconsin,
        1878-1880), 112.

129.   Course of Study of the Public Schools.   (Minneapolis,
        1871), 1-12.

130.   Course of Study of the Public Schools.   (Minneapolis,
        1888).

131.   Report of the United States Commissioner of Education.
        (Washington, D. C., 1872), 275.

132.   Annual Reports of the State Commissioner of Common
        Schools.   (Ohio, 1855/1856/1886), 6, 22, 67-69 re-
        spectively.

133.   Cleveland Public Schools, Thirty-Third Annual Report of
        the Board of Education for the School Year Ending August
        31, 1869.   18.

134.   Ibid., 67.

135.   Ibid., 67-69.

136.   Cleveland Public Schools.   Thirty-Fourth Annual Report
        of the Board of Education for the School Year Ending
        August 31, 1870.   92-93.

137. Ibid., 89-90.

138. Thirty-Ninth Annual Report of the Superintendent of Public Instruction of Michigan, 1875. 310.

139. Ibid., 302.

140. Forty-Fourth Annual Report of the Superintendent of Public Instruction of Michigan, 1880. 333.

141. Fourteenth Annual Report of the Board of Education of the City of Grand Rapids, 1886. 78-93.

142. First Annual Report of the Superintendent of Public Instruction of the State of Nevada, 1865. 32-33.

143. Report of the United States Commissioner of Education, 1871. 91-92.

144. Report of the United States Commissioner of Education, 1873. 23.

145. Report of the United States Commission of Education, 1874. 24.

146. Report of the United States Commissioner of Education, 1878. 17.

147. Report of the United States Commissioner of Education, 1877. lxxviii-lxxix.

148. Third Biennial Report of the Superintendent of Public Instruction of the State of Colorado, 1881/1882. 19-27.

149. Biennial Report of the Utah Territorial Superintendent of District Schools, 1878/1879. 23-24.

150. First Annual Report of the City Superintendent of the Public Schools of Seattle, Washington Territory, 1885. 16.

151. Report of the Superintendent of Public Instruction of Washington Territory, 1887. 34.

152. American Education as Described by the French Commissioner to the International Exhibition of 1876. (Washington, D.C.: Bureau of Education, Circulars of Information, No. 5. 1879), 28-29.

153. Report of the United States Commissioner of Education, 1878. 446-482.

154. "The Study of Music in Public Schools," Circulars of
      Information.   (Washington, D. C. , Bureau of Education,
      Government Printing Office, 1886), 5-6.

155. Ibid. , 4-54.

IX.   EDUCATIONAL CONVENTIONS: THEIR INFLUENCE ON
      EARLY AMERICAN MUSIC EDUCATION

Early American educational conventions may be divided into
at least three divisions: 1) Institutes,   2) Conventions, and
3) Lyceums.   Those that we cite were primarily interested in
popularizing the teaching of singing in early American schools.
Birge says that as early as 1829 singing-schools met in Concord,
New Hampshire, holding what they called a Singing-School
Convention.   These singing-school conventions were undoubtedly
among the first of American music teacher-training institutions.
They were interested in diffusing adult learning in the United States.

One of the early Lyceums was the result of the ability and
enthusiasm of Josiah Holbrook of Derby, Connecticut, who organized
the first Lyceum in 1826.   Holbrook outlined the purposes of
Lyceums in one of the Old South Leaflets in which he stated that
they were designed 1) "To improve conversation by introducing
worthwhile topics into the daily intercourse of families, neighbors
and friends.   2) To elevate the amusements of the community by
making weekly exercises of the Lyceum both instructive and enjoyable.   3) To provide a seminary for teachers.   4) To encourage
and assist existing academies. "[1]   The American Institute of
Instruction which met August 19, 1830, in Representatives' Hall,
Boston provided the occasion for Woodbridge and his declaration on
"Vocal Music as a Branch of Common Education. "[2]   It is he who
made the first extensive plea in behalf of vocal music for American
school children.   The 1830 meeting of The American Institute of
Instruction was attended by several hundred people, most of whom
were actual teachers, coming from at least eleven states.   It is
difficult to believe that this address by Woodbridge came from a
geographer and not a musician!

<u>Convention of Vocal Teachers Meeting in Boston.</u> The great
ferment initiated by William Woodbridge, Elam Ives, Jr., Lowell
Mason, and the officers of The Boston Academy of Music was
certain to profoundly affect the future course of vocal music in
American schools. Such a vigorous campaign may have been
responsible for the meeting of the first Convention of Vocal Teachers
in America, which was held on August 19, 1836 in Boston, when
vocal teachers from all the "New England States except Rhode
Island and New York"[3] came to Boston for the purpose of discussing
questions related to vocal music teaching in the public schools.
The teachers in attendance at the convention were to be interested
in the following considerations:

1. <u>Resolved.</u> That the introduction and application of the
Pestalozzian System of teaching music form a new era in the
science of musical education in this country; and, that in
pursuring our labors as teachers, we will conform ourselves
as far as circumstances will admit, to that system as published in the Manual of the Boston Academy of Music.

2. That in order to diffuse a knowledge of Music through
the community, it is necessary to teach it to our youth; and
that it is desirable and practicable to introduce it into all
our schools, as a branch of elementary education.

3. That it is the special duty of the Christian Church to
cultivate and encourage the cultivation of Sacred Music generally, as a powerful auxiliary to devotion.

4. That it is a source of deep regret to this Convention,
that, in so many instances, Religious Societies and Parishes,
instead of exerting a fostering care and influence over the
cause of Sacred Music, neglect it, suffer it to fall into un-
skilful hands, and thus, not only would the cause itself, but
make it a detriment, rather than a help, to the best interests
of the Church.

5. That Singing Choirs too frequently, in conducting their
part of divine worship, attempt the performance of music too
difficult, and with which they are not sufficiently familiar;
thereby detracting from the solemnity and devotion of the
exercise.

6. That in pursuing our labors as Teachers and Choristers,
we will strive to avoid, as far as in us lies, anything like
invidious rivalry; and that we will assist each other in our
profession, as we have opportunity.

7.   That, notwithstanding we have to contend with the prejudice of some, the opposition of others, and the indifference of many, yet we find in the progress of musical education for a few years past, abundant encouragement to persevere in our labors, and not to become weary in well-doing.

8.   That the sentiment which prevails in some places, that to occupy a place in the Choir, is not respectable, and, therefore, to assist in one of the most delightful services of the house of God, is not an honorable and dignified employment, is a sentiment founded in ignorance and prejudice; and that those who cherish such a sentiment themselves, or give countenance to it in any way, are endeavoring to subvert an ordianance which God himself has established.

9.   That in the opinion of this Convention, a good moral character, is an indispensable qualification for a Teacher of Sacred Music, for a Chorister. [4]

Although the Lyceum as a formal movement ceased to exist by 1840, it influenced educational activities throughout America for succeeding decades.   It was a powerful agent for the establishment of public schools.   Some of the topics for discussion at Lyceum meetings involved school organization, curricula, and school improvement.   At some of the meetings music was included among the topics for study and discussion.

In 1836 under the leadership of Lowell Mason and George J. Webb many teachers' conventions like the one at New Braintree, Massachusetts were held in various cities.   These teachers' conventions, or teachers' classes as they were called, evolved into musical conventions.

The early music teachers' convention served many purposes: 1) It made possible systematic instruction in voice culture;   2) It served to professionalize public school music;   3) It became a teacher-training institution for those interested in school music teaching;   4) It was an important factor in creating enthusiasm for lay and professional choral singing.

During the latter part of August, 1836 at the Vermont Convention of Teachers, Montpelier, Vermont, one of the topics for discussion was, "Can Music be successfully and usefully taught in common-schools."[5]   A lecture was also presented on the subject,

entitled "Music in Common Schools.[6] At the Fourth Annual Meeting of the Western Literary Institute in Cincinnati, during October,
1834, Professor Nixon of that city gave a talk entitled "On the
Influence of Music. "[7] The Convention of Teachers held in 1835 at
Carthage, Ohio, formulated the following resolution: "Resolved,
That Vocal Music should be made a part of common elementary
education, for boys and girls. "[8]

The Sixth Annual Meeting of the Western Literary Institute
and College of Professional Teachers was held the first week of
October, 1836, in Cincinnati. At that time, a committee was
appointed to report at the next annual meeting on "On Vocal Music
as a Branch of Common School Education. "[9] Even the State
Education Convention, held in Utica, New York May 11, 1837,
featured an address delivered by Professor S. N. Sweet. [10] It was
reported that music had been taught at an Academy in Utica as
early as 1827.

The Journal of the Rhode Island Institute of Instruction,
edited by Henry Barnard, Commissioner of Public Schools, included in the First Annual Report of its Executive Committee a
report by Professor Gammell, who stated the purpose of the
Institute was to further the cause of common school education. [11]
Meetings of the Institute had been held in different districts of the
state. They were held in Providence, Newport, Bristol, Warren,
Woonsocket, East Greenwich, Chepatchet, Pawtucket, Foster, and
Kingston. Some of the meetings lasted for two days. Among the
subjects discussed at these meetings throughout the state, was "Music
as a branch of education in schools. "[12] The first Institute for
teachers in the state of Massachusetts (1845) was an eminent
success. At the Institute, instruction in vocal music was given
by Lowell Mason and A. Fitz. [13]

John Sullivan Dwight reported a Musical Convention in progress at the Melodeon in Boston on August 16, 1852. [14] Benjamin
F. Baker and A. N. Johnson were conducting sessions on various
aspects of music study. Baker's emphasis was upon the Cultivation
of Voice and its relationship to the improvement of singing tone. [15]

Birge stated that the musical convention was "our first national school of music pedagogy, harmony, conducting, and voice culture."[16] The Otsego County Teachers' Institute which was held at Cooperstown, New York, commencing September 20, 1869 and lasting for two weeks, had singing as a part of the exercises at the day meetings of the institute.[17]

In the Fifteenth Annual Report (1848) the Superintendent of the Common Schools of Connecticut, Merrill Richardson, reported that conventions had been held for teachers in several counties of his state. Those reported by Richardson during 1847 were Middletown, Tolland, New London, Norwich, Goshen, and Farmington. The topic "Singing and Methods of Teaching the Science" were discussed at Farmington by a Mr. Ward who had experience teaching Juvenile singing schools. One of the methods suggested for administrating the teaching of the science, was for the singing teacher to go from school to school in the same town and spend an appropriate and somewhat equalized amount of time in each school. Teachers were giving more attention to the subject of music (1848). Richardson further stated that in the future teachers in taking their examinations will be asked as to whether or not they can sing.

Charles Ansorge of Chicago, Illinois stated in 1864, in a contribution entitled, "Singing in Schools," that "the following resolutions were passed unanimously at the last meeting of the National Teachers' Convention, held in Chicago last August (1863).

> Whereas, The power of music over the human soul has been proved beyond question, both by reason and experience; and whereas singing is the simplest as well as the most popular and effective kinds of music; therefore,
>
> Resolved, That singing should be taught to some extent in every public school, and that public teachers by whom in most cases this branch of instruction will be cultivated, should cultivate their musical faculties as much as circumstances will permit.
>
> Resolved, That the publication of a suitable collection for teachers, containing songs of a professional, social, patriotic and religious character, would supply an acknowledged want and be likely to meet with favor.[18]

Later during the same year at the Illinois Teachers' Convention, held in Springfield, Illinois the teachers voted unanimously that:

> Whereas, Music draws out and develops man's noblest faculties, exerting a great influence upon mind and character; and
>
> Whereas, Singing is the most effective and popular branch of music; therefore,
>
> Resolved, That Vocal Music should be taught in all our schools on a equal footing with the other branches of education. [19]

For a Teachers' Convention to consider music and advocate its introduction twice during the same year is evidence that prior to the Civil War its advocacy was beginning to be felt in Illinois. Music was championed because it had proven its value in the education of youth. The school boards of Boston, New York, Chicago, Buffalo and Cincinnati, had said a "yes" to this curriculum consideration; it now remained for the teachers in Illinois to warmly encourage its adoption. Ansorge in the same article to which we have referred stated that two things remained to be done by the assembled teachers of the conventions before real action would be forthcoming. "1) Every teacher by action, encouragement, advice and example should see to it that music is made the most popular subject possible; 2) There should be more singing at the Teachers' Conventions in order that a musical experience could definitely take hold of that person who is to teach music, the teacher. "[20]

The Shenandoah Musical Association was to hold its first meeting at Woodstock, Virginia, December 24-27, 1867. [21] Dr. Everett was to lecture on "The History, Utility and Influence of Sacred Music. " The leader of the convention was to be Professor R. M. McIntosh.

When the National Teachers' Association met August 18, 1870 at the Central High School, Cleveland, Ohio, [22] the records have it that a very fine paper on "Music in its relations to Common School Education" was delivered by Professor Eben Tourjee, Director of the New England Conservatory of Music, Boston. It was in his address that this eminent educator stated that music should enter into common school education, because:

> It is an aid to other studies.
>
> It assists the teacher in maintaining the discipline of the school.
>
> It cultivates the aesthetic nature of the child.
>
> It is valuable as a means of mental discipline.
>
> It lays a favorable foundation for the more advanced culture of later life.
>
> It is a positive economy.
>
> It is of the highest value as a sanitary measure.
>
> It prepares for participation in the church service.

At this same session a model lesson in vocal music was presented by Professor Miller of Illinois. In addition, a musical exercise was exhibited for study purposes with a group of girls. Professor N. C. Stewart of Cleveland presented and directed the demonstration.

These early teachers' conventions or teachers' classes, as they were called, evolved into musical conventions. The music educator was not alone, for other interested people were attending the sessions which were held for periods of from two to five weeks. Because the musical convention idea had somewhat lost sight of the objectives of the original teachers' conventions, a new venture was started in New York City known as the Normal Musical Institute. Later, its headquarters were removed to North Reading, Massachusetts, where it was in full operation for approximately three months each year. The term of the Normal Musical Institute at North Reading for 1860 commenced July 11, 1860 and continued for six weeks. [23] The purposes of the Institute were to be found in an announcement which stated that

> The leading object of this School is to afford aid to such persons, male or female, as desire to prepare themselves for teaching, or who wish to make higher attainments in the art of teaching vocal music, either in juvenile or in adult classes. The instructions will be adapted to the want of such female teachers of primary, or more advanced

schools, as wish to introduce singing as an exercise, or
music as a study; or, to teach in seminaries where music
is made one of the regular branches of instruction; or, to
teachers, male or female, who desire to teach music in
schools generally, or in classes, juvenile or adult, formed
expressly to receive instruction.   Also to gentlemen who
desire to qualify themselves to conduct Musical Conventions,
especially such as are of a school character, which are
now becoming common to some parts of the country, in
which many people, young and old, come together and
devote several successive days, perhaps a week or more,
meeting several times each day for the special purpose
of improving in singing.   Often with direct references to
the psalmody of public worship, and where it is properly
expected that much, comparatively, will be done in a short
space of time.   For teachers of Singing - Schools, or
Classes of all kinds, (be it repeated), the Normal Institute
is especially designed.

In carrying out this object of the school, the exercises
will, in a very general manner, be divided into four
departments:

I.	Elemental	III.	Vocal Training
II.	Choral Song	IV.	Musical Composition.

During 1860, the other Normal Institute which Lowell Mason,
Wm. B. Bradbury, and George F. Root were directly interested
in was to be conducted in Chicago, commencing Wednesday,
September 12, 1860, and continuing the term for six weeks. [24]

Not only did the triumvirate, Mason, Bradbury, and Root
work together, they also participated individually in Institute work.
In 1859, an Institute was conducted by William Bradbury at Geneseo
New York.

Some of the leading Institute conductors in America about
1860 were:

Bailey, E. H.	Portland, Michigan
Cady, C. M.	Chicago, Illinois
Collister, Samuel	Worcester, Massachusetts
Cook, T. J.	New York City, N. Y.
Foote, E. M.	Lockport, New York.
Greene, Charles H.	St. Louis, Missouri.
Killip, W. W.	Geneseo, New York
Loomis, George B.	Providence, R. I.
Marvin, E.	Jackson, Tennessee
Miller, L. B.	Galesburg, Illinois
Peck, J. Bidwell	Great Barrington, Mass.

Perkins, Theo. E.	Tunkhannock, Pennsylvania
Perkins, W. O.	Boston, Massachusetts
Sherwin, W. F.	Albany, New York
Snyder, D. D.	Warsaw, New York
Tillinghast, William	Chicago, Illinois
Warren, S. W.	Coventryville, New York
Williams, A. C.	Orange, New Jersey

Another Institute which prepared music students for teaching purposes was the one known as the Normal Academy of Music, Painesville, Ohio. This was in session July 2, 1867 to August 27, 1867.

City Institutes were becoming exceedingly popular by 1885. The United States Government Circulars on Information pertaining to education were produced in 1885[25] for the purpose of revealing the extent of City or Teachers' Institutes in American cities. The Superintendent in Lancaster, Pennsylvania, stated in 1885 that "all cities should provide for at least one week's instruction annually, just before the opening of the schools, by specialists, in some one branch especially necessary in each grade - the primary, (teachers might profit) object lessons, vocal music, etc. "[26] It was further suggested that these Institutes might become more effective if they were held before the opening of the school year. The Superintendent in Lynn, Massachusetts, concluded that "These institutes are termed teachers' meetings by us and are of no additional expense other than for simple apparatus occasionally or to defray car fare from Boston or some lecturer once in six months. "[27]   Each month they had an institute known as a monthly institute. At the first Normal Institute of South Carolina, which was held at Wofford College, Spartanburg, instruction in singing was offered, with nearly all of the members of the Institute taking part (date before 1885). [28]   The first Institute for Colored Teachers, which was held at Howard College, (Howard School) Columbia, S. C., offered vocal music instruction under H. F. Grant for a four week period between July 5 and July 29, 1881. [29]

Whether it was a lyceum, teachers' convention, or an institute, it is seen from the evidence presented that each offered music instruction, lectures, or both as part of their educational program. The music teachers' convention and institute proved to be an institution which made possible the professionalization of early American school music teaching. Its inspirational vigor permeated nineteenth century public school music teaching. From the Atlantic Seaboard to Midwestern Illinois, and into the Southern States considerable agitation through these mediums had manifested itself during the period 1830-1885. It was at these meetings that the missionaries of American music education formulated worthwhile and stimulating conceptions of a functional music teaching philosophy. Prior to 1885 the summer and short term school music teaching institute had become an established reality. Surely the nineteenth century musical institute gave American school music a practical knowledge of how to teach music to every child. No study can afford to pass lightly over the influence of the institute upon the historical development of school music education.

Notes

1. Hoffsinger, John F., Correspondence Schools, Lyceums, Chautauquas. 99.

2. Woodbridge, William C., "On Vocal Music as a Branch of Common Education," The American Institute of Instruction, 1831. 231-235.

3. "Convention of Teachers of Vocal Music," American Annals of Education and Instruction, 6: (October, 1836). 473-474.

4. Ibid., 473-474.

5. Ibid., (June, 1836). 283.

6. Ibid., (September, 1836). 423.

7. Nixon, Professor, "On the Influence of Music," The American Annals of Education and Instruction, 5: (November, 1835). 507-510.

8. "Western Literary Institute," The American Annals of Education and Instruction, 7: (January, 1837). 40.

9. "Convention of Teachers at Carthage," The American Annals of Education and Instruction, 5: (June, 1835). 281-282.

10. "State Education Convention, " American Annals of
     Education and Instruction, 7: (July, 1837). 329.

11. Journal of The Rhode Island Institute of Instruction,
     1845-46. 1: 58.

12. Ibid., 58-59.

13. Ninth Annual Report of the Superintendent of Public
     Instruction of the Ninth Annual Report of the Secretary
     of the Board, 1846 Boston, 55, 60.

14. Dwight, John Sullivan. Dwight's Journal of Music, Vol: 1.
     No. 19 (August 14, 1852). 149-150.

15. Ibid., Vol: 1 No. 20 (August 21, 1852). 157-158.

16. Birge, Edward B. History of Public School Music In The
     United States. (Boston, Mass.: Oliver Ditson Co.,
     1928). 28.

17. Sixteenth Annual Report of the Superintendent of Public
     Instruction of the State of New York, 1870. 251.

18. Ansorge, Charles. "Singing in Schools, " The Illinois
     Teacher, 10: (March, 1864). 115-119.

19. Ibid.

20. Ibid.

21. "A Musical Convention at the South, " The Musical Pio-
     neer. 12: (January, 1867). 2.

22. Report of the United States Commissioner of Education,
     1871. 536.

23. "The Normal Musical Institute at North Reading. "
     New York Musical Review and Gazette. 11: (April 14,
     1860). 115-120.

24. Ibid., 153.

25. Teachers' Institutes. Bureau of Education. Circulars
     of Information, No. 2, 1885. 65.

26. Ibid.

27. Ibid.

28. Ibid., 74, 107.

29. Ibid.

X. THE ADVENT OF METHOD IN MUSIC EDUCATION[1]

The introduction of vocal music into American public schools brought with it a method for teaching music. Earlier we learned that Woodbridge was the first person to communicate to Elam Ives of Philadelphia and then to Lowell Mason, various German methods based on Pestalozzian principles for teaching elementary instruction in vocal music. This chapter will treat this European influence upon American methods of school music teaching. Included is a detailed examination and interpretation of those methods employed during the first sixty years of American music education.

Ives published in 1831 A Manual of Instruction in the Art of Singing, which was "constructed on the principles of the inductive system of music originally devised and published by Pfeiffer & Nägeli, under the direction of Pestalozzi." A year later, he published The American Elementary Singing Book, further carrying out the general plan of Pfeiffer and Nägeli, but he was taken to task for not indicating that the authors of the instructional plan were not mentioned. The reviewing critic, probably Woodbridge, admits that Ives had made some improvements over the original works. [2]

It remained for Lowell Mason to become the first successful interpreter and standard-bearer of public school music in this country. Mason, like Ives, had seen the German works on elementary music instruction which were introduced into America by Woodbridge. Beginning in 1833, Mason, as professor of the Boston Academy of Music, extended the use of the methods throughout the eastern United States. He was aided by George James Webb.

In 1834 Mason published his Manual of the Boston Academy of Music, for Instruction in the Elements of Vocal Music, on the System of Pestalozzi. In this work he states that the system of instruction which he has used may be traced to Pestalozzi.

190

M. T. Pfeiffer and H. G. Nägeli published an extensive work entitled, Gesangbildungslehre nach Pestalozzischen Grundsätzen, which embodied the Pestalozzian system of teaching the elements of elementary music.   Mason also used works on elementary music instruction by Kübler and other German teachers.   In the preface to his "Carmina Sacra," he said that his Manual of Instruction may be considered a translation of Kübler's work. [3]

The Pestalozzian system of teaching vocal music as Mason saw it was a systematization of the elements of music, so that one thing at a time was taken up for study.   When that was mastered the pupil proceeded to the next.   The elements of music were presented so simply that pupils could learn without the aid of the teacher.   The teacher was to refrain from telling the pupils everything, hoping that they would, by a series of questions, learn the answers for themselves.   This technique was supposed to aid independent thinking and satisfaction would come to the student when he learned things for himself.   Mason maintained that, by applying such a procedure to a study of the elements of music, interest in the subject could be maintained for a period of years.   The old illogical and jumbled order of presenting the elements of music was confusing, uninteresting, and not conducive to rapid learning. The Pestalozzian method was a way of teaching the rudiments of music. [4]

In Mason's Manual of Instruction published in 1834, he included the principles of teaching music formulated by Pestalozzi.   They were:

1. To teach sounds before signs -- to make the child sing before he learns the written notes, or their names.

2. To lead him to observe -- by hearing and imitating sounds, their resemblances and differences, their agreeable and disagreeable effect, instead of explaining these things to him: - in short, to make him active instead of passive in learning.

3. In teaching but one thing at a time -- rhythm, melody, expression are taught and practiced separately, before the child is called to the difficult task of attending to

all at once.

4. In making them practice each step of each of these divisions, until they are masters of it, before passing to the next.

5. In giving the principles and theory after practice, and as an induction from it.

6. In analyzing and practicing the elements of articulate sound, in order to apply them to music.

7. Another peculiarity, which is not, however, essential to the system, is, that the names of the notes correspond to those employed in instrumental music, and are derived from the letters with variation from flats and sharps; a method whose utility is questioned by some, but which is deemed very important by others. [5]

In addition to making popular the Pestalozzian methods of instruction, Mason published in his Manual of Instruction, specific steps to be followed in teaching the elements or rudiments of music. The study of music was divided into three parts: Part I, Rhythm; Part II, Melody; Part III, Dynamics. Parts I and II were divided into first, second, and third courses of study. Part III was divided into first and second courses of study. An outline of the material covered in each Part follows:[6]

Part I --- Rhythm

First Course

1). Divisions of time into measures, 2). Measuring time by beats, 3). Practice accent, 4). Notes applied to measure, 5). Value and names of notes, 6). Variation of measure, 7). Different notes in measure, 8). Different notes in same measure, 9). Derivation and relation of notes, 10). Rests.

Second Course

1). Relations of divided notes, 2). Divided notes continued, 3). United notes continued, 4). Rests continued, 5). Triplets.

Third Course

1). Divided notes four to a beat, 2). Rests continued, 3). Thirty-seconds, and sixty-fourths, 4). Grades of time.

Part II -- Melody

First Course

1). Pitch, or sounds high or low, 2). Tones and semitones, 3). Tetrachord, 4). Scale, 5). Staff,
6). Letters applied to the staff, 7). Exercise on
the third, 8). Exercises on the fifth, 9). Exercises
on the eighth, 10). Combinations of these four principal sounds (Chord, Concord, Discord, Harmony),
11). Exercises on the seventh, 12). Exercises of
the fourth, 13). Exercises on the second, 14).
Exercises of the sixth, 15). Extension of the scale
(Eight becomes one for scale above, and one becomes
eight for scale below).

Second Course

1). Chromatic scale, 2). Exercises on the semitones,
3). Diatonic intervals, 4). Major and minor intervals, 5). Common chords, 6). Harmony, 7).
Essential and transient notes, 8). Transposition of
the scale, 9). Key of G, or of one sharp, 10). Key
of D, or of two sharps, 11). Key of A, or of three
sharps, 12). Key of E, or of four sharps, 13). Key
of B, or 5 sharps, and of F sharp or 6 sharps, 14).
Key of F, or of one flat, 15). Key of B flat, or of
two flats, 16). Key of E flat or of three flats, 17).
Key of A flat, or of four flats, 18). Keys of D flat
and G flat.

Third Course

1). Modulation into relative keys, 2). Modulation to the
fifth, 3). Modulation to the fourth, 4). Minor scale.
(Only two parts were indicated for study during the
Third Course.)

Part III --- Dynamics

First Course

1). Loud, soft, and medium sound, 2). Very loud and
very soft sounds.

Second Course

1). Organ, increasing, diminishing, pressure, and explosive
tones, 2). Exercises on the force of sounds. (It was
stated that a proper application of all the different

phases of the study of dynamics would result in what
is called expression.)[7]

Each lesson was to include a study of rhythm, melody, and harmony.   All topics under the sub-heading, <u>First Course</u> (Parts I,
II, III) were to be studied before proceeding to the second course.
All topics were to be studied in the order listed.   The lessons
were to be short.   The teacher was requested to give frequent
reviews.   Approximately one half to two thirds of each lesson was
devoted to a study of the elements of music, the remaining time
being spent in singing songs.

Under the classification, "Dynamics," there was a discussion
of "expression of words, in connexion with sound."   This section
of music instruction included the following: 1).   Articulation,   2).
Emphasis,   3).   Connexion of syllables and words,   4).   Sentiment.
These phases of music study were to be introduced near the beginning of instruction and carefully attended to throughout the course
of study. [8]

The equipment necessary for instruction was simple.   Blackboards 6' x 4' 6" were recommended.   The staff should be drawn
three or four times across it, the lines being one and one half
inches apart; a rod or pointer was necessary.   Mason suggested
the piano as the most suitable instrument for giving a pitch; a
violin could be used.   Blank music books should be provided the
students in order that exercises in music could be written. [9]

Mason said that before receiving instruction in music children
should be taught to sing easy songs by rote.   Children could receive
this instruction in their homes, or in infant schools.   The aim of
this pre-school training was to develop their singing ability.   After
this training, the child of 6-8 years would be ready for the formal
instruction of music.   The course was completed at the age of
fourteen or fifteen.   These methods of music teaching outlined in
the preceding pages were used by Mason in the Boston Public
Schools.

Henry Barnard, Secretary of the Connecticut Board of Commissioners for Common Schools published articles on vocal music

in his <u>Connecticut Common School Journal.</u> In 1838 the journal
carried an article entitled "The Elements of Music." It pointed
out the merits and demerits of the old and new way of teaching
vocal music. It stated that the old way was to find out the intellectual and factual material, such as <u>definitions, signs, names of</u>
<u>the notes, rules for finding do, etc.</u>

The new way of teaching music said the writer, was used
differently by each teacher. In general advocates of the new
method were divided into two groups: 1. The <u>rudimentists</u> were
those who felt it imperative to instruct the pupil adquately in the
elements of music; 2. The <u>combinationists</u> were those who would
rather forego the learning of the elements of music in order that
interest may be maintained through song singing. It was a question
of the intellectual procedure against the more emotional and enjoyable. The first group spent a great deal of time intensively drilling
intonation, time, harmony, etc. separately, while the second group
felt that both the rudimentary and song singing approach could be
conveniently and efficiently combined. Lowell Mason of Boston
belonged to the <u>rudimentists,</u> while Elam Ives of Philadelphia was a
combinationist. [10]

The writer of the article indicated that the new way of teaching (Pestalozzian or German methods) had considerably increased
the effectiveness of school music instruction. [11]

It may be worthwhile to note the exact steps involved in the
early method of teaching music. The writer of the article mentioned above described the method as he had seen it used in 1839;

> To give an idea of the manner in which this system may
> be adapted to a common school, we will here sketch, in
> as brief a manner as we can, such a lesson as we have
> often witnessed, and given among schools in our neighbor-
> hood.
>
> Standing by a blackboard, we ask, who can tell me how
> he makes a noise in talking? Then we describe the little
> musical instrument in the throat, and ask the children to
> feel their throats with the thumb and finger; sound a note
> and observe how it jars like a musical instrument, calling
> upon them to admire it as a work of God. We then say,
> some sounds appear to go up, and some down, as in asking

a question, and in making a simple declaration . Now we
may make a spot for each sound, putting those above which
stand for high notes, etc.   But to show exactly where they
are intended to be, we draw five lines, and place the dots
on or between them (It is well if the pupils have slates
and write everything down).   Now the teacher may sing
up the scale, and ask where each note is to be written.
Then sing down, and ask the same.   Then sound the
common chords, and ask the same.

The pupils may then be requested to sing up and down, till
they do it together.   Then the semi-breve, minim crotchet,
etc. , may be written, and called whole, half, quarter
notes, etc. and the time spent in singing them briefly
shown, with a little practice in singing and beating.   The
use of bars and rests may also be briefly explained; and
if questions were asked of the whole school, after these
steps are explained, the impressions will be made clearer
on the mind.

The teacher should inform the pupils that the musical
scale is like a ladder or staircase (as scala means in
Italian,) of seven steps, two of which, (viz. the third and
seventh), are only about half as high as the others; and
that, although we do not know why it is, everybody naturally
sings in that manner, and cannot easily sing in any other
way.   He may then try to sing some familiar tune, beginning at a wrong part of the scale, (as "Wells, " beginning
on the third, instead of the first,) and say that before we
begin to sing, we must know where the first note is, and
how far from it the tune begins.   He then may show that
the sound belonging to a particular line or space is fixed
the whole scale being moveable up or down on the staff.
This may be familiarly illustrated by beginning with singing
one, two, three, etc., or do, re, mi, etc., on difficult
lines and spaces successively, but taking the correct pitch
in all cases.

It is probably better, in the first lesson to use the numbers
1, 2, 3, etc. , in singing, rather than the syllables, do, re,
etc. , as every unnecessary obstacle to the pupils' progress
should be avoided, that his courage may be increased by
successful progress.   The exercises sketched here, and
others on dynamics, (or singing loud and soft,) as well
as on harmony, may be extended through several lessons,
or condensed, as far as may be, in one.   They should,
at any rate, be often repeated, as the teacher must not be
discouraged, if he finds the pupils easily forget what they
may have seemed to learn with avidity and distinctly.   They
will at least make some progress in the rudiments, and the
exercises will necessarily prove useful to the moral feelings,
the lungs and muscles of the chest, even among the most

volatile and inattentive of the number. They will also be
prepared to regard this branch with pleasure and interest;
and the watchful and faithful instructor may find many
opportunities, in the momentary intervals, to drop affectionate and pungent remarks, with the fairest prospect of
permanent benefit. [12]

In the preceding pages our discussion has dealt with the
modern school music teaching methods as developed by Ives and
Mason. Another leader in American school music teaching was
Luther Whiting Mason, supervisor of primary school music in
Boston. He, like Lowell Mason, used the song as a basis for
teaching the elementary principles of music. He believed that the
methods used in teaching language, based upon teaching by rote,
could be applied to the teaching of music. A good foundation for
learning to read has been laid before a child enters school and
this is not true of music.

Mason thought that there should be an organized course in
rote singing; the songs to be written within a child's range and of
simple rhythm. He taught music notation, step by step. Blackboards and charts were used to train the ear and eye for sight-
reading. No clef signs or key signatures were used. In short,
the material was presented: "first, by rote; second, step by step
from the blackboard; third, from the charts; and, fourth, from the
printed page of the book. "[13]

In direct contrast to the methods employed by Lowell Mason
and Luther Whiting Mason, Hosea H. Holt, supervisor of music
in the Boston Public Schools (1869-1898), did not believe in using
the song as a basis for teaching the rudiments of music. His
method was based on a series of technical exercises which were in
no way related to a song. Holt employed the exercise plan, whereas, the Masons used the song plan. [14]

From the beginnings of method in American music education
to the Civil War, no fundamental change had been made in the
teaching of school music. Whether music was being taught in San
Francisco, Chicago, Cleveland, Buffalo, Oswego, or New York,
music teaching to a greater or lesser degree followed the system

as outlined in Mason's <u>Manual of Instruction.</u>   In order to indicate
the type of instruction pursued in these cities, there will be a
discussion of some of the more interesting phases of the methods
of music teaching in Chicago during the period 1858-1874.

During the school year 1857-58 W. H. Wells, the Chicago
superintendent of schools, reported that lessons in vocal music
were being given once a week in all its schools.   The primary
music lessons were devoted to the singing of rote songs; the singing by rote of various scale exercises, and the dictation of scale
exercises.   A major objective was to be able to appreciate pitch
relationships.   Chicago, like a majority of other American cities,
long retained sight-singing (reading) as a major school music teaching objective. [15]

By 1869 the pupils in the grammar department of the Chicago
schools under E. E. Whittemore were learning music by rote.   Even
to learn music by rote was a task.   The committee on music for
1869 pointed out that in the grammar department pupils had developed their ability to sing at sight the songs which <u>one year ago</u> were
being taught by the rote method.   Sight-reading of music was a new
adventure for the music department of the Chicago Public Schools
in 1869.   In that year the committee on music indicated that the
singing of music at sight was introduced by the music teacher. [16]

By 1870 Whittemore had introduced three part music in the
grammar department.   In addition, attempts were being made to
introduce the key signatures of four sharps and seven flats into the
third and fourth grades, but the results were not gratifying.   The
method of placing voices in three part work was as follows: the
boys sang the lower or third part; the girls the first or second.
Mention is made of the fact that at the end of the school term the
boys were able to sing creditably their third part in "Lift Thine
Eyes" by Mendelssohn.

Later in 1871 the committee on music stated that much progress had been made in the music work.   A summary of achievements follows: "1) Music teaching is not entirely confined to rote
singing: instead we find those who are singing two or three part

songs;   2)   Persistent efforts are being made to create an artistic
musical performance.   Emphasis is placed on good tone quality as
being conducive to throat protection.   3)   Sight-singing has become
a definite goal to be attained; it was practiced with considerable
success.   4)   The primary department music teacher was examining
all voices and classifying them into their proper registers.   5)
Music was rapidly becoming a potent factor in the educational life of
Chicago school children. "[17]

During 1873 the board of education stated that harmony had
been attempted with success in the high and normal schools.   A
year later the three important features of the Chicago public school
music program were:

First.   Theory of Music.   --   It is necessary for pupils to
           understand the use of all characters in this grade.
           This will give them the ability to pursue their study
           with intelligence.

Second.   Chorus Singing.   --   It is certainly important that
           the chorus singing be excellent, in order that a
           correct musical taste may be formed.   The influence
           of the songs, when all join, is very beneficial and a
           source of recreation to the pupils.

Third.   Individual Singing.   --   Theory and chorus singing
           secure to the pupils a certain degree of proficiency,
           but the greatest benefit is derived from requiring
           him to sing alone. [18]

After the Civil War music teaching in Chicago emphasized a
study of the rudiments of music.   More attention was given to
sight-singing.   The music program was being expanded.   Harmony
as a technical subject was offered in some of the high schools.
Individual opportunity for singing was receiving greater stress.
Selected choral groups were being organized for special performances.   Music study in Chicago was becoming more satisfactory
from year to year.

In summarizing the beginnings of method in American school
music teaching it is noted that during the period 1830-1870 there
was little change in the methods employed in teaching vocal music.
It is shown that Elam Ives and Lowell Mason were the earliest to

formulate methods of teaching elementary music.   The evidence
presented indicates Mason was the most important figure in school
music during this period.

As pointed out, early American methodologists of school music
were divided into two camps, the rudimentists, and combinationists.
After 1870 the breach between the two widened. The discussion of music
teaching in Chicago during the period 1858-1874 illustrates the
increased emphasis given to sight-singing or music-reading.   Music-
reading became the summum bonum of school music.   Luther
Whiting Mason represented the song-singing plan, whereby the child
learned an abundance of fine songs by rote, afterwards learning
them by note.

Hosea Holt had faith in the exercise plan which required the
child to be drilled in a host of musical exercises.   These were
taught independently of songs, but were later applied to music-
reading.

Notes

1. Sunderman, Lloyd F.   "The Advent of Method in Music
   Education, " Education.   Vol. 61: No. 9 (May, 1941).   555-561.
   Reprinted with the permission of Education Magazine, The
   Bobbs-Merrill Company, Inc. , Indianapolis, Indiana.

2. The American Annals of Education and Instruction, 1832.
   136.   (Book Review).

3. Mason, Lowell.   Manual of the Boston Academy of Music,
   for Instruction in the Elements of Vocal Music, on the
   System of Pestalozzi.   14-15.

4. Ibid. , 13-14, 32.

5. Woodbridge, William C.   "On Vocal Music as a Branch of
   Common Education, " American Institute of Instruction, 1:
   231-255.

6. Mason, Lowell.   Ibid. , 40-232.

7. Ibid. , 232.

8. Ibid. , 233-241.

9. Ibid. , 34.

10. "The Elements of Music." The Connecticut Common School Journal, 1: 100-109.

11. Ibid.

12. Ibid., 108-109.

13. Lawrence, Clara E. "Early School Music Methods," Music Educators Journal, 25: (December, 1938). 21-22.

14. Coburn, E. L. "Music in the United States for the Last Twenty-Five Years," Journal of Proceedings of the Third Annual Meeting of the Music Supervisors' Conference, 16-19.

15. Fourth Annual Report of the Superintendent of the Public Schools of the City of Chicago, 1858. 41.

16. Fifteenth Annual Report of the Chicago Board of Education, 1869. 118-121.

17. Seventeenth Annual Report of the Chicago Board of Education, 1871. 64-70.

18. Twentieth Annual Report of the Chicago Board of Education, 1874. 191-201.

XI. SOME EARLY CONCEPTS OF THE EDUCATIONAL VALUES OF MUSIC EDUCATION[1]

The embroyonic developments of seventeenth and eighteenth century American music education have been traced in the preceding chapters. It has been seen that early music was tolerated solely in light of its religious consecration. Following that time was a period when the omnipresent physical and economic considerations gave little time for cultural pursuits. With the passing of the Revolutionary period there began to appear in the daily program of the American citizen's activities an opportunity for some cultural meditation and aspiration. The concern of a group of lay and professional educators and musical enthusiasts fused with an evangelizing spirit which found its expression through the medium of periodicals, books, and public lectures. Some of the concepts promulgated by these early leaders are surveyed in the following pages.

Vocal music as a part of the school curriculum was not popular in the early nineteenth century. In order for an educator to secure its inclusion he had to submit convincing educational reasons. The cause of school music instruction traversed a thorny pathway beset by economic stringency, and moral and religious intolerance. The added expense which attended the addition of music to the school curriculum was a big factor in thwarting its progress. The opponents of music education claimed that it was devitalizing and injurious to the moral and religious sensibilities of young minds. All notions of music's harmful effects were in some degree traceable to religious fanaticism. Any phase of music education which in any way secularized the religious sensibilities of the child was vigorously opposed, and any music permitted in the schoolroom was almost uniformly religious in character.

Beginning about 1825 there was much discussion in favor of

free public schools.   The early protagonists of popular education
did not realize that by 1850 free public schools would become
realities in most of the northern states.   It is natural that this
era brought educational propaganda, and with it an increased
emphasis upon curriculum content and a re-evaluation of the school
as a servant of the public.   The philosophy of phrenology and mind
improvement did much to hinder the growth of those subjects which
would not claim mind improvement potentialities.   All the subjects
which demanded a hearing for inclusion into public school curriculums
claimed intellectual connotations in order to command a respect
from the people in charge of school administration.   It was quite
plausible in view of early nineteenth century educational philosophy,
that music teachers should advocate intellectual advantages to be
derived from the study of music.   In many cases the early music
educator and sympathetic school administrator advanced claims which
were gross exaggerations.   Music was not at fault; it was a condition inherent in the educational profession.

During the period 1830-1865, vocal music instruction was
often considered an educational extravaganza.   Few of the children
in American public schools had experienced systematic vocal music
instruction before 1838.   If the period 1830-1838 bore fruit, the
available records do not reveal much evidence of the fact.   This
was a period of philosophical and educational preparation.

William Woodbridge, Lowell Mason, and George J. Webb
were the stalwart early advocates of music study.   They argued
that music produced a changed rather than a static condition in
the intellectual, social, emotional, and moral faculties of man.
They believed that school music education was an avenue toward
achieving the betterment of the social, intellectual, and emotional
well-being of mankind.

Two of the more pressing questions that begged for resolution
were   1) What salutary educational gains are to be achieved by the
introduction of vocal music into the public schools? and   2) How
can the expenditure of time and money on school music be justified?
A third question of major consideration also arose: What arguments

should be used to attain a sympathetic ear from the school
authorities responsible for the administration of public school
education?   The following pages attempt to provide some of the
answers given by music education proponents during the last
century.

One of the supposedly remarkable concomitants of vocal
music study was that it furnished an intellectual exercise, or
rather, provided a salutary discipline of the mind.[2]   Lowell Mason
contended that music did serve as an intellectualizing force.   Learning the science of music notation demanded an orderly thought
process which was certain to prove beneficial to the development
of man's intellect.   Although quite different as to function, nature,
and content, music as a mental discipline was in no way intellectually inferior to the study of mathematics.   Horace Mann stated
that

> Vocal music furnishes the means of intellectual exercises.
> All the musical tones have mathematical relations.[3]

It was claimed that all music reading required brain functions
which were of a high order.

Many of the early writers on education encouraged the study
of vocal music because its cultivation would materially aid the
general physical well-being of those taking up its study.   It was
the one tenet which received constant emphasis and elaboration
during the period beginning with 1830 and lasting well into the
post-Civil War era.   Dr. Rush, a medical authority, stated that
singing was a means of "protection from the pulmonary diseases
so common in our climate; ... the German were seldom afflicted
with consumption, ... singing (was) employed with success as a
means of arresting the progress of pulmonary complaints."[4]

During the period 1830-1860, there appeared a relentless
barrage of literature devoted to the physio-therapeutic values to
be derived from the study of vocal music.   Horace Mann's 1844
report stated: "Vocal music, by exercising and strengthening the
lungs, and by imparting gayety to the spirits, would tend to diminish
the number of that sad procession whom we daily see hastening to

an early tomb. "[5] Not only were pulmonary considerations of prime
physical import, but other writers stressed the salutary benefits
accruing to the muscular development of the chest and throat. [6]

Mann vigorously championed the cause of vocal music education. He was convinced that its study would aid in promoting
a general healthful condition of the person undertaking a period
of vocal study. Again he stated that among the claims for vocal
music, the first is "that Vocal music promotes health. It accom-
plishes this object directly, by the exercise which it gives to the
lungs and other vital organs, and indirectly, by the cheerfulness
and genial flow of spirits, which it is the especial prerogative of
music to bestow. Vocal Music cannot be performed without an
increased action of the lungs; and an increased action of the heart
and of all the organs of digestion and nutrition. The singer brings
a greater quantity of air in contact with blood. Hence the blood
is better purified and vitalized.... "[7] Later in 1860, Professor
Chamberlin, of the Young Ladies' Seminary in Monroe, Michigan,
predicted that "singing will (not only) form a part on all the
devotional exercises of our schools, but also a pleasing and healthful recreation during the hours of the day. "[8]

It is not very difficult to ascertain why there was so much
emphasis placed upon the physical benefits to be derived from
music study. The Industrial Revolution which began to make its
appearance during the latter half of the eighteenth century brought
with it great social and economic changes. The development of
the spinning jenny (1764), the spinning machine (1769), the power
loom (1784), the first steam engine (1785), and countless other
industrial mechanical devices, brought about a greater concentration
of factory workers in urban areas. The rise of factories and the
accompanying evils of child labor, low wages, long hours, unsanitary
places of employment, all tended to militate against the physical well-
being of the workers. The cities were found to be inadequately
prepared to handle the great increment in population; overcrowding
ensued. The question of health became a topic of popular discussion.
Devices for ameliorating the lack of sanitary conditions commanded

the attention of those interested in humanitarian needs. It can thus
be seen that the subject of vocal music study and health would
strike a concordant note in the thinking of contemporary educators.

Dr. Alexander Bache of Philadelphia reported in 1838 in an
account devoted to the school organization of Berlin, that in none
of the public elementary schools of the city was physical education
attended to by the school governors. [9] The subject of physical
education and vocal music were frills that had received little
educational support prior to 1840 in the United States. Most of
the educational leaders in this country were influenced by the
writings of those few who had the privilege of witnessing first-
hand the school systems of Europe and in particular those of
Switzerland, Germany, France, and England.

There was, however, a virtue in that great trio of spirit,
mind, and body, which above all others would be certain to elicit
the discriminating attention of those religious zealots who did much
to curb the development of seventeenth, eighteenth, and early nineteenth-century music education. This virtue, of course, was the
moralizing potency of music. The Puritanical spirit kept religion
and beauty looking askance at each other. When early writers began to see in music study possibilities for moral rectitude and
spiritual elevation, the deaf ear of the religious patriot was mar-
shalled to attention.

Horace Mann contended in 1844 that the social and moral
influences of music far outstripped all other values to be acquired
from vocal music instruction. [10] Mann was in that group of people
who were convinced that music was "a moral means of great
efficacy. "[11]

The American Association for the Advancement of Education,
in 1855 passed a resolution which stated that "Vocal Music is one
of the best means of quickening the moral sensibilities and elevating
the affections of the young..."[12] In 1883 another writer elaborated
on the theme of "Music a Prime Factor in Education" and stressed
the importance of music in the "moral, intellectual, and physical
nature, harmonizing all branches of knowledge, and manifesting

itself not only in thought and action, but in language, manners, and bearing. "[13]

When the proponents indicated the effect that the study of vocal music would have upon the disciplinary problems of the school-room, a sympathetic chord was struck in every administrator's thinking.   American school administrators had the testimony of such writers in Vehrli and Pfeiffer as to the almost one hundred per cent desirable disciplinary results to be obtained from teaching children how to sing.   Vehrli, an instructor in the Agricultural School of Hofwyl, was constantly observing that as the barometer of musical performance, ability, and participation increased, there was a like increment of "spirit and kindness and devotion among his pupils. "[14]

During a visit to a village in Switzerland, William C. Wood-bridge found that the cultivation of vocal music had been so effective as to set aright a group of disorderly drunken men. [15] He insisted that music study inculcated and even necessitated the formation of the habits of order, obedience, and union.   His pronouncement was that in musical performance all individuals function according to rule, acting as a collective body under the direction of a leader. [16] In 1840 George L. Foote, a teacher at New Town, Connecticut, wrote to Henry Barnard that music aided in harmonizing the school and served as an aid to discipline. [17]

When the advocates of vocal music propounded the idea that as a study in the school curriculum, music would improve the pupil-teacher relationships, the idea of including music as a branch of common education was beginning to make rapid strides.   Rev. John M. Allis in 1874 was advocating the disciplinary value of music, when he said that "music is an excellent help in maintaining discipline and decorum in a school. "[18]

At the 1896 South Dakota Educational Association meeting, held at Vermillion, South Dakota, an address given by S. L. Brown emphasized the role music played in maintaining classroom esprit de corps.   He said that vocal music or musical training was a factor in obtaining a "condition of easy control. " He further noted

"A school may be ever so noisy and disorderly, whispering, seat-leaving, question asking, and other disorderly things known all too well to the teacher may reign supreme, but the introduction of music will change all this to order and quiet. "[19]

Margaret Smith, in an address delivered before the same educational body, likewise emphasized music because of its disciplinary value.   She pointed out that our lives, governed as they are by emotions, would be directly affected by music because it is an educator of emotions.   Music would aid in eliciting the finest of deportment from pupils. [20]

The early nineteenth-century proponents of music education stressed the pleasure, the worthwhileness, and the inherent ability of all to derive gain from vocal music study.   It was an emotional experience to be enjoyed in the home, church, and in the school-room.   It could be experienced universally because it was believed that as many could learn to sing as could learn to read or write.

Prior to 1835, congregational singing in many American churches was deplorably unmusical.   Most of the churches were employing the lining out method of singing hymns and psalm tunes. Lowell Mason and George J. Webb were among those who advocated public school music as the major hope for improving the succeeding generations of lay church singers.   Not only would school music improve church singing, but it would aid in bringing about an attitude of reverence in the church service.   C. A. Fyke said: "Music is a spiritual interpretation of Man's inner nature. "[21]

A tenet vigorously supported and believed by most nineteenth-century music educators was that the object of song in the church service was to aid the individual in expressing religious feelings. Church music, Mason said, would "animate the feelings of de-votion. "[22]   Mason believed that there was no religion in music but he agreed that it could serve religion. [23]   Educators saw in music an opportunity for childhood expression of faith, love, praise, and gratitude.

Music study fraternalizes mankind.   This all-encompassing generalization attracted the early advocates of music instruction.

What subject, indeed, could be quite so beneficial for mankind as this unifying medium? As late as 1913, F. H. Westhoff stated that music was an "elevating and refining diversion for the leisure hours of all classes, kinds, and conditions of people."[24]

Another argument in favor of music instruction was that in the home, music would aid in strengthening family ties. Parents would find that a singing home circle would be conducive in creating an appealing home environment for their children. Culturally, this was important because the home, as the source of first education for the child, provided the wealth of experiences the individual would draw upon in later years.

Music would aid those persons who experience periods of physical and mental debility. Music is a therapeutic. Lowell Mason maintained that music induced a tranquility and mental relaxation which in many cases resulted in very definite physical and mental improvement. He believed music to be an agency for harmonizing the affinity between body and mind and felt that the dull mind could be beneficially stimulated by music study.

Notes

1. Sunderman, Lloyd F. "Some Early Concepts of the Value of Music Education," The School Music News 10: (June, 1947). 20-22, 24-25, 27-28. This chapter first appeared as an article as indicated. Corrections and changes have been made. Reprinted with the permission of The New York State School Music News.

2. Andrews, E. A. "Letter of Communication," The American Annals of Education and Instruction. 4: (July, 1834). 330-331.

3. Eighth Annual Report of the Massachusetts Board of Education. 1844. 125.

4. The American Annals of Education and Instruction, 1: (February, 1831), (Editorial). 64-65.

5. Eighth Annual Report of the Massachusetts Board of Education, 1844. 125.

6. The Connecticut Common School Journal, 1: (September, 1838). (Editorial).

7.   Eighth Annual Report of the Massachusetts Board of
     Education.   1844.   124-125.

8.   Chamberlin, Prof.   "Singing in the Common Schools,"
     Michigan Journal of Education.   7: (May, 1860).   183-185.

9.   Bache, A. D.   "Elementary Schools," The American
     Journal of Education,   8: (June, 1860).   444.

10. Eighth Annual Report of the Massachusetts Board of
     Education, 1844.   126.

11. Ibid. ,   126-127.

12. Proceedings of the Fifth Session of the American
     Association for the Advancement of Education, 1855.   16.

13. "Music a Prime Factor in Education," Musical Herald,
     4: (February, 1883).   40.

14. Woodbridge, William C.   "On Vocal Music as a Branch
     of Common Education," The American Institute of
     Instruction,   1830.   231-255.

15. The American Annals of Education and Instruction,   1:
     (February, 1831).   67.   (Editorial).

16. Woodbridge, William C.   "On Vocal Music as a Branch
     of Common Education."   1:   (1830).   231-255.

17. Barnard, Henry.   New York University Manuscript No.
     359.   George L. Foote to Henry Barnard, January 28,
     1840.

18. Allis, John M.   "Music in our Public Schools," The
     Michigan Teacher,   9: (November, 1874).   391-392.

19. Fourth Biennial Report of the Superintendent of Public
     Instruction of the State of South Dakota,   1897-1898.
     187-191.

20. Ibid. ,   292-296.

21. Fyke, C. A.   "Music," Indiana School Journal,   26:
     (September, 1881).   432.

22. Mason, Lowell.   Address on Church Music.   1826.   2.

23. Ibid. ,   6-30.

24. Westhoff, F. W.   "Education," The Illinois Music Teachers'
     Association Official Report.   Twenty-Fifth Annual Convention.
     1913.   45-47.

XII. SUPERVISIONAL AND INSTRUCTIONAL ASPECTS OF
EARLY AMERICAN MUSIC EDUCATION[1]

The pioneers of American public school music made their
contribution by acquainting professional and lay educators with
the salutary benefits to be derived from the study of music.
To arouse interest was not enough. After the introduction of
music into the public school curriculum, it soon became apparent
that special music teachers who were adequately prepared to
teach music capably to young children had to be trained. As the
public school music program expanded, the special music teacher
found it impossible to teach each day in each room of his school
system. It then became imperative to instruct the regular grade
teacher how to teach music.

Some of the supervisional and instructional ramifications of
nineteenth century school music teaching will be discussed in the
following pages. The more important aspects of the problem may
be conveniently grouped under the following sub-headings:
1). Dual supervision; 2). The classroom teacher as a teacher
of music; 3). Optional instruction; 4). Instructional obstacles;
5). Instructional period; 6). Examinations; 7). Textbooks.

Dual Supervision. With but few exceptions, music supervisors prior to 1885 were men. Beginning about 1860, a few
women were hired as assistant teachers; many of them were known
as assistants to the music superintendent or supervisor.

The introduction of vocal music into a school system was
made by an individual who was supposed to be trained or at least
talented in music. If we were to compare the academic qualifications of the first and second generation music instructors (1830-
1890) with the academic preparation of their contemporary colleagues,
the results would be most illuminating. The early music teacher
was usually a product of the singing-school. Prior to 1890 some

music teachers may have received additional training in a summer
institute conducted by private individuals who were in most cases
active public school music teachers. The early music supervisor
was distinctly a conservatory trained musician.

In many cities a dual-system of supervision and teaching
existed. This meant that the superintendent (supervisor) of vocal
music would instruct music once or twice a week, while the
regular classroom teacher taught the remaining time. The plan
adopted usually depended upon the musical ability and training of
the classroom teachers.

Orlando Blackman, music supervisor for the Chicago public
schools in 1865, stated that the upper grades of the grammar department were to receive music instruction under the direction of
the city music teachers. These teachers visited the lower grades
and instructed the pupils as time permitted. The regular teachers
of the primary and grammar divisions were to receive music
instruction one hour each month. [2]

N. Coe Stewart of Cleveland has been credited with the idea
of requiring the regular classroom teachers to teach music lessons.
In 1867 the Cleveland Public Schools employed one special teacher
of music. The following year, however, no music teacher was
hired, because the board of education found no satisfactory candidate. This necessitated the regular teachers teach music. [3]
Superintendent Andrew J. Rickoff doubted the wisdom of allowing
special teachers to go into the schoolroom to teach a twenty or
thirty minute lesson once each week. He was of the opinion that
the pupils would feel no responsibility to the regular teachers. [4]

The Classroom Teacher as a Teacher of Music. Before 1885
it became apparent to educational administrators that a music
supervisor could not adequately teach the music program without
getting some assistance from the classroom teacher; such assistance
implied a need for giving music instruction to the classroom
teacher, and for hiring teachers who had received some training
in how to teach music. It was urged that such preparation should
become a part of their normal school or college curriculum.

Requiring the regular teacher to teach music received increasing emphasis after the Civil War. The larger school systems were undoubtedly among the first to sense such a need. They saw the impossibility of one or two instructions adequately offering music instruction in 100 or 200 classrooms; it was sheer nonsense.

Cleveland, Ohio was among the earlier school systems to grapple with the problem of the regular teacher teaching music in her schoolroom. As in many other cities, Cleveland's system had a very limited music teaching staff. In 1869 their superintendent of schools stated what steps were being taken to improve the opportunities for vocal music study.

> To remedy this state of affairs, the committee to which
> the matter was referred reported in favor of the instruction
> of all classes by their regular teachers, and the Board of
> Education, after due deliberation, quite unanimously adopted
> the recommendation. It was then determined to secure
> the services of a music master, whose duty it should be
> 1) to give instruction to the teachers; 2) to teach the
> High Schools and highest grades in the Grammar Schools;
> 3) to direct the work in all the rest of the classes. [5]

The new plan suggested by Andrew J. Rickoff met with enthusiastic response from both teacher and pupil. The music committee in 1869 recommended that one teacher of music be employed and that he spend most of his time giving music instruction to the classrooom teachers. The music teacher employed was N. Coe Stewart. [6]

Dayton, Ohio, likewise adopted the plan of having the regular classroom teacher offer music instruction. Warren Highly, Superintendent of the Dayton Public Schools, reported in 1872 that their music program was under the direction of a music professor who taught the regular teachers how to teach music. Every grade school teacher in Dayton was teaching music to her own classes. [7]

What was being accomplished in Cleveland and Dayton was not possible in many cities before 1875. Some schools were less fortunate in having on their staff, teachers who were qualified to teach music. Then too, many of the regular classroom teachers manifested no interest toward the subject. Upon many occasions

they demonstrated their dislike for the music master.   Teachers
in some schools petitioned that they be relieved of music making
responsibilities.

Chicago, as well as other cities, was asking if the time had
not arrived when in selecting the regular classroom teacher, music
qualifications should not receive consideration.[8]   It was a fore-
shadowing of teaching requirements asked today by the progressive
child-centered education group.   The teacher of today must be the
complete teacher, able to adequately handle all the work of the
classroom.   Where were these classroom teachers with music
teaching qualifications to be found?   It is a known fact that prior
to 1865 a few of the normal and teacher-training institutions were
offering music instruction.   The State Normal School, Albany,
New York, was giving teacher-training in primary and elementary
school music prior to 1850.

The plan conceived by Chicago was epoch-making.   It brought
to the attention of teachers and teacher-training institutions the
importance of the complete teaching personality.   The committee on
music for the Brooklyn Public Schools reported in 1877 that their
Board of Education had previously asked several local committees
to inquire into the status of music teaching by the regular classroom
teacher.   The report proposed that all class teachers be expected
to teach their own music.   A survey showed that five hundred
eighty-seven of nine hundred eighty-four Brooklyn teachers were
competent under proper supervision to teach music to some degree.[9]

In a speech delivered in 1871 before the American Social
Science Association, J. Baxter Upham stated that all regular teachers were capable of doing their part in the instruction of music.[10]
It was suggested that the class teacher needed no special ability
and only an aptness to teach was essential.   H. E. Holt, in his
Boston School Report of 1869, stated that of the two hundred fifty-
one teachers under his direction, only seven found it impossible
to teach music in a satisfactory fashion.   In the Brooklyn survey
one of the school principals reported that: "the A B C of music
will never be imparted to the great mass of pupils unless their

regular class teachers are employed to do the work.   This I am quite sure of.   There is no other way to reach the individuals of the great army assembled within the walls of our great school buildings. "[11]

Optional Instruction.   Such an arrangement made it possible for the student to choose whether or not he wanted to take music. The operation of the optional factor in music study appeared very definitely as an adjustment in the music program for the Chicago Public Schools during the school year 1875-1878.   The wisdom of making the study of vocal music a matter of personal choice was evidently doubted by many.   The report for 1878 stated that eighty-five per cent of the pupils joined singing classes, whereas under the ruling of optional choice they might have refused to do so. [12] The operation of the optional choice of music study in Chicago unquestionably marks the early beginnings of such permissive legislation.   Likewise, it definitely pointed out that educators of the Chicago Schools during the 1870's were grappling with the question of vocal music and its rightful emphasis in the curriculum. The rules and regulations of the Chicago Schools, Section 56, stated that "It shall be optional with the parents or guardians of pupils to let their children or wards pursue" the study of vocal music.   The optional privilege in vocal music started in the first grade. [13]   This sole evidence indicates the priority of such permissive legislation.   Investigation of thousands of source materials have revealed that any discussion of elective music study in the elementary grades was limited to the Chicago account.   Elective vocal music was not common until after 1915.

Instructional Obstacles.   There were many problems or obstacles in the development of music education.   The most frequent ones were: 1) The lack of musical training on the part of the regular classroom teacher;   2) The lack of supervision and technical advice;   3) Local lay opposition;   4) The lack of textbooks and desirable music materials;   5) Lack of a sympathetic attitude on the part of educational groups, boards of education, and school administrations.

Opposition from the classroom teacher was most vehement in some cities. These antagonistic pedants waged a battle which surely did not help the cause of music education during its early introduction into the public schools of America. Some of the statements which teachers used for the purpose of indicating their unsympathetic attitude were: 1) I cannot sing; 2) I have no time; 3) I can sing, but have failed in my endeavors to introduce music into my school.

In order that the classroom teacher might teach music successfully, one writer suggested what the school song should be, if it were properly conceived for children.

> First, your songs must be school-songs. By a school-song we do not mean that it necessarily sings of school, of scholars, of teacher, or of any thing connected with school, although it may sing of all these.... A school-song must have pleasant words, often funny. They must be such as will be comprehended easily. Comic songs have no place in the school-room. The music must be as new and fresh as possible, and that of a lively character is mostly needed. [14]

John Monteith, State Superintendent of Missouri, stated in 1872 that two objections raised against the introduction of vocal music were: 1) That vocal music is an unnecessary luxury; 2) That there are only a few teachers qualified to impart such instruction. [15]

Beginning with the 1870's, obstacles in the progress of American public school music education began to give ground. This era ushered in provisions for graded songbooks, a lessening of lay opposition, and a slight shifting of emphasis from the intellectual to the enjoyment opportunities which public school music could offer American school children.

The Instructional Period. The board of education of Chicago announced in its report of 1859-60 that two vocal lessons were being given each week in the high school, whereas, the primary and grammar schools received one lesson. The periods of instruction for the high school were forty-five minutes, in the grammar school forty minutes, and in the primary schools thirty minutes. [16]

By 1871 the primary schools were receiving less than twenty minutes per day.[17]

What was true of Chicago was somewhat applicable to Newport, Rhode Island. During 1872-1873, James F. O. Smith, the supervisor of music, was offering instruction of one half-hour each week below the first grammar level; in the higher grades, one hour each week.[18]

The rules for the government of the St. Louis Public Schools in 1870 specified that the teachers should require their pupils to practice music fifteen minutes each day. It was also stated that when the music teacher was in the room, the regular classroom teacher should be responsible for discipline.[19]

The committee on music and drawing for the city of Albany, New York recommended for adoption on October 1, 1877, a resolution which stated that the professor of music should visit each school once every two weeks, devoting ten minutes to the study of the science of music.[20]

John Esputa, the supervisor of music for the public schools of the District of Columbia, related in 1875 that he was teaching vocal music once a week in one of the two district schools. By alternating with his assistant teacher, Henry F. Grant, he was able to superintend the other district by alternating monthly with his assistant teacher, bringing both district schools under his supervision.[21] The music teachers were spending forty minutes per week teaching the pupils the theory of music.[22]

Examinations. Prior to 1885, examinations in public school music fell under three main headings: 1) Those used for the purpose of evaluating instruction; 2) Those that were used as a part of teacher certification requirements; 3) Those that became a part of entrance examinations for high school candidacy.

Examinations for the purpose of evaluating instruction were in vogue during the latter half of the nineteenth century. Newport, Rhode Island, during 1872 was asking students in the first class grammar school division the following questions:

1. Give the pitch-names of the scale of A.
2. What letter is sharped to form this scale?
3. Draw a staff and write upon it the names of the
    lines and spaces, as pitch-names of the scale of E.
4. Give the pitch-names of the keys of B and F sharp.
5. Give the pitch-names of the keys in transposition
    by flats.
6. Write upon the treble staff the following musical
    phrases in G; 3 - 3, 3, 2, 1, 4, 3, 2.
    Place all the necessary marks upon the staff; divide
    into measures; and indicate the time.   The figures
    are scale-names, the dash placed after figure
    indicates a half-note, and the comma indicates a
    quarter note.
7. Draw the chromatic music ladder.
8. How many transpositions by sharps have you had?
9. How many by flats?
10. What other key is there, and what is it called to
    distinguish it from the transposed keys?[23]

Terre Haute, Indiana, by 1873 had become steeped in the art
of teaching the science of vocal music.   The children were required
to study assigned lessons and make recitations.   They had to under-
go music examinations at the end of each term.   It was a question
of learning music.   If there was any enjoyment of the music in
the learning process that fact was merely incidental. [24]

One major consideration in evaluating the success of a music
program was its ability to teach children to sing.   What is meant
is that all should be able to approximate the tones of the scale.
The annual reports of various Connecticut school superintendents
for 1871 indicated how effective some school music programs were
in eliminating non-singers.   Ariel Parish, the superintendent of
schools for New Haven, indicated that examinations in music for
his school system revealed that only 248 out of over 6,000 students
were unable to sing the scale; of the non-singer group, 140 belonged to the primary grades. [25]

Benjamin Jepson, supervisor of music in New Haven at this
time, pointed out some evidence of good musical performance
that examinations revealed.   He said in part

> If one point has been more strongly developed than another,
> in the experience of the past year, it is the fact that the
> teachers in primary rooms, really need a more correct
> musical ear, and more careful preparation for their daily

> class practice, than any other grade of teaching. Wrong
> ideas of sounds, imparted at the outset, may, and prob-
> ably will prove an impediment in musical progress ever
> after.
>
> The 'quality of tone' in singing is very much improved
> throughout the schools, but I trust I may be pardoned
> for saying, that if the same pains were taken at every
> exercise through the year, as were used in the pre-
> paration of children for examination, the 'screaming'
> quality of tone would soon disappear.
>
> 'Accuracy in time,' is steadily improving. The 'drawling'
> style of singing is seldom heard, but wherever it pre-
> vails, the children cannot be held wholly responsible. It
> cannot be too strongly urged upon the teachers, to pay the
> most scrupulous attention to time, not only during the
> fifteen minutes daily allotted for the practice of the music
> lesson, but at the opening exercises of the school, and
> at all the exercises, when the children are permitted to
> sing. [26]

Jepson had indicated some of the foci of music objectives of
his period. In stressing the importance of primary teachers having
good musical ears, and to the daily preparation of lessons, vigilant
guarding against the dragging of tempi, continually demanding an
improvement of tone quality, minute attention to notational values,
and deploring the screaming of the musical tones, he has indicated
that music education up to the period 1871, demanded a perfection
of the mechanics of music instruction. A proper characterization
of this type of music education could undoubtedly be the science of
music education.

In the Cincinnati Public Schools after the Civil War period,
music teaching and the organization for its successful promotion
had been somewhat systematically arranged under the direction of
Charles Aiken, supervisor of music. Regulations of the public
schools had provided for an evaluation of musical achievement.
Periodically tests were given.   The school regulations stated:

> In Music there shall be four examinations in each school
> year, as follows: At the expiration of the first and third
> quarters, written examinations by the respective teachers
> of Music, the questions prepared by the Music teachers to
> be submitted to the Committee on Music, for their approval.
> At the expiration of the second and fourth quarters, oral

and written examinations combined under the immediate supervision of the Committee on Music. [27]

Some of Aiken's reports clearly indicate the emphasis had been placed upon music examinations in Cincinnati. The supervisor of music was required to mark classrooms on their ability to attain moderate, good, very good, or excellent on exercises in music submitted by the supervisor. The results of the examinations were reported to the office of the superintendent of schools. [28]

Chicago, like Cincinnati, gave periodic music examinations for the purpose of testing the student's knowledge of the science of music. If in the test the boys and girls displayed a mastery of musical knowledge, it was considered that desired ends had been achieved. It is our purpose in this section to show that the music education program of the nineteenth century was fundamentally an intellectual exercise. The opportunity for pleasurable musical experience was a secondary consideration

In the Chicago Public Schools the customary procedure was to submit yearly music examinations to the students. The examination covered sight-reading material. The pupil's marks were recorded and a total average was obtained for each school. [29]

The following averages indicate the condition of the Chicago Public Schools for the year 1868-1869.

Chicago Public Schools

Washington	99. 2	Dearborn	90. 4
Foster	99. 2	Jones	89. 0
Brown	99. 2	Cottage Grove	88. 4
Hayes	98. 8	Clarke	86. 8
Scammon	98. 2	Carpenter	84. 2
Newberry	97. 2	Wells	83. 8
Dore	95. 8	Ogden	80. 8
Kinzie	95. 6	Franklin	77. 6
Haven	93. 6	Holden	71. 6
Moseley	93. 2		

The report of the committee on the High School for July, 1869 stated that the following music examination had been submitted to that division in June, 1869.

1) Give three varieties of measure; the length of the dotted quarter note in each variety; and the department to which the dot belongs.

2) Write the scales of C, D, E, B-flat, and A-flat in double measure, writing under each note the name of its pitch.

3) Give the names of the pitches in the scale of A, between which the half steps occur.

4) Define syncopation and illustrate it in triple measure in the key of G.

5) Write four measures of quadruple measure, using three kinds of dotted notes. [31]

(The time for the examination was not to exceed fifty minutes.)

These questions give us a very definite idea of the technical knowledge required in the high school music examination. It is apparent from the superintendent's report for the same year that the annual examination in a measure satisfied the demands for measuring what had been considered as obtainable objectives. [32]

The practice of reporting classroom and school averages made on sight-reading tests was continued from year to year as a way of measuring the ability attained in this particular department of music study. No level of school grade, whether it be primary, grammar, or high school was left untouched.

Methods of evaluating instruction unquestionably varied from place to place. In Washington, F. H. Butterfield, Director, and J. H. Daniel, Assistant Director of Music, reported for the year 1886-1887 that they had

examined three hundred fifty-four classes since the 26th of April (going together), notwithstanding the extra number of holidays and the fact that the director of music has given eight lessons to the High School in the meantime. We have also spent three days in revisiting the schools. We find that while some teachers have kept the work up, others have dropped it since the examination and have given the time to other studies.

Our method of examining was as follows: The pupils were required to sing two or three pieces from the charts or books under the direction of the teacher, and were asked such questions as were suggested by the manner in which the pieces were performed. We then put a piece of music (especially prepared for the grade) on the board to test the pupils in sight-singing. At the close of the examination we made such suggestions to the teacher as we thought would improve the work. The great majority of the schools marked excellent on these test exercises correctly at first sight, while the remainder needed only a suggestion here and there to enable them to sing them correctly the second time trying. The summary of our rating is as follows: Number of schools considered excellent, 72; good, 118; fair, 146; poor, 18. [33]

<u>Examination for Teacher Certification.</u> In 1855 a writer urged teachers of the future to consider their ability to teach vocal music at the elementary level. He felt that music for school purposes would never be adequately realized until the "qualifications demanded at the hands of common school teachers, shall embrace <u>an ability to teach vocal music</u>...." He predicted that vocal music in the future would be one of the requirements for teacher certification. [34]

Applicants for certification to teach music in Albany in 1877 were given the following examination:

Music

1. What is a staff?
2. What is the Diatonic Scale?
3. What is the Chromatic Scale?
4. What is the difference between a major and a minor scale?
5. What is the key note of the natural scale?
6. - 8. What is the key note of a tune in three sharps? In one flat? In four flats?
9. Give the notes of the scale of two sharps.
10. Into how many departments may the elementary principles of music be divided?
11. What varieties of time are in common use?
12. - 13. On what line or space does F occur in the treble staff? In the bass staff?
14. What is an interval?
15. Of what value is a dot after a note?
16. What is an octave?
17. What is a third?
18. What is a tie?
19. What is a leger line?
20. How is a "repeat" indicated? [35]

By 1881 the state and county board of examiners of Ohio had constructed an examination which was used as a basis for teacher certification. The examination laid great stress upon the technical aspects of music study.

1. What is a scale, the diatonic scale, the mode of expressing the duration, and pitch of musical sounds? Write the notes in common use, with the corresponding rests.
2. Write and state the use of the G, and F clef.
3. What are bars, and measures? How is the kind of time shown? Where does the accent fall in measures containing two, three, four, and six parts?
4. What is the use of a dot after a note, of a double dot? What is meant by the tonic, the leading tone, a tetrachord, and a triad?
5. Write the signature of the different major scales, and tell how the tonic is found in scales of sharps, in scales of flats.
6. Write the ascending and descending chromatic scale of G clef.
7. What is a major sixth, a minor sixth? When does a major sixth become an inversion?
8. What is the difference between a major and a minor key? Write the ascending and descending scale of the relative minor to the key of D, giving both forms.
9. Write the triads of C major, and in its relative minor.
10. Define the following terms, and write their abbreviations, viz: piano, pianissimo, dolce, forte, fortissimo, mezzo forte, diminuendo and ad libitum. Name or write minor thirds, major thirds, fifths, and leading notes to E, B sharp, F, G flat, and E sharp. [36]

By 1867 it had become the custom in Providence, Rhode Island to submit music questions to the boy or girl who was to be a candidate for admission to the high school. Those that were examined on May 8 and 10, 1867, were asked the following questions: [37]

Music

1. What is a Diatonic Scale?
2. What is a semitone?
3. In what order do the tones and semitones occur in the Diatonic Scale?
4. Why is a scale of eight notes, starting with Do, called the natural scale?
5. What are the names of the notes in the natural scale, between which the semitones occur?
6. If we commence on Sol, what numbers are Mi, Fa, and Si, Do?
7. How then do we get the semitones between 7 and 8?
8. What sign is used to denote that the 7th is to be raised a semitone?
9. What is the name of the 7th note in the scale of Sol?
10. What is a Chromatic Scale?

> N. B. - The average per cent of correct answers given
> to the above questions, by 100 pupils, was a
> fraction over eighty.

Because music is more an emotional experience rather than
an intellectual exercise, there is little wonder that twentieth
century music education brought about a reaction to the factual-
intellectual aspects of the nineteenth century school music program.
Today's school music program has to some degree divorced itself
from a plan of study involving serious consideration of music
rudiments.   The modern music program has minimized music
examinations at the primary and elementary levels.   Today,
children are being given more opportunity for self-expression
through musical experiences.   A good music program not only
includes singing, but also the creation of simple melodies, piano
playing, instrument making, listening, etc.   The learning of the
factual aspects of music is an outcome of enjoyable musical
experiences.

Textbooks.   The adoption of music textbooks by a school
system was not a frequent occurrence anywhere in the United States
prior to 1865.   Much of the music work was handled by means
of the rote and blackboard methods.   If the pupils had no books,
the teacher could write musical exercises on the blackboard.   Such
was the pre-Civil War custom.

In 1860, Chicago was using Mason's Normal Singer in the
grammar school and Bradbury's School Melodist in the primary
divisions. [38]   Under the heading of State Series of Text Books
adopted by the state board of education of Nevada in 1865, music
was not incorporated as a separate study, and no text-book for
music was recommended.   The state superintendent suggested,
however, that the teachers would find useful among other reference
books, Russell's Vocal Culture. [39]

In Washington, D. C., the pupils were using music readers
prior to 1866.   The board of trustees in cooperation with the
committee on vocal music had become interested in the Song-Garden,
a series of three song books by Lowell Mason.   Of the three books

the second had been adopted in some of their schools by 1866. [40]

Music books were used during the territorial days of the State of Washington. In 1871, P. Phillips' Day-School Singer was being recommended for adoption. Phillips' book was listed and recommended with others in compliance with the school-law. The significance to be noted is that the State of Washington along with California and Nevada, were among the earliest of the western states to suggest vocal music materials in recommended book-lists for state-wide usage. [41]

Newport, Rhode Island, had introduced into the upper classes some music readers prior to 1872. In the primary school, music readers were not required. It was claimed that music charts were better than books for use in the primary divisions. In each room a set of charts was a part of standard music equipment. [42]

Prior to 1873 no general music textbook adoption had been made in Buffalo. Baker, the supervisor of music in 1873, was sent to New Haven for the purpose of seeing the work of Benjamin Jepson. Upon the basis of recommendations by Baker, Jepson's Music Reader was adopted as a basic text in the Buffalo elementary schools. The new music textbook tended to hold in common the objectives of their elementary music program. Baker was most enthusiastic about the textbook. The music reader aided in bringing about a systematic study of the rudiments of music. Learning was more interesting and rapid. [43]

The science of music captivated and permeated the thinking of the music staff of Buffalo down to the close of the nineteenth century. In 1886, Baker was annually preparing a Manual of Elementary Music, which contained "not only progressive lessons in the elementary principles of music, illustrations and characters and signs employed in musical notation, but also pages with staff lines for transcriptions of songs, part exercises, scale forms, etc." [44]

Exercise books and music charts were recommended for New York City in 1877. [45] In the following year the Brooklyn Board of Education suggested that Mason's Fourth Music Readers

and blank staff music books be adopted as textbooks for use in the
Central Grammar Schools. [46] During the same year the Albany
Board of Education passed a resolution which required the purchase
of one hundred fifty copies of the Graded Music Reader, (Part I)
by H. S. Perkins. [47]

In 1870 Luther Mason published his National Music Course.
The publisher was Edwin Ginn, who was the founder of Ginn and
Company.   In 1859 Mason had an English translation made of some
fifth edition song books by Christian Heinrich Hohmann.   They
were published by Oliver Ditson.   Hohmann's works were based
upon the system devised by Hans Georg Nägeli who had been a co-
worker with Pestalozzi.

Earlier works produced in this country by Ives, Phillips,
Bradbury, Lowell Mason and others were used for three purposes:
1) As school-singers or song books; 2) As singing-school books;
3) As church and Sunday-school music readers.

The National Music Course offered a planned music series
designed to supply song materials for all grade levels.   Mason's
Readers were a milestone in American school music.   As a
systematic graded course of study it was probably the first.
It set criteria for most of the succeeding courses for another half
a century.   The National Music Course was translated and used
in Germany.   Mason, who had been supervisor of music for the
Japanese government for three years, had established his methods
in that country.

In 1883 there appeared the Normal Music Course by Hosea E.
Holt and John W. Tufts, which was published by D. Appleton and
Company.   Holt was supervisor of music in Boston from 1869 until
his death in 1898.   Tufts was an outstanding organist, conductor,
and oratorio coach, residing in Boston after 1880 where he was an
organist at King's Chapel.   Holt was the methodologist while Tufts
composed and edited the music to be found in the Normal Music
Course.   The course consisted of First, Second, and Third Readers;
for high schools, they prepared the Euterpean Song Book.   Charts
were prepared and used for drill purposes in the elementary grades.

The series met with widespread usage in the United States.   In
1885 the publishing rights for the Normal Music Course were procured by Silver, Burdett and Company.[48]

The National Music Course, and its revised edition under the
name, the New National Music Course published in 1885 by Ginn
and Company, along with the Normal Music Course, were the outstanding graded school music reader series on the market prior
to 1886.   An era of methodology was ushered in when it was
determined that a child should learn the factual knowledge of
music.   It was an age of music reading rather than singing.

Notes

1. Sunderman, Lloyd F. "Supervisional and Instructional
    Aspects of Early American Music Education," Educational
    Administration and Supervision, Vol. 37: No. 6
    (October, 1951).   337-354.   Chapter appeared as article
    indicated above.

2. Twelfth Annual Report of the Board of Education of
    Chicago, 1865-66.   184.

3. Thirty-Third Annual Report of the Board of Education of
    Cleveland, 1869.   18.

4. Ibid., 67.

5. Ibid., 67-69.

6. Thirty-Fourth Annual Report of the Cleveland Public
    Schools, 1870.   92-93.

7. Report of the United States Commissioner of Education,
    1873.   318.

8. Eighth Annual Report of the Board of Education of
    Chicago, 1861.   22-23.

9. Proceedings of the Board of Education of the City of
    Brooklyn, 1877.   98-100.

10. Ibid., 100-102.

11. Ibid.

12. Twenty-Fourth Annual Report of the Board of Education,
    Chicago, 1878.   28.

13. Twenty-Ninth Annual Report of the Board of Education, Chicago, 1883. 32-33.

14. "Music in Schools, " The Illinois Teacher, 11:78. March, 1865.

15. Sixth Annual Report of the Superintendent of Public Schools of the State of Missouri, 1872. 16-17.

16. Sixth Annual Report of the Board of Education, of Chicago, 1860. 91.

17. Fifteenth Annual Report of the Board of Education of Chicago, 1869. 118-121.

18. Annual Report of the School Committee of the City of Newport, R. I. , 1876-1877. 75-83.

19. Sixteenth Annual Report of the Board of Directors of St. Louis Public Schools, 1870. xliii.

20. Proceedings of the Board of Public Instruction of the City of Albany. Vol. VI. 1877. 456.

21. First Report of the Board of Trustees of Public Schools of the District of Columbia, 1874-75. 310-316.

22. Report of the United States Commissioner of Education, 1873. 436.

23. Fourth Annual Report of the Board of Education, Together With the Twenty-Ninth Annual Report of the Commissioner of Public Schools of Rhode Island, 1874. 168.

24. Twelfth Annual Report of the Terre Haute Public Schools, 1875. 40.

25. Annual Report of the Board of Education of the State of Connecticut, 1871. 119.

26. Ibid. , 172.

27. Forty-Second Annual Report of the Common Schools of Cincinnati, 1871. 217.

28. Forty-Seventh Annual Report of the Common Schools of Cincinnati, 1876. 174-176.

29. Fifteenth Annual Report of the Board of Education of Chicago, 1869. 118-121.

30. Ibid.

31. Ibid., 123-124.

32. Ibid., 169.

33. Report of the Board of Trustees of Public Schools of the District of Columbia, 1887. 90-91.

34. "Music for Schools," The Ohio Journal of Education, 4:357-8. December, 1855.

35. Twelfth Annual Report of the Board of Public Instruction of the City of Albany, 1878. 45.

36. Twenty-Eighth Annual Report of the State Commissioner of Common Schools of Ohio, 1881. 297-298.

37. Annual Report of the School Committee of the City of Providence, 1867. 54-58.

38. Sixth Annual Report of the Board of Education of Chicago, 1860.

39. Fourth Annual Report of the Superintendent of Public Instruction of Nevada, 1868. 35.

40. Twenty-First Annual Report of the Board of Trustees of the Public Schools of Washington, 1866. 28-29.

41. Report of the Territorial Superintendent of Common Schools of the Territory of Washington, 1871-73. 4.

42. Annual Report of the School Committee of the City of Newport, Rhode Island, 1873. 44.

43. "A Century of Music in Buffalo Schools," Music Educators Journal, 23:81. March, 1937.

44. Ibid., 81.

45. Thirty-Sixth Annual Report of the Board of Education of the City and County of New York, 1877. 164.

46. Proceedings of the Board of Education of the City of Brooklyn, 1878. 407.

47. Twelfth Annual Report of the Board of Public Instruction of the City of Albany, 1878. 45.

48. Birge, Edward B. History of Public School Music in the United States. 119.

XIII. EARLY MUSIC INSTRUCTION IN HIGHER EDUCATION[1]

Vocal music instruction was offered in institutions of higher learning in the early part of the nineteenth century for two fundamental reasons: 1) in the normal schools so that the students would be qualified to teach it; 2) in colleges and universities as a cultural study. It must not be assumed that collegiate institutions did not prepare people for music teaching; they did, but they emphasized music study as cultural training rather than as preparation for teaching in public schools. This chapter aims to describe the work of both types of institutions, including a story of the growth of music teaching in American colleges and universities.

It is singularly important that only one year after the official introduction of vocal music in the Boston Public Schools, that the first normal school in America, located at Lexington, Massachusetts, offered vocal music.[2] The extent of music instruction in the norma schools is indicated in the Report of the State Board of Education for 1844, which recorded the fact that instruction in vocal music was being given every week at the Westfield Normal School, Westfield, Massachusetts.[3] Those people who pursued more than a one year course of study were offered a more elaborate program of study, including music.[4]

In 1846 vocal music instruction was offered as a part of the regular course of study for teachers at the State Normal School at Albany, New York, Previously emphasis had been placed upon the elements of music and upon collecting a repertoire of songs that could be taught to little children. The teacher of vocal music was F. I. Ilsley.[5]

Before 1870 other Normal Schools had been established in the state. Table I indicates the instructors, years of appointment, early stipends, and the catalogue title of duties for the music

230

instructors in nine different institutions of the state between 1865-
1885.

Table I[6]

Status of New York State Normal School
Music Instructors
1867-1887

Teacher	Subject	Year	Salary
Oswego State Normal			
Redington, J. C. O.	Vocal Music	1867	
McLean, John B.	Vocal Music	1870-71	$ 200.
Davis, Mary	Vocal Music	1872	200.
Parkhurst, John G.	Vocal Music	1873-74	
Baker, James N.	Vocal Music	1875	
Lester, Ordelia A.	Composition, Rhetoric, Spelling, Vocal Music	1880	
Myers, Amelia B.	Vocal Music, Reading, Calisthenics, Rehearsals, Methods of Teaching Reading and Vocal Music	1882-87.	
		1886	600.
Brockport State Normal			
Richmond, Elizabeth	Reading and Vocal Music	1867	600.
Alling, Mrs. F. C.	Teacher of Instrumental Music	1871	
Richmond, Libbie S.	Teacher of Reading and Vocal Music	1871	
Potsdam State Normal			
Dutton, Robert H.	Vocal Music	1869	300.
Holcomb, Julia	Vocal Music	1871	300.
Hawley, Giles P. (A. B.)	Vocal Music and Elocution	1872-4.	700.
Hathorne, Frank E.	Vocal and Instrumental Music	1875	
Howe, Mrs. H. H.	Vocal Music	1873-75	200.
Kimball, Kittie M.	Vocal Music	1872	
Haynes, Phebe M.	Vocal and Instrumental Music and Methods	1882-84.	

Table 1 cont.

Teacher	Subject	Year	Salary
Cortland State Normal			
Bates, Marianne	Vocal Music	1869	$ 300.
Douglass, O. S. Mrs.	Vocal Music	1869	
Marsh, Mary	Vocal Music	1869-72	300.
Drake, M. Auzolette	Vocal Music and Drawing	1874	
Halbert, E. P. Mrs.	Vocal Music and Drawing	1874	
Whitney, Clara S.	Vocal Music	1875	
Fredonia State Normal			
Whitney, Clara S.	Vocal Music	1870-74	
Whiting, M. Antoinette	Vocal Music	1882-84	
Norton, Alida	Instrumental Music	1883	
Buffalo State Normal			
Sykes, Charles M.	Vocal Music	1871-73	500.
Mischka, Joseph	Vocal Music	1874-86	500.
Geneseo State Normal			
Killip, Lizzie	Instrumental Music	1872	
Parks, Mary E.	Vocal Music	1872	500.
Walker, W. K.	Instrumental Music	1873	
Parks, Mary E.	Vocal Music	1873-83	300.
Fraley, J. L. Mrs.	Instrumental Music	1882-84	
Albany State Normal			
Marsh, John B.	Vocal Music	1874-84	600.
Belding, John B.	Vocal Music	1886	600.
New Paltz State Normal			
Roberts, Timothy L.	Vocal Music	1886	350.

Early information about preparation was difficult to obtain. That of Timothy L. Roberts of the New Paltz Normal School may be cited. He had previously studied at the New England Conservatory of Music in Boston, having personally worked under H. E. Holt, John W. Tufts, and W. H. Daniell. It is likely that other early normal school music instructors had received comparable training. Before coming to New Paltz, Roberts was for several years Director of Music at Newton, Massachusetts.

The phrase "glee class" appeared in 1875 in the report of
Joseph Mischka, teacher of vocal music at the Buffalo State Normal
School.   The class was of ten weeks duration, having a twofold
purpose: 1) to instruct the members in advanced music, 2) and
to prepare music for the annual commencement exercises. [7]

During the school year 1847-48 the normal school in Philadelphia was offering music as David P. Allen was receiving $100
for his services. [8]

In the midwest a normal school in St. Louis was offering a
course in vocal music and modes for its teaching during the school
year 1867-68. [9] Henry M. Butler was the teacher giving two music
lessons a week.   They were using The Song Garden, written by
Mason. [10]

Likewise, Michigan State Normal School, Ypsilanti, under
the leadership of J. M. B. Sill, announced in 1859 that their policy
was "to give to every student such a knowledge of the art of Music
as will enable him to teach it with success in Primary Schools,
and to such as desire it a thorough knowledge of both the science
and the art.   Instruction in this department has been attended with
abundant and gratifying success. [11]

Just prior to and closely following the Civil War increasing
numbers of Normal Schools were reporting the instructing of vocal
music in their teacher-training programs.   The State Normal School
established in 1850 at New Britain, Connecticut, reported in 1861
that all divisions of the course of instruction offered vocal music. [12]
In 1863 the Superintendent of Public Instruction of California reported that vocal music was a part of the regular curriculum for
the sub-junior, junior, and senior class. [13] The normal school
which opened in Baltimore in 1866, gave immediate attention to
vocal music. [14]

Beginning with the decade of 1860-1870 Institutes as well as
Normal Schools were offering instruction to prospective teachers.
The Vermont Board of Education in 1867 ruled that

> In view of a possible conflict in the practical working
> of this law and that for the establishment of Normal
> Schools, by reason of the provision that certificates of

> precisely the same character and scope might be granted
> at the Institutes as at the Normal Schools, the Board was
> unanimously and decidedly of the opinion that the examina-
> tions ought to be quite as rigid and exacting in the one
> case as in the other. The same courses of study were
> therefore arranged with reference to both classes of
> examinations, as follows: For the first course, candidates
> might be examined in eight distinct subjects, and the
> examination in the first seven must be partly written.
> Reading, including the elements of elocution and vocal
> culture. [15]

Herein we have evidence that those people taking normal school
work would of necessity by school law, take vocal culture.

In 1870 the Emporia State Normal School, Emporia, Kansas
offered vocal music instruction during the second term of the first
year program. This plan has been continued down to the present
day, freshmen music being the course required by teacher-training
institutions in many states. [16]

In 1872 the Central Female Institute, Clinton, Mississippi,
offered theoretical and practical instruction in vocal music. The piano
and guitar pupils received private lessons in singing. The institution
was proud of its continuous record of operation during the Civil War
period, not missing its regular exercises a single day. [17]

The Pine Bluff Normal Institute at Pine Bluff, Arkansas,
which was primarily devoted to the training of teachers for colored
schools, reported to The American Missionary Society in 1875 that
it was offering vocal and instrumental music. [18]

In Fayetteville, North Carolina, the State Colored Normal
School (organized in September, 1877), gave special attention to
vocal music. [19] That same year, the University Normal School
announced daily drill in vocal music. [20] During the summer term
in 1884 Hosea F. Holt of Boston was a guest lecturer. [21] Wilson
Normal School during 1881 had Vaillant de La Croix (formerly of
Paris), teaching vocal music one hour and a half each day. [22] At
the Newton Normal School, P. J. Leonard of Lexington was teaching
music. [23] In 1883 music was taught at the Newbern Colored Normal
School by Mamie E. Nichols. [24] The Elizabeth City Normal School
reported the employment of a music instructor in 1884. [25] A year

later, The Asheville State Normal School was employing Charles L.
Wilson as vocal teacher.[26] The Normal Schools of North Carolina
were so progressive that by 1887, all were offering vocal study
and some were giving instrumental music instruction in addition.

The number of Normal Schools in the United States offering
vocal and instrumental music by 1878 was widespread. (See Table
II.) The data reveals that in thirty-three states and the District
of Columbia, 123 schools offered vocal and 74 provided instrumental music.[27]

During the school year 1877-1878 the Wisconsin Normal
Schools at Platteville, Whitewater, and River Falls were employing
teachers of music. The teachers for these institutions were:

Platteville Normal School, Platteville, D. E. Gardner,
Mathematics and Vocal Music.

Whitewater Normal School, Whitewater, Mrs. E. M. Knapp,
Vocal Music.

River Falls Normal School, River Falls, Miss Anna
S. Clark,
Music, Drawing, Penmanship.[28]

The Sam Houston Normal Institute, at Huntsville, Texas, had
a music professor on its faculty during the period 1879-1882. The
duties of the professor of music were not enumerated.[29]

Normal Schools prior to 1890 were usually short term summer
sessions lasting from four to six weeks. Throughout the United
States there were some programs lasting two, three, and occasionally four academic years. The State Female School, Farmville,
Virginia, as early as 1887 offered vocal music in each of the three
years of its curriculum.[30] The Staunton Institute had a choir of
about twenty-five voices during the summer session of 1887. A
year later, the Roanoke Colored Institute which was in session from
July 17 to August 16, offered vocal music.[31]

TABLE II

Music Teaching in Normal Schools, 1878

| | Number of Schools | |
States	Vocal Music	Instrumental Music
Alabama	3	3
Arkansas	3	3
California	2	–
Connecticut	1	–
Georgia	2	1
Illinois	7	5
Indiana	5	2
Iowa	3	3
Kansas	2	1
Kentucky	4	4
Louisiana	2	1
Maine	3	1
Maryland	4	3
Massachusetts	6	–
Michigan	1	–
Minnesota	3	–
Mississippi	2	2
Missouri	7	6
Nebraska	1	1
New Hampshire	–	–
New Jersey	1	1
New York	9	2
North Carolina	6	2
Ohio	10	6
Pennsylvania	12	10
Rhode Island	1	–
South Carolina	1	1
Tennessee	7	4
Vermont	1	2
Virginia	4	3
West Virginia	2	5
Wisconsin	5	2
District of Columbia	3	–
Utah	–	–
Total	123	74

The growth of music instruction in Normal Schools and Institutes is directly related to the growth of music teacher education in institutions of higher learning.

Oberlin College, recognized by the Ohio Legislature in 1834, was probably one of the first of collegiate institutions to give professorial status to a musician. There was reported to be a professor of sacred music on its faculty; however, the position was abolished the following year for financial reasons. Sometime about 1838, George N. Allen, a former pupil of Lowell Mason, was appointed teacher of sacred music. He became professor in 1841 and systematic music instruction was offered to all those who desired it. It was not until 1849 that instrumental instruction was added to the curriculum. Because grave objections were urged against the use of a piano at the college, it was decided not wise to give piano instruction, but a piano did arrive a year later and another the following year. Oberlin was one of the earliest colleges to start publication of song books. In 1844 The Social and Sabbath School Hymn Book was published, eventually going through seven editions. Subsequently, in 1875, came Sacred Songs For Social Worship and in 1890, Manual of Praise. The Oberlin Conservatory was established in 1865, and its growth is reflected in a report which stated that 264 students were studying music by 1871.

The Harvard Musical Association, made up of Harvard College Alumni, apparently started in 1837. The purpose of the organization was the development of music within Harvard. During the academic year 1870 Harvard University began to grant credit for music work toward the A. B. degree,[32] with eleven students being registered in the music department.[33] John Knowles Paine was appointed instructor in 1862, attaining full professorship in 1876.

In 1864 music teaching at the Kansas State Agricultural College was being taught by J. Evarts Platt, Professor of Vocal Music and Principal of the Preparatory Department; Dr. Hubzman, Professor of Instrumental Music; and Mrs. Eliza C. Beckwith, Teacher of Instrumental Music.[34] This music staff would indicate a breadth of offerings which was uncommon prior to 1870. The University of Iowa was offering some vocal music by 1865. A report dated 1866 stated that to provide "students an opportunity of studying Vocal Music, [they] have engaged the services of a competent teacher. Instruction is given in this branch once each week in the University Chapel free of charge to the students."[35]

Some early attempts in Illinois are reflected in a report of the following educational institutions:

Lombard University Galesburg, established in 1852.	Music and drawing, or French, offered each of three terms in the Ladies' Collegiate Course First Year.
Jacksonville Female Academy, Jacksonville, established in 1830.	Vocal Music. In the Senior Year.
Monticello Seminary Monticello (Godfrey P. O.) established in 1838.	Provision is made for Vocal Music, Music Instruction in Piano, Guitar, and Organ.
Illinois State Normal University, Normal, Established, 1857.	C. M. Cady, Instructor in Music.[36]

During the third term of the second year music and gymnastics were offered to students of the County Normal Schools.[37] Eureka College, founded as Walnut Grove Academy in 1849 and chartered as a college in 1855, had on its faculty during 1871, E. H. Plowe, professor of vocal and instrumental music. Plowe was a revered member of the Eureka College faculty and was "connected for several years with the institution."[38] In 1880 the Illinois Industrial University at Champaign was offering instruction in vocal and instrumental music, Mrs. Abbie Wilkinson being the teacher.[39] In 1883 the Southern Illinois Normal University at Carbondale employed James H. Brownlee, M. A., as the teacher of English literature, elocution, vocal music, and calisthenics.[40]

Straight University, New Orleans, Louisiana, was giving vocal and instrumental music instruction before 1872.[41] Centenary College, Jackson, had an elaborate music program in 1877, offering piano, guitar, organ, and vocalization.[42]

In the First Annual Circular and Catalogue of the Arkansas
Industrial University, (Fayetteville?) 1872-1873, it was stated that
music was given as a part of the regular course of study.   The
catalogue stated "Special instruction in vocal and instrumental music
will be given, two lessons a week, by W. D. C. Botefuhr, Professor
of Music, to such students as may desire it.   Tuition, fifteen
dollars per term. "[43]   Arkansas College, Batesville, announced at
its opening that instruction would be given in vocal and instrumental
music.   These were considered as additional offerings to a regular
collegiate program.[44]   During the period 1880-1882 Mrs. P. E.
Northern was teaching instrumental music at Marianna College and
Normal Institute, Marianna.[45]

In 1875, the United States Commissioner of Education reported
under the heading of Superior Instruction of Women, that vocal and
Instrumental music were being offered in some schools of Vermont.[46]
The Vermont Methodist Seminary and Female College, Montpelier,
reported in 1876 that its four year course included vocal and
instrumental music.[47]   The University of Colorado, Boulder, was
employing W. H. Mershon as a licensed instructor of music in 1879.[48]
It is probable that a music teacher may have been employed even
earlier.

The growth of music education in American normal schools,
colleges, and universities runs parallel with the development of
public school music in primary, elementary, and secondary schools.
In 1835 music had become a subject for study at Oberlin College.
It is significant to note that this was before the official introduction
of music into the Boston Public Schools.   Although the American
colleges and universities were established earlier than the normal
schools, they offered music instruction no earlier.   It had to wait
for the appearance of the music education movement which came
after 1830.

With the first normal schools offering music as a part of
their teacher-training programs, by 1870 vocal music had been
ushered into the programs of city and state normal schools in
Massachusetts, New York, Pennsylvania, Michigan, Connecticut,

Maryland, and Kansas. By 1860 there were twelve state normal schools in nine states[49] offering music instruction. Thus, the inclusion of music as a part of the teacher-training curriculum was necessarily dependent upon the growth of the normal school movement. The period 1865-1890 saw a great increase in the number of new state normal schools. Music education during the same period became a part of the teacher-training program because of the increased recognition it was receiving in primary, elementary, and secondary schools. In some cities the teacher with training in music was looked upon with great favor. Music instruction in institutions of higher learning as either cultural or professional training was distinctly a nineteenth century development.

A Résumé of Music Education in Normal Schools and Colleges

> (Note: Chronologically arranged in order of earliest record of music instruction found by the writer.)

Oberlin College, Oberlin, Ohio   1835
    A professor of sacred music employed.

Harvard University, Cambridge, Massachusetts   1837
    The Harvard Musical Association for improve-
    ment and development of music was underway.

State Normal School, Lexington, Massachusetts.   1839
    Offered vocal music instruction.   (Later
    located at West Newton.)

State Normal School, Westfield, Massachusetts.   1845
    Was offering vocal music instruction as part
    of the curriculum before 1845.

State Normal School, Bridgewater, Massachusetts.   1845
    Was offering vocal music before 1845.

State Normal School, Albany, New York.   1845
    Established in 1844.   Offered vocal music.

Normal School, Philadelphia, Pennsylvania.   1847
    Was offering music instruction under
    David P. Allen.

Baker University, Baldwin, Kansas.   1858
    Had a music professor.

Michigan State Normal School, Ypsilanti, Michigan   1859
    Had a well-developed music program before.

State Normal School, New Britain, Connecticut   1861
    Was offering vocal music in all divisions of
    their course of study.

Kansas State Agricultural College, Manhattan, Kansas.   1864
    Had three instructors in music.

University of Iowa, Iowa City, Iowa.   1865
    Had a teacher of vocal music.

Oberlin College, Oberlin, Ohio.   1865
    Their conservatory was established.

Normal School, Baltimore, Maryland.   1866
    In 1866, during the first year of the school's
    history, they were offering vocal music
    instruction.

Normal School, St. Louis, Missouri.   1867
    Henry M. Butler was teaching vocal music.

Lombard University, Galesburg, Illinois.   1867
    Offered music.

Illinois State Normal University, Normal, Illinois.   1867
    C. M. Cady, Instructor of Music during 1867.

Vassar College, Poughkeepsie, New York.   1867
    Frederick Louis Ritter was offering music
    courses.

University of Kansas, Lawrence, Kansas.   1870
    J. E. Bartlett, Instructor of Music; he
    received $400 per annum.

Emporia State Normal School, Emporia, Kansas.   1870
    Offered music.

Harvard University, Cambridge, Massachusetts.   1870
    Began to grant credit for music work which
    could be applied toward academic degrees.

State Agricultural College, Manhattan, Kansas.   1870
    Offered instrumental instruction.

Eureka College, Eureka, Illinois.   1871
    Employed E. H. Plowe, Professor of Vocal
    and Instrumental music.

University of Michigan, Ann Arbor, Michigan.   1871
    Professor Frieze was offering vocal music
    at Chapel exercises.

Straight University, New Orleans, Louisiana.   1872
    Music instruction was given before this date.

Arkansas Industrial University, Fayetteville,
Arkansas.   1872
    Music was offered as a regular subject.

Olivet College, Olivet, Michigan.   1874
    Conservatory of Music established.

Northwestern University, Evanston, Illinois.   1874
    Had a Conservatory of Music before this date.   .

Fort Wayne College, Fort Wayne, Indiana.   1874.
    Offered music before this date.

Hartsville University, Hartsville, Indiana.   1874
    Offered music before this date.

Moore's Hill College, Moore's Hill, Indiana.   1874
    Offered music before this date.

Palatinate College, Myerstown, Pennsylvania.   1874.
    Offered vocal and instrumental music.

Greeneville and Tusculum College, Greeneville,
Tennessee.   1874.
    Music was offered as an elective subject.

Ridgeville College, Ridgeville, Indiana.   1874
    Had a music department.

Albermarle Female Institute, Charlottesville,
Virginia.   1874
    Offered music.

Vermont Methodist Seminary and Female College,
Montpelier, Vermont.   1875
    Offered vocal and instrumental music.

Upper Iowa University, Fayette, Iowa.   1875
    Offered music instruction.

Western College, Western, Iowa.   1875
    Offered instruction in music.

Adrian College, Adrian, Michigan.   1875
    Had a school of music offering vocal and
    instrumental music.

Hillsdale College, Hillsdale, Michigan.   1875
    Had a school of music.

Olivet College, Olivet, Michigan.   1875
    Had a music department which was called
    the Michigan Conservatory of Music.

St. John's College, St. Joseph, Minnesota.   1875.
    Offered instruction in music.

State Normal School, Trenton, New Jersey.   1875
    Required vocal music courses of their students
    and offered instrumental music as an optional
    study.

Farmer's College, College Hill, Ohio.   1875
    Offered music instruction.

Mt. Union College, Mt. Union, Ohio.   1875
    Offered music instruction.

Neophogen College, Gallatin, Tennessee.   1875
    Offered music instruction.

Chapel Hill Female College, Chapel Hill, Texas.   1875
    Offered music instruction.

Smith College, Northampton, Massachusetts.   1875
    Was offering some music instruction.

University of Pennsylvania, Philadelphia.   1875
Pennsylvania.
    Professor Hugh A. Clarke was appointed
    to the chair of music. The requirements
    for entrance were a knowledge of the
    rudiments, and the ability to play some instrument.

Lincoln University, Lincoln, Illinois.   1875
    Had a conservatory before 1875.

Monmouth College, Monmouth, Illinois.   1875
    Offered music before 1875.

Arkansas College, Batesville, Arkansas.   1876
    Offered vocal and instrumental music in 1876,
    the year of the school's opening.

University of Wisconsin, Madison, Wisconsin.   1876
    Beginning with 1876, the University started
    to recognize a place for music teachers on
    its faculty.

University of Nashville, Nashville, Tennessee.   1877
    The State Normal College Division was
    offering instruction in vocal music under the
    direction of John E. Bailey.

University of Nebraska, Lincoln, Nebraska.   1877
    Vocal and instrumental music was offered
    by a faculty member.

University of Illinois, Urbana, Illinois.   1877
    Formerly known as Illinois Industrial University.
    They were offering piano instruction; became a
    university in 1885.

Ohio Wesleyan University, Delaware, Ohio.   1877
    School of Music established as a part of the
    University in 1877.

Centenary College, Jackson, Louisiana.   1877
    Had an elaborate applied music program.

State Normal Colored School, Fayetteville, North
Carolina.   1877
    Giving attention to vocal music.

State Normal School, Platteville, Wisconsin.   1877
    Offering vocal music.

State Normal School, River Falls, Wisconsin.   1877
    Was offering vocal music.

State Normal School, Whitewater, Wisconsin.   1877
    Was offering vocal music.

University Normal School, Chapel Hill, North
Carolina.   1877
    Was offering vocal music.

University of Deseret, State of Utah.   1879
    Had one music student.

University of Colorado, Boulder, Colorado.   1879
    A licensed instructor in music.

Sam Houston Normal Institute, Huntsville, Texas.   1879
    A professor of music.

Marianna College, Marianna, Arkansas.   1880
    Offering instrumental instruction.

University of Michigan, Ann Arbor, Michigan.   1880
    In 1880 School of Music established.

University of Nebraska, Lincoln, Nebraska.   1880
    In 1880 a director of the Music Conservatory
    was appointed.

State Normal School, Wilson, North Carolina.   1881
    Was offering music.

State Normal School, Newton, North Carolina.   1881
    Was offering music.

Southern Illinois Normal University, Carbondale,
Illinois.   1883
    James H. Brownlee, M.A., teacher of
    vocal music.

Knox College, Galesburg, Illinois.   1883
    Music Conservatory established in 1883.

Newbern Colored Normal School, Newbern, North
Carolina.   1883
    Offering vocal music.

Elizabeth City Normal School, Elizabeth,
North Carolina.   1884
    Offering music instruction.

State Normal School, Franklin, North Carolina.   1884
    Music during summer normal school session.

Creighton University, Omaha, Nebraska.   1885
    They had a glee club organized in 1885.

University of Colorado, Boulder, Colorado.   1885
    In 1885 started giving special attention
    to music instruction.

Fisk University, Nashville, Tennesse.   1885
    Chair of music established in 1885.

State Normal School, Asheville, North Carolina.   1885
    Offering music instruction.

Augustana College and Theological Seminary, Rock Island,
Illinois.   1887
    Had a Conservatory established in 1887.

Roanoke Colored Institute, Roanoke, Virginia.   1888
    Offering vocal music instruction in curriculum.

Staunton Institute, Staunton, Virginia.   1888
    Had a choir.

Mt. Holyoke College, Mt. Holyoke, Massachusetts.   1889.
    Was offering some music in 1889.

South Dakota University, Mitchell, South Dakota.   1890
    Music was being offered by 1890.

University of Wisconsin, Madison, Wisconsin.   1894
    Music school opened.

Chronological Evidences of Early Leaders of Music Education in the State Normal Schools.

Date	Institution	Teacher
1844	Albany	Mr. J. C. O. Redington, A. M.
1866	Oswego	Mr. J. C. O. Redington, A. M.
1869	Potsdam	Robert H. Dutton
	Oswego	John B. McLean
	Brockport	Elizabeth Richmond
	Cortland	Mrs. O. S. Douglass also Marianne Bates
1870	Cortland	Miss M. Marsch (Services 1869-73)
	Potsdam	Julia Holcomb (Also 1871)
	Fredonia	Clara S. Whitney (1870-73)
	Brockport	Mrs. F. C. Alling (Teacher of Instrumental Music)
1871	Buffalo	Charles M. Sykes (1871-1872)
	Geneseo	Lizzie Killip (Teacher of Instrumental music).

Date	Institution	Teacher
		Mary E. Parks (1871-74, 1883- Teacher of Vocal music.)
1872	Oswego	Mary Davis, resigned
	Geneseo	Mrs. W. K. Walker (Teacher of instrumental music)
	Oswego	John G. Parkhurst (1872-3)
	Potsdam	Giles P. Hawley, A. B. (1872-3)
1873	Cortland	Mrs. E. P. Halbert
	Potsdam	Mrs. H. H. Howe (1873-4)
1874	Albany	John B. Marsh (1874, 1879-1883)
	Buffalo	Joseph Mischka (1874-5, 1879-85)
	Cortland	Clara S. Whitney
	Oswego	James N. Baker
1879	Oswego	Ordelia Lester
1882	Fredonia	M. Antoinette Whiting
	Fredonia	Alida Norton (1883-85) Instrumental Teacher
	Oswego	Amelia B. Myers (1882-83) Teacher of Vocal Music
	Potsdam	Phebe M. Haynes (Teacher of Vocal and Instrumental Music)
1883	Albany	John B. Marsh
	Geneseo	Mrs. J. L. Fraley (Teacher of Instrumental Music)
	Fredonia	Miss M. Antoinette Whiting
1886	Albany	John B. Belding (Teacher of Vocal Music)
	New Paltz	Timothy L. Roberts

Notes

1. Sunderman, Lloyd F.   "Sign Posts in the History of
    American Music Education, " Education, Vol. 62: No. 9
    (May, 1942).   536-542.   Reprinted with the permission
    of Education Magazine, The Bobbs-Merrill Company, Inc. ,
    Indianapolis, Indiana.

2. "Normal Schools In Massachusetts, " The Connecticut
    Common School Journal.   1: (March, 1839).   97.

3. Eighth Annual Report of the Massachusetts State Board
    of Education, 1845.   20.

4. Tenth Annual Report of the Massachusetts State Board of
    Education, 1847.   220-221.

5. "Report of the Executive Committee of the State Normal
    School, " Journal of the Rhode Island Institute of Instruc-
    tion, 1: (March 16, 1846).   108.

6. Twenty-Second Annual Report of the Superintendent of
    Public Instruction of the State of New York, 1876.   172.

7. Annual Reports of the Superintendent of Public Instruction
    of the State of New York, 1867-1887.   passim.

8. Thirteenth Annual Report of the Controllers of the Public
    Schools of the City and County of Philadelphia, 1848.   22.

9. Fourteenth Annual Report of the Board of Directors of
    St. Louis Public Schools, 1868.   27-28.

10. Ibid. , Appendix, lxxx.

11. Twenty-Third Annual Report of the Superintendent of
    Public Instruction of the State of Michigan, 1859.   140.

12. Report of the Superintendent of Common Schools of
    Connecticut, 1862.   (In annual report of the trustees of
    the state normal school).   23-26.

13. Thirteenth Annual Report of the Superintendent of Public
    Instruction of California, 1863.   211-212.

14. First Annual Report of the Maryland State Superintendent
    of Public Instruction, 1866.   53.

15. Eleventh Annual Report of the Vermont Board of
    Education, 1867.   3-4.

16. Tenth Annual Report of the Department of Public
    Instruction of the State of Kansas, 1870.   157.

17. Annual Report of the Superintendent of Public Education for the State of Mississippi. 1871.

18. Report of the United States Commissioner of Education, 1875. 18.

19. Report of the Superintendent of Public Instruction of North Carolina, 1877. 42.

20. Ibid., 9-11.

21. Biennial Report of the Superintendent of Public Instruction of North Carolina, 1883, 1884. 124.

22. Biennial Report of the Superintendent of Public Instruction of North Carolina, 1881, 1882. 88.

23. Ibid., 90.

24. Biennial Report of the Superintendent of Public Instruction of North Carolina, 1883, 1884. 94.

25. Ibid., 147.

26. Biennial Report of the Superintendent of Public Instruction of North Carolina, 1885, 1886. 48.

27. Report of the United States Commissioner of Education, 1878. lxviii-lxix.

28. Annual Report of the State Superintendent of the State of Wisconsin, 1878. 367.

29. Third Biennial Report of the State Board of Education of the State of Texas, 1881/1882.

30. Eighteenth Annual Report of the Superintendent of Public Instruction of the Commonwealth of Virginia, 1888. 42-43.

31. Ibid., 75, 81.

32. Dickinson, Edward. "Music in America Fifty Years Ago and its Significance in the light of the Present," Volume of Proceedings of the Music Teachers' National Association, Twenty-Third Series, 1928. 9-26.

33. Yont, Rose. Status and Value of Music in Education, Chapter V.

34. Fourth Annual Report of the Superintendent of Public Instruction of State of Kansas, 1864. 31.

35. Biennial Report of the Iowa Superintendent of Public
     Instruction, 1866. 10.

36. Seventh Biennial Report of the Superintendent of Public
     Instruction of the State of Illinois, 1867/1868. 232, 265,
     270, 376.

37. Ibid., 377.

38. Ninth Biennial Report of the Superintendent of Public
     Instruction of the State of Illinois, 1871/1872. 313.

39. Fourteenth Biennial Report of the Superintendent of Public
     Instruction of the State of Illinois, 1880/1882. 21.

40. Fifteenth Biennial Report of the Superintendent of Public
     Instruction of the State of Illinois, 1882/1884. 33.

41. Annual Report of the State Superintendent of Public
     Education of the State of Louisiana, 1872. 29.

42. Annual Report of the State Superintendent of Public
     Education of the State of Louisiana, 1877. 235.

43. Biennial Report of the Superintendent of Public Instruction
     for the State of Arkansas, 1870/1872. 88.

44. Report of the United States Commissioner of Education,
     1876. 20.

45. Report of the State Superintendent of Public Instruction
     of the State of Arkansas, 1880/1882. 109-110.

46. Report of the United States Commissioner of Education,
     1875. 418.

47. Report of the United States Commissioner of Education,
     1876. 396.

48. Fourth Biennial Report of the Superintendent of Public
     Instruction of the State of Colorado, 1883/1884. 3.

49. Cubberley, Ellwood P. Public Education in the United
     States. 293.

XIV. EARLY MUSIC EDUCATION FOR THE PHYSICALLY HANDICAPPED

The science of music instruction was made intelligible to the blind when Louis Braille simplified the Barbier system of fundamental signs employed by the blind in communication. A September, 1857 account by Henry Barnard stated:

> His (Braille's) plan is based upon a series of fundamental signs comprising the first ten letters of the alphabet; none of these consist of less than two, nor more than four dots. A second series is formed by placing one dot at the left of each fundamental sign; a third by placing two dots under each sign; a fourth by placing one under the right side of each. By prefixing a character comprised of three dots, the first ten are used as figures; by prefixing another the last seven of the fundamental signs represent musical characters, and here, by a sign peculiar to each octave, he avoids the necessity of designating the key of each musical sentence. The apparatus consists of a board in a frame like that of a double slate, the surface of which is grooved horizontally, and vertically, by lines one-eighth of an inch apart; on this the paper is fastened, by shutting down the upper half of the frame, and the points are made with an awl or bodkin through a piece of tin perforated with six holes, 1/8 of an inch apart. The perforations are made from right to left, in order that the writing when reversed may be read from left to right. [1]

There was also definite evidence that such a system of reading music had been incorporated into the French, Austrian, Belgian, Swedish and Dutch schools; in America, New York, Maryland, and Illinois were represented with one or more institutions pursuing a like procedure. Even South America by 1857 had the Imperial Institute for the Blind at Rio de Janeiro.

The school for The Deaf and Dumb, located at Cedar Spring, South Carolina, established a department of musical instruction in 1871 for the purpose of serving its patients. Professor W. B. North was offering vocal and instrumental music as a part of their regular course of instruction. [2] The Maryland State Board of Education revealed that fifty students were receiving vocal and thirty were

enjoying instrumental instruction at the Maryland Institute for Blind
at Baltimore in 1872. [3]

The Trustees' Report of the Perkins Institution in
Massachusetts reported in 1874 that one of the objects of its
school was to instruct non-seeing children "in vocal and instrumental music, as will be an accomplishment, and a source of
pleasure to themselves and to others.   Then, to give special
instruction to those who possess talent and taste for music, and
a special fitness for teaching music, or for playing the organ, or
tuning pianos, to the end that they may be fitted to teach some
branch of music as a profession. "[4]

The Superintendent of Public Instruction of the State of Illinois
reported in 1880 that[5] the Illinois Asylum for the feeble-minded
presented for the first time in the history of the institution a
musical performance at the exercises marking the closing of the
school year; thirty-two students participated in the performance.
Although this was the first public manifestation of music for these
people, it is possible that physically handicapped individuals had
appeared in music programs in other institutions.   Evidence concerning the effectiveness of music instruction for feeble-minded
individuals is lacking.   The Illinois Asylum underscored the fact
that

> Music and Amusements hold an important place in our
> course of training.   Such children as are susceptible of
> instruction in singing received daily lessons.   Monday
> evenings are devoted to dancing and amusements, and at
> different times during the school year entertainments of
> various kinds are provided for the children.

The music performed by the Fourth Class of Girls, the thirty-
two pupils mentioned above, included selections from Pinafore:

Over the Bright Blue Sea	Chorus
Little Buttercup	Solo
Bell Trio	Chorus

The Singing Class performed the following:

Children's Te Deum	Solo, Quartet, and Chorus
In The Starlight	Duet
The Strolling Minstrels	Song and Chorus
Gaudeamus	
America	

In addition there were some miscellaneous instrumental numbers which no doubt included piano, violin, guitar, or organ.

The Illinois Institution for the education of the blind which was founded at Jacksonville in 1849 was making singular musical contributions to its inmates by the close of the '60s. The Illinois State Superintendent of Public Instruction 1868 devoted some space in his annual report to a discussion of music for the blind. Joshua Rhoads, Superintendent of the Jacksonville school, had some comments about music instruction for the blind.

> The ability of the blind as musicians, and their devotion
> to its study, are great; but there prevails, in the minds
> of a great many persons an exaggerated idea of this
> subject. Many suppose that all blind persons are musical,
> and that one whose eyes are closed to the impression of
> the light must of course have an ear open to the harmonies
> of sound.... In a given number of blind and seeing per-
> sons, there will certainly be about the same number of
> each qualified by nature to excell in music. But in
> institutions for the blind, whether from the propensity to
> imitation, or from the hope of future reward, the desire
> to study music is almost universal among the pupils, while
> the musical ear, necessary to attain to skill in performance,
> is rare.... This institution, as in literature, pursues
> a more enlarged policy, and endeavors to cultivate any
> musical taste existing in a pupil, however feeble it may
> be. The talent of a pupil is sometimes small, and his
> desire for learning music proportionally great. In this
> case we find it adds essentially to his happiness to aid
> him in his efforts to become a musician. If he fails to
> succeed he has the consolation of feeling that he has tried,
> and that no exertion has been spared for his benefit. [7]

According to a report of 1880, The Superintendent of the New York Institution for the Blind, New York City, was offering music instruction as "heretofore";[8] in other words before 1880. Later in 1883,[9] it was revealed that the musical program for the institution included the following activities by the two classes that are indicated.

<u>Elementary Classes:</u>	Singing by interval and rudiments.
<u>Advanced Classes:</u>	Voice culture, chorus singing, piano and organ playing, harmony, theory and practice of teaching. Staff and New York Point Systems of musical notation, piano tuning.

It is the observation of the author that prior to 1885, the science of vocal music and its rudiments was being preferred to blind, deaf, and dumb patients in some American institutions.

Notes

1. Barnard, Henry. American Journal of Education. IV: No. 10 (September, 1857). 137.

2. Third Annual Report of the State Superintendent of Education of the State of South Carolina. 1871. 82.

3. Annual Report of the State Board of Education, Showing The Condition of the Public Schools of Maryland, With The Reports of the School Commissioners of Baltimore City and the Several Counties, for Year Ending September 30, 1873. 1874. 39.

4. Thirty-Ninth Annual Report of the Board of Education, Together With the Ninth Annual Report of the Secretary of the Board, 1874-75. January, 1876. Boston: 1876. 163.

5. Fourteenth Biennial Report of the Superintendent of Public Instruction of the State of Illinois, July 1, 1882 - June 30, 1882. Springfield, Illinois: 1883. 275-276.

6. Fifteenth Biennial Report of the Superintendent of Public Instruction of the State of Illinois, July 1, 1882 - June 30, 1884. Springfield, Illinois: 1884. 68.

7. Seventh Biennial Report of the Superintendent of Public Instruction of the State of Illinois, 1867 - 1868. 194-195.

8. Twenty-Seventh Annual Report of the Superintendent of Public Instruction of the State of New York. Transmitted to the Legislature, January 5, 1881. Albany: 1881. 115.

9. Thirtieth Annual Report of the Superintendent of Public Instruction of the State of New York. Transmitted to the Legislature, January 9, 1884. 139.

XV. POST-WORLD WAR I: MUSIC EDUCATION'S FORWARD THRUST

The potent force for modern American music has been the school music movement. Its great strength lay in its mass of personnel, sponteneity, youth, competitive spirit, and the potential nucleus for a vast creative and consuming audience. The growth of the movement in United States, although over a century in development, made felt its significant birth of new achievements shortly after the end of World War I.

Competitive music contests were an outgrowth of music in twentieth century education. A national or even a sectional competitive music program was unknown before 1900. Although the Magna Charta of music education was signed in Boston in 1838, regularly scheduled high school orchestras and bands were of no consequence prior to 1917.

In 1917 John Phillip Sousa, "The March King" was still alive and had been singled out as America's leading exponent of the concert band. He lived during an era when a band was for many people something of a novelty. To see it meant, in some cases, long tedious travel to a large center to witness a holiday celebration. Of course there were the street corner efforts of The Salvation Army Bands, or perhaps the appearance of a traveling band making a stand at some state or county fair. The American school music program had yet to experience the tremendous impetus imbedded in instrumental music. After the first World War there was a marked ascendency in the development of instrumental music, and bands in particular, in public and private schools.

Prior to 1917 the embryonic state of development of school bands and orchestras could be pin-pointed by naming isolated instances where their organization had brought local, state, and in some cases national recognition. Reputedly one of the earliest high school bands was organized in 1858 on Thompson Island in

Boston Harbor, Massachusetts.   Under the direction of John Ripley
Morse it made its first public appearance in 1859. [1]   Significant
among its early achievements was that in 1869 it took part in the
Patrick Gilmore Peace Jubilee, where fine musicians from five
countries performed.   In 1933 the band had a personnel count of
fifty with a supporting drum and bugle corps. [2]

An orchestra which attained eventual distinction was started
by Will Earhart in 1898.   Meeting for one rehearsal a week after
school, its members received one-half credit per semester.   Class
instruction was instituted in 1910 and by 1912 it had attained full
orchestral proportions of sixty-four players.

Some Early bands were: [3]

City	Organized	Information
Stockton, California	1901	
Wellington, Kansas		(About the same time)
Rockford, Illinois	1907	John T. Haight, Director
Belle Fourche, S. Dak.	1908	H. A. Moddie, Director
Joliet, Illinois	1913	A. R. McAllister, Director
Oakland, California	1913	It had twenty-nine band members by 1915
Lincoln, Nebraska	1916	Experimented with the establishment of a band
Richland Center, Wisconsin	1916	Victor Gravel
Grand Rapids, Michigan	1916	By 1917 free instruction on any band or orchestral instrument.
Evansville, Indiana	1918	
Rochester, New York	1918	Three hundred instruments given by George A. Eastman. Joseph E. Maddy was hired as instrumental teacher.
Fostoria, Ohio	1919	This band in 1923 won first place in the First National Band Contest held at Chicago. J. W. Wainwright was the director.

City	Organized	Information
Aurora, Illinois	1919	East High School organized its band
Parsons, Kansas	1920	Probably the first known school band to have daily rehearsals during the regular school day.

In addition to the above mentioned scattered firsts, the generalization is justified that between 1895 and 1915 there were increasing numbers of bands and orchestras. Among the locations of these were Wichita, Kansas; Indianapolis, Indiana; New London and Hartford, Connecticut, and Chelsea, Massachusetts. Beginning about 1915 credit for music was being allowed. Boys and girls taking music courses in secondary schools began to receive credit for regularly offered instruction.

With the appointment by the Music Educators National Conference of a Committee on Instrumental Affairs in 1922 much constructive organizational work was accomplished for the cause of instrumental music in American schools. Although currently we have highly organized music programs in American schools, 1924 represents the beginning of the band contest movement as we know it today. In 1924 there were 13 state contests with 104 bands participating; the number had grown to approximately 1500 bands in 1936. [4]

A Committee on Vocal Affairs was appointed in 1928. These Committees continued until 1934 when their responsibilities were fused into one organization, the Committee on Festivals and Contests. Later in 1936 this group was replaced by the Committee on School Music Competition-Festivals.

The first official national school music contest was held for bands in 1926. In 1929 the first official National School Orchestra Contest was held at Mason City, Iowa. In 1937 some vocal events were sponsored by The National School Vocal Association, and in cooperation with the National School Band and Orchestra Association met at Lawrence, Kansas. That same year The National Vocal Association held a choral competition festival in conjunction with the

North Central Conference at Minneapolis, Minnesota.

The growth of the festival movement had been astounding.
The sixteenth year of festival activity (1941) showed that 80, 897
students representing 2, 400 schools were entered in the finals of
National School Music Competition.   An aggregate of about 900, 000
boys and girls from American high schools participated. [5]

A recent survey indicated that there were over 2, 000, 000
players registered in approximately 25, 000 bands and 40, 000
orchestras in the American public schools. [6]   During the decade
1940-1950 thousands of instrumentalists had taken their place in
our national life.

Music In Our National Life.   In the symphonic field there
likewise had been considerable growth.   With less than fifty
orchestras of symphonic proportions in 1923, there were more
than 300 in 1931.   In cities of less than 25, 000 population there
were fine orchestras though not necessarily symphonic in size. [7]

By 1930 public school music programs had developed to such
a point that it was estimated that over 500, 000 boys and girls were
in bands and 400, 000 in orchestras.   There was an ever-increasing
demand for musical compositions.   Like all compositional production there were increasingly new works expressing a new found
American medium of creative effort.   In 1930 it was reported that
there were "in the United States, 150, 000 musicians who are
affiliated with the American Federation of Musicians -- all identified
with the organized labor movement. "[8]

Additionally great sums of money had been entrusted to foundations, organized for the expressed purpose of encouraging music
education in America.   Three foundations of outstanding importance
and in existance during the 1930's were Julliard of New York,
Presser Foundation of Philadelphia, and the Curtis Institute of
Philadelphia. [9]

This was the period when millions of people were listening
to music every hour of the day by means of the radio; this medium
for transmitting music started about 1921.   In 1930 George Engles
stated that the radio has "not lessened but immeasurably increased"

opportunities for the professional musician. [10]

> Over the networks of the National Broadcasting Company
> alone more than six thousand appearances are made every
> month, more than are made in public concerts in any four
> of our largest cities during an entire concert season.
> Three-fourths (3,750) of these appearances are by
> musicians.   One may realize, therefore, what tremendously
> greater possibilities radio, in conjunction with individual
> concert appearances, offers in the furthering of the careers
> of musicians than would (result if there were) concert
> appearances alone.
>
> Go into any community, no matter how small or how
> isolated, and you will find, not one or two, but dozens
> (of persons) who have heard of Ganz, Lhevinne, Chemet,
> Kochanski, Schumann-Heink, Giannini, Iturbi, and many
> others, who know the music they are best fitted to inter-
> pret, who know their technical limitations, and who are
> anxious to see them in the flesh on the concert stage. [11]

In the orchestral field great progress was being made.   The
Philharmonic Symphony Orchestra of New York, Detroit Symphony,
Minneapolis Symphony, and Boston Symphony Orchestras were
ranked with the most superior musical organizations in the world
of orchestral art.   Our American commercialism had left little
undone -- even our orchestras were among the best.   A London
critic once said that the Philharmonic was composed mostly of
Europeans and therefore nothing was remarkable about its superiority.   The Philharmonic, which the European audiences heard during
1930, was composed of 114 musicians only 8 of which were not
American citizens. [12]

From the turn of the nineteenth century, down to World War
I, Americans were primarily interested in expanding the industrial,
social, and material frontiers within our borders.   Up to the time
of the Great War, the foreign artist dominated the American plat-
form.   With the signing of the Armistice, hundreds of thousands
of men came back from the war convinced that within our borders
were to be found opportunities second to none which they had seen
offered on the European continent.   Americans were fused with the
idea of doing things, big things.   This was the musician's point of
view in the United States.   Post World War I found   1)   fine
orchestras coming into being, particularly the Detroit and Cleveland

organizations,   2)   music conservatories expanding at a rapid rate,
3)   theatres employing vast numbers of professional instrumentalists
who depended upon such appointments for their livelihood,   4)   piano
production hitting an all time high in 1929, when approximately
600, 000 units were produced,   5)   theatres installing expensive
pipe organs, which provided positions for organists with salaries
sometimes approaching $15, 000 per year,   6)   music departments
and music classes in the universities beginning to emphasize music.

Then came the financial erosion of 1929 which had a de-
vastating affect upon the social and economic structure of society.
It brought about technological changes which took place in the field
of industrial and cultural music.   Mechanical sound producers
had been gaining momentum from about 1921; what had been
"ritually called canned music" was fast becoming ruinous to theatre
music positions.   Gradually the organist was finding his position
taken over by mechanically produced sound mechanisms.   The
organist was being relegated to just "week-end feature programs. "
The orchestras in many theatres were completely eliminated.
Where the theatres of Washington, D. C. , at one time employed
65 organists, in 1931 there were but 4. [13]

The effects of the depression caused some symphony orchestras
to disappear from the music scene, due to smaller subscription
lists and concert artists were increasingly finding it difficult to
secure bookings.   In the struggle for a type of "splash" supremacy,
the thought of training the "star" performer left little time and
understanding for the average appreciator who was to buy the product.

The upheaval of '29 and the production of the "mechanical
music maker" wreaked havoc with those men who has spent a
lifetime in devotion to the development of manipulatory skills.   The
man who used his hands -- the violinist, cellist, and pianist --
could not afford to do hard labor even if the opportunity presented
itself.   The player of these instruments take as great care of his
hands as does the singer of his throat.   The fact remained also
that the people who had chosen music as a vocation were not trained

for entry into other professions.

Properly coordinating nation-wide projects to aid in the huge task of alleviating the situation proved difficult and challenging. There was need to secure competent leaders to properly direct the activities of smaller performing units in many communities, but salary scales prohibited compensation commensurate with the work and genius required in achieving good results.   Another difficulty was supervision of work at points distant from organization head-quarters.   Politics offered "barbed wire entanglements" in the carrying out of objectives; the possibility of corrupt management raised its ugly head.

Music in Higher Education.   Music had failed to carry out its universalization concept in institutions of higher education--with one out of every 120 persons matriculated in such schools.   American educators had partially failed to give music a place of significant importance.   Instructors were still somewhat 'high bound' by the money making potential of private music teaching.   It was strongley urged that music instruction must be provided for all those who desired it.   The prevalent slogan for that era was "Music for every child and every child for music"--but should it not have been "Opportunities for all those who desire music instruction"?

It was felt that institutions of higher learning should make music instruction available to all of its students.   In many schools private instruction was offered but fees were frequently prohibitive. In some cases individuals felt that their talents did not justify the expenditure, yet innately these same people enjoyed music as much, if not more than some who may be taking music to satisfy their personal desires.   The day of greater music opportunities in these institutions was predicted for the near future.   The music depart-ment of the future featuring four or more bands and choruses, aug-mented by smaller instrumental and vocal groups, was the hope. In finalizing this philosophy, many music educators were predicting a great future for music in all educational institutions.

Music in American Cultural Life.   The decade 1929-38 was not one which fostered a highly developed sensibility toward aesthetic

pursuits.   Some significant attemps to sustain music during this
period included   1)   The Federal Music Program of the Works
Progress Administration;   2)   The Federal Government and Music
Education;   3)   Legislation relating to music;   4)   The Keyboard
Business;   5)   The Impetus of Radio;   6)   Some Mechanical In-
novations;   7)   Grand Opera;   8)   The Psychotherapeutic Values
of Music;   9)   Music in Rural Life;   10)   Urban Music; and   11)
Music and Industrial Fatigue.

During the bleak years of the 1930's many Americans began
to feel the need to plan and evaluate their social and economic
futures.   Music had a definite design in weaving the fabric of the
future.

One use of music used extensively by concerns in stimulating
new business was as minister of the "get acquainted plan. "   A
comparable plan to interest youth in the arts was presented
for parental consideration.   It was felt that parents needed some
plan through which children could become more integrated in home
life.   Music was urged because of its invaluable service as being
therapeutic leading to the full life.   It was thought that home musical groups might be the amalgam which could keep the home together.   Since the beginning of the century the home, as an institution,
had suffered disintegration.   Expanded educational and social
agencies were offering children greater advantages than had been
realized in the family group.   When the young people began to
participate in the larger community, the home no longer served
as the center of their existence.

During the 18th and 19th century the boy or girl found a program of music was one attempt to bring them back to the family
group.

The Federal Music Project of the Works Progress Administration.   Government sponsored music started in July, 1935, when
The Federal Music Project (WPA) was inaugurated.   Countless
millions enjoyed good performances of all types of music when 273
communities in forty-two states became beneficiaries of this govern-
ment-sponsored play.   In June 1936, approximately 15, 000 musicians

were enrolled in various types of performing music. [14]

The importance of the Federal Music Project, which offered music opportunities to Americans in 1937, has been little realized. The original director of the project, Nikolai Sokoloff, said it would try "to employ, to retain, and rehabilitate musicians who lost employment in the depression. " It was

> nation-wide, functioning in forty-two states and the District of Columbia.... More than thirty-two million persons had heard 'in the flesh' concerts or performances by units of the Federal Music Project since October, 1935. It reported approximately thirty-six thousand performances in the period between January 1 and July 31, 1936. [15]

It had a National Advisory Committee composed of outstanding leaders in the field of music throughout the United States. The membership list included such names as Dr. Howard Hanson, Dr. Frederick Stock, Paul Whitman, and Mrs. John Alexander Jardine. There were twenty-four members altogether.

In 1936, nine months after the inauguration of its music projects, it was reported that this unit of the WPA employed some 15, 000 individuals. Between March 31, and June 30, 1936, approximately 700 musicians left relief rolls. A tabulation as of August 31st reported 694 projects, incorporating a relief personnel of 13, 317 plus a non-relief group of 1, 587. In all, there were 14, 904 who found constructive employment. The distributions for various types of music occupations were as follows:

Recapitulation as of August 31, 1936

Projects		Personnel		
Number	Types	Relief	Non-Relief	Total
162	Symphony and Concert Orchestras	5005	832	5837
97	Bands	2758	226	2984
26	Chamber Music Ensenbles..............	231	24	255
122	Dance, Theatre and Novelty Orchestras....	1679	141	1820
33	Vocal, Chorus, Quartets, etc.........	1122	124	1246
4	Opera Groups.........	252	50	302
202	Teaching Projects.....	1377	118	1495
27	Copyists, Librarians...	428	42	470

Recapitualation as of August 31, 1936 cont.

Projects		Personnel		
Number	Types	Relief	Non-Relief	Total
1	Composer Project......	1		1
2	Soloists Projects.......	181		181
18	Miscellaneous (Coordinating, Administrative, Supervisory, Labor)....	283	30	313
694		13, 317	1, 587	14,904

The co-operating sponsors for the programs included major universities, city commissions, city councils, school districts and boards of education, civic organizations of all descriptions, and the National Federation of Music Clubs, with more than 5, 000 affiliated organizations in forty-eight states. Outstanding orchestral conductors offered their services in order to stimulate and bring a tinge of professionalism to the Federal interest in the professional musician.

The importance of this agency's work can be more vividly appreciated by an inventory of activities which reveals that more than 4, 500 musical performances per month were presented to over 3, 100, 000 people. In addition to these musical performances as many as 1, 600 WPA music teachers were employed in teaching more than 140, 000 musically interested people. Not only re-creators but creators of American music found expression through 5, 300 compositions by 1, 500 composers. From October, 1935, to the same month in 1939, approximately 148, 000, 000 persons witnessed music programs of all types. As of December, 1941, the program was being conducted in 40 states, New York City, and the District of Columbia, employing 7, 000 musicians. [16]

More than half of those employed were performing in defense work at army, navy, marine bases, and in other service centers. The remainder were appearing in approximately 5, 000 concerts a month to an audience well in excess of 2, 000,000. The musicians serving the teaching centers had enrolled 250, 000 students per week. From the program's inception up to July 1, 1941, a total of 8, 000 different American compositions by 2, 300 American composers had been performed. [17]

The Federal Music Project was organized to serve the musical tastes of people in all walks of life. The thousands of performances during the above seven year period certainly had done much to instill within Americans an appreciation for musical art and particularly so, American music. Much had been done to give courage to indigenous musical composition.

The Federal Government and Music Education. John W. Studebaker, United States Commissioner of Education during this era, suggested "A Plan for the Development of the Fine Arts through Education."[18] His office was attempting

> to maintain the advances made in education and to promote further gains by organizing a service centered in Washington which will bring to the attention of every state and local school and every parent and teacher in America the best thought and the most valuable experiences in all fields of education including the so-called cultural activities. This is the purpose of the Office of Education. [19]

In the summer of 1936, persons interested in music education and other arts were called to Washington in order to aid the Office of Education in planning a program for those interested in various areas of cultural development. The resulting recommendations of the group were formulated by Mrs. Frances E. Clark. The Office of Education was urged to have a Division of Fine Arts projecting the following objectives:

a) To provide for the promotion of education through the arts.

b) To cooperate with all existing organizations in an effort to bring to the attention of educators, parents, and citizens the need for greater development of aesthetics in education, the value of appreciation of beauty in all things, the need of culturing the pleasurable emotions in the education of future citizens.

c) To carry over into education through the arts the same procedure as now obtains in the general and vocational phases, viz., gathering facts and information, making surveys and studies, dissemination of the findings and interpretation through bulletins, letters, pamphlets, conferences, etc.

d) To maintain a national comprehensive, indexed compendium of statistics of these arts in both school and adult education, also a card file of a library of information on these subjects, including cooperation with the indexed system of the music division of the Library of Congress.

e) To secure, if possible, funds to organize a large national advisory board or to formulate plans, to make regional surveys, gather information for presentation to the division head, and through public addresses, magazine articles and contacts with large groups to build up public support. [20]

This ambitious program demanded an efficient director and divisional personnel, and coordination of all vocational, avocational, and cultural groups. The proposed division was intended to deal with all fine arts, not music alone, and its purpose was to stimulate rather than dictate to those interested in fine arts agencies. Heretofore, it seems, the government had been feeding only "skim milk" to the finer arts.

Legislation Relating To Music. It was Alfredo Salmaggi who stated that "just like spaghetti, grand opera comes from Italy, and belongs to the Italians."[21] Statements similar to this one and the complications resulting from the age of "canned music" and the depression had of course, irked the American artistic community no little, and in due time legislation was presented which, had it been passed upon favorably, would actually have had a limiting character upon Italian Spaghetti and grand opera music.

One of the first pieces of legislation introduced into the House of Representatives was the bill presented by Representative Hoeppel of California, in July of 1935. It was designed "to protect the artistic and earning opportunities of American musicians...." [22] This bill lacked support, but was brought before the House with another bill designed by Representative Samuel Dickstein of New York during the 1936 sessions. The Dickstein bill stirred a furor in artistic circles, resulting in two opposing camps. The legislator made the following statements concerning the purposes and provisions of his measure:

> The Dickstein Bill, introduced by me in the House of Representatives on Jan. 5, and referred to the Committee on Immigration and Naturalization, of which I am chairman, provides that, notwithstanding any other provision of the immigration law to the contrary, no alien vocal musician, operatic singer, solo instrumentalist, solo dancer, orchestral conductor, or actor shall be admitted

> to the United States, for either temporary or permanent
> residence, unless prior to the issuance of the visa the
> Secretary of Labor has received an application from such
> artist for permission to enter the country for professional
> engagements, and such permission has been granted prior
> to his or her departure from foreign territory.
>
> The bill further provides that the number of these admiss-
> ible alien artists admitted during any calendar year shall
> be limited to the number of American artists of similar
> qualifications which the government of such foreign country
> has granted permission to enter such foreign country for
> professional engagements during the same calendar year.
>
> In the event that an American artist having similar
> qualifications to those of an alien applicant for admission
> as a non-immigrant cannot be found among unemployed
> citizens in the United States, the Secretary of Labor may,
> upon full hearing and investigation, admit such foreign
> artist for temporary professional engagements during
> specified periods.
>
> The purpose of these provisions is that protection be given
> American artists to the extent that the foreign artist does
> not displace or prevent employment of the citizen or lawful
> permanent resident alien having similar professional
> qualifications.
>
> Instrumental musicians, as such, are not admissible under
> the terms of the proposed law, although vocal musicians,
> opera singers, instrumental soloists, and orchestral con-
> ductors are included. [23]

The Hoeppel Bill had a reciprocal clause which permitted the
impresario to employ or import foreign artists equal in number to
American artists in his employ.

Implications of the Dickstein Bill were that 1) Artist immigration would be based on employment conditions in this country.
2) The Secretary of Labor would of necessity be the reviewing
board or he would have to set up such for the purpose of determining the qualifications of both American born and alien artists.
(The implication of artist determination as a first, second, or
third rater would be difficult.) 3) The population would be protected from its own gullibility regarding aesthetic choices. (The
highest priced performer may be the one who offers a minimum of
artistic worth.) 4) Self-sufficiency protective measures were
beginning to take shape.

Favoring the bill was Lawrence Tibbett, President of The American Guild of Musical Artists and well-known operatic baritone of the era. He championed the bill by declaring that 1) "The basis of the Guild's policy is one of protection against immigration restrictions that have long been in practice against Americans in Europe. 2) Examination of the bill would disclose the fact that it is in no sense restrictive after the manner of the arbitrary restrictions of European countries, but rather that it is reciprocative, calling for the admission of artists from those countries which allow the admission of Americans. (He claimed elasticity of provisions.) 3) Unprincipled and irresponsible producers are bringing to America musicians who are in no way qualified to compete with the recognized artists, American and European, who are legitimately in America. 4) At the present moment certain European nations, acting under misguided policy of isolation, are creating conditions which have an unfortunate repercussion here."[24]

F. C. Schang, Secretary of The Concerts Association of America stated an opposite point of view:

1) There are two major concert managements in the United States: the Columbia Concerts Corporation and the NBC Artists Service. An analysis of the lists of artists of these two managements, which handle the business of about 200 artists and organizations, shows that 75 per cent of them are either American-born or American citizens. This would represent the two lists which include the most foreign artists. Artists under other managements will show a much higher American average, because foreign artists prefer to come with these two leading agencies. 2) There are so few drawing-cards alive now that they can readily be named without much challenge. For obvious reasons their names are withheld here; but within the classifications of the Dickstein Bill, i.e., vocal musicians, operatic singers, solo dancers, solo instrumentalists, and orchestral conductors, there are only fifteen living drawing-cards, divided as follows: instrumentalists, five; male singers, four; female singers, three; orchestral conductors, three; dancers, none. 3) The point of this argument revolves about these two ratios; while the concert managements are managing three Americans to every one alien, the ratio of the drawing-cards is one American to two aliens. Of fifteen drawing-cards mentioned above, five are American-born and ten foreign-born. Of sixteen drawing-cards listed as living in the last quarter century, thirteen are foreign born and only three American-born.

4) European representatives of the Columbia Concerts
Corporation and the NBC management report that there is
a much greater demand for American artists in Europe
now than there is for European artists in America. Artists
such as Lawrence Tibbett, Nelson Eddy, Richard Crooks,
Grace Moore, Jeanette MacDonald, and Gladys Swarthout
can secure immediate and extensive engagements at high
fees abroad. Actually, they have turned a deaf ear.
5) What decides whether an American artist is going to
get engagements in Europe is exactly what decides whether
a European artist is going to get engagements in America,
i. e. , Are they any good? and, Does the public like them?
The growth of musical appreciation in this country has been
extraordinary, but it is still in its infancy. The vitality
of musical life here is dependent to a large extent upon
the great musical personalities who can draw audiences to
hear the message of this subtle art. The country at present is in no condition whatsoever to place any limitations
on its normal growth. The shutting of the market or the
restriction on it can have only one effect: that of arresting its progress. [25]

Legislation of this character was epoch-making. It fore-
shadowed the musicians' protective groups and unions of the mid-
century. What about protecting our academically trained college
and university professors? (These movements of the depression
era did have a salutary effect upon all non-professional and professional employable people of the period 1945-1965). [26]

In addition, great numbers of refugee doctors of both the
medical and academic ranks had arrived from Europe and Germany
due to Hitler's purge in the medical profession and university
teaching ranks.

Prior to the depression academic growth was on the increase.
During the period 1925-1935, 20,580 doctorates were offered; 1935
saw but 2,588 doctorates offered in the same 90 schools; 19,339
masters degrees were proferred in 1932. [27] During this era there
was the beginning of a new concept of professional protection for
the teaching profession. Mass production without a market presents
an evil whether the individual be a singer, violinist, or a doctorate
of philosophy in education or chemistry.

The Keyboard Business. It had been long recognized by music
educators that the piano is the primary musical instrument. A
mark of good musicianship presupposes more than a passing

familiarity. It requires thorough understanding. As an instrument
it can become functionally more easily adapted for the layman. All
music is reducible to the piano. It can become the accompaniment
for all instruments. More music has been written for it than any
other single instrument.

The piano during the decade (1920-1930) had been increasing
in public favor. Recent statistics would indicate a piano shortage
in this country; in 1933 approximately 27,000 pianos were shipped
by manufacturers; shipments rose to about 138,000 in 1941. This
increase of over 500 percent strongly indicates that the piano was
finding a lively market in the canned-dial-turning civilization. The
reason for such a resurgence of popularity lay in a variety of
things. Certainly the radio has done much to encourage appreciation
for it as a musical producer. Radio courses in teaching people
how to play chordwise or in a musicianly fashion had created a
host of new tyro performers. Then too, the piano manufacturers
had created a new type of moderately priced lightweight, compact,
and attractive instrument that blended into modern home designing.
The ponderous models of a past era were beyond the needs of the
average American. The musical laity needed instruments that
served their enjoyment needs. The popularity of the models attested
to their satisfactoriness.

The abundance of musical course offerings in the modern
public schools of that era had served to stimulate in thousands
of people a desire to be creators as well as listeners and modern
mass production methods make it possible for people to experiment
musically, and less expensively.

R. C. Rolfing, President of the National Piano Manufacturers
Association stated that in 1933 at least 15,000,000 people in America
could play some musical instrument. He further claimed that of
these, 9,000,000 could play the piano and 2,000,000 more were
studying the violin.

Thus, music education had become a more significant factor
in the cultural and aesthetic growth of the American way of life.
The musical development of children was advancing nearer the ulti-

mate goal of plentiful musical experiences for all those who desire it.   American music education, through its democratic processes, permitted individual initiative for creative expression.

The Impetus of Radio.   The advent of radio broadcasting of educational programs had done much to give impetus to all forms of music education.   The radio had become a major factor in the upsurge of lay interest in music for recreation.   People derive self-satisfaction from doing what others are doing.   Radio had popularized the doing.   In proportion to ability manifest by man, he instinctively desired the imitative whether the task be of an intellectual, semi-intellectual, or non-intellectual nature.

As an illustration of what was being done in radio, The School of The Air of the Americas by the Columbia Broadcasting Company is cited.   During 1941-42, audiences in the Western Hemisphere were being educated weekly through the Music of the Americas programs.   The CBC estimated that in the United States and Canada "several million" school children heard programs in their classrooms; an additional estimated 3, 500, 000 adults were benefited in their homes.   The programs instead of eliminating teaching, were designed specifically to supplement and vitalize teaching.   Teaching materials in the form of manuals were furnished which provided lesson outlines, bibliographical information, and lists of recordings which were correlated with each lesson.   They served a purpose which was both educational and purposeful for hemispheric solidarity.

Some Mechanical Innovations.   Of significance was the appearance in 1935 of the Hammond Electric Organ.   This instrument was exhibited by Laurens Hammond its inventor, at the Industrial Arts Exposition, in Rockefeller Center with Pietro Yon at the console. This marked a significant milestone in the development of electronically produced instruments.

A new piano keyboard, with 17 intervals in an octave, instead of twelve, appeared in 1936.   This ingenious device was the product of the Russian musician, A. S. Ogolevets.   He claimed that it would be possible to perform on this 17 toned octave, Eastern music, such

as Arabic and Iranian. The quarter toned piano had been demonstrated by Alois Saba, Czechoslovakian composer, Rimsky-Korsakoff
the Soviet musician, and Hans Barth. Julian Carillo, the Mexican
composer employed 16 tones to the octave as a medium of tonal
expression and his experiments caused much interest.

Grand Opera During The Depression Era. When Giulio-Gatti
Casazza, who for 27 years was director of the Metropolitan Opera
Company, tendered his resignation, Herbert Witherspoon, former
Basso of the same organization was appointed director. He died
suddenly in 1935 and was succeeded by Edward Johnson, who guided
the company to many successes during the latter part of the depression era. The Chicago Civic Opera Company which shriveled
up and closed its doors early in the depression found new hope and
gave a five week season in 1936 and looked forward to a brighter
future. A new found hope was engendered by the management
through featuring popular priced opera performances.

The Psychotherapeutic Value of Music. Psychotherapy began
its significant pioneering work shortly after World War I. Dr.
Frankwood E. Williams, of the National Committee of Mental
Hygiene, pointed out some interesting statistics for that era:
"...from every 7,000 children born in the United States each year,
269 will become definitely diseased in the course of their lives. "
Looking backward, he said "50,000 Americans were admitted last
year (1923) as new patients in the mental hospitals of the United
States, and this does not include the readmissions.... Looking
forward, this means that 250,000 people carrying the burdens of
life today will break down mentally under the load within five years
and that half a million men and women will be registered in the
mental hospitals as new patients within ten years at an increasing
rate of admission each year. Who among our acquaintances will
be among them?[28] Pennsylvania was first among the states to
employ music for educating and ameliorating the mentally unstable.

About 1922, the Central Islip State Hospital in New York
started employing music with a couple of patients once a week;
1925 saw 1,772 patients at Central Islip participate each week in a

seven days-a-week rotating program of activities, directly and indirectly employing music.   The State Hospital at Allentown, Pa.
had a program incorporating music. [29]   Van De Wall declared that
music as created by the composer and performed by the artist
could become a helper in mental reconstruction of human personalities.   He further insisted that those mental unfortunates would
have a brighter chance if music were offered as a companion aid.
Music could stimulate the physiological and psychological structure
either positively or negatively.   He felt that if music could stimulate
lethargic individuals to activity from nonparticipation into constructive socialized activities, its beneficial effects should be
sought.   The judicious use of music for unstable individuals offered
potent psychotherapeutic value.

Van De Wall spoke of a Washington Birthday Pageant which
took place at the Allentown State Hospital, Allentown, Pennsylvania.
The cast consisted of "25 dementia praecox cases, 7 cases of
maniac depression, 5 cases of general paresis, 18 psychopathic
cases of which some were feeble-minded, 4 epileptics, 1 drug
addict -- all together forming a cast of 26 women and 34 men. "[30]

Was music of any therapeutic benefit to them?   The individuals
in this cast were required to function in an orderly systematic
manner.   The repetition of each individual's little performance during rehearsals had a tendency to cause conditioned reflexes.   These
people had to make possible the performance of their music, and
participate in many other additional activities which were essential
to the success of their performance--such things as make up and
preparations involved in putting on a dress rehearsal.   Some of the
reflexes developed into habits and therefore much dress rehearsal
was unnecessary.

Van De Wall concluded that music was the guiding factor in
the net results of these experiments.   Among his conclusions were
the following:

> 1)   Music is a system of constructive normal and idealistic
> mental suggestions, supplying from the outside an
> initiative and a force which is missing within the patient....
> A system which:

2) Makes him leave his place of self-sufficiency and seclu-
   sion and raise him to the level of sociability....

3) He proves another point and very important one in mental
   therapy, that the abnormal individual 'has not only a great
   desire to function normally, but that he wants to learn, to
   acquire new ideas and new skill, to master a new repertoire and to fill up his mind with new happiness-bringing
   notions'. [31]

4) Music naturally cannot rebuild a broken mentality--but
   musical joys alone could easily turn into a sedative, a
   dope and even intensify abnormal automatisms and intro-
   vert phantasies. [32]

During this early publicized usage of music as a therapeutic
had been the program carried out as a part of the Federal Music
Project actvities.   "Under strict scientific control music therapy
classes are being conducted in eight New York hospitals, a training
school for girls and a house of detention for women, covering approximately 6, 200 patients a month.   This work was begun in the
psychiatric ward for children at Bellevue Hospital. [33]

"In the Jacksonville Memorial Hospital in Florida other
experiments to determine the value of music along therapeutic
lines were being made.   These experiments also are under scientific
control."[34]   Increasingly it became more common to employ psychotherapy in wards where the mentally deficient were detained.   This
is indicative of the early beginnings of this work.

Music In Rural Life.   Modern transportation had suburbanized
much rural social life.   Modern communication media on wheels
and through the air had created a rejuvenated consumer of modern
music.   Modern civilization had given the farmer many more winter
hours of leisure time.   Musical experiences for rural people had
not been offered to one cintillianth of its inherent possibilities.

Evidence of Lay Participation and Urban Music.   Unquestionably the Chicagoland Music Festival which held its twelfth annual
festival at Soldiers' Field, August 16, 1941, was one of the greatest
single lay municipal music efforts in this country.   Sponsored by
the Chicago Tribune Charities, Inc., it cooperated with newspapers,
civic, and musical organizations to bring together musical laity who
participated in the festival for fun.   Beyond the enjoyment stage,
prizes were offered for those who wished to participate in contests

covering thirteen categories:

Vocal	--	Men and Women
Choral	--	Men, Women, Mixed
Band	--	Adult and Juvenile
Trombone		
Accordion		
Flag Swinging	--	Individual and Team
Baton Twirling	--	Adult, Junior, and Juvenile
Hawaiian Guitar		
Spanish Guitar		
Mandolin		
Tenor Banjo		
Accordion Band		
Fretted Band		

During a period of eleven years more than 1, 000, 000 had attended these mass spectacles which had been participated in by over 75, 000 men, women, and children. Money derived from the festivals served charitable purposes. This event was certainly the greatest and most spectacular lay music effort of its kind that probably appeared on the American musical scene. The richness of man's experiences are in exact proportion to his recreativeness for self-experience. As a great art expression of man, music must be created by or entirely consumed by Mr. and Mrs. City Dweller. The Chicagoland Music Festival is evidence of great lay music participation and enjoyment during the pre World-War II period.

Music and Industrial Fatigue. A large eastern manufacturing company used music to promote efficiency and alleviate industrial fatigue. This firm furnishes four hours of music each day: one hour in the morning, two during the lunch hour, and one during the later afternoon. The company stated: "We believe that music will be an aid in enabling plant and office workers to go through the day with a minimum of fatigue from a good day's work. "

There were significant achievements made in American music during this era: 1) National legislation was initiated for the purpose of protecting the professional and vocational status of musicians; 2) The Federal government became interested in the fine arts; 3) Artistic talent arriving in America in many cases was not deemed worthy of the financial support they received, while American artists of comparable ability could not qualify because they were

not foreign;   4)   The immigration of European musicians had a
tendency to make distinctions against American musicians and
artists;   5)   Grand opera made hesitant strides during the era
1929-1938;   6)   The creation of mechanical music reproducers
created both beneficial and detrimental economic problems (Enjoyment and temporary unemployment very frequently are the hand-
maidens of science);   7)   Psychotherapy had opened up new vistas
of opportunity for the power of music to have a salutary affect
upon the intellectual and emotional life of man;   8)   Music could
play an important role in utilizing the ever-increasing amounts of
leisure time;   9)   Music had the potentiality for uniting community
and home interests into one big civic unit--functioning in the
interest of all;   10)   There was developed a new concept of the
meaning of the "tolerant professional attitude";   11)   Music in
higher education had not passed entirely from the private money
concept into the realm of more public and governmental support
for education.

       During the pre World War II era, progressive community
music had actually functioned in American life.   Many city supervisors had failed to integrate the music program with the com-
munity--music was yet to attain a civic concept.   The need was
not always that of creating more types of musical organizations,
but rather to find resolutions to   1)   How was music leadership
in the community going to achieve dynamic programs of music
for all its citizens?   2)   How would it be possible to unite the
school music programs with community life programs?   If music
education had a grip on both problems, music education would more
likely become more functional for all members of society.   The
pupil must have the encouragement and support of the parent and
the school.   The child must be allowed to experience the functional
power of music in his life,   3)   There was need for developing a
professionalized spirit among all musicians.   There was need for
a high sense of dedicated professionalism.   Without it the cause
of music's growth would be stunted.   Professional attitudes were
expounded to help the cause of all music education.

Notes

1. Swift, E. Hargrave. "A Historical Study of the Develop-
    ment of the High School Band." Unpublished Master's
    Thesis. University of Southern California, 1939. 12-13.

2. Ibid., 13.

3. Ibid., 13-18.

4. Ibid., 98.

5. Letter from Secretary of Music Educators National
    Conference, November 18, 1941; Also: "The Competition-
    Festivals," Music Educators Journal, 28:35. (January,
    1942). 71-72.

6. After Fifteen Years of School Bands and Orchestras.
    C. G. Conn, Ltd., Educational Department, (Elkhart,
    Indiana.: C. G. Conn, Ltd.,). 1.

7. Ibid., 1.

8. Editorial, Musician. Vol. XXXV. No. 1 (January, 1930).

9. Galloway, Judge Tod B. "Millions and Millions for
    Musical Education," The Etude. Vol. L. No. 9
    (September, 1932). 620-622.

10. Engles, George. "Radio Friend or Enemy of the Music
    Profession?" The Musician. Vol. XXXV. No. 9
    (September, 1930).

11. Ibid.

12. Ibid.

13. Music, Leaflet No. 17. United States Office of Education,
    (Washington, D. C.: U. S. Government Printing Office,
    1931). 3.

14. "The Federal Music Project, Dr. Nikolai Sokoloff,
    Director." Division Women's and Professional Projects,
    Ellen S. Woodward, Assistant Administrator. 1500
    I Street, Washington, D. C. 2-4.

15. Ibid., 3-8.

16. Ibid.

17. Ibid.

18. Studebaker, John W. "A Federal Note in Music
     Education," Music Educators Journal, Chicago. Vol.
     XXIII. No. 4. 22.

19. Ibid., 22.

20. Ibid., 23.

21. "The World of Music," Musical Digest. Vol. XXI:
     No. 4 (April, 1936). 25.

22. Ibid., 25.

23. "The Problem of the Foreign Born Artist," Musical
     Courier. Vol. LVII, No. 3. (February 10, 1937). 16.

24. "Controversial View of Dickstein Bill," Musical Courier.
     Vol. LVII, No. 3 (February 10, 1937). 17.

25. Ibid., 17.

26. American Universities and Colleges. (Edited by Clarence
     Stephan Marsh) Washington: American Council on
     Education, 1936. 74.

27. "Degrees," The Phi Delta Kappan. Chicago XIX. No. 5
     (January, 1937). 123.

28. Van De Wall, William. Psychotherapeutic Value of Music.
     (New York: National Bureau For The Advancement of
     Music, 1925). 3.

29. Ibid., 6.

30. Ibid., 8.

31. Ibid., 9.

32. Ibid., 13.

33. "The Federal Music Project. Dr. Nikolai Sokoloff,
     Director." Division of Women's and Professional Pro-
     jects, Ellen S. Woodward, Assistant Administrator,
     1500 I Street, Washington, D. C. 21.

34. Ibid.

XVI. THE DEPRESSION YEARS:
      MUSIC EDUCATION MARCHES FORWARD

This was a period of social and economic upheaval that had
a profound effect upon music education in America. During this
era (1929-1939) many pertinent questions were asked about school
music education. Some of them were: 1) What affect did
financial stress during the period have upon sustaining music
education in school curricula? 2) Was the depression era a
"trial ground" for justification of its inclusion or elimination in
the curriculum? 3) How well did music fare in its own right?
4) Did music curricula sustainment and curtailment reflect a
general curricula rather than an extra curricula curtailment?

Many school boards, superintendents, teachers, lay, and
professional people were having discussions which included the
advisability of including and continuing music as a part of the
regular school program. School men pointed out on numerous
occasions that great changes had taken place in the amount and
quality of music education which was being offered in schools.
A study during that period revealed that music was still holding
its own favorably with academic subjects. Had its status changed
since 1929?

Research reflects situations where some supervisors found
salary, budget, and position curtailed or eliminated. Though
justifiable in some cases, it is unfair to give the general impression that music was being ruthlessly wiped out of school programs. Obviously there is concern to hear individuals interpret
such instances as being indicative of general practice.

In 1933 the United States Commissioner of education, George
F. Zook, published a report of the effects of the economic crisis
on general education in United States. The report depicts a picture
of the outlook for the school year 1933-34. So provocative of

concern were the results that an attempt should be made to understand the relationship of conditions to music education.   He compared the financial situation, teaching load, departmental eliminations, curtailments and staff withdrawals in the "frill" subjects
with comparable criteria in basic curricular subjects. [1]

Under the leadership of C. M. Tremaine, a Commission was
appointed to study costs and economic-social values of music
education. [2]   The study indicated that music education was to remain a part of the educational program.

The commission sent out 3, 330 questionnaires to superintendents of schools in America.   Of the original number sent
53 percent or 1, 761 were returned.   Of the number returned,
94 percent were filled out by superintendents; the remaining 6 percent included "a few music supervisors, teachers of music, supervisors of music and art, and directors of research. "[3]

Replies were received from every state.   Tabulation and
interpretation was as follows:

Group I.   Towns of less than 5, 000 from which 685
               questionnaires were received.

Group II.   Towns of 5, 000 to 15, 000 from which 637
               questionnaires were received.

Group III.   Towns of 15, 000 to 100, 000 from which 353
               questionnaires were received.

Group IV.   Towns of 100, 000 or more from which 86
               replies were received.

The first question asked: "Have the cultural subjects (music,
art, dramatics) been eliminated in your school system, or recently
curtailed as compared with the academic subjects?   State which,
if either, in a, b, c, or d below:

a.   In the elementary school?
b.   In the junior high school?
c.   In the senior high school?
d.   Has the curtailment been greater in some
     of the cultural subjects than in others?"[4]

The commission report provided information for the following
table (Table I) which serves as a résumé for Question 1.

Table I[5]

Question: Have the cultural subjects (music, art, dramatics) been eliminated in your school system, or recently curtailed as compared with the academic subjects?

1,761 schools reporting

	(A) Number of Replies	(B) Number of No Change, Music, Art, Dramatics	(C) Number of No Change Music Only	(D) Number of Curtailments	(E) Number of Eliminations	Combined No. of Curtailments and Eliminations
Group I . . .	685	303 or 44%	369 or 54%	276 or 40%	40 or 6%	316 or 46%
Group II . .	637	270 or 42%	323 or 51%	299 or 47%	15 or 2%	314 or 49%
Group III . .	353	163 or 47%	176 or 50%	172 or 49%	5 or 1%	177 or 50%
Group IV . .	86	31 or 36%	36 or 42%	50 or 58%	. . . .	50 or 58%
Grand Total .	1761	767 or 44%	904 or 51%	797 or 45%	60 or 4%	857 or 49%

Reflections and Some Prognostications.   Column (A) presents
the number of replies to the various questions by population groups;
(B) It cannot be justified to say that the larger communities made
a fewer "Number of No Changes in Music, Art, and Drama. "   In
all probability larger communities are less likely to make artistic
curtailments; (C) There was apparently no high relationship between size of city and the extent of "No Change Music Only. "
From the facts we might conclude that the smaller cities retained
their music program nearly as tenaciously as did the larger cities;
(D) Number of curtailments.   Cities of greater size probably did
no better job of retaining music departmental activities.   Group IV
indicates a 58 percent curtailment, this percentage being somewhat
higher than percentage cuts for Groups I, II, or III.   Consideration
must be given to the meaning of curtailment in the smaller communities when compared with a like statement for larger cities.

Cuts in the music program for cities of 100, 000 population
may still provide considerable music for each individual student.
What happens in a city of 5, 000 or less may be more far-reaching
in its drastic nature, if a comparable percentage of curtailment is
made with the larger cities affected.   (E) If the fewer number of
replies are sufficiently significant to indicate "Departmental Eliminations, " it may be that the smaller communities made more;
however, absolute evidence is not represented by this study.
Further investigation bears out the trend as manifested in the
study as reported by the commission; (F) When "Combined Number
of Curtailments and Eliminations" are considered, there is justification for the statement that no great relationship exists between
size of community and the number of departmental curtailments
and eliminations.

Grand Total figures for Table I in order of greatest percentage frequency are:

Column	Replies	Per Cent
(C) Number of No Change in Music Only	904	51
(F) Combined Number of Curtailments and Eliminations........	857	49
(D) Number of Curtailments.......	797	45
(B) Number of No Change in Music, Art, or Drama..............	767	44
(E) Number of Eliminations.......	60	4

This summary of 1,761 replies is self-evident. For one to generalize that "wholesale extirpation" of music departments had taken place during the depression was a gross exaggeration of facts, especially in view of these findings.

Table II presents the situation as revealed in a report of 700 typical cities. According to this chart, music education apparently did not suffer much greater departmental curtailment or elimination than did other special subjects popularly known as "frill" subjects.

TABLE II

Distribution of Curtailed School Services in
Seven Hundred Typical American Cities*

Curtailment and Eliminations				
Subject	Numbers Curtailed	Per Cent	Numbers Eliminated	Per Cent
Art Education	67	9.5	36	5.1
Music Program	110	15.7	29	4.1
Physical Education	81	11.5	28	4.0
Home Ec. Education	65	9.2	19	2.7
Art Education	58	8.2	24	3.4
Health Service Education	89	12.7	22	3.1

* Table Constructed from report by Zook, George F. United States Commissioner of Education, Department of Interior, Office of Education, November 10, 1933.

Obtaining facts about a person's salary by the questionnaire method sometimes results in unreliable information of negligible value. The commission headed by Tremaine probably secured from Question 2, their most incomplete data:

Question 2: "If the Music Department has been curtailed, to what extent has this been done? (Include here any reductions in personnel and salaries; also material and time allotment)."[6]

Table III[6]

Question: If the Music Department
has been curtailed, to what
extent has this been done?

1,761 schools reporting

	Total Replies	Less than 10%	10-20%	21-33%	33 1/3-50%	Undefined	No Salary Cut	Number Replies
Group I . . .	685	6 or .9%	63 or 9%	19 or 3%	7 or 9%	63 or .9%	15 or 2%	75% or 512
Group II. . .	637	4 or .6%	55 or 8%	16 or 3%	4 or .6%	69 or 11%	20 or 3%	74% or 469
Group III . .	353	1 or .3%	33 or 9%	10 or 3%	5 or 1%	27 or 8%	10 or 3%	76% or 267
Group IV . .	86	1 or 1%	10 or 12%	2 or 2%	0 or 0%	7 or 8%	4 or 5%	72% or 62
Grand Total	1761	12 or .7%	161 or 9%	47 or 3%	16 or .9%	166 or 9%	49 or 3%	74% or1310

Prognostication on the basis of Table III, would be unwise. The few returns must be taken at face value.

A questionnaire study of Wisconsin, South Dakota, and North Dakota in 1934 reporting salary reduction <u>indicate no relationship</u> <u>between the size of the salary and the per cent cut.</u>   An instructor receiving a high salary did not necessarily receive a high per-cent salary reduction. [7]   Reductions for Wisconsin Music Super-visors' salaries were so generalized that they were not itemized in a manner acceptable for table distribution.   Forty-eight replies revealed the following data: eighty-three percent of the teachers reported that they had received salary cuts since 1930.   The cuts ranged from two percent to fifty percent, the average being ap-proximately twenty percent.

TABLE IV

Distribution of Per Cent Salary Reductions
for North Dakota Music Supervisors

Per Cent Reductions	Number of Teachers
60-69	2
50-59	-
40-49	2
30-39	15
20-29	10
10-19	1
1- 9	2
0	5
	$\overline{37}$

N_3

Q 36. 50%

Mdn   30. 66%

Q_1 21. 75%

TABLE V

Distribution of Per Cent Salary Reductions
for South Dakota Music Supervisors

Per Cent Reductions	Number of Teachers
50	1
35	3
32 1/2	9
27 1/2	4
25	3
22 1/2	8
15	3
11	2
0	8
	41

N
Q_3 32. %
Mdn   22. %
Q_1 15. %

Tables IV and V present a frequency distribution of salary reductions obtained from North and South Dakota; North Dakota's median reduction was 31 percent while South Dakota's was 22 percent.   Of the forty-two percent who returned questionnaires from North Dakota, seven percent stated "we have no music supervisor now" or "we have eliminated our music supervisor as a depression measure."   Other towns were sustaining music teachers and supervisors, making this possible by salary reductions.   One city of prominence in North Dakota stated that the music supervisor's salary of $900.00 was being raised this year (1933-34) by service club subscriptions.   Another supervisor stated:

> For what the information is worth to you, I will say that
> my position formerly paid $3000.00 per annum (to my
> predecessor).   I began at $2550.00, now cut to $1980.00

> Besides my work as instrumental director was expanded
> to include vocal music (in Senior High School) and the
> vocal supervisor (salary $1800.00) was dropped. 8

Music teacher's salaries in Minnesota during the same period
indicated a median stipend of $130 per month for nine months or
$1170 for the period.   These figures reflect salary reductions;
the median in 1931 was $1388 (See Table VIII).   These data do
depict the situation typical of the area and the era.

The Dakotas apparently weathered pitiable circumstances, as
some of its communities although large, had a median which was
roughly $100 per year less than that of Minnesota for the same
period.   All cities reported in the studies gave reports from
accredited high schools and the towns in Wisconsin and Minnesota
were of less than 25,000 population.

The study further revealed that approximately fifty percent
of the music teachers in Wisconsin, North and South Dakota had
college degrees. The percentage in Minnesota was a little higher--
about sixty percent.   The music teacher was gradually eliminating
the question of academic ridicule concerning his competency
qualifications.   Table VI indicates comparatively the music-
academic qualifications of music teachers on the basis of a 1934
study. 9

TABLE VI

Degree Qualifications of Music Teachers
in Public Schools of Wisconsin,
North Dakota, and Minnesota.

Name of Degree	Wisc.	Degree Frequency No. Dak.	Minn. *
M. Music	2	–	–
B. Arts	6	–	52
B. Ed.	3	–	–
B. Mus.	20	20**	12
B. Mus. Ed.	3	–	–
B. Sc.	6	–	34
Diploma (4 years)	–	–	5
Diploma (3 years)	2	–	15
Diploma (2 years)	–	20***	21
Diploma (1 years)	–	–	–
No Degrees	7	–	2
No. Cases	49	40	141

*   Figures based on 1931 Survey
**   Total includes the various kinds of Bachelor's Degrees
***   Total includes two year academic and music conservatory
       work

TABLE VII

Distribution of Per Cent Salary Reductions*
Based on Statistics Derived from
700 Typical Cities[10]

State	Proportion of Teachers	Per Cent Reductions Range or Amount	Per Cent Loss in Warrants
Arizona	All	20-40	10
Colorado	All	5-20	Some
Illinois	All	10	Much
Iowa	50%	(8)	
Kansas	All	30 Approx.	
Louisiana	All	20 Aver. 10-40	
Michigan	All	1-60	Additional
Missouri	All (Rural...	25 loss of from one to four months salary.)	
	75%	Less than "Blanket Code" minimum unskilled factory labor $728 per year.	
	97%	Rural..will receive less than $728 per year.	
	10%	Rural...will work for less than $320 per year.	
Nebraska	All	40	
Oklahoma	All	24 Approx.	
Tennessee	All	25	
Virginia	All	20 Approx.	
Washington	All	220 Approx.	

* "One-half of all teacher (1933-34) will receive $750 per year or less; legal minimum now $40 per month."

TABLE VIII

Distribution of Salaries Statistically Compared for South Dakota, North Dakota, Wisconsin and Minnesota During School Years 1930-31, 1933-34, 1934-35.

State	Number Teachers	Source of Information	Date of Study	Mdn.	Q₃	Average	Low	High
So. Dakota	41	Ques.	May 1934	$1075	$1355	$ 891.27	$ 450	$ 1800
Wisconsin*	48	Ques.	May 1934			1293.60	900	2390
No. Dakota*	39	Ques.	May 1934			910.70	600	1980
Minnesota**	162	Ques.	1930-31	1388				
Minnesota***	404x	St. D.	1934-35	1170			800	2800
N	694							

Legend:

*   Median and Q₃ not obtainable due to manner in which the salaries were reported for these two states.

**   Figures based on facts derived from Mr. A. N. Jones, Master's thesis 1931. University of Minnesota Library.

***   Facts based on 1934-35 salaries obtained from records, Department of Education, St. Paul, Minn.

x   Represents full time salaried supervisors.

Table IX reveals changes (eliminations and additions in ten academic and one non-academic subject) in the program of studies of Illinois High Schools accredited by the North Central Association of Colleges and Secondary Schools since June 30, 1929. Of the eleven secondary school subjects, five are strictly academic fields and six may be considered special subject matter classifications. These findings indicate that

1) Remarkable similarity exists between the Illinois survey of "Changes which have been made in the program of studies, " and the findings of the National Research Council and studies by Sunderman and Jones;

2) To some degree one may postulate on the basis of the 379 schools reported in the Illinois survey that special subject matter fields are doing a better job than just "holding their own" as compared with the academic subjects;

3) We also observe that all schools considered in Group III and IV made appreciably more departmental additions than eliminations;

4) Group II had one academic subject manifesting more eliminations than additions;

5) In Group I, we find the same situation as mentioned in (4) with the additional feature of one academic subject having an equal number of eliminations and additions. [11]

TABLE IX: Changes Made in the Program of Studies of Illinois High Schools Since June 30, 1929

	Group I: Less Than 200 Pupils		Group II: Less 200-499 Pupils		Group III: 500-999 Pupils		Group IV: 1000 or more Pupils		All Schools		Ratio
Total No. of Schs.	138		125		47		69		379		
No. add. no. Subjs.	29		29		9		10		77		
No. elim. no. Subjs.	63		54		24		25		166		
Subjects by Fields	No. Schs. Elim.	Add.	No. Schs. Elim.	Add.	No. Schs. Elim.	Add.	No. Schs. Elim.	Add.	No. Schs. Elim.	Add.	
English	3	15	2	19	0	16	4	26	9	76	8-1
For. Lang.	36	17	47	19	5	12	9	34	97	82	39-1
Agric.	0	18	0	18	1	2	0	1	1	39	1.7-1
Soc. Studies	47	77	23	34	11	23	21	43	102	177	1.8-1
Science	29	40	13	21	7	14	0	12	49	87	1.8-1
Comm.	19	97	20	55	11	31	0	42	50	225	5-1
Math.	6	17	2	11	0	16	0	3	8	47	6-1
Indust. Arts	7	7	3	15	4	6	4	20	18	48	3-1
Home Econ.	19	13	5	25	3	8	4	9	31	55	1.8-1
Art / Drawing	4	6	5	7	3	7	1	5	13	25	2-1
Phys. Educ.	0	7	0	11	0	5	3	4	3	27	9-1
Aggreg. No. Schools Adding/Elim. Courses	174	332	124	253	45	157	46	212	389	954	
	8/		10/		11/		11/		10/		

TABLE X

Showing Names of Subjects Offered, Administrative Unit Values of Subjects, and Percentages of Schools Offering These Subjects During the Years, 1932-1933, 1933-1934, and 1934-1935 in Over 550 Accredited Public Schools in Illinois

Percentage of Schools Offering Different Subjects

Names of Subjects	Unit Values of Subjects	Group I 100 or Fewer			Group II 101-250			Group III 251-500			Group IV 500-1000			Group V 1000 and Over		
		32-33	33-34	34-35	32-33	33-34	34-35	32-33	33-34	34-35	32-33	33-34	34-35	32-33	33-34	34-35
MUSIC																
Harmony I	1	3.5	3.3	3.3	5.9	5.8	5.6	11.3	10.6	12.6	18.6	16.7	28.5	51.5	40.	50.
Harmony I	1/2	1.	.4	.4	.5			5.	1.2	1.2				6.4	5.7	5.8
Hist. of Mus.	1	1.5	.9	5.1	5.9	6.3	5.1	11.3	8.2	8.8	9.3	2.8	8.5	19.3	17.1	19.4
Hist. of Mus.	1/2				1.8	1.5	1.5	2.5	3.5		2.3			3.2		
Appreciation	1	1.	1.5	1.5	5.5	3.9		8.8	4.2	13.9	18.6	13.9	20.	32.2	14.3	27.8
Appreciation	1/2		.4	.4	1.3	1.5	5.6	2.5	1.5		2.3	2.8	2.8	6.4	8.6	2.8
Composite Course	1	2.5	2.9	2.9	5.	4.3	8.4	6.3	7.1	7.5	25.6	11.1	22.8	16.1	8.6	8.3
Applied Music	1	17.	32.8	32.8	22.4	45.1	20.6	32.5			51.2	72.2	42.7	51.5	54.3	33.3
Applied Music	1/2	2.	.9	.9	1.3	2.4		2.5			4.7	16.7	5.7	5.8	5.8	2.8
Band	1/4; 1/2, 1		.9	23.9					61.2	54.4					96.3	83.4
Orchestra	1/4; 1/2, 1		1.9	21.6					48.3	40.4					94.2	80.5
Glee Club	1/4; 1/2, 1		2.4	31.4					68.3	40.4					58.8	69.4

Tables IX and X, tabulating the results of the Illinois Survey of Accredited Public High Schools offering music, give credence to the statement that "music education is marching on." These tables indicate the schools offering the subjects suggested for academic credit for 1933-1935. Some conclusions are:

1) The 1934 report revealed that all schools suffered some retrenchment;

2) Advances were made in 1935 over 1934;

3) The omnibus course idea which incorporates a conglomeration of music history, music appreciation, and theory or harmony was rapidly losing its hold in the larger school systems. This music course is difficult to organize;

4) In 1935 all high schools offering the courses requiring less financial outlay, (harmony, appreciation, history of music, glee clubs) indicated greater come back strength than did either band or orchestra.

Members of the Tremaine commission in their study on "Costs and Economic-Social Values of Music Education" submitted the following as the third question.

"If there has been curtailment, which of the following do you consider the chief cause, and which one subsidiary cause:

a) Pressure from taxpayers demanding reduction in school subjects?
b) Lack of appreciation of the value of the department?
c) Unsatisfactory supervisors or teachers?
d) Other causes? (Please State.)[12]

The replies to the four parts of the third question were largely in the form of check marks with, however, frequent naming of other causes beside the first three specified. No definite date, however, was given as to which were the chief and which the subsidiary causes. In many, if not all cases, there were evidently several causes, since we find frequently check marks under two, three, or even four headings. Consequently, the four parts of the tabulation must be interpreted independently, and it is impossible to check on the results in the sense that the sum of the causes given will equal 100%. [13]

Table XI reveals the following: 1) Schools in all group classifications indicate that of the 904 school systems checked "no curtailment" was made. This figure representing as it does 51 percent of all the replies is consistent with other studies; 2) "Pressure from Taxation" adjustments evidently were a big factor in curtailment

TABLE XI

Question: If There Has Been Curtailment, What Are the Chief Reasons?

Group Total Replies	Total Curtailment	Pressure from Taxation	Lack of Appreciation	Unsatisfactory Supervisors	Other Causes	Causes Not Specific	No Curtailment
Group I... 685	316 or 46%	256 or 81%	52 or 17%	38 or 12%	58 or 18%	43 or 14%	369 or 54%
Group II.. 637	314 or 49%	227 or 72%	41 or 13%	38 or 12%	77 or 25%	41 or 13%	323 or 51%
Group III..353	177 or 50%	101 or 57%	18 or 11%	14 or 8%	53 or 30%	20 or 11%	176 or 50%
Group IV.. 86	50 or 58%	35 or 72%	2 or 4%	1 or 2%	17 or 34%	7 or 14%	36 or 42%
Grand Total 1761	857 or 49%	619 or 72%	113 or 13%	91 or 11%	205 or 24%	111 or 13%	904 or 51%

of school music programs; 3) "Lack of Appreciation" by community and school boards revealed that there was still a great
opportunity for music educators to prove to the community the
values of a music education; 4) "Unsatisfactory Supervisors"
will always be a ubiquitous problem for school superintendents
to surmount. Who should share the responsibility for this particular
problem? There are at least three major conflicting agencies
who may aid in its amelioration:

    a) Educational institutions which have sometimes been over
       zealous in crowding music education departments with
       numbers rather than fully considering the candidate's
       potential as a teacher;

    b) Music faculties that are often composed of non-academic
       members who are interested in a conservatory type of
       music education;

    c) Parents who, misguided by pride or other extraneous
       motives, bring undue pressure upon their child's selection
       of music as a career.

Professional Honesty. If highly selected and trained people
are to be hired for the teaching of music in educational institutions,
then the selection process must begin at the moment an individual
applies for entrance into the training program. Too many music
schools admit and encourage individuals with minor musical talents.
Early in the 1920's, for example, matriculation to a music program in many schools was effected merely by the desire to become a music supervisor. This sort of situation in any era is
deplorable and can only bring disaster to music education.

The answer to the problem lies in the tightening up of basic
prerequisite qualifications before a prospective music teacher
candidate is allowed to embark on a career. Entrance requirements, testing programs, and evidence of talent in the field are
not too much to ask. It is necessary that professional honesty
prevail in the training institutions.

A study by the author found that institutions in the same state
were at variance to the extent of from 15 to 30 quarter hours in

music academic work required for a major in public school music.
It was found that one major would have as much more additional
work as another individual had for his entire major requirement.
One student parades the country with a "baccalaureate sheet" and,
when comparison is made with another on the basis of name, both
individuals would apparently be comparably qualified.   "Bachelors"
they may be, and baccalaureates they become irrespective of any
great training standardization requirements.   Administrators were
encouraged to seriously evaluate the 'sheets' offered as evidence
of adequate preparation.

This author further found that of 104 majors in a music
department, sixty-six percent were there because their parents
thought it culturally desirable and probably professionally remunerative.   In all probability music education majors represent
a talent selection which is far above the median of mass population
scores; talent was one of the many considerations.   It is not
infrequent to find a student entering music education whose back-
ground or musical development is inferior to the musical performance of superior high school juniors and seniors.

Academic vs. Conservatory Perspectives.   The rapidly changing
panorama of education during this era impinged upon music teachers
the need for becoming educators.   In 1934 Jones and Sunderman
found that there were departments of music offering baccalaureates
in music education with no member of the faculties in question
(which consisted of nine in one case) having such a degree.
Further, it was found that a state institution was offering a master
of music degree with less than 10 percent of the faculty possessing
a comparable degree.   How could guidance be given research unless
the faculties offering such degrees had training with the tools and
techniques pertinent to educational investigation?

Music Education vs the Concert Perfection Objective.   Music
education met a need for mass education which could be attained
through concert performance objectives.   The music teaching
profession had been partially responsible for some of the false
objectives which had been established in the minds of some credulous

individuals.   Concert perfection and 'star' ideas had permeated
lay and professional thinking.   Thousands were ready to perform,
but the profession was so overcrowded with wealth and fortune
seekers, that many music appreciators found it impossible to pay
admission prices for concerts.

The Great Change.   The depression had wrought change in the
picture.   The 64,000 millionaires of 1929 had dwindled to 34,000
in 1932; some organized symphony orchestras ceased to exist;
opera companies which were once the pride of the genteel had
disappeared; great numbers of concert artists ceased to have
thirty and forty season bookings at $1,500 to $5,000 per booking;
favored few were they who were finding it possible to book a busy
concert season; prices of opera tickets had fallen considerably;
concert and operatic personages were finding incomes affected by
prevailing conditions.   Professional musicians, who prior to 1929
experienced monetary security, were experiencing difficulty in
obtaining remunerative employment.   The art that was the
expression of all was back in the control of the masses; it never
was any other place, except in the perfected art which found an
audience through the box-office.   Those who govern and control
mediums of musical expression must remember that they deal
with an art, which issues forth as an expression without major
pecuniary considerations.   Music will live if it is able to give
back its lovely expression and experiences at a price which all
can afford to pay.

Philosophy of The Era.   The idea expounded was that man has
an inherent right to music because it is a universal heritage.   Some
leaders of musical thought conceived music as an art with universal
expression not dependent upon any group for its realization.   The
countless thousands who still retained high hopes of artistic achievement needed caution not to lose sight of the fact that the masses
and not the genteel will always be the great reservoir of appreciators.   Another obstacle to greater strides of artistic music production in this country was the lack of acceptance of the fact that
music is universal.

TABLE XII

Grand Total Frequency Distribution of 1761 Returned Questionnaires of Tax
Payer, School Board, and Superintendent Attitudes

Grand Total for Groups I, II, III, IV	No Ans.	%	No. Ans. Rec'd.	%	Very Favorable	%	Favorable	%	Unfavorable	%
Taxpayer	149	8	1612	92	300	19	923	57	389	24
School Board	127	7	1634	93	471	29	1032	63	131	8
Superintendent	118	6	1643	94	695	42	920	56	28	2

The grand total frequency distribution of 1761 returned
questionnaires of tax payer, school board, and superintendent
attitudes toward music (Table XII) is indeed most enlightening.
The questionnaire study attempted to find an answer to the question

What is the general attitude in your community toward the
cultural subjects, and especially towards music:

(a) On the part of the taxpayers;

(b) On the part of the school board;

(c) On the part of the superintendent?

Is there a distinction in the general attitude between music
and other cultural subjects? If so, is it favorable or
unfavorable to music? [14]

The then current attitudes revealed that (1) At the present time
the superintendent is apparently more favorable to music education
than either the school board or taxpayer; (2) However, there is
reported 24 percent of "unfavorable" attitudes of the taxpayer toward
music which is altogether too great; (3) There appeared an urgency
on the part of music educators to expend greater efforts in demonstrating the important place music played in the education of
children. The taxpayer was not emotional about music and often
demanded a cold, unemotional demonstration of the necessity for
incorporating music in school curriculums. [15]

Table XIII shows a summary of collegiate graduates and teacher
placements in secondary major field interests for 1934 (Summer
session included). [16] The evidence reveals the demand for music
educators. During the period (1929-1934) when teacher placements
were still at a low ebb, the secondary school special fields,
particularly music education, demonstrated placement strength--
sometimes decidedly better than did the academic fields.

Of 11, 401 graduates qualified for academic fields, 5, 120 placements were made, or approximately 45 per cent. In the special
fields, 5, 717 were given degrees and 3, 280 were successful in
securing appointments, or 58 per cent. The academic fields
reported four fields marked thus ('), indicating areas of instruction
(text continued on p. 303)

TABLE XIII

Summary Distribution of Collegiate Graduates
and Teacher Placements in Secondary Major Field
Interests for 1933-34--Summer Session Included

Academic Fields	No. Qualified to Teach*	Positions Secured	Per Cent
Biology	659*	236	36
Botany	66	13	20
Chemistry	600*	175	29
Economics	114	14	12
Education	164	112	68-*(')
English	3,042	1,524*	50-*
"Foreign Language"	19	15	79-*(')
French	573*	203*	35
Geography	141*	63	45
German	106	28	26
Greek	7	. . .	. .
History	1,784*	793*	44
"Jr. High School"	283	160	67-*(')
Latin	453*	190*	42
Mathematics	1,189*	601*	51-*
"Modern Language"	17	7	41
"Natural Science"	583	235	40
Philosophy	19	6	32
Physics	61	14	23
Psychology	47	15	32
"Romance Language"	26	15	58-*
"Secondary"	76	51	67-*(')
Sociology	223	37	17
Social Studies	836	462	55-*
Spanish	126*	66	52-*
Speech	142*	66*	46
Zoology	90	19	21
Total Academic Fields	11,401*	5,120	45
Special Fields:			
Agriculture	242	171	71-*(')
Art Education	372*	167*	45
Bible & Religious Ed.	43	8	19
Child Welfare	30	18	60-*
Commercial Ed.	888*	490*	55-*
"Fine Arts"	13	10	77-*(')
Guidance	1	1	100-*(')
Home Economics	1,159	733*	63*
Industrial Ed.	611*	353	58-*
Journalism	11	7	64*
Library Methods	223*	91*	41

TABLE XIII cont.

Academic Fields	No. Qualified to Teach*	Positions Secured	Per Cent
Nursing	30	15	50-*
Physical Education	1, 169	607*	52-*
"Practical Arts"	21	18	86-*(')
Public School Music	896*	588*	66-*
Religious Education	2	1	50-*
School Health Work	2	1	50-*
Special Work	4	1	25
Total Special Fields	5, 717*	3, 280*	58-*
Total Secondary School	17, 118*	8, 400*	49

Legend:
*   Of the 394 institutions, 67 reported only grand totals of
-*   50 per cent placements or more.   (Grads and placements)
(')   2/3 placements or more.

attaining placement for 66 percent or more of those receiving their baccalaureates. The special fields including public school music had the same percent of placement, 896 graduates and 588 positions filled. The placements in the so-called 'fill fields' supported the fact that music education was moving forward. Music education during the depression era did move forward although sometimes uncertainly and haltingly.

Notes

1. United States Department of the Interior, Office of
    Education, Mr. George F. Zook, Report, November 10,
    1933.   Washington, D. C.

2. "The Present Status of School Music Instruction, " Music
    Educators National Conference Bulletin No. 16. , April,
    1934.   3.

3. Ibid. , 3.

4. Ibid. , 6.

5. Ibid. , 13.

6. Ibid. , 15.

7. One person, receiving $1, 000 had received a fifty per
    cent cut whereas another person receiving $2, 390 had
    sustained a reduction of only ten per cent.

8. Jones, Archie N. and Sunderman, Lloyd F.   "Degrees
    and Salaries of Music Teachers in Wisconsin, North
    Dakota, and Minnesota. " (Private Circular, University
    of Minnesota).

9. Senior Music Education Students Study, College of
    Education, University of Minnesota, Minneapolis,
    Minnesota, 1934.

10. "The Present States of School Music Instruction. " 3-17.

11. Ibid. , 8

12. Ibid.

13. Ibid. , 17.

14. Ibid. , 10.

15. Ibid. , 11.

16. Umstattd, J. G.   "Placement Success of the 1933-34
    Education Graduates of Three Hundred Seventy-Four
    Collegiate Institutions, " Bulletin of The National
    Institutional Teacher Placement Associations, I: No. 1
    (March 15, 1935).   (Minneapolis, Minn. : University of
    Minnesota, 1935).   16.

XVII: AFTER WORLD WAR II

Plans for music education at the end of World War II had their beginnings in the early 1940's. There was resistance, of course, from those of a conservative nature who doubted the wisdom of projected planning, especially when the fruition of proposed projects was seemingly so far-distant, but the need for an organized, well-planned and concerted effort toward planning for the future of music education was strong enough to overcome these objections.

With an eye toward the "New World" which was promised after the war, educators began to think in terms of a musical democracy: one that would have something for everyone regardless of his level of talent or ability. There was a need for the development of a new philosophy. It was suggested that music education concentrate its efforts not on making music masters of children, but on opening doors to music appreciation for the non-specialist--the average child.

Some Concepts. Some of the concepts developed in the 1940's regarding the future pattern of music education were as follows:

1) The music program should permit greater freedom of individual expression through music.

2) Children in primary grades should have more latitude for self-expression through music.

3) The child must be aided by sympathetic understanding and, through intelligently employed techniques, must be assisted in learning to respond to music's inherent beauty.

4) There should be available a masterful teacher who can assist the child in expressing himself through music.

Actual Planning. Based on the above concepts, actual planning for post-war music education was begun. Educators suggested the following:

1)   Cooperative studies be carried on with those educational
     agencies who could assist in the tabulation of statistical
     music data regarding the immediate music service needs
     at all educational levels.

2)   The establishment of music teacher-education courses
     be encouraged in teacher-training institutions which
     devote a major share of their course requirements for
     the preparation of elementary school music supervisors.

3)   A campaign be started utilizing the press and radio--
     through local, state, and national organizations for
     supporting state-wide rural school music programs.

4)   More elective music units be encouraged in the area of
     secondary education curriculums; suggestion that more
     units be acceptable toward credit for graduation from
     secondary schools.   (Some schools at that time permitted
     two units; many, just one.)

5)   A greater cooperative support be secured for music
     from administrators, educational specialists, and lay
     leaders.

6)   Music through various educational organizations both
     local and national in character be encouraged.

7)   Greater responsibility be assumed by teacher-education
     institutions for the preparation of better prepared music
     educators.   These centers of learning must enlarge
     their cultural influence.

8)   Campaigns be conducted through press and radio for
     the purpose of championing general music education
     for all members of society.

9)   Fitting slogans be disseminated.

10) State-wide coordinated programs of music supervision
     be instituted for all grades.   Music education should be
     available for both the juvenile and the adult.

11) The use of music as a social rehabilitator be encouraged.

Problems--financial and otherwise.   Plans, however well
formulated, are only valuable if they can be put into effect.   For
music education the bridge between planning and doing was money.
Educators were aware that the end of the war would bring a slow-
down of the economy and the country would be faced for a time
with instability in this respect.

Public supported programs, it was feared, were sure to be among the first to feel the pressures of a stepped down economy. Those on the side of music argued that because of its intrinsic value to mankind, music would surely receive public support and monies. The opposition argued that excessive public support of the arts was unnecessary, an argument that was countered with the opinion that no amount of money would be too great for those art forms which had been, and still were, a major force in the cultural development of man.

There were problems other than finance to be dealt with, however. The country was changing and the population was shifting. There was a widespread demand for educational retrenchment in some quarters because of a rather pronounced drop in school enroll- ments. The following reveals the basis for this demand:

> The proportion of the population under twenty years of age in 1930 was 38. 8 percent; in 1940, 34. 5 percent. It is estimated by the Census Bureau that by 1960 it will be 29 percent.

The birthrate had dipped to a low of 16. 6 percent per 1, 000 population in 1940, but by 1941 it showed only a small increase-- 18. 5 percent per 1, 000. [1]

It was feared that a cut in public support for education would mean a shifting in the per capita ratio of music educators: inadequate compensation could cause them to gravitate to better paying occupations, leaving their jobs to be filled by the inexperi- enced and less competent.

More than one-fourth of the large urban centers (population 100, 000 or more) lost population to the suburbs and rural areas during the period 1930-1940. In general, these were the cities which were providing security and higher salaries to their music educators, but even that factor could not mitigate the problems prompted by the tide of shifting population.

One further problem of the times, and unfortunately, one that is still present in many areas today, was that of local governments ignoring or only partially assuming their responsibilities toward education.

Agencies Basic to America's Musical Culture.   While the area
of education, and music education in particular, was struggling
for survival during these years, there were agencies and publications which directly aided the cause.   Some of these were   1)
The Music Educators' National Conference,   2) locally and
nationally supported educational organizations and institutions,
3)   privately endowed and state-supported institutions of learning--
colleges, music schools, etc. ,   4) music periodicals--publications
that were either in brochure or book form which devoted space to
music,   5)   private and commercial enterprises, and   6) community concerts and independently organized concert bureaus.

Demobilization and Music.   The signing of the G. I. Bill by
President Roosevelt in 1944 brought a new challenge to American
educators.   This Bill provided for the honorably discharged G. I.
an opportunity to pursue education where he left off or to review
already learned skills through a refresher course if he desired
it.   The Bill provided one year of refresher education or one year
of education.   The latter choice could be extended to a period
not exceeding four years, this extention being governed by the
veteran's length of service.   Ex-soldiers were soon taking
advantage of the provisions of the Bill and many of them registered
in music courses.   It would appear that cultural as well as
technical education was desired by the returning G. I.

Municipal Support of Music.   In 1925 legislation was passed
in 21 states which gave specific statutory permission to cities
and towns for the appropriation of funds for free public concerts.
These twenty-one states were

Alabama	Massachusetts	New York
California	Michigan	Ohio
Colorado	Minnesota	Pennsylvania
Illinois	Mississippi	South Dakota
Indiana	Montana	Texas
Iowa	Nebraska	Vermont
Kansas	New Hampshire	Wisconsin

In twelve of these states the laws specified band concerts
and the levy was generally set at 2 mills.

Some areas also found public support for symphony concerts and free "pop" concerts. The Detroit Symphony was known to have been given $30,000 from the city treasury for its pop concerts and Indianapolis Symphony funding in the amount of $50,000 was at one time shared by the city and the state. Cleveland, San Francisco, Minneapolis and Denver also had free pop concerts offered by their orchestras. Minneapolis boasted music appreciation concerts in addition.

Many cities around the country supported municipal organs. Among those cities supporting and enjoying this kind of musical activity were Portland (Oregon), Denver, St. Paul, Minneapolis, Dallas, San Antonio, Atlantic City, Atlanta, Springfield (Mass.), Westchester County (N.Y.), Cleveland, Toledo, Detroit and the Morman Tabernacle in Salt Lake City.

Municipal support of music could even be found in such activities as adult education. Much had been done under the old WPA programs of the thirties, but the post-war years provided even greater opportunities for music education. Municipalities and boards of education began to recognize that a community's responsibilities toward the education of its citizens does not end at age 18. The institution of adult education provided many people a "second chance" toward learning new skills, music being among them.

Church Music. Tours were made by internationally known colleges and church choirs. Among these were groups such as the St. Olaf College Choir, Northwestern University's A Cappella Choir and the Westminister Choir.

Music in the Home. Family musical groups were common during this time. Public libraries in Evanston, Indianapolis, Cleveland, Chicago, Detroit, Philadelphia, New York and an increasing number of smaller cities made available for circulation vocal and instrumental music. Many families took advantage of this free access to music scores and were able to enjoy a "togetherness" not afforded by many other activities.

Music in the Summer Camps.   By 1930 more than 1, 117, 000 boys and girls of elementary and secondary ages were attending summer music camps.   Some of the special activities which engaged their attention were

Glee Club	Light Opera
Choir	Folk Dancing
Vocal Quartet	Singing Games
Orchestra	Harmonica Bands
Band	Ukelele Groups
Chamber Music	

In their home communities children of this age were also exposed to music through settlement and community centers, neighborhood social centers, the YMCA and the YWCA.

Music in Art Museums.   Eleven museums offered 89 orchestral concerts for which the average attendance was 1, 555.   A sixty-five member orchestra at the Metropolitan Art Museum in New York had an average attendance of 8, 000, with 11, 000 being the peak for any one concert.   A small orchestra at the Art Institute of Chicago gave two identical concerts on Sunday afternoons from October to May for a total of fifty concerts.   Many of these were free while others required a nominal charge.   There were thirty choral concerts offered in ten museums, performances being given by organizations such as the Harvard Glee Club.   Five museums were the scenes of 165 recitals by professional organists.

American Opera.   There were two outstanding American opera companies, one each in New York and Chicago.   In addition, there were civic opera companies such as the American Grand Opera Company of Portland and the Atlanta Grand Opera Company.   Other cities sponsoring opera included Boston, Canton, Cincinnati, Cleveland, Dallas, Denver, Kansas City, Los Angeles, New Orleans, Oakland, Rochester, Salt Lake City, San Diego, San Francisco, Savannah, Seattle, St. Louis, Washington and the Cincinnati Zoo Opera Company.

Operatic works written by American composers prior to 1930 with their dates of performance were as follows:

Damrosch, Walter	The Scarlet Letter	1896
	Cyrano de Bergerac	1913
DeKoven, Reginald	Robinhood	1890
	Rip Van Winkle	1920
Hadley, Henry	Safie	1909
	Bianca	1916
Parker, Horatio	Mona	1912
Taylor, Deems	The King's Henchmen	1927
Bimboni, Alberto	Winona (All-Indian Opera)	
Breil, Joseph	Love Laughs at Lock-smiths	1910
	The Legend	1919
Coerne, Louis	Zenobia	1905

(First American opera by an American composer to have a performance in Europe: Bremen, Germany in December of 1905)

American composers were also working creatively in areas other than opera. Among the more distinguished of the period were

Chadwick, George	1854-1931
MacDowell, Edward	1861-1908
Parker, Horatio	1863-1919
Mason, Daniel Gregory	1873-1953
Ives, Charles	1874-1954
Taylor, Deems	1885-1966
Piston, Walter	1894-
Hanson, Howard	1896-
Sessions, Roger	1896-
Porter, Quincy	1897-1966
Harris, Roy	1898-
Gershwin, George	1898-1937
Thompson, Randall	1899-
Copland, Aaron	1900-

Status of Musical Growth 1941-1950. Great strides in music education were made during the decade of the 1940's. Measurable evidence points to more than 22,000,000 elementary school children, but of whom there was only one in every four who had the opportunity of having a school music lesson once a week. In spite of that statistic, there was evidence of accomplishments which read like

this: 1)   In 1941, 80, 897 boys and girls representing 2, 400 schools
were entered in the finals of the National School Music Competition,
2)   Among other surveys more than 2, 000, 000 players were
registered in 40, 000 bands and 25, 000 orchestras in American
Public Schools,   3)   An additional 900, 000 boys and girls from
American high schools participated in school music competition
or festivals of some kind,   4)   Colleges and conservatories in
1948 reported 2, 430, 000 students who were pursuing special, private
and specially conducted ecclesiastical courses,   5)   The Inter-
collegiate Musical Council numbered 6, 000 singers among its 100
participating college glee clubs.   There were another 130 colleges
who had applied for membership with an additional enrollment of
10, 000 singers,   6)   There were Women's College glee clubs with
large registrations at Smith, Vassar and Wellesley,   7)   The
National Federation of Music Clubs had over 400, 000 members
registered in nearly 5, 000 clubs who conducted local, state, and
national contests for the purpose of selecting winners in both vocal
and instrumental divisions,   8)   In innumerable communities thousands of high school and college musicians played in dance bands;
they were earning money which partially or wholly defrayed the
expenses of their education; most professional groups were
unionized,   9)   More than 1, 500, 000 adults participated yearly in
home study courses.   More adults attended public evening school
classes.   These were found in hundreds of cities and towns throughout the nation,   10)   Playground music reported from 766 cities in
1940 indicated that 7, 677 outdoor playgrounds were conducted under
trained leadership.   Nearly 25, 000 men and women were employed
as recreation leaders.   The largest proportion of the average daily
summer attendance of 3, 722, 358 was by children from seven to
fourteen years of age.   Activities included bands, harmonica bands,
orchestras, toy orchestras, and choral groups.   In 1946 there were
61, 500 cities with less than 50, 000 population and 53, 000 with less
than 1, 000.   Other categories of music activities indicate the vigor
of musical growth in America.

A National Music Education Society.   Prior to 1950 a vigorous start had been made in promoting a national music education organization.   There were six main concerns of this group:

1) State-wide coordinated programs of music supervision for all levels of education

2) De-emphasis upon the professionalization of musical talent and encouragement of music for the masses (Professionalization would be a natural concomitant of lay consumption and education during the latter half of the twentieth century)

3) Development of well-balanced school music programs that would emphasize total participation of educational forces at the local, state, and national levels

4) Retainment of the culture of the past, and through our composers, music educators, and professional musicians, the development of a national musical expression which would function as an expression of American creative talent

5) Encouragement of American educators to champion the idea of securing public support for making educational institutions serve the community beyond the generally accepted four o'clock school day

6) Enlistment of the aid of adults and service to them in ways only partially envisioned through adult training programs.

America had made tremendous strides in music education during the period prior to 1950 but the job was only begun; its success was dependent upon reaching all men and stressing the function of music in life.

Notes

1. The total number of births in 1942 was 2, 808, 996; for 1943 it was 2, 767, 081.   (Census Bureau Publication, Vital Statistics).   The United States Bureau of the Census estimates show 1945 as having the greatest number of the population under twenty-four years of age.   Until 1960 there will annually be a decreasing number of people under twenty-four years of age.

XVIII: THE PROFESSIONAL MUSICIAN AND THE
         PROFESSIONAL MUSIC EDUCATOR

The professional musician may have many individualized
characteristics.   His musical training is usually extensive.   There
is a possibility that he may not have a college degree.   A great
virtuoso must spend long hours in perfecting techniques which are
in keeping with the dignity of the phrase "Professional Musicianship, " and any academic endeavors he may engage in are relegated
to the few hours left him each day.   His defense for the lack of a
formal higher education lies in the plea "lack of time. "   It must
not be implied that he is disinterested in or incapable of scholar-
ship.   The musician of stature must have intelligence in keeping
with the demands of significant performance.

Frequently, the professional musician as a member of the
American community is probably a private studio teacher who may
also direct choral and instrumental ogranizations.   The larger
communities may offer him limited opportunities for directing
symphonic and operatic groups.   Often the remuneration is dis-
appointing.   Another outlet for his talents and a source of profit-
able professional employment are the television and radio programs
broadcast from five major metropolitan centers in America.   Not
every professional musician is able or prefers to live in one of
these five metropolitan areas and those who choose to live elsewhere find the market for their talents very limited.   Opportunities
for private teaching are numerous, but guaranteed remuneration
is almost non-existent.   The professional's income is often limited
to scattered employment in bands, choirs, orchestras, churches,
opera companies and various types of dance orchestras.

This kind of crisis in American music and the "economic
blight" for the professional which had been caused in the fifties
by canned music moved James C. Petrillo, President of the

International Board of Directors of The American Federation of
Musicians in 1954 to state:

> Of nearly 249, 000 A F of M members, slightly more than
> half are even largely supported by music. The 32 major
> symphony orchestras in the United States and Canada employ
> fewer than 2, 270 musicians. These elite instrumentalists
> of the music world work an average of only 22. 4 weeks a
> year at an average weekly pay of $81. Not more than
> 2, 000 musicians in the 2, 636 broadcasting stations of the
> United States (or less than one musician per station) enjoy
> a full year's employment. Between three and four thousand
> more are used with fair regularity in single broadcasting
> engagements.
>
> Theaters provide jobs for about 2, 000 musicians. The
> motion picture industry affords more or less steady work
> to about 350 staff musicians and for some 4, 000 non-
> traveling musicians. An indeterminate number of traveling
> musicians, numbering perhaps 50, 000, work most of a year.
>
> These are the favored few whose livelihood is fairly secure.
> Others, in addition, are among the 60, 000 musicians who
> share an income of approximately $2 million a year for
> making recordings. Their product, by contrast, earns for
> the machine music vendors a gross income of some $164
> millions annually.
>
> Those who earn the major part of their livelihood from
> music may be said to number 72, 000. Thus it is apparent
> that a staggering total of some 175, 000 professional
> musicians must supplement their income by other means. 1

As an illustration of what was being done in concert, radio,
television, and hi-fi phonograph and tape equipment, the following
1958 report vividly portrays what was being accomplished by these
media in the United States.

> Of the approximately 2, 000 symphony orchestras in the
> world, 1, 055 symphony orchestras are in the United States
> today, (1958) compared with less than 100 in 1920!
>
> There are an estimated 35, 000, 000 or more individual
> Americans actively interested in one form or another of
> concert music!
>
> In 1957, Americans continued to spend more money at the
> box office for concert music than they did for baseball!

Americans spent as much money for the purchase of recordings of concert music and high fidelity equipment on which
to play these recordings as they did on all spectator sports
in 1956!

During 1957, American radio stations planned to carry more
concert music than they did in previous years. One thou-
sand, two hundred and seventy-three stations programmed
an average of 8,780 hours of concert music each week
during 1956, an average of 6.9 hours per station per week!

As radio is greater today than it has been at any time in
its 36 year history, with 135 million radio sets in operation
and the average American family listening approximately
15.4 hours per week, broadcasters continue to play a major
role in bringing concert music to large audiences. An
indication of the tremendous audience for concert music
available to radio is the fact that more people hear a broadcast of the New York Philharmonic on a single Sunday than
could have heard it in Carnegie Hall in 110 years.

About $240,000,000 was spent on spectator sports in 1957.
In contrast to this Variety reported that $50,000,000 is
spent averagely at the concert music box office. About
$80,000,000 was spent for the purchase of concert music
on recordings. More than $166,000,000 was spent for the
purchase of high fidelity phonograph and tape equipment.
More than $40,000,000 was spent at retail for the purchase
of printed concert music and teaching pieces.

Sales of classical platters have soared to where they now
account for an astounding 35% ($70,000,000 plus) to 40% of
the industry's total business. As recently as 1946 'long
hair' discs represented a modest 15% of all record sales.
(from The Wall Street Journal)

The Institute of High Fidelity Manufacturers reported that
total volume of audio component business in 1956 was
$166,220,000. The breakdown is as follows: speaker
systems and enclosures, $42,000,000; amplifiers and pre-
amplifiers, $42,000,000; record changers, turntables and
accessories, $25,000,000; tape recorders, $16,000,000;
FM and AM tuners, $25,000,000. It was estimated that
the 1957 volume would go over the $200,000,000 mark. [2]

Petrillo further emphasized the plight of the professional
musician by indicating that "there is some hope that most of the
32 major symphonic organizations subsisting in metropolitan centers
may be able to survive. But in most cities of 300,000 population
or less, the days of serious music and skilled music and skilled

musicians are numbered. [3] Even now, the best that some of these
groups can offer is 10 weeks of employment at near starvation
wages to musicians of demonstrated ability.   These must seek
supplemental income, accepting for the sake of their art the flimsy
security of part-time jobs.   Without some minimum guarantee of
security for musicians serious music in America can only degenerate
into a 'second class' product.   That is unthinkable. "[4] He further
posits the idea that subsidy may "not be a pretty work in our
language" but such support may be the only remaining economic
hope for professional musicians under existing economic conditions.
Petrillo argued that the salvation of great music culture was at
stake.

In Cleveland, Ohio, Rudolph Bing, manager of the Metropolitan
Opera Association, stated that that organization would have to close
its doors unless they would be able to raise $1, 500, 000 by 1954.
Imagine such a statement from the manager of the only opera house
in America (with a lengthy season of opera)--actually pleading for
a pittance in order to continue giving operatic performances to the
people of this country.

Facts cannot be denied.   The Metropolitan has resorted to
every form of appeal (even to the stopping of a performance) in
order to emphasize its plight.   It would seem fair to maintain that
if the 169, 000, 000 Americans wanted such art, they would not have
lacked in their enthusiasm by barely supporting the drives the
Association conducted for maintenance.

But there are encouraging evidences of progress.   The mid-
century reports gave rise to much encouragement regarding
American operatic activity.   Twelve months prior to October 15,
1956, there were "600 performing organizations in forty-seven
states, plus the District of Columbia, [presenting] 3, 581 stage
performances of opera, overwhelmingly in English.   Three
organizations in five were educational--colleges, high and elementary
schools, conservatories.   Of the remainder, about 15% were likewise non-professional; clubs, churches, studios, settlement houses,
a hotel.   That leaves 25% of the companies professional, or one in

four. " Continuing, this report relates: "The survey published two
years ago listed 444 companies in forty-five states, of which 40%
were professional.   Three years ago the total of the companies was
386.   The number of performances has grown, but not sensationally.
Last year the figure was 3, 217; three years ago, 2, 704. "[5]   Among
colleges there were 184 performing organizations.   Last year this
category recorded 167 and three years ago 111.   It remained for
the high school and church groups to indicate the greatest growth.
At the high school level there were 110 performing organizations
and among the churches 35.   Last year these figures were 96 and
23 respectively.   Three years ago there were 43 high school
organizations. [6]

This evidence of operatic activity is the type of development
which must take place before it can be said that a healthy music
productivity characterizes our culture.   An imbalance between
artistic productivity and its consumption will occur whenever our
public schools have ceased to create within its future citizens a
passionate appreciation for musical beauty and understanding.
Music must become a pulsating vital need in the lives of Americans.
Music educators must keep their eye focused on the major task--
the musical education of the 230, 000, 000 or more who are expected
to be its citizens by the end of the present century.   Such a
population portends the task that lies ahead.

Musical Growth.   The countless opportunities for musical
enjoyment provide sources of instruction to be pursued both in the
classroom and the home.   These experiences in music should be
functional in the life of the child and should not stop in the school.
There should be a constant check on the part of the teacher to
determine to what use each child is making of his musical endowment and interest.   Does the teacher encourage the child to evaluate
the quality of the music that is being permitted in the home?   Is
the child stimulated to become interested in singing or playing
with home mechanical producers?   Urge them to sing with their
parents and the radio.   If whistling or humming is more successful,
such a technique is stimulating and pleasurable.   It is the active

participator that knows the thrill of musical enjoyment; knowledge comes from familiarity with the tools of music. Musical experiences to be stimulating cannot be passive. There must be recreative moments.

The School Music Educator. The music educator, as he functions in the American school system, may be designated by various titles. He may be known as an administrator, supervisor, consultant, specialist, or teacher of music. The professional school music educator is that person who, by demonstrated musicianship and understanding of educational theory as applied to the teaching of music, should have developed an expertness for imparting music instruction to the youth in our public and private schools. It bears noting that the purist's determination of the professional musician is often characterized by the requirement for excellence of performance. Excellence, it may be added, is usually achieved at the expense of much practice and dedicated attention to technical minutiae. However, this definition may not be sufficiently broad to include the school music educator who must be both musician and teacher. He must possess those qualifications that will enable him to perform competently, even though he does not always possess those qualifications that are characteristic of the concert artist.

The typical school music educator is qualified to teach music in both public and private schools. He has graduated from an accredited college, university, or private conservatory. He has had four or more years of collegiate training, having pursued a music major consisting of from forty to ninety semester hours of credit, containing academic, music, and professional music education courses. As a performer, he usually excels as a singer or as a performer on one or more instruments. His musical training has included some keyboard study. He must have been certified by a state department of education in order to qualify to teach in public schools.

Typically, the position occupied by the school music educator provides him with a steady income, tenurial privileges, and retire-

ment income.   He often pursues his music avocationally as well
as vocationally--he may very likely be earning additional income
as a member of a symphony orchestra, or as a choir singer, band
director, or choral director.   Many music educators maintain
private music studios where they teach music during after-school
hours.   The music educator is usually more interested in serving
the creative needs of many people than he is in promoting the
personal performance ambitions of a few.   In conclusion, professional music educators are (or should be) intensely interested
in aiding others how to learn.   It was Prescott who said, "Children
cannot be taught but they can learn. "[7]

All administrative, supervisory, and teaching personnel to whom
we refer as music educators, must have intelligence, musicianship,
emotional stability, and physical well-being if they are to be successfu
in the capacity in which they are to serve.   Neither the music
administrator nor the teacher should have a heart like an iceberg
nor a mind like a volcano.   Rather, the personalities of both should
be characterized by understanding, warmth, and humaneness in
order that they may be effective in acquainting individuals with all
forms of musical art.   Certain significant personality traits and
understandings are required of those who would successfully pursue
the musical arts.   Among these are: 1) Music educators must be
well-trained musicians possessed of acknowledged musicianship,   2)
They must constantly evince high professional idealisms which are
properly tempered by a practicality making for philosophical understandings which are suited to the needs of individuals of varying
abilities,   3) They must have a genuine desire to understand all
those who come under their tutelage,   4) They must champion a
philosophy of education that is all-encompassing in its usefulness
for practical daily living.

The music educator must be a leader, and in order to fill
this place in his community he must possess the admirable traits
we have just indicated.   As a leader, his success will be dependent
upon his ability to attract others who will be willing, if necessary,
to make sacrifices of time, effort, and even money, in order to

achieve an artistic ideal. Knowledge and imagination are not enough; without the faculty for imparting his ideas and without the ability to arouse in others a desire to achieve and to understand, the teacher will fail.

Professional Musicians and The Music Educator. The music educator is a professional musician. If his profession is to survive it must be reinforced by all musicians who earn their livelihood from musical pursuits. The music profession includes that great body of professional musicians, the members of The American Federation of Musicians, and all music educators, either publicly or privately employed, who pursue music as a means of personal and aesthetic satisfaction and occupational livelihood.

With the great development of school bands, choirs, and orchestras, during the last twenty-five years, and with the inception of the mechanization of music -- television, radio, and mechanized music reproduction -- the American Federation of Musicians, Music Educators National Conference, and the American Association of School Administrators adopted a Code of Ethics[8] or policy of Professional Relations. It was first adopted jointly in 1947 and renewed by the co-partners again in 1948. It has continued in force since the original signing and its original Code structure is still in force with little change.

Under the heading of Music, the Code states:

> The field of music education, including the teaching of music and such demonstrations of music education as do not directly conflict with the interests of the professional musician, is the province of the music educator. It is the primary purpose of all the parties signatory hereto that the professional musician shall have the fullest protection in his efforts to earn his living from the rendition of music; to that end it is recognized and accepted that all music performances by school students under the "Code of Ethics" herein set forth shall be in connection with non-profit, non-commercial enterprises. Under the heading of "Music Education" should be included the following:
>
> (1) School Functions initiated by the schools as a part of a school program, whether in a school building or other buildings.

(2) Community Functions organized in the interest of the schools strictly for educational purposes, such as those that might be originated by the Parent-Teacher Association.

(3) School Exhibits prepared as a part of the school district's courtesies for educational organizations or educational conventions being entertained in the district.

(4) Educational Broadcasts which have the purpose of demonstrating or illustrating pupils' achievements in music study, or which represent the culmination of a period of study and rehearsal. Included in this category are local, state, regional and national school music festivals and competitions held under the auspices of schools, colleges, and/or educational organizations on a non-profit basis and broadcast to acquaint the public with the results of music instruction in the schools.

(5) Civic Occasions of local, state or national patriotic interest, of sufficient breadth to enlist the sympathies and cooperation of all persons, such as those held by the G. A. R., American Legion, and Veterans of Foreign Wars in connection with their Memorial Day services in the cemeteries. It is understood that affairs of this kind may be participated in only when such participation does not in the least usurp the rights and privileges of local professional musicians.

(6) Benefit Performances for local charities, such as the Welfare Federations, Red Cross, hospitals, etc., when and where local professional musicians would like-wise donate their services.

(7) Educational or Civic Services that might beforehand be mutually agreed upon by the school authorities and official representatives of local professional musicians.

(8) Audition Recordings for study purposes made in the classroom or in connection with contest or festival performances by students, such recordings to be limited to exclusive use by the students and their teachers, and not offered for general sale or other public distribution. This definition pertains only to the purpose and utilization of audition recordings and not to matters concerned with copyright regulations. Compliance with copyright requirements applying to recording of compositions not in the public domain is the responsibility of the school, college or educational organizations under whose auspices the recordings are made.

Pertaining to music education and classified as Entertainment, the Code of Ethics continues:

The field of entertainment is the province of the professional musician.   Under this heading are the following:

(1) Civic parades, ceremonies, expositions, community
concerts, and community-center activities (see I, paragraph
2 for further definition); regattas, non-scholastic contests,
festivals, athletic games, activities or celebrations, and
the like; national, state and county fairs (See I, paragraph
5 for further definition).

(2) Functions for the furtherance, directly or indirectly, of
any public or private enterprise; functions by chambers of
commerce, boards of trade, and commercial clubs or
associations.

(3) Any occasion that is partisan or sectarian in character
or purpose.

(4) Functions of clubs, societies, civic or fraternal
organizations.

Statements that funds are not available for the employment
of professional musicians, or that if the talents of amateur
musical organizations cannot be had, other musicians cannot
or will not be employed, or that the amateur musicians are
to play without remuneration of any kind, are all immaterial.

This code was originally signed by James C. Petrillo for
the American Federation of Musicians, Luther A Richman,
for The Music Educators National Conference, and Herold C.
Hunt For the American Association of School Administrators,
and originally dated at Chicago, September 22, 1947. [9]

This portion of a momentous document for protecting the
integrity, prestige, employment and eventual preservation of
individual musical talents indicates the impact of the growing
profession of music in America during an age of great industrial
development.   The seriousness of the professional musician's
plight was stated recently by James C. Petrillo, President of the
American Federation of Musicians, when he said:

The day fast approaches when there will be no adequate
supply of skilled musicians.   The present dearth of competent string instrumentalists is desperate enough to evoke
immediate concern.   Without orchestras and ensembles to
employ them the incentive for students to play stringed
instruments will disappear completely.   One depends on
the other and without them, our nation's heritage of music
eventually will consist only of historical libraries of
recordings.   There will be no new music, no youthful talent

coming along to man our symphonies or make new records.
There will be only memories of a better day when musical
culture was a cherished part of the American way of life.
We can hope that our generation won't see the debacle, but
it approaches so fast that even we may see that sorry
day. [10]

The Professional Musician - A Challenge To The Music
Educator.   Undoubtedly a deterrent to progress in music education
currently is the ill effect of early twentieth century professionalism.
The great emphasis and insistence upon performance for "winning"
developed rapidly during the era 1926-1945.   The idea of winning
resulted in a type of specialization which was understood and more
easily attainable by the musically gifted.   The less talented were
often forced to stand by and lose the joyous experience which music
participation provided.   Individuals who did not possess the minimum
talent requirements necessary to specialized performance very
often developed a distaste for that music education which was
designed for the performing few.   Too often the professional
musician and only less so the music educator have lost a vision
of the musical needs of our school population.

In a generation we developed a stage full of performers and an
audience that had not grown in proportionate numbers to those who
discriminate the understandings of musical art.   A gulf had developed
between the performer and the spectator because the ideals of
the former and the lack of musical knowledge of the latter were
unrealistic.   Very often the musical performance was too "long-
haired" for the consumer.   This conflicting understanding of needs
on the part of the performers, lacking a practical philosophy of
music education for every individual has been a deterrent to
musical growth.   The ideal is still attempting to develop a
generation of individuals who have a desire to derive enjoyment
from music through self-expression.   It must be realized that solo
art is reserved for but a limited proportion of society.

When a program of music education is designed for mass
participation and enjoyment it will then begin to serve with greater
effectiveness.   The experiences derived from singing, playing an

instrument, dancing, and composing provide innumerable opportunities for growth in musical knowledge. It is about these
experiences that a good program of music education can be
constructed. If the program is an imaginative one, every individual will experience varied music experiences. Whenever an
art gets too far removed from the participative experiences of
the society it serves, it easily becomes relegated to serve the
talented few.

No brief is held against the philosophy that professionalism
is not essential to the progress of musical art. The long existent
belief that participation in music study must of necessity entail
HANON AND CZERNY before the enjoyment of musical art may be
realized is no longer educationally valid.

The professional musician is the inspiration and creative
backbone of all music--music in any form needs a creator and
re-creator. Both the professional musician and the music educator
are creatively and re-creatively productive. Musicians have been
known to build concentric circles of egotism and importance about
themselves which may do injustice to the significance of their
contribution to the cause of music education.

Music education does not need more objectives, attainments,
curriculums or programs, but it needs educators who can relevel
their sights on a philosophy of music education which is designed
for all men. This philosophy must envision the aspirations of the
musician, but it must never lose sight of the great segment of our
population whose aesthetic needs, artistic capacities, and musical
creativity are in keeping with their limited artistic capacities to
comprehend music. Musical enjoyment and creativeness are much
like other intellectual creations. Creativity and the use to which
it is put is usually proportional to the inherent intellectual and
artistic capacities of the individual.

An individual's concept of musical performance standards
varies with his intellectual capacity, training, and cultural back-
ground. Quality of performance varies within these related factors.
Among individuals these capacities are somewhat evenly distributed.

Great variation does exist in training opportunities and in the
accumulation of cultural backgrounds. These two factors do much
to alter the nature -- the true quality of an artistic musical
performance.

If our thesis is sound, then levels of quality of musical
performance must of necessity vary widely among the communities,
states, and nations of the world. Frequently there appears to
exist a chasm between the musical idealisms of the professional
musician and the school music educator. This undoubtedly occurs
because the professional musician perceives his achievements as
idealized performance, whereas, the school music educator con-
ceives mass music education superior to that of isolated instances
of highly specialized performance. The level of performance to
which the competent professional aspires is excellence in technique
and performance; whereas the music educator, recognizing that his
field of endeavor requires him to create inspiring musical experiences for great numbers possessed of varying degrees of talent,
often seeks his success on a musical level that may fall far short
of artistic excellence.

The professional musician is often critical about the quality
of the performance obtained by the music educator in our public
schools. Conversely, the music educator looks upon the professional musician as an artistic and oftentimes impractical
dreamer, far removed from educational reality. Schuman, speaking of these divergent philosophies of the professional musician
and the music educator, believes that "many professional musicians
do, in fact, evaluate school music from a narrow point of view.
Let me assure you, however, that my own experience with school
music has given me a realistic understanding of the problems
you face. I recognize, for example, that music-making in the
schools often has a goal which is not that of musical excellence
alone. Music is used for other purposes. "[11] He continues by
positing the thesis "that school music affords opportunities for
group activities and has the capacity for aiding in the general
development of students, both individually and as a social entity,

which other subject areas do not as effectively provide. But is there anything inconsistent between this approach and that of the achievement of high musical standards? Not if the difference between the uses of music for social values and the standards required for the performance of music in public schools is clearly understood. The performance of music in public demands meeting an objective standard. "[12] We insist that music's attainments in realms of human satisfactions must be achieved rather than assumed. Schuman's assertion that school music has the capacity for aiding general development more effectively than other academic areas is a claim for the intellectual superiority of music which might be difficult to support.

Schuman recognizes that "the problems of school music are many, " and he asks "what solution can be proposed which will preserve the social values for which music is used in the schools and at the same time achieve acceptable musical standards?" Would you not agree that no musical performance should be given in public which does not meet acceptable standards; that, however socially valuable the musical training has been for a particular group of students, there should not be a public performance which is not valid musically? A poor performance of a piece of music does a disservice to the art of music, regardless of what developmental benefits may accrue to the students taking part in such a performance. No musical performance should be given in public which cannot meet acceptable musical standards. [13] We vigorously support his general thesis that standards in music education must be maintained at all costs, but there can be much argument over his last statement that, "No musical performance should be given in public which cannot meet acceptable standards. "

The state of American music education is such that much school music performance is not acceptable. Schuman evaluates performance excellence by those criteria which he has learned to use in his determination of acceptability. It is obvious that there are many mitigating factors involved in the determination of what is acceptable musical performance for elementary and secondary

school. It is highly probable that some phases of school music
performance will always be that way -- the music educator will
always deal with those who are young in training and experience!
It is important to be an idealist, but it is likewise important to
be be a practical idealist. If all school music is to be "acceptable"
before the child enjoys the experience of performance, many school
music organizations may only infrequently appear in public. Who
is to determine what is acceptable? Will it be William Schuman,
other professional musicians, or will it be a teacher in a self-
contained school? Quality of musical performance depends upon
good literature that is well performed. Literature cannot be good
unless it is well written. Good performance implies intelligent
artistic interpretation and presentation. We are inclined to
attribute poor musical performance not entirely to the quality of
the literature, but rather to the inadequacy of the musician inter-
preting the music.

There are many mitigating circumstances which must be
evaluated before an assessment can be made of Schuman's statements. The following tempering facts may modify his evaluation
of American school music performance standards:

> 1. It is estimated that only one out of every four children
> in American elementary schools has music intruction
> under the supervision of a music educator once each week.

> 2. Elementary music instruction is no more regular than
> the appearance of the music instructor. We know of one
> community of over 300, 000 population that does not provide
> music supervision (instruction) or a lesson taught by a
> qualified musician for its classroom teachers more than
> three times a year!

> 3. Most American elementary school music is taught by
> regular inservice classroom teachers who teach music under
> duress, or more certainly do not profess to be musicians,
> and who even avoid such instruction whenever possible.

> 4. These in-service teachers have had at most but six
> semesters (on the average) of collegiate level music training
> as preparation for teaching their classroom music.

5.   In-service teachers are usually selected for their
positions because of academic training, ability, and probable
promise for teaching successfully a dozen subject areas,
which are "bread and butter" subjects for the pupils' eventual
economic and social well being.   (Availability is often the
sole criterion for selection).   To be sure there are even
a few among these elementary and secondary school teachers
who graduated from music conservatories and professional
music schools, but who failed economically as concert
artists and who have turned to the more stable financial
outlook which elementary and secondary teaching provides!
Apparently they did not measure up to the standards demanded of those who attain success as professional musicians.
Then too, there may have been an insufficient number of
individuals who had been well trained musically.   Music
administrators have been known to be incapable of understanding the economic needs of trained musicians for social
living.   Eventually someone will have to accept some
responsibility for intellectual dishonesty.   Professional
guidance in teacher-training institutions will help to eliminate
those candidates who are pursuing music careers, but who
are woefully lacking in musicianship and ability.

6.   Both the pupil and the in-service classroom teacher
often achieve musical satisfactions which are satisfying to
them, but which may be artistically unrewarding to the
professional musician.   Always keep in mind that simple
musical expression in song and dance is in keeping with
their talents and elementary knowledge of music.

This author has always insisted that it is just as absurd to
assume music for every child and every child for music[14] as it
is to demand standard attainments in mathematics, physics, and
chemistry for every child intrigued by test tubes.   Psychological
measurement of individual differences has amply attested to the
truth of the statement that whether it be in the artistic, academic,
or in physical motor expressional areas of man's potentialities,
his achievement is determined by his ability.   In no area of human
endeavor is one able to say that all have attained acceptable
standards.   For everybody, "acceptable" may be impossible!

It is a sad commentary on American music education, if
music teaching is conducted as Schuman declares: He states
that he has "heard it stated over and over again by many teachers
that the band room is first of all a place for the boys and girls
to blow off steam.   If, they argue, the musical results are not

always what they should be, the results in social values are
sufficient justification.   In other words, school music is often
regarded as a social force and, if you wish, as a therapeutic
agent.   These uses are often considered more important than
musical excellence itself. "[15] To all this we counter by stating
that the competent music educators and teachers of school music
do have high professional ideals.   Those who are not making a
contribution to high musical standards may be ineffectual for
many reasons: (1) They are not musicians,   (2) They may
reflect the unfortunate teacher-training programs which are in
part responsible for the poor quality of their teaching,   (3) Music
departments in conservatories and colleges have not assumed their
responsibility by discouraging the less gifted musically from entering the profession.   Institutions such as the one that Schuman
directed must shoulder their share of the responsibility for the
existence of the condition which he so severely criticizes.   Music
departments must discourage those individuals who are potentially
ill-equipped by talent, training, and idealisms, to achieve the
musical excellence to which Schuman alludes.   The music excellence
which he envisions will be more readily resolved by the more
selective recruitment of teacher-musicians.

Schuman is on the right track when he states that an insufficient amount of contemporary music is being used by school
music educators.   There is much contemporary music available
that is worthwhile and to which youth in our schools will respond.
If the music educator received his professional training in an
environment of classicism, he may become desensitized or wholly
unfamiliar with contemporary music because he lacked familiarity
with it.   The contemporary musician is capable of producing music
of artistic merit.   The professional music school must assume full
responsibility for nurturing its students in the contemporary medium.
It is a sine qua non that educational theory is often delayed in its
practice by a generation or more.   There is an ever-increasing
amount of good contemporary music being produced.   The well-
trained musician must become familiar with it.

The aforementioned circumstances have done much to militate
against the quality of music teaching in American schools.   The
"qualitative range of their (public school music groups) musical
performance is often astonishing. "[16]   Unfortunately we cannot
agree with Schuman's logic when he says "If students in the
schools do not vary greatly in terms of their general musicality,
what is it then that causes this wide quantitative gamut in school
music performance?   The answer is simple in the extreme.   The
quality of performance in school music is in direct proportion to
the musical skills of the teacher. "[17]   Schuman's thesis is ill-
conceived--students in music schools vary in ability and intelligence.
the normal probability curve of musical ability and intelligence.
Performance results will gravitate about the median of the curve.
The good teacher working with a wide range of musical ability
will atempt to produce performances in keeping with his skill as
a teacher.   It is obvious that results are dependent upon the
talent available and the "musical skills of the teacher. "[18]

The Music Critic And The Music Educator.   Great musical
art has always thrived in an environment where there were many
standards.   But in a society made up of countless appreciative
understandings, it naturally follows that there can be no fixed
standard measurement of musical performance.   An educational
measurement that is sound must succeed in evaluating with fidelity
what it purports to measure, but often the wrong evaluation is
made of the educational objective that is to be attained.

The educator and the professional music critic are often poles
apart hurling the invective "impractical dreamer, " at each other
because each believes the other person is not capable of properly
evaluating musical achievement nor does he understand the problem.
We contend that there is both an educational and professional
standard.   The professional musician and the professional school
music teacher are confronted with qualitative and quantitative
performance problems.   The music critic is able to adjudicate a
professional's performance, but he may do a great disservice to
amateur performance, because he may be most inept at applying

qualitative measurement to primary, elementary, and secondary
school music.   Until an individual or group has attained professional
stature, achievement must be evaluated accordingly.

The professional music critic plays an important role in
society.   Through his musical criticisms and literary evaluations,
he reveals his musical stature.   His criticisms are usually
evaluations of performances by outstanding musical organizations
and personalities.   Criticism should reflect and interpret his
opinion based upon judgments seasoned in the cauldron of training
and extensive experience.   His standards are man made.   His
evaluations reveal either objectivity or the lack of it in determining
integrity of performance.   The music critic must reveal his
scholarly judgments through spoken and written criticism and they
in turn should become guideposts for charting new avenues for
greater musical achievement.   He who has attained the stature
of a competent critic cannot assume that he is also qualified to
interpret the educational objectives of a good school music program.
Unless he has been actively associated with the problems concerned
with developing primary, elementary, and secondary school programs, it would seem wise that he learn what they are.   Frequently
a chasm of misunderstanding exists between the music critic and
the school music educator.

School music education is designed to meet the artistic needs
and developmental growth patterns of youth.   Music educators must
attempt to discern how music can serve the healthy development of
the psychological and emotional growth of individuals.   Unless the
professional music critic has been associated with youth, their
training, their attainments, and what they may be capable of
achieving, he is likely to make erroneous appraisals.   Standards
for evaluating performance cannot be understood nor established
without close study of all these facets of child growth.

An improper standard of achievement imposed upon youth may
cause much individual and artistic maladjustment.   It may bring
about personality frustrations and thwart the development of a
child's artistic nature.   A child needs patient tolerance and under-

standing through the formative years of mental and physical growth.
The professional musician, although ordinarily without training in
psychology or psychometrics, must nevertheless have some knowledge and understanding of the levels of achievement which are
practical and possible for the child.

The professional music critic is often severely criticized for
being too far removed from reality in evaluating public school
achievements.   Conversely the music educator is frequently blamed
by professionals as being musically incompetent.   By implication
the professional often asserts that the "school music teacher" is
just a school teacher with little serious music training.   The music
educator is more often reproved for his inability to perform than
for any other deficiency in his musical ability.

To the professional musician, musicianship and qualifications
for teaching music must always be associated with performance.
Since 1945, there has been an increased emphasis upon securing
more and better qualified teachers.   There has been an increasing
number of professional musicians entering the teaching professions.
Many institutions of higher learning have been emphasizing the
importance of good teaching and the necessity for encouraging
people of outstanding musical ability to enter the profession.

Much of the professional antipathy which the critic and school
music teacher may have for each other is due in part to the nature
of the work they pursue.   Whereas the music critic objectively
attempts to evaluate professional performances, the school music
educator is concerned with initiating those early music experiences
for the child, which although often discouraging, aid him in attaining eventual satisfaction.   To initiate the early experiences in
individual and ensemble choral, band, and orchestral playing
requires teacher inspirations which transcend the comprehension
of those who witness the fruits of such efforts.   The musician
who has "arrived" often finds it difficult to appreciate the child's
early frustrations in trying to make his instrument perform satisfactorily.   This accomplished musician's attitude of disdain could
not prevent a child from becoming discouraged to the point of

discontinuing all efforts to learn.   Such a level of performance and
skill is poles removed from the professional who is deriving
satisfactions which the beginner has not experienced.

When professional evaluations are made, they must be formed
in proper perspective.   If the music critic is to participate in the
evaluation of pupil performance, he must understand what constitutes
reasonable achievement.   The music educator in the schools must
constantly encourage achievement in a manner that is both encouraging and challenging.   An attainable objective must always appear
to be within the child's grasp.   Professional criticism should never
overwhelm a child at any stage of development to the point that
he gives up.   Millions of instruments are set aside and banished to
the attics of American homes long before their owners have had
the joy of experiencing music.   The learning stage in the acquisition
of any skill is often discouraging.   Only the exceptionally talented
child is by nature endowed with those personality traits which will
carry him beyond disparagement in his attempt to achieve performance success.   The child with less talent needs a sympathetic
teacher who can bring about enjoyment during the learning process.

Notes

1.   Diminuendo.   American Federation of Musicians of The
     United States and Canada, New York, 1954.   9.   (Section
     One, "The Crisis in Live Music Today").   James C.
     Petrillo, President.   It is reported that since 1954, the
     average weekly salary of $81. has become larger.   The
     socalled recession of 1958 may have again altered the
     reported increase.

2.   "Concert Music U.S.A. 1958."   (New York, N.Y.:
     Broadcast Music, Inc., 1958).   1-8.

3.   Italics are the writers.

4.   Diminuendo.   11.

5.   "U.S. Opera Compass 1955-1956."   Opera News.   (New
     York, N.Y.:   The Metropolitan Opera Guild, Inc., 21:
     No. 3 (November 19, 1956).   4.

6.   Ibid., 4-5.

7. Education 2000 A. D.   C. W. Hunnicut, editor.   (Syracuse,
    N. Y.: Syracuse University Press, 1956).   52.

8. "For Understanding and Cooperation Between School and
    Professional Musicians," Music Educators Journal, 41:
    No. 5 (April-May, 1955).   37.

9. Ibid.

10. Ibid., "The Crisis in Live Music Today."   23.

11. Schuman, William.   "The Responsibility of Music Education
    to Music," Music Educators Journal, 42: No. 6 (June-
    July, 1956).   17.

12. Ibid.

13. Ibid.

14. Slogan for American Music Educators and adopted by the
    Music Educators National Conference.

15. Schuman, Ibid., 17.

16. Ibid., 18.

17. Ibid.,

18. Ibid.

XIX. THE PROFESSIONAL ORGANIZATION OF MUSIC EDUCATORS

The Music Educators National Conference today stands as a
monument to the heroic efforts of many individuals.   Music
educators are indebted to the early trio of vocal music teachers,
Elam Ives, George J. Webb, and Lowell Mason.   It was under
their leadership, and especially that of Mason, that the first
experimental attempts at introducing music into many of the Boston
schools were started in 1832 and 1833.   Later, the pioneer efforts
of Lowell Mason were consummated by the official introduction of
music into the Boston schools in 1838.   Throughout the nineteenth
century individuals and organized groups did much to further the
development of music in American schools.

However, it was not until 1907, when the Music Supervisors'
National Conference came into being, that the phenomenal growth
of school music was started on its way.   Later, in 1934 its name
was changed to the Music Educators' National Conference.   The
present stature of the Conference has been attained through its
many national and international functions.   Today the MENC is
undoubtedly the only organization of its kind that so completely
serves the cause of music through its many official organizations
and representatives.

Just how has the MENC attained this status and become the
mobilizer of the creative energies of more than 55,000 school
music educators in the United States?   Just what has it proclaimed
through its many organizational offices that gives it such an
important place in modern education?   In all of the activities
participated in by the MENC, there has been slowly but surely
developing a consciousness on the part of educators that music
education is a profession in its own right.   It has evolved a
philosophy of education that brings into its orbit of activity all
aspects of those arts which are directly or indirectly related to

music.

Although the official introduction of music into our American schools came with its inclusion in the curriculum of the schools of Boston in 1838, a permanent organizational unit for the professionalization of activities related to school music was not initiated until 1907 when a small group of 67 people met in Keokuk, Iowa to discuss their mutual problems in conference.

The MENC has carried its influence into various service and humanitarian organizations. As a result of a project with the American Junior Red Cross, children in chapters all over the world are listening to recordings made by American high school bands, orchestras, choruses, and instrumental and vocal ensembles. A special MENC committee, appointed in 1948, screened over 300 recordings made by fifty groups in the United States; enough were selected to make up 1,000 albums of six records each. These were sent to Junior Red Cross chapters throughout the world.

The MENC is effectively meeting the problems confronting music education through its many affiliate organizations and especially through its co-operative efforts with the National Education Association. Through a professional feeling of belonging, the members of the Conference have found personal expression in their work with State, Division, and National organizational units. In another direction, there is close liaison with the Musicians Union and National Congress of Parents and Teachers.

Under the aegis of UNESCO, there has been established an International Society for Music Education. The General Conference on Music in General Education, which was devoted to an appraisal of the "role of music in the education of youth and adults,"[1] held its first meeting in Brussels in 1953. It was this meeting that the functioning commissions issued resolutions and recommendations which indicated the Society's breadth of interests. The principal commissions were (1) Music in General Education in School and Community, and (2) Education of the Professional Musician, whether as teacher, performer, composer, musicologist, or otherwise.[2] The resolutions and recommendations issued by all commissions were:

1. Music education is a part of general education.

2. Every child, no matter what degree of talent he possesses, is entitled to basic instruction and participation in music as part of his education.

3. Private teachers and composers should be more closely linked with the general system of music education.

4. Listing of opportunities for teacher training in various countries should be provided and exchange of music educators facilitated.

5. UNESCO is requested to publish a series of monographs on the status of music education in each of its member states.

6. Greater consideration should be given to the choice and transmission of works of the highest quality. [3]

Later, in the summer of 1955, the First General Assembly of the International Society for Music Education met in Lindau, Germany and in Zurich, Switzerland. A meeting was held in Hamburg, Germany in June of 1957. The prime objective of these movements is the promotion of music education opportunities for people throughout the entire world. It is believed that this international understanding of the objectives of the "profession" of music education should be shared by people of all nations. The United States under the leadership of the MENC has given great impetus and encouragement to these projects.

Bengt Franzen, a Swedish delegate to the 1953 Brussels Conference on Music Education, related that in June 1952 delegates to a conference on music education from four Scandinavian countries had assembled in Stockholm for discussions on the music educator and the composer. Their deliberations resulted in the formation of a Scandinavian union for music education. [4] They pursued a reevaluation of the importance of the composer, educator, and performer in enriched musical experiences for all.

The leaders in music education in Southeast Asia held a regional meeting in Manila in 1953, sponsored by the Philippine

Government.   Nordic Music Teachers convened in Helsinki,
Finland in August, 1955.   Cities such as Montevideo in Uruguay,
South America, and Melbourne, Australia, hosted meetings in
1956.   Lawler states that, "The International Society of Music
Education belongs to the music educators all over the world.   It
should be borne in mind that the principal commissions of ISME
are (1) Music in General Education in School and Community, and
(2) Education of the Professional Musician, whether as teacher,
performer, composer, musicologist, or otherwise.   This is a
broad program, to be sure, and yet it is inevitable that there
must be a common meeting ground for those responsible for the
education of children through and in music, and those responsible
for the education of the professional musician.   Members of the
Society representing both the fields of music in general education
and the education of the professional musician who were in Brussels
in 1953, and in Lindau and Zurich in 1955, were unanimous in the
all-inclusiveness of the program of the Society. "[5]

Inter-American and Inter-Hemisphere Music Education.   Inter-
American and Inter-Hemisphere music education were inaugurated
just prior to 1940.   This was just a century after the first introduction of music into American public schools.   The exchange of
cultural relations between North Americans and South Americans
was unquestionably an outgrowth of the good neighbor policy which
was largely initiated by the United States Government.

The Coolidge administration did much to start an improvement
in our relations with Latin America.   Hoover, as President-elect,
made a good-will tour of Latin America.   When Herbert Hoover
left the White House, "our cultural relations with Latin America
were better than they had been at any time in the past thirty
years. "[6]   President Franklin Roosevelt further strengthened the
work of his two predecessors and declared in his first inaugural
address that he "would dedicate this nation to the policy of the
good neighbor. "[7]   Thus, there was established a positive program
of governmental policy toward the encouragement of better cultural
exchange with Latin America.   Prior to this effort on the part of

the United States Government, Latin and South American countries usually looked to Europeans for cultural inspiration and leadership. "Then with the threat of World War II, the political and economic interests and finally, the cultural, began to be drawn together through the Good Neighbor Policy. Artists, writers, dancers, poets, and musicians were sent to Latin America and were invited from Latin America to visit the United States. The Pan American Union, the international organization representing all of the American Republics including the United States, established a Division of Music (after fifty-two years of existence!). With this flow of persons north and south, there emerged a unique situation. The vanguard of North American musicians (composers, musicologists, performers) who first went south, discovered the all-inclusive music interests of Latin American musicians -- that the Latin American musicians (musicologist, composer and performer) were also interested in music teaching in the schools, an interest not generally common ten years ago among North American composers, musicologists and performers. The Latin American musicians, musicologists, composers and performers who came north made a discovery. They found a new profession of music, namely, music education, not musical education, as they had experienced it in their own countries and in European schools and conservatories. They found boys and girls in many United States schools receiving education in music as part of their general education. They saw for the first time teacher education in music in our state teachers colleges and universities as contrasted with the conservatory plan of training, so prevalent in Latin America and Europe. [8] Undoubtedly the major purpose of the inter-American movement and the good neighbor policy was the interchange of the forementioned cultural relations -- it brought together large groups of professional peoples.

It was Charles Seeger, who as Chief of the Division of Music of the Pan American Union, envisioned the great opportunities for music education on an inter-American cultural exchange basis. He enlisted the support of the largest professional music education organization in the United States -- the Music Educators National Conference.

Naturally, the progress that was achieved was further aided by "the Government of the United States through its Department of State and the special wartime organization of the United States then known as the Office of the Coordinator of Inter-American Affairs -- the international organization, the Pan American Union (now the Organization of American States) and the private, professional organization, and the Music Educators' National Conference. "[9]

The Outcomes.   This was the era of the "One World" of Wendell Wilkie.   It is the beginning of a shattering of the concept that the Americas were insular in their interrelationships.   Below are listed some of the outcomes which were influential in accomplishing this far-reaching cultural expansion.

1.   There was increased cultural exchange which included artists, writers, dancers, poets, and musicians, who were sent by the United States to Latin America; the Latin American countries, in turn, reciprocated by sending representative artists to the United States.

The inter-hemisphere cultural exchange emphasized the leadership of the United States in music education. The nations of the Western Hemisphere looked to America rather than to Europe for significant music leadership.

2.   Under the leadership of the Pan American Union and in cooperation with the Music Educators National Conference and American publishers, more than one hundred and fifty Latin American music publications had been produced by 1949. [10]

3.   The Latin and South American Countries have found appreciation in the United States for the products of their musical creativity.

4.   Unquestionably the exchange of musicians and music educators brought to the attention of our sister countries the great school music developments which had taken place in the United States.

5. It was in Latin America that music education through
the Music Educators National Conference had made
its first appearance outside of the United States. [11]

There were many interesting expansions of these outcomes
through the observance of widespread development of music
education in South America. Music educators and musicians in
Chile, Colombia, Venezuela, Uruguay, Argentina, Brazil, and Peru,
showed much interest and even acceptance of various aspects of
the philosophy of music teaching as practiced in the United States.
Further reforms have taken place in their teacher-training curriculums as evidenced by reports from Chile and Peru. Lawler
says that,

> The music educators of the United States and their
> professional organization can justifiably be proud of their
> contribution. They have started their philosophy and
> technique of music education on its way around the
> world -- with other peoples and in other countries whose
> customs, heritage and way of life are quite different
> from ours.... Our hope in the United States should be
> that we can continue to expand our horizons -- our
> advancement program -- so that music education can
> open doors for itself and for music educators, not alone
> in this hemisphere, but in countries all over the world. [12]

Continuing Growth of The Music Educators National Conference.
The MENC, through its vast organizational structure, is making
it possible for every member educator in our public schools to look
to it with pride and for help. Its many regional administrative
and organizational units (Eastern, North Central, Northwest,
Southern, Southwestern, and Western Division) are persevering
in their efforts to sponsor every worthwhile professional music
education enterprise. Among the many organizations, there are
associated The National Interscholastic Music Activities Commission,
Music Industry Council, College and Directors National Association,
National Association of College Wind and Percussion Instructors,
Council of Past-Presidents, Music Education Research Council,
Music Educators' Journal, Editorial Board, Journal of Research
in Music Education Editorial Committee, MENC Student Membership
Counselors, State Presidents' National Assembly, Council of State
Editors, Council of State Supervisors of Music, Council of In- and

About Clubs, State Music Educators Associations (State Units of
the Music Educators National Conference), State Music Education
Periodicals and Editors, State Supervisors of Music, International
Society for Music Education, and Music in American Life Commissions and Committees. The latter mentioned Commissions
are as follows:

Commission	I:	Basic Concepts in Music Education
Commission	II:	Standards of Music Literature and Performance
Commission	III:	Music in General School Administration
Commission	IV:	Music in Pre-School, Kindergarten, and Elementary Schools
Commission	V:	Music in Junior High School
Commission	VI:	Music in Senior High School
Commission	VII:	Music in Higher Education
Commission	VIII:	Music in The Community
Commission	IX:	Music in Media of Mass Communications
Commission	X:	Accreditation and Certification[13]

There are other Standing Committees in Music Education, such as:
Music for Exceptional Children, Music in International Relations,
Organ Instruction in the Schools, Piano Instruction in the Schools,
and String Instruction in the Schools. This comprehensive
organization of the MENC aids American music educators in becoming a dynamic force for implementing the concept of music
education for all.   Through this vast network there is an actual
association of music educators that brings them into intimate
relation with a great number of their collegues in the great musical
centers of the world.   The MENC is the "great cohesive association of educators that is working for the common objective of
securing better music teaching. With better teaching will come
variations in procedures, expanded uses for new equipment, and
music suited to the functional needs of tomorrow's citizens. "[14]

     The Music Educators National Conference through its many
regional and organizational units was the product of a reevaluation
of the basic philosophy of National, Divisional, and State Music
Educators Associations.   The Commission and Committee plan
"provides for (1) participation of MENC members at national,
division, and state levels, (2) participation by MENC auxiliary
and associated organizations, and (3) cooperation through joint

committees with other organizations representing professional,
educational, governmental, inter-governmental, and lay groups. "[15]
Choate has said that "the Music in American Life plan (The
Commission and Committee Plan) is not regarded as a new departure but rather as the basis for a period of renewed activity
and productivity in the continuing pursuit of the MENC purpose --
the advancement of music education. "[16] The Music in American
Life Plan was "set up to provide for participation of music
educators on an organizational-wide basis. The MENC state,
division, and national pattern provides for Commission and
Committee organization at the national level, with participation
at the state level on a strictly voluntary basis, depending on the
needs and wishes of the state leadership. Division coordinators
are appointed for each Commission area and for each Standing
Committee to assist in joint planning by state Commission and
Committee chairmen in connection with Division biennial programs. "[17]

  Music Education's Great Cultural Contributions. In a
democratic society every child -- every adult -- should be assured
the opportunity of enjoying the social, intellectual, and spiritual
contributions of music to the societal unit. The proviso appended
to such an opportunity is that every individual can enjoy these
benefits provided that he seeks them and that they are in keeping
with the "Common Good. " This concept is expressed in the Bill
of Rights which was adopted by the General Assembly of the United
Nations. Among its many Articles we find the declaration that
"Everyone has the right to education which shall be directed to
the full development of human personality and to the strengthening
of respect for human rights and fundamental freedom, "[18] and
further that, "Everyone has the right freely to participate in the
cultural life of the community, to enjoy the arts and to share in
scientific advancement and its benefits. "[19] These assertions,
sections of the preamble, and other articles of the Declaration
of Human Rights became the basis for the formulation of The
Child's Bill of Rights in Music which was part of the resolutions

adopted by the Music Educators National Conference at its biennial convention, in 1950.[20]   Prepared by its Council of Past Presidents it is set forth in article form:

The Child's Bill of Rights in Music

I

Every child has the right to full and free opportunity to explore and develop his capacities in the field of music in such ways as may bring him happiness and a sense of well-being; stimulate his imagination and stir his creative activities; and make him so responsive that he will cherish and seek to renew the fine feelings induced by music.

II

As his right, every child shall have the opportunity to experience music with other people so that his own enjoyment shall be heightened and he shall be led into greater appreciation of the feelings and aspirations of others.

III

As his right, every child shall have the opportunity to make music through being guided and instructed in singing, in playing at least one instrument both alone and with others, and, so far as his powers and interests permit, in composing music.

IV

As his right, every child shall have opportunity to grow in musical appreciation, knowledge, and skill, through instruction equal to that given in any other subject in all the free public educational programs that may be offered to children and youths.

V

As his right, every child shall be given the opportunity to have his interest and power in music explored and developed to the end that unusual talent may be utilized for the enrichment of the individual and society.

VI

Every child has the right to such teaching as will sensitize, refine, elevate, and enlarge not only his appreciation of music, but also his whole affective nature, to the end that the high part such developed feeling may play in raising the stature of mankind may be revealed to him.

Postlude

> A philosophy of the arts is mainly concerned with a set of values
> different from the material ones . . . of general education.
> Although current general educational concepts are often strongly
> materialistic, they are frequently given authority in moral and
> aesthetic fields in which they are inapplicable. Since moral,
> aesthetic, and material interests co-exist in life and are not
> mutually exclusive, those who would promote the arts, including
> music, should . . . advocate a philosophy which affirms that
> moral and aesthetic elements are part of the whole, equally
> with physical elements.

These postulates may be more broadly stated as the 1) Social Contributions, 2) Intellectual Contributions, and 3) Spiritual Contributions.

1.   The Social Contributions.   The socializing aspect of music
education is probably its greatest asset.   Man is gregariously
minded -- he craves attention, success, sense of belonging, and
a reasonable amount of approbation.   The singular contribution of
music to the socialization of man is its great capacity for creativity.
Thus, the socialization factor is always a dynamic experience.   The
reading about music is like playing baseball while lying in bed
reading about the rules of the game.   Music cannot touch the soul
of man unless he hears its message.   Man must always become a
participant in order to derive its great aesthetic benefits.   He is
perforce socialized with himself.

Socialization always includes the individual participative factor.
Of the great structural components of music -- rhythm, melody,
and harmony -- the play factor is strongly incorporated into rhythm.
The dance which is so great a part of lay enjoyment and social
participation always involves individual participation.   We believe
that participation in dancing undoubtedly employs some degree of
musical skill for all participants.   The number of people able to
enjoy such experience is very great.

2.   The Intellectual Contributions.   There are significant
intellectual opportunities afforded by musical composition which
encompass the gamut of creativity.   Music specialization envelops
many individuals with an all consuming desire for creative activity
which is capable of challenging the utmost of intellectual endeavor.
The creation of musical composition, the accomplishment of

meritorious skills in instrumental performance, the intelligent
performance of vocal literature gives its creator an intellectual
experience worthy of challenging his best abilities.   There are
manifold illustrations where the intellectual aspects of music have
challenged men of great mental acumen -- Schweitzer, Paderewski,
and Mozart are illustrious examples of varied intellectual creativity
of distinction.

    3.   The Spiritual Contributions.   All music has a message
which speaks to the soul of man through the unalterable impact
of sound and tonal beauty.   Sound does not have a verbalism which
man can understand, but if there be any intelligibility it is communicated in such a manner that all men who experience it are
able to feel its spiritualizing impact.   Verbalism is often inadequate to express man's most fundamental feelings and desires,
but the martial music of a band has often moved men to great
emotional fervor and collective action; the dynamic force of an
incessant drum-beat pattern has stirred the heart in the savage
breast; a certain rhythmic pattern repeated over and over will
often create elements of great joy; a religious song with words of
great spiritual meaning has moved individuals to moments of great
spiritual joy; slow or soft music has often been associated with
tranquility or sadness; the minor mode has created moods of
sombre atmosphere.   These tell-tale reactions have brought music
closer to the individual.   The music educator must be ever aware
of the potency of these dynamic forces.

    The cultural factors supplied by music indicates the basic and
comprehensive part it plays in the cultural education of all men.
But this is consummate culture -- all of music's great contributions
to learning.   Willis contends that "The stake of music in education
can be analyzed from many viewpoints. "[21]   He believes three
important aspects to be: (1) "the artistic implications of music
in education; (2) the general educative value of music in education;
(3) the place of music in education from a functional standpoint. "[22]
He further contends that music "incorporates artistic values in its
methods and techniques, " resulting in a "technical proficiency un-

matched by any other country in the world. "[23]   Along with these
educative values of helping people find expression for the creative
ability in maturity, Willis continues by stating five functional values
which he believes music education fulfills:

> First, music offers an opportunity for self-expression
> through a group activity.

> Second, music offers an opportunity to develop moral and
> spiritual values and to satisfy aesthetic needs.

> Third, music provides a medium through which boys and
> girls can make direct contributions to the community
> during their school days, and thus acquire a
> consciousness of the responsibility of the individual
> to the community.

> Fourth, music offers a medium for understanding other
> people -- their culture, and their problems.

> Finally, through music the student is led to a realization
> that the arts, of which music is one, have been
> of indisputable importance throughout all history. [24]

Willis' thesis presents to the music educator the professional
challenge of aiding in the determination of music as a medium of
self-expression, developing moral and spiritual values, which will
contribute to boys' and girls' preparation for community and world
living.   But even more important is the responsibility that the
music educator must coordinate the professionalization of its
contributive cultural assets for the betterment of man.   The music
educator must assume responsiblity for supporting all efforts
toward improving the cultural understanding of mankind through the
arts.   He must stand aloof to this challenge but must become an
expendable force for helping music education attain an understanding
which is commensurate with the leadership it envisions.

These contributions we believe are in keeping with statements
of belief articulated through a spokesman for the Music Educators
National Conference.   Six fundamental purposes are set forth in
credo form:

These Things We Believe

1. Music education's sacred concern is with lives - not life as an abstract concept, but with life as it is spent in homes, on streets and playgrounds, in school and out, at all ages and at every school level.

2. Music is a powerful personal and social force in the development of the maximum human and spiritual power from which the promises of our democratic ideal will be realized with increasing effectiveness.

3. Musical experiences rightly planned and guided are capable of liberating bodies, hearts and minds in ways that make children, youths, and adults freer to work toward newer, richer, and more valuable expressive and social ends.

4. Every child, every person in our American schools, is privileged -- therefore obligated -- to do his bit in improving musical and cultural life in America by improving himself.

5. Improving oneself musically, or otherwise, is an active process of giving out, as well as taking in; a child or adult develops more fully when these two principles of growth are given due consideration.

6. Music education can fulfill its highest purpose (1) by seeking the most effective interrelations possible with every other relevant area of public education, and (2) by examining all current issues and problems within the field of music in a spirit of constructive and open inquiry. [25]

These implications of music education's contribution to the development of society may be quite completely realized if their impact can be transmitted to individuals -- it is the sole hope if music as a cultural force is to survive -- this is the responsibility of tomorrow's music educator. A democratic music program implies that all peoples must have the chance to experience functional music -- a dilettante social music program is destined to utter failure. Music education cannot succeed if it is a veneer -- it can not be poured on from above, hoping that an overflow of its creativity will be distributed according to the needs of all men. The administration of such a program makes it imperative that such an opportunity is provided equally among all the members of society.

On the occasion of its Golden Anniversary, The Music Educator
National Conference expressed a Declaration of Faith[26] which had
a humanizing and spiritualizing tone in its statements:

> We believe that music has a special mission in a world torn
> with anxiety and doubt, dissension and fear; in a world in
> danger of being dehumanized and disillusioned by materialism
> mechanization and skepticism.
>
> We believe that by its innermost nature, music is closely
> related to ideal aspirations and purposes; and, being
> symbolic in its expressive language, it has the power to
> lead the human spirit further than any other art.
>
> We believe that we can make Music In American Life a
> living reality of the great American dream -- the inalienable
> right of every human being to the pursuit of happiness --
> realizing, of course, that happiness cannot be caught,
> nor taught or brought at any price; nor can it be given, no
> matter how much we may wish to bestow it upon others.
>
> We believe that happiness is a by-product of a way of living
> and learning that creates more life by adding to one's store
> of inner resources of heart, mind, and spirit, on the one
> hand, and skill in their outward expression, on the other
> hand.
>
> We believe that all phases of our school music program can
> be planned, administered and taught in ways that will bring
> happiness into the lives of the many -- not limiting the
> benefits of musical experience to the especially blessed few.
>
> We believe that those of great talent and those of small
> gifts have need of each other and that making music together
> is an ideal way of satisfying "deep hungers from which great
> dreams grow. "
>
> Finally, we believe that the years to come will bring "Many
> Happy Returns" to our beloved MENC. If this birthday wish
> is to come true, you and I have the promises of our faith
> to keep -- faith in the intrinsic worth of every man, every
> woman, and every child; faith in the values to be found in
> the timeless art of music.

Significant Events in the Development of The Music Supervisors National Conference -- The Music Educators National Conference[27]

1907 -- Music Supervisors National Conference organized--an
outgrowth of a conference attended by 104 persons from sixteen
states, who had responded to an invitiation to come to Keokuk,
Iowa, April 10-12, to discuss matters of mutual interest to
school music teachers.   69 enrolled as members.

1908 -- No separate meeting of the new organization as such.... Effort and participation concentrated in Cleveland convention of the National Education Association and its Music Education Department (established by the NEA in 1884), of which most of the Conference group were members ... From its beginning the Music Supervisors Conference worked closely with the NEA, and the membership and leadership of the Conference interlocked with membership in the NEA Music Education Dept.

1909 -- Second meeting of the Music Supervisors National Conference at Indianapolis, Indiana, with about 100 in attendance.... Chief discussion pertained to grammar grade requirements of music teaching.

1910 -- Meeting in Cincinnati.... Membership reaches 150.... Constitution was adopted and the name Music Supervisors National Conference made official.... First recorded committee report-- by Committee on Formulation of a Music Course for High School.... First book of proceedings published.... Established affiliate relationship with National Federation of Music Clubs.

1911 -- Meeting in Detroit.... The first report made by the Committee on High School Music was presented.... Membership nearly 200.

1912 -- Meeting held at St. Louis, Missouri.... This was the first of five meetings held in St. Louis; the last (thus far!) the Golden Anniversary Year inaugural in 1956.

1913 -- Meeting at Rochester, New York.... High school orchestras stressed for the first time.... Appointment of Committee on Songs for Community Singing, Peter W. Dykema, chairman.

1914 -- Meeting in Minneapolis.... Music Supervisors Bulletin, now Music Educators Journal, authorized.... First report of Committee on Community Songs.... Discussion of report of music committee of the NEA Commission on the Reorganization of Secondary Education.... 350 members.

1915 -- Pittsburgh meeting.... Beginning of emphasis on community music activities and community service by school music supervisors and school music teachers.... Inauguration of informal singing at the convention -- now the traditional "lobby sings."

1916 -- Meeting at Lincoln, Nebraska.... First choral concert by the whole membership under the leadership of William L. Tomlins.... Introduction of violin class teaching.

1917 -- First National Music Supervisors Chorus.... Demonstration of violin class instruction attracts considerable attention

at the convention.... Attention directed to more adequate preparation for school music teachers. Participation in civilian
cooperation. World War I.

1918. -- National Education Council established.... Eastern
Music Supervisors Conference organized.

1919 -- Music appreciation comes into the foreground ....
"Service Version" of the Star Spangled Banner accepted by War
Department upon recommendation of Conference-sponsored
"Committee of Twelve."

1920 -- State Advisory Committees established.... Instrumental
music instruction receiving more attention.... Need recognized
for giving special attention to music in rural schools.

1921 -- Education Council completes Standard Course in Music
for Elementary Grades and Training Courses for Supervisors,
later published as Educational Council Bulletin No. 1.

1922 -- Southern Conference for Music Education organized....
First National Music Supervisors Orchestra give concert with
sixth National Music Supervisors Chorus.... Establishment of
National Committee on Instrumental Music (later named
Committee on Instrumental Affairs).

1923 -- Acceptance of goal to make music available to all
children in the schools indicated by introduction of slogan
"Music for Every Child--Every Child for Music".... National
Research Council of Music Education replaces Educational
Council.

1924 -- Biennial plan proposed for meetings of National and
Sectional Conferences.... Discussion of development of Sectional
Conferences in regions not organized in order to cover all states.

1925 -- Serious attention given to radio in education.... Interstate band, orchestra and choral contests introduced on national
convention program.... Committee on Music Contests appointed.

1926 -- First National High School Orchestra creates sensation
at Detroit Convention.... Music Education Exhibitors Association
organized.... Committee on Vocal Affairs established....
First official National High School Band Contest, sponsored by
MENC. Committee on Instrumental Affairs and National Bureau
for the Advancement of Music.

1927 -- North Central and Southwestern Conference hold first
meetings.... National High School Orchestra plays for NEA
Department of Superintendence (now American Association of
School Administrators) at Dallas, Texas.... Superintendents
go on record that "...we are rightly coming to regard music,

art, and other similar subjects as fundamental in the education of American children. We recommend that they be given everywhere equal consideration and support with other basic subjects" (Article XII, 1927 Resolutions of the Department of Superintendence).... MENC Committee on Instrumental Affairs sets up and introduces instrumentation for symphonic band, which became the standard for school band contests; now is basis for band instrumentation throughout the world.

1928 -- First National High School Chorus.... A cappella choirs capture National Convention.... Piano section added to Instrumental Affairs Committee.

1929 -- First meeting of Northwest Conference.... A cappella choirs capture Sectional Conferences; new era for choral music.

1930 -- New Constitution adopted providing for business office and paid staff.... Office opened in Chicago at 64 E. Jackson Blvd.

1931 -- California-Western (now Western) Conference hold first meeting, completing the circuit of six Sectional Conferences.

1932 -- Beginning of emphasis on widespread committee participation in the over-all program.... Twenty-fifth Anniversary Convention at Cleveland, Ohio.

1933 -- Beginning of state affiliation plan.... National High School Band and Orchestra Association become auxiliaries of the Conference; take over responsibility for national contests.... Depression time--aggressive program of service and promotion authorized by Executive Committee; lowest ebb for membership enrollments--highest degree of enthusiasm, vigor and constructive results.

1934 -- Name changed from Music Supervisors National Conference to Music Educators National Conference.... Music in American Youth NBC network radio programs inaugurated.... First official state music education periodical established (Ohio Music Education Association's Triad).... NEA reinstates its music section at annual convention after several years discontinuance. MENC takes cooperating responsibilities.... Emergence of music education as a profession.

1935 -- More states become interested in MENC state affiliation plan. Depression program of service and promotion by MENC pays dividends in achievements and membership enrollments.

1936 -- Great convention in New York City marks upswing in organized effort.... National School Vocal Association organized and joins forces with Band and Orchestra Associations as a unit under name of National School Band, Orchestra and Vocal Association; rating plan for contest adjudication replaces ranking system.... Further development of nationwide participation in MENC Committee program.

1937 -- State affiliation plan progresses. Participating in early developments: Louisiana, Ohio, Delaware, Michigan, Connecticut, Illinois, Missouri, Colorado, Alaska, Florida, Georgia, Idaho, Kansas, Massachusetts, Kentucky, Maine, Minnesota.

1938 -- NSBOVA divides national school music competions into ten regions supervised by ten regional boards under aegis of NSBOVA National Board of Control.... NEA officially invites MENC to become a department of NEA.

1939 -- Increasing acceptance of music as a factor in general education. Accelerated progress in extension of state unit affiliation plan.

1940 -- MENC becomes the Department of Music of the National Education Association.... "Music in American Unity" hemisphere program.... Beginning of cooperation with Pan American Union and State Department in "Good Neighbor" program.... First meeting of College Band Directors National Conference as an outgrowth of the MENC Committee on College Bands, first established in 1938.

1941 -- Beginning of full operation of state unit (federation) plan. State, division and national dues combined. State presidents with elected officers comprise the respective MENC Division Boards.... Climax of participation in National School Music Competition-Festivals as finals for state competitons held in nearly all states; 75,000 students enrolled in the ten regions.

1942 -- "Music Education in Wartime" period. Intensive cooperation with Government and Military Departments and agencies, especially State Department, Treasury Department, War Department, Joint Army and Navy Committee on Welfare and Recreation, Library of Congress Music Division.... Interstate (regional) competitions discontinued because of wartime conditions. (Competitions beyond state level were not resumed). ...Beginning of widespread recognition and acceptance in music education of American folk music, as well as contemporary music.

1943 -- "Wartime" meetings held by the six MENC Divisions-- geared to cooperation with State, War, and Treasury Departments, other Government agencies, and Pan American Union.

1944 -- Wartime Division and National meetings continue; "Widening Horizons for Music Education" program.... Preparation for post-war years.... Nationwide Curriculum Committee organization activated; thirty-eight committee work-groups form core of National Convention at St. Louis; produce and distribute on the spot preliminary (workdraft) edition of first Source Book.

1945 -- Severe wartime travel restrictions.... Six MENC Division Consultants Councils (the "Six Fifties") replace Division Conventions and lay foundation for post-war Music Education Advancement Program.... Twelve projects launched within framework of the Advancement Program with nationwide state-division-national committee organization setup.... Increasing provision for piano and string class teaching in schools; corresponding attention in teacher education.

1946 -- First State Presidents National Assembly.... Interim issue of Music Education Source Book published.... Authorization of student membership plan.

1947 -- Completion of Music Education Source Book, representing the work of nearly 2,000 participants in the three periods of the state-division-national curriculum committee organization. ... Student membership plan established; first chapters enrolled. Total student members 2,034 in 157 institutions.... Code for relationships of school music teachers and students with professional musicians signed for American Association of School Administrators, Music Educators National Conference and American Federation of Musicians by the respective presidents of the three organizations.

1948 -- Music Education Advancement Program continues. State units participate.... MENC publication program expanded.

1949 -- MENC begins active cooperation with UNESCO.... College Band Directors Conference adopts Constitution as College Band Directors National Association, an associated organization of the MENC.

1950 -- Child's Bill of Rights adopted.... Third major revision of MENC Constitution and By-Laws makes provision for needs caused by growth of the organization and extension of activities. MENC Washington office opened in NEA headquarters....

1951 -- "Music in American Education" program initiated.... First raise in MENC active membership dues in twenty-five years (from $3.00 to $4.00).... Collaboration with National Association of Secondary School Principals in preparation of contents of special issue of the NASSP Bulletin devoted to "Music Education in Secondary Schools." ... Beginning cooperation with American Association of School Administrators in planning music programs.... MENC joins MTNA and NASM in establishing a permanent liaison committee headed by the presidents of the respective organizations.

1952 -- MENC Board of Directors votes to consolidate Chicago office with Washington office in NEA Education Center, Washington, D.C., "as soon as expedient." ...MENC Commission on Accreditation and Certification in Music Education develops

Standards for the Evaluation of the College Curriculum for the
Training of the School Music Teacher, Collaborating organizations:
NASM, and MTNA.   Committee on Studies and Standards of the
American Association of Colleges for Teacher Education approves
the materials and adds them to the evaluation schedules of the
AACTE for use in connection with their inter-visitation program....
National School Band, Orchestra, and Vocal Association adopts
new Bylaws as the National Interscholastic Music Activities
Commission of the MENC, with responsibility as official spokes-
man of the MENC for interscholastic affairs in music education....
Plans consummated for Journal of Research in Music Education
(first issue published 1953).

1953 -- Many MENC members participate in UNESCO sponsored
International Music Education Conference in Brussels, Belgium,
where International Society of Music Education is organized.

1954 -- All states represented at State Presidents National
Assembly.... Music Education Exhibitors Association in its
28th year adopts new Constitution and becomes Music Industry
Council of the MENC.... Newly organized National Association
of College Wind and Percussion Instructors becomes a MENC
associated organization.... MENC appointed to United States
National Commission on UNESCO.... Organization-wide
participation in laying groundwork for five-year Music in
American Life Commission-Committee Organization.

1955 -- Membership reaches 27,829, including nearly 8,000
college student members in 342 institutions.... Music Educators
Journal circulation continues growth--33,750 printing for September-October 1955 issue.... Forty-one state music educators
association periodicals now being published.... Two major MENC
books published: Music in American Education (Source Book
Two); Music Buildings, Rooms and Equipment.... MENC becomes
member of National Music Council.... Northwest Association
of College Choral Directors becomes an associated organization,
attached to MENC Northwest Division.... Plans being completed
to move Chicago office to Washington, D.C. during summer of
1956.... Board of Directors, with heads of auxiliary and
associated organizations, other official groups, plan program
for official nationwide Observance of the Fiftieth Anniversary,
April 1956 through April 1957.... Golden Anniversary Commission appointed.... Music in American Life Commission
and Committee organization completed and at work.... Joint
planning by the respective Anniversary Commissions for the
one-hundredth anniversary of the National Education Association
and the fiftieth anniversary of the MENC, both of which occur
in 1957.

1956 -- Golden Anniversary Observance Year inaugurated at
St. Louis convention (April 13-18, 1956) with many special
features including the NIMAC sponsored Golden Anniversary

National High School Band, Chorus and Orchestra with students
enrolled from forty-six states, the Golden Anniversary Historical
Center, and the Golden Anniversary Conference Breakfast....
Work begun on joint publication project with the National Society
for the Study of Education by the Music in American Education
Commission on Basic Concepts in Music Education, a subsidiary
of the Music Education Research Council.   The "Basic Concepts
in Music Education" book is scheduled for publication as one
book of the two-volume 1958 Yearbook of NSSE.... Arkansas
Music Educators Association becomes the forty-eigth state in
the MENC federation which, with the District of Columbia and
Hawaii, totals exactly fifty in the fiftieth anniversary year of
the MENC....   Golden Anniversary observances, local and state-
wide, continue throught the year.   ...Removal of the headquarters
office from Chicago to Washington completed September 1.

1957 -- Golden Anniversary observance climaxed by the six
division conventions, March 5 through April 30, at Atlantic
City, Omaha, Denver, Boise, Pasadena, Miami....   Plans
completed for participation in the NEA Centennial Observance
convention in Philadelphia, June 30 to July 5....   World premiere
April 9 by National Symphony Orchestra and Howard University
Chorus of Howard Hanson's NEA commissioned "Song of
Democrary, " dedicated to the "Music Educators of Ameria for
their 50th anniversary and the 100th anniversary of the National
Education Association. " ...The Golden Anniversary life membership project more than trebles the enrollment of life members....
North Central Association of Colleges and Secondary Schools
adopts guiding principles for school music group activities
recommended by a joint committee representing the NCA
Activities Committee, the Contest and Activities Committee
of the National Association of Secondary School Principals, and
the Executive Committee of the MENC....   Indications that
when count for 1957 is all recorded, the original membership
enrollment of 69 at Keokuk in 1907 will have grown to more
than 33, 000.

Notes

1. Dennis, Charles M.   "The Brussels Conference in
    Retrospect, " Music Educators Journal, 40: No. 3,
    (January, 1954), 35.

2. Lawler, Vanett.   "The International Society for Music
    Education, " Education, (March, 1956).   418.

3. Dennis, op. cit. , 35.

4. Franzen, Bengt.   "The Professional Musician and the
    Music Educator, " Music Educators Journal, 41: No. 2.
    (November-December, 1954), 34.

5. Lawler, Vanett.   op. cit. , 414-418.

6. Gavian, Ruth Wood and Hamm, William A.   The American
    Story.   (Boston, Mass. : D. C. Heath and Company, 1947),
    575-576.

7. Ibid. , 576.

8. Lawler, Vanett.   "Music Education in the Americas, "
    Education.   69: No. 7.   (March, 1949), 392.

9. Ibid.

10. Ibid.

11. Ibid.

12. Ibid.

13. "Official Directory, 1956-1957.   Music Educators National
    Conference and Associated Organizations. "   Music
    Educators Journal, 42, No. 3 (January, 1956), 66-70.

14. Sunderman, Lloyd F.   "The Music Educators National
    Conference, " Education.   72: No. 1 (September, 1951).
    3-4.

15. Editorial.   "Music In American Life, " Music Educators
    Journal, 41: No. 2 (November-December, 1954).   17.

16. Ibid.

17. Ibid.

18. Article XXVI of Bill of Rights adopted by the General
    Assembly of the United Nations.

19. Ibid.

20. Music In American Education.   Music Educator Source
    Book Number Two.   (Washington, D. C. : Music Educators
    National Conference, 1955).   298-299.   Resolutions adopted
    by the Music Educators National Conference at its biennial
    convention, St. Louis, Missouri, March, 1950.   Prepared
    by the MENC Council of Past Presidents (Official MENC
    Committee on Resolutions, Peter W. Dykema, chairman,
    1948-1950.   This declaration was incorporated as Part
    One in the report adopted in 1951 by the North Central
    Association of Colleges and Secondary Schools.

21. Willis, Benjamin C.   "The Stake of Music in Education, "
    Music Educators Journal, 40: No. 6 (June-July, 1954), 9.

22. Ibid.

23. Ibid.

24. Ibid., 11.

25. Pitts, Lilla Belle. "The Golden Anniversary Observance,"
Music Educators Journal, 42: No. 4 (February-March,
1956), 24.

26. Pitts, Lilla Belle. "Open Letter to Music Educators,"
Music Educators Journal, 43: No. 3 (January, 1957), 7.

27. "Mileposts and Stepping Stones," (1907-1957) MENC
Progress Report From The Records. Music Educators
Journal, 43: No. 5 (April-May, 1957). 40-41. Re-
produced in its entirety.

APPENDICES

I.   Some Early Leaders and Educators in American Music Education

II. Some Significant Events in Music Education 1603-1895

III. Cities Which Pioneered in Music Education: A Chronological List by Earliest Date Known

IV. Some Statistical Evidences of the Growth of American Music Education before 1890

APPENDIX I

Some Early Leaders and Educators in American Music

Aiken, Charles
Aiken, Walter H.
Allen, Anna H.
Allen, David
Ansorge, Charles
Bailey, J. E.
Baker, Benjamin Franklin
Baker, Everett L.
Ballard, Levi W.
Ballou, E. P.
Bancroft, S. C. (Miss)
Barr, Colonel
Bingham, Silas
Blackman, Orlando
Butler, Henry M.
Butterfield, F. H.
Carter, Henry
Clark, J. H.
Clarke, Charles M.
Cogswell, Hamlin E.
Colburn, William F.
Cole, Samuel W.
Cooke, M. D. (Mrs.)
Daniel, J. H.
Davis, Warren
Doyle, Charlotte O. (Miss)
Eichberg, Julius
Emerson, Irving
Esputa, John
Fallen, William
Gilbert, N.
Glover, Nathan L.
Godfrey, Charles
Gould, Anna L. (Mrs.)
Gould, Nathaniel D.
Grant, Henry F.
Greene, Professor
Hanks, J. F.
Hodgdon, William A.
Holt, Hosea Edson
Howard, Francis E.

Huntington, Charles W.
Ives, Elam
Jantz, A.
Jepson, Benjamin
Jones, Darius E.
Junkermann, G. F.
Kingsley, George
Lincoln, L. P.
Locke, Elisha
Lombard, Frank
Loomis, George B.
Mason, Lowell
Mason, Luther W.
Mason, T. B.
Meade, Walter S.
Mower, Nathaniel L.
Oliver, H. K.
Paige, W. H.
Perkins, H. S.
Plagge, Christopher
Powell, Joseph P.
Sharland, John B.
Slayton, J. L.
Stewart, N. Coe
Stowe, Calvin E. (Rev.)
Sumner, Seth
Tillinghast, William
Tinker, M. Z.
Thurston, Samuel
Trowbridge, Edward
Van Meter, W. C.
Vining, George V.
Weaver, Sterrie, A.
Webb, George J.
Webster, William C.
White, Jason
Whittemore, Edward E.
Wilsey, Alvin
Wood, Benjamin W.
Woodbridge, William Channing
Zinker, M. Z.

363

Some Significant Events in the History of Music in
America 1603-1895.

Date   Event

1603   The Franciscan Friars began a school in St. Augustine,
Florida, in which they taught vocal and instrumental music.

1604   The first celebration of mass in New England took
place on Holy Cross Island in the St. Croix River.

1640   The Bay Psalm Book was printed at Cambridge, Massachusetts.

c1693   Father Rale formed a robed choir of forty Indians at
Norridgewock, Maine.

1700   First pipe organ in America was imported from Europe
and placed in the Anglican Church at Port Royal, Virginia.

c1717   First singing school was conducted in Brattle Street, Boston,
Massachusetts. The leader was Dr. Coleman.

1721   First music book in America to be printed with bars:
Rev. Thomas Walter's The Grounds and Rules of Musick
explained: Or an Introduction to the Art of Singing by Note:
Fitted to the meanest capacities.

1740   Musical Association in Philadelphia.

1742   Musical Instrument manufacture established in America.

c1745   Father Schneider had incorporated singing into the schools
of Goshenhoppen, Pennsylvania.

1746   Birth of America's first native composer, William Billings.
One of his tunes, "Chester," was called the battle hymn of
the Revolution.

1759   Earliest singing-society or choral organization, the Orpheus
Club, begun in Philadelphia.

1761   Boys were used in the singing service of the Old Trinity
Church in New York City.

1762   St. Cecilia Society organized in Charleston, S. C.

1765   A community orchestra was organized at Lititz, Pennsylvania, to supplement the music of the church service.

1770   The Messiah was performed at Trinity Church, New York City, on January 9, 1770.

1773   The 70th and last edition of The Bay Psalm Book was printed.

1780   The Handel Society of Dartmouth College was formed at Hanover, N. H.

1781   Birth of Nathaniel D. Gould. He entered the field of juvenile music instruction before Lowell Mason. He was born at Chelmsford, Massachusetts, in 1781, dying in Boston, in 1864.

1786   Stoughton Musical Society formed at Stoughton, Massachusetts.

c1790   Probable date of the first singing contest in America.

1792   Birth of Lowell Mason the father of the American Musical Convention. First salaried teacher of music instruction in the Boston Public Schools.

1798   Date of the appearance of a male vested choir in St. Michaels Church, Charleston, S. C.

c1809   Father Gabriel Richard of Detroit advocates music education in an educational scheme which he presented to the United States Government.

1811   The Moravians at Bethlehem, Pennsylvania, gave a performance of Haydn's Creation in 1811.

1815   Beginning of the Handel and Haydn Society, Boston, Massachusetts.

1818   Handel and Haydn Society of Boston gives the first complete performance of an oratorio in the United States. It was a performance of Handel's Messiah.

c1820   At Nazareth, Kentucky, Sister Scholastica was the first to teach music.

1824   Singing instruction was offered to school children in South Boston, Massachusetts as early as 1824. The instructor was N. D. Gould.

1825 The Musical Fund Society of Philadelphia started the first important music school in America. It opened in May, 1825 with twenty-five pupils.

1827 Utica Gymnasium, Utica, New York, which was founded in 1827 and which later became Utica High School had on its first faculty a teacher of music, Ebenezer Leach.

1830 Elam Ives was the first teacher to instruct vocal music in this country, according to Pestalozzian principles.

1830 William C. Woodbridge gave the first lecture in America; "On Vocal Music as a Branch of Common Education. "

1831 In Park Street Church in Boston, Massachusetts on July 4, 1831, Lowell Mason directed the first performance in America of the "original hymn" written by Samuel Francis Smith; he was a student at Andover Seminary. The song is known as "America. "

1832 The American Elementary Singing Book, produced in 1832 by Elam Ives was the first book for a serious study of music in public schools.

1833 The Boston Academy of Music was formally organized January 8, 1833.

1833 Music was taught in nine Boston schools during 1833-1834.

1833 Probably two of the earliest juvenile music concerts in America were held in Boston in the spring of 1833.

1834 Consideration was given to music teacher preparation by the Boston Academy of Music as early as 1834.

1834 Lowell Mason's Manual of Instruction was produced. It was used extensively by singing school teachers.

1836 First meeting of the Convention of Teachers of Vocal Music in Boston, Massachusetts took place August 19, 1836.

1838 Lowell Mason taught gratuitously from January to August in the Boston Public Schools.

1838 Represents the official year of the introduction of vocal music into the Boston Public Schools.

1844 The Musical Institute, the first important choral society of New York City, was established in this year.

1847 The Boston Academy of Music ceases to exist.

1850   New York Harmonic Society gave its first concert on May
        10, 1850.

1855   The first honorary degree, Doctor of Music, conferred in
        1855. It was given to Lowell Mason by New York University.

1857   Louis M. Braille invented a system of musical characters
        for blind music readers.

1858   The Worcester Musical Convention came into being under
        the leadership of B. F. Baker and Edward Hamilton.

1866   The Handel and Haydn Society of San Francisco, California,
        was organized.

1868   The Peabody Conservatory of Music, Baltimore, Maryland,
        was established by George Peabody.

1869   H. E. Holt, born February 20, 1836, at Ashburnham,
        Massachusetts, begins his long tenure as supervisor of
        music in Boston. It covered the years 1869-1898.

1870   Luther W. Mason brought out the National Music Course.

1870   Music made a part of the course of study for all grades in
        Philadelphia, Pennsylvania.

1874   Detroit Conservatory of Music was established in 1874 by
        J. H. Hahn.

1876   Music Teachers' National Association founded at Delaware,
        Ohio in 1876.

1877   Indiana Music Teachers' Association was formed.

1878   Organization of the Cincinnati College of Music. Theodore
        Thomas was its great musical director.

1878   The Ohio Music Teachers' Association was formed in 1878
        by Nathan L. Glover.

1883   The Normal Music Course by H. E. Holt and John W. Tufts
        was published by D. Appleton and Company. It was taken
        over by Silver, Burdett and Company in 1885.

1884   Under the leadership of Julia Ettie Crane, one of the
        earliest normal school teacher-training departments for
        music supervisors and teachers was established at Potsdam
        Normal School, Potsdam, New York.

1884   H. E. Holt in 1884 opened a summer school at Lexington,
        Massachusetts for the study of texts and materials.   Begin-
        ning and experienced music teachers came for additional
        training.

1885   The Coombs Conservatory of Music was established in
        Philadelphia in 1885.

APPENDIX III

Cities which Pioneered in Music Education:
A Chronological list by Earliest Date Known.

(An asterisk beside a date indicates that discrepancies exist as to
the year in which music education was introduced into the public
schools.)

Location	Date
South Boston, Mass.	1824
Utica, New York	1827*
New York City, N. Y.	1829*
Palmyra, N. Y.	1831
Boston, Mass.	1832*
Shrewsbury, Pa.	1836
Buffalo, N. Y.	1837*
Charlestown, Conn.	1839
Lancaster, Pa.	1840
Northampton, Mass.	1840
Philadelphia, Pa.	1840*
Salem, Mass.	1841*
Lowell, Mass.	1841
Chicago, Ill.	1841*
Duanesburgh, N. Y.	1842
Cincinnati, O.	1842*
Zanesville, O.	1842
New Orleans, La.	1842
Baltimore, Md.	1843
Rochester, N. Y.	1844*
Oberlin, O.	1844
Pittsburg, Pa.	1844
Louisville, Ky.	1844
Providence, R. I.	1844
Wirt, N. Y.	1844
Bolivar, N. Y.	1844
Washington, D. C.	1845
Cleveland, O.	1846*
Jersey City, N. J.	1848
Dayton, O.	1849
Sandusky, O.	1850
Geneva, Wis.	1850
San Francisco, Cal.	1851*
Columbus, O.	1851
St. Louis, Mo.	1852

Location	Date
Syracuse, N. Y.	1852*
Ripley, O.	1853
Wellesville, O.	1853
Detroit, Mich.	1853
Terre Haute, Ind.	1853*
Joliet, Ill.	1855
Chillicothe, O.	1855
Hartford, Conn.	1856
Brooklyn, N. Y.	1856
Barret, Vt.	1858
Toledo, O.	1858
Memphis, Tenn.	1858
Carlisle, Pa.	1858
St. Tammany, La	1860
Newark, O.	1861
Galesburg, Ill.	1862
New Haven, Conn.	1862
Middletown, Conn.	1862*
West Winfield, N. Y.	1862
Mexico, N. Y.	1863
Milwaukee, Wis.	1864*
Phillipsburg, N. J.	1864
Newport, R. I.	1865*
Oswego, N. Y.	1866
Troy, N. Y.	1866
Windham, Conn.	1866
Meriden, Conn.	1866
Canterbury, Conn.	1868*
Aurora, Ind.	1869
Lewiston, Me.	1870
Lawrence, Kan.	1870
Davenport, Ia.	1871
Minneapolis, Minn.	1871
Chattanooga, Tenn.	1872
Columbus, Ga.	1872
Atlanta, Ga.	1872
Wallingford, Conn.	1872
Norwalk, Conn.	1872
New London, Conn.	1872
Manchester, Conn.	1872
Denver, Colo.	1872
Allegheny, Pa.	1873
Bath, Me.	1873
Oakland, Cal.	1873
Selma, Ala.	1873
Opelika, Ala.	1873
Montgomery, Ala.	1873
Paterson, N. J.	1874
Nashua, N. H.	1874
Grand Rapids, Mich.	1874

Location	Date
Atchinson, Kan.	1874
Peoria, Ill.	1874
Belleville, Ill.	1874

Table I is a recapitulation of the sources found on pages 371-373. The Table arranges the information by five year periods and shows the number of introductions of music into community public schools by states. The period of great acceleration was 1870-1874 when twenty-four additional cities were reported from fourteen states. Fifty per cent, or seven of the states for the same period were states never before represented. Sources offering information for the period after 1874 proved to be unreliable and therefore were not included in this table.

TABLE I

Frequency Distribution of Significant Dates in the
History of Public School Music by Five Year Periods†

State	1820-1824	1825-1829	1830-1834	1835-1839	1840-1844	1845-1849	1850-1854	1855-1859	1860-1864	1865-1869	1870-1874
Massachusetts	1		1		2						
New York		2		1	4		1	1	2	2	
Pennsylvania				1	3			1			1
Connecticut				1				1	2	3	4
Illinois					1			1	1		2
Ohio					3	3	3	2	1		
Louisiana					1				1		
Maryland					1						
Kentucky					1						
Rhode Island					1					1	
Washington, D. C.						1					
New Jersey						1			1		2
Wisconsin							1		1		
California							1				1
Missouri							1				
Michigan							1				1
Indiana							1			1	
Vermont								1			
Tennessee								1			1
Maine											2
Kansas											2
Iowa											1
Minnesota											1
Georgia											2
Colorado											1
Alabama											3
No. Community Introductions	1	2	1	3	17	5	9	8	9	7	24
No. States Represented	1	1	1	3	9	3	7	7	7	4	14

Note to Table I:-

†How to read: During the period 1825-29, two additional cities throughout the United States indicated that they were offering music in their schools. During the period 1870-1874, there were twenty-four additional cities representing fourteen states.

APPENDIX IV

Some Statistical Evidences of the Growth of
American Music Education Before 1890

Notable developments had taken place in music education before
1890. The teaching of vocal music according to some formal
method of instruction had become a reality. The teaching of the
science of music was the prevalent practice. Definite courses
of music study existed in many cities. The music reader, at
first a one-book course, had become graded. At the secondary
level the optional instead of the compulsory feature had become
a working reality. Music education, while a feature in enter-
prising and progressive areas, most certainly was not an accepted
subject for study in any large percentage of school programs. The
period of determining the worthwhileness of music instruction had
not entirely passed. In a host of cases the battle for free education
for the masses was still being fought. To suggest that music
study be included before the acceptance of free education was
strategically unwise, unless there was a demand for music
instruction. When that was the case the cause of music education
actually strengthened the demand for free public schools in which
such instruction could be given.

In the 1880's there appeared an attempt to shift some of the
emphasis from music as a science or study to music as an
emotional language where enjoyment predominates. The period
1830-1885 is one of the growth of acceptance with concomitant
developments. The purpose of this section is to show some of
the achievements of this period. The first topic to be treated
is that of the salaried supervisor as a special music teacher.

The salaried supervisor had become a definite reality prior
to the Civil War. Early public school music instructor's yearly

377

stipends were small.   Data reported by the United States Commissioner of Education, John Eaton, for 1874, in part dealt with
the "average annual salaries of special teachers. "[1] This information presents a picture of 63 communities with salaries based
on 1874 tabulations: the population figures were taken from the
1870 census.   Only cities with 10, 000 or more population were
considered.

If we add to the above, the cities of 7, 500 inhabitants or over,
we naturally find an additional number of communities in which
music was being taught by a special teacher.   Those cities with
that population, and who employed a special music teacher during
1870, 1872, 1874, 1875, 1876, 1877, 1878, or 1879 have been
tabulated in Table I.   A study of the evidence reveals that there
is but a low positive correlation between size of city and amount
of the salary received.

On a comparative basis it would appear that there was as great
a lack of uniformity among the salaried supervisors of the East as
there was in the Midwest and Far-West.   A point of interest is the
fact that the music teachers were receiving as great and in many
cases a greater annual stipend than the regular teacher.   It does
appear that the supervisor of music in Boston was receiving the
highest yearly salary.   In general it would appear that the salaries
in the eastern part of the United States were larger than those
offered in the West.

How to read Table I using New Haven as an illustration.   The
fact that it is listed means that it had a special music teacher
before 1880.   During 1870 he was receiving $2, 000 per year;
during 1874 through 1877 he was receiving $2, 500.   Some cities
have only one salary indicated, which of course means that the
sources were limited to the single date reference.

TABLE I

120 Cities of 7, 500 or More Indicating a Special
Music Teacher Prior to 1880

City	Misc. Reports	Salary Based on Report Indicated		
		1874[4]	1876[5]	1877[6]
Oakland, Cal.	(1879)[8] $1, 350			
San Francisco, Cal.	(1879) 137b	$1, 800	$1, 950	$1, 800
Stockton, Cal.	(1879) 1, 100	1, 100	1, 200	1, 200
Denver, Col.		1, 000		
Bridgeport, Conn.			1, 200	
New Haven, Conn.		2, 500	2, 500	2, 500
New London, Conn.			500	300a
Norwich, Conn.	(1878)[7] 1, 200a			
Wilmington, Del.	(1872)[3] .01k			
Columbus, Ga.			90	90
Belleville, Ill.	8	1, 200	850	
Chicago, Ill.	(1879) 1, 248	2, 200	1, 800	1, 500
Peoria, Ill.		1, 200		
Evansville, Ind.		1, 500		
Fort Wayne, Ind.	(1879)[8] 1, 200	1, 000	1, 200	1, 200
Indianapolis, Ind.	(1879) 1, 150	1, 800	1, 600	1, 600
Richmond, Ind.			1, 000	900
Terre Haute, Ind.		900	960	891a
Vincennes, Ind.	(1879) 650			
Burlington, Ia.			1, 200	1, 200
Council Bluffs, Ia.				1, 000
Davenport, Ia.				582e
Keokuk, Ia.		1, 200		1, 000a
Ottumwa, Ia.	(1879) 500			
Atchison, Kan.		350		
Lawrence, Kan.				70c
Louisville, Ky.			1, 025	1, 025
Newport, Ky.			600	
Bangor, Me.			400	
Lewiston, Me.		900	900	900a
Portland, Me.			1, 000	1, 000

TABLE I cont.

City	Misc. Reports		1874[4]	1876[5]	1877[6]
Baltimore, Md.			$1,500		$1,250a
Adams, Mass.			2,512	$3,300a	
Cambridge, Mass.	(1879)[8]	$1,500a		2,250	2,000a
Fall River, Mass.				1,200	
Fitchburg, Mass.			1,200	1,200	800
Gloucester, Mass.	(1878)[7]	700			
Haverhill, Mass.				1,100	
Holyoke, Mass.			700	700	700
Lawrence, Mass.			1,000	600f	
Lowell, Mass.			2,000	1,500	1,447
Lynn, Mass.			800	700	
Malden, Mass.	(1879)[8]	800a			
New Bedford, Mass.				1,650	
Newton, Mass.				1,500	
Northampton, Mass.	(1878)[7]	800			
Pittsfield, Mass.			250	1,200	
Salem, Mass.			1,650	1,600	1,600
Somerville, Mass.	(1878)	1,050			
Springfield, Mass.			1,200	1,200	900
Taunton, Mass.			1,500	1,200	1,200
Waltham, Mass.	(1878)	800a			
Woburn, Mass.			600	600	500a
Worcester, Mass.			1,900	1,900	1,500
Ann Arbor, Mich.					600
Detroit, Mich.				1,500	1,200a
East Siginaw, Mich.				800	500a
Flint, Mich.	(1879)[8]	400a			
Grand Rapids, Mich.			1,000	1,200	1,000
Saginaw, Mich.				500	500
Minneapolis, Minn.			1,200	1,300j	1,300
St. Paul, Minn.					1,000g

TABLE I cont.

City	Misc. Reports	1874[4]	1876[5]	1877[6]
St. Louis, Mo.		$1,925	$1,900	$1,500
Dover, N.H.	(1879)[8] $ 396			
Manchester, N.H.		1,600	1,200	
Nashua, N.H.		1,000	800	1,200
Newark, N.J.		2,000	1,500	
Orange, N.J.			750	750
Paterson, N.J.		600	600	
Trenton, N.J.			800	
Albany, N.Y.		1,650		
Auburn, N.Y.		1,000	750	800
Buffalo, N.Y.			1,100	
Cohoes, N.Y.		750	750	750
Elmira, N.Y.			500	
Ithaca, N.Y.				500
Lockport, N.Y.			1,200	1,200
New York, N.Y.		90d		
Oswego, N.Y.		800	800	
Poughkeepsie, N.Y.			700	700
Rochester, N.Y.		1,500		
Saratoga Springs, N.Y.			1,000	1,000a
Syracuse, N.Y.		1,300	1,300	
Troy, N.Y.			1,400	
Utica, N.Y.		1,200	1,200	1,200
Yonkers, N.Y.			200	400
Akron, O.		700	700	600
Canton, O.		600	650	600
Cincinnati, O.		1,850	1,860	1,860
Cleveland, O.		2,500	2,500	2,500
Columbus, O.		1,500	1,600	1,600
Dayton, O.		1,500	1,500	1,500
Fremont, O.	(1879)[8] 500a			
Hamilton, O.			750	800
Mansfield, O.				480
Newark, O.			1,000e	
Sandusky, O.		750	900	900
Springfield, O.		950	1,500	1,500
Steubenville, O.		900	500	500
Toledo, O.		575	1,250	1,250a
Zanesville, O.		525	525	

TABLE I cont.

City	Misc. Reports	1874[4]	1876[5]	1877[6]
Allegheny, Pa.		$1, 250	$1, 200	$1, 000
Erie, Pa.		1, 000	1, 000	
Harrisburg, Pa.		800	700	700
Lancaster, Pa.			1, 000	
Morristown, Pa.		300	300	300
Pittsburg, Pa.		1, 200	1, 200	
Titusville, Pa.			400	380
Newport, R. I.		1, 000	900	800
Providence, R. I.	(1879)[8] $1, 700a		1, 800	
Woonsocket, R. I.		400	300	500
Charleston, S. C.	(1878)[7] 900			
Nashville, Tenn.		1, 100	1, 300	1, 170
Burlington, Vt.			600	
Wheeling, W. Va.	(1878)[8] 25b			
Milwaukee, Wis.			1, 800f	
La Crosse, Wis.				1, 100
Georgetown, D. C.		200i		
Washington, D. C.	(1870)[2] 1, 200	800i	625i	675i

Legend: a. Maxium salary.
          b. Per month.
          c. Per month maximum.
          d. 1 cent per week from each scholar.
          D. Salary per year for each hour taught per week employee
          e. For music and German.
          f. 1875 Commissioner report.
          g. For French and German also.
          i. White schools only.
          j. West division.

A geographical distribution of the cities tabulated in Table I
would show that the Northeastern section of the United States far
outstripped all other sections in the employment of a special music
teacher.   The South and Southwest had practically no representation,
while the Midwest and Farwest had some.   The four states having
the largest number of special music teachers were Massachusetts,
New York, Pennsylvania, and Ohio.   It is probable that some
cities having special music teachers did not report to the Commissioner.   It does seem reasonable to suppose, however, that
most of them did report.

Table 2 presents a frequency distribution of secondary school
vocal and instrumental music instruction based upon reports
gathered by the United States Commissioner of Education for 1874.
The schools are divided into three classifications: 1) Schools for
boys;   2) Schools for girls;   3) Schools for boys and girls. [9]

By referring to Table 2 it is apparent that the schools for
girls were offering considerably more music instruction than those
for boys.   No information is available for determining the exact
nature of the instrumental music instruction.   School board reports
of the period reveal that piano and guitar lessons usually constituted
the instrumental music program.   The high school orchestra before
1885 did not exist in numbers.

TABLE 2

Frequency Distribution of Secondary Schools
Offering Music Instruction in 1874. [10]

Type of School	Total No. of Schs.	No. Schs. Having Voc. Music	Per Cent of Total No. Schs. Having Voc. Music	No. Schs. Having Instru- mental Music	Per Cent of Total No. of Schs. Having Instru. Music
Schs. for boys	195	80	41	82	42
Schs. for girls	275	223	81	247	89
Schs. for boys and girls	561	345	61	362	64

An important survey was made by a commission appointed by
John Eaton, United States Commissioner of Education in 1885. Its
primary impetus was a request from the Music Teachers' National
Association. Cooperation for the survey came from many other
sources. The members of the National Association who worked in
cooperation with the Commissioner were Theodore Presser, Charles
W. Landon, H. E. Holt, N. C. Stewart, George F. Bristow, and
Luther Whiting Mason. Their findings provide a storehouse of facts
concerning the teaching of music education in the United States as of
1886. Reflected are the great strides accomplished fifty-five years
after the original efforts of Woodbridge, Mason, Webb, Ives, and
others. [11]

The Bureau by means of the questionnaire received replies from
343 (344) cities and towns. These cities embraced a population
of 7,933,193, with a school population of 2,181,634, and with a
public school enrollment of 1,209,677. The questions submitted
were as follows:

> Is music taught? In what grades?
> By special teacher? By regular teacher?
> By both regular and special teachers?
> Number of hours per week?
> Please state what, if any, instrument is used to
>   lead the singing.
> Which system is used of the three commonly known
>   as "fixed do," "movable do," or "tonic sol-fa,"
>   or are different ones used in different schools?
> If different systems are used, which finds most favor?
> What text-books or charts are used?
> Are there stated musical examinations or exhibitions,
>   are both?
> Is notation required in music books?
> Please send copy of regulations, if any have been
>   printed.
> Please state, if possible, whether any established
>   vocal societies (independent of church choirs)
>   are now in active operation in your city; if so,
>   please give names of societies and full addresses
>   of conductors.
> If music is not taught in your schools, what objections,
>   if any, would probably be urged against the intro-
>   duction of systematic instruction in it? [12]

Of the reporting cities, 96 indicated no instruction, whereas,
132 (sic 133) said that the regular teacher offers the instruction,
19 stated only special teachers of music were used, while 96
suggested the employment of both ordinary and special teachers
for instruction.

If we take an analysis of the report verbatim, we learn first-
hand of the equipment, methods of instruction, and teaching
personnel under four different categories.

> Of the 96 cities where no instruction in music is given,
> 6 report that singing is permitted, 15 that it is encouraged;
> 12 of them have organs, 2 have pianos and organs, and 1
> has melodeons, which instruments are used to lead in
> occasional rote singing, while the other 81 places possess
> no musical instruments for such use. Of these 96 cities
> where no instruction is given, 76 give reasons. In one
> the school board considers the community too poverty-
> stricken; another finds no reason except the lack of time;
> a third, that the organization is immature; a fourth, the
> population is reported to be mainly made up of manufacturing
> operatives, and it is a common remark that the children
> are too poor to occupy the time spent out of the mills in
> learning music; some members of the board class music
> as among the 'brass ornaments;' a fifth give lack of interest;
> a sixth, the community considers the 'three R's' are the
> only subjects that should occupy a permanent place in public
> instruction; seventh, music has been taught poorly in the
> past and failed lamentably; eight, no objection is offered
> to music, but the board is not financially able to introduce
> it; ninth, special teachers in music were dropped because
> the people were heavily taxed to erect necessary buildings;
> tenth, though there is no music taught, there is no special
> reason assigned. And so the objections go on ringing the
> changes on these various negations, sometimes repeating
> the lack of qualification on the part of the teachers.

> Next there follow replies from 132 (133) superintendents of
> cities where instruction is given exclusively by the ordinary
> teaching force. Of these, 59 appear to teach either by rote
> or without system; 14 use the fixed do; 51 the movable do;
> 2 use the tonic sol-fa only; the rest use two or more of
> these methods variously combined and modified. Most of
> these have musical instruments, and 73 of them mention
> various text-books, charts, etc. The time devoted to
> music varies from one to three and three-quarter hours,
> according to the degree of importance attached to this study.

> Nineteen superintendents of cities report only special teachers
> for music in their public schools; 2 of these teach by fixed

do, 13 by movable do, and the other 4 use mixed methods.

Of the 96 cities and towns employing special instructors
in addition to the ordinary teachers for regular instruction
in music, 65 use movable do; 6 use fixed do; 3 use tonic
sol-fa; and the other 22 use various combinations or
modifications.

Among the 247 places teaching vocal music, 171 have it in
"all grades;" 43 use pianos; 69 use organs; 55 use pianos
and organs; 20 use other instruments; 36 use none.

As to the number of hours per week devoted to training
in music, the reports of the several superintendents of
schools where there are no special teachers of music
show that, in 86 of these places reporting, the time
varies from thirty minutes to five hours per week; but the
favorite time seems to be from one to two hours per
week. "[13]

The committee in charge of the study certainly found some
reasons for satisfaction in the data which revealed the strides
which had been made in American music education.   They were,
however, not unaware of the great need for further growth.   They
concluded:

This inquiry is still in progress, but the returns to come
in can hardly change essentially the basis here furnished
for inference.   The time has not yet come when musicians
and the friends of their art in the United States can lay
aside their harps with the sweet assurance that there re-
mains nothing for them to do.   Certainly it is clear that
there is not likely to be a musical millennium in our city
schools before Christmas. [14]

Table 3 (p. 387) is a tabulation of the commission's report
dealing with "Places in Which Music is Not Taught. " It reveals
some discrepencies with information tabulated in Table I.
The cities of East Saginaw, Michigan, Rochester, New York,
Steubenville, Ohio, and Woonsocket, Rhode Island were reported
by the commission as not having music, whereas, the United States
Commissioner in his reports of 1874, 1876, and 1877 revealed that
these cities had music instruction in their public schools.

TABLE 3

Places in Which Music Was Not Taught in 1885[15]

City	Population 1885
Fort Smith, Ark.	9, 000
Nevada, Cal.	4, 022
Pueblo, Col.	13, 500†
Augusta, Ga.	21, 891
Savannah, Ga.	34, 789
Auburn, Ill.	900
Carlyle, Ill.	2, 218
Dwight, Ill.	1, 400
Freeport, Ill.	10, 000
Joliet, Ill.	19, 000
Meredosia, Ill.	950
Mount Vernon, Ill.	3, 000
Princeton, Ill.	3, 500
Sycamore, Ill.	3, 030
Anderson, Ind.	5, 000
Butler, Ind.	1, 500
Cannelton, Ind.	2, 000
Hammond, Ind.	2, 500
Seymour, Ind.	5, 981
Spencer, Ind.	1, 800
South Bend, Ind.	13, 324
Cedar Rapids, Ia.	18, 000
Clear Lake, Ia.	1, 100
Clinton, Ia.	12, 000†
Decorah, Ia.	4, 000
Iowa City, Ia.	10, 000
Marshaltown, Ia.	10, 000
Muscatine, Ia.	10, 000
Augusta, Kan.	1, 500
Beloit, Kan.	1, 835
Independence, Kan.	5, 200
Leavenworth, Kan.	26, 000
Covington, Ky.	30, 000
Rockland, Me.	7, 599
Billerica, Mass.	3, 000
Chicopee, Mass.	11, 416†††††
Milford, Mass.	9, 310
Williamstown, Mass.	3, 394

TABLE 3 cont.

City	Population 1885
Byron, Mich.	374
Coldwater, Mich.	5, 099
East Saginaw, Mich.	29, 100
Fenton, Mich.	2, 434
Frankfort, Mich.	1, 100
Jackson, Mich.	20, 000
Duluth, Minn.	20, 000†
Fairbault, Minn.	5, 760
Fergus Falls, Minn.	1, 635
Owatonna, Minn.	3, 300
Sauk Center, Minn.	2, 500
Lexington, Mo.	4, 050
Louisiana, Mo.	4, 325
Helena, Mont.	8, 000
Virginia, Nev.	10, 917
Kingston, N. C.	3, 000
Bow, N. H.	700
Dunbarton, N. H.	350
Fremont, N. H.	623
Gorham, N. H.	1, 800
Jackson, N. H.	464
Marlow, N. H.	716
New Market, N. H.	2, 400
Ossipee, N. H.	1, 782
Peterborough, N. H.	2, 300
Binghamton, N. Y.	17, 315
Rochester, N. Y.	89, 363
Little Falls, N. Y.	8, 000
Ashtabula, O.	4, 445
Barnesville, O.	2, 438
Bellefontaine, O.	4, 001
Cadiz, O.	1, 896
Chillicothe, O.	13, 000
Ironton, O.	8, 857
Lancaster, O.	7, 000
Marietta, O.	5, 444
Salem, O.	4, 041
Steubenville, O.	12, 093
Wauseon, O.	2, 000

TABLE 3 cont.

City	Population 1885
Eugene City, Ore.	1, 850†
Altoona, Pa.	19, 764
Johnstown, Pa.	8, 330††
McKeesport, Pa.	12, 000
West Chester, Pa.	7, 000†††
Williamsport, Pa.	18, 934
Cumberland, R. I.	6, 445†††††
Little Compton, R. I.	1, 202
Tiverton, R. I.	2, 810
Woonsocket, R. I.	16, 050††
Andover, Vt.	564
Jamaica, Vt.	856
Lyndonville, Vt.	788
Norwich, Vt.	809††††
Royalton, Vt.	1, 679
Seattle, Wash.	9, 827
Fond du Lac, Wis.	13, 094
Janesville, Wis.	9, 000
Oshkosh, Wis.	15, 758

Legend:
> †Estimated
> ††Education Report 1882-1883
> †††Education Report 1883-1884
> ††††Census, 1880
> †††††Township

Tables III, IV, V, VI, reproduced from United States Commissioner of Education John Eaton's study, The Study of Music in Public Schools.   10.

The 96 cities though reporting No were divided into sixteen divisions, each having some qualification.   They are quoted directly from the study.

11 cities that answer, without qualification, No.

17 cities answer No, giving expense as the reason.

2 cities answer No, giving want of money.

7 cities answer No, whose schools have a crude organization.

4 cities answer No, where importance of music is misunderstood.

3 cities answer No, because of public opposition or indifference.

2 cities answer No, failure in former attempts.

2 cities answer No, lack of time for music in addition to other studies.

10 cities answer No, because of inability of teaching force, expense, lack of means, public opposition, crude organization, injurious results, lack of time.

4 cities answer No, because of indifferent results, crude organization, public indifference, public misapprehension as to value of music.

3 cities answer No, Lack of means, lack of time and public misapprehension.

1 city answered No, because of lack of means.

3 cities answer No, because of local and temporary reasons, not specified.

6 cities answer No, yet stating that there is no existing objection.

6 cities answer No, in which singing by rote, etc., is permitted.

15 cities answer No, in which singing by rote and to accompaniment by instruments are mentioned. [16]

Table 4 treating the materials gathered under the heading "Places in Which Music is Taught by the Usual Teaching Force," significantly shows that small and large communities were administering music instruction.   Of the 132 cities (sic 133), it appears that the Midwestern states, Illinois, Iowa, Missouri, Wisconsin, and Minnesota, were beginning to offer music education after 1850. Down to 1885 the Southern states were still feebly represented.

TABLE 4

Places in Which Music Was Taught by the Usual
Teaching Force in 1885. [17]

City	Population 1885
Birmingham, Ala.	21, 000
Lonoke, Ark.	1, 200
Texarkana, Ark.	6, 000
Vallejo, Cal.	6, 800†
Bridgeport, Conn.	37, 000
Meriden, Conn.	20, 000
New Britain, Conn.	17, 000
Central City, Col.	2, 600
South Pueblo, Col.	12, 500†
Wilmington, Del.	42, 600
Atlanta, Ga.	40, 000
Arcola, Ill.	1, 641
Charleston, Ill.	3, 500
Chester, Ill.	3, 500
Decatur, Ill.	9, 548
Edwardsville, Ill.	2, 790
Elgin, Ill.	14, 351
Galena, Ill.	6, 460
Highland, Ill.	1, 963
Morris, Ill.	4, 000
Paris, Ill.	4, 343
Pekin, Ill.	7, 000
Pullman, Ill.	7, 000
Rantoul, Ill.	1, 000
Rockford, Ill.	19, 576
Sparta, Ill.	1, 800
Springfield, Ill.	19, 746
Attica, Ind.	3, 000
Crown Point, Ind.	3, 730
Garrett, Ind.	1, 800
Rushville, Ind.	3, 600
Warsaw, Ind.	3, 123
East Waterloo, Ia.	6, 500
Knoxville, Ia.	2, 766
Malvern, Ia.	1, 000
Marengo, Ia.	2, 500

TABLE 4 cont.

City	Population 1885
Marian, Ia.	4, 000
Waterloo, Ia.	6, 000
Cherryvale, Kan.	4, 000
Holton, Kan.	2, 000
Lawrence, Kan.	12, 000
Manhattan, Kan.	3, 000
Henderson, Ky.	8, 178
New Orleans, La.	216, 000
Farmington, Me.	3, 353
Amesbury, Mass.	3, 500
Canton, Mass.	5, 000
Fall River, Mass.	55, 000
Falmouth, Mass.	2, 422
Northborough, Mass.	1, 676
Westfield, Mass.	7, 587
Armada, Mich.	800
Bronson, Mich.	1, 000
Cedar Springs, Mich.	1, 141
Detroit, Mich.	134, 834
Ludington, Mich.	5, 433
Mason, Mich.	1, 907
Menominee, Mich.	5, 057
Mount Clemens, Mich.	3, 850
Saint Joseph, Mich.	3, 500
Spring Lake, Mich.	2, 480
Three Rivers, Mich.	2, 700
West Bay City, Mich.	10, 000
Albert Lea, Minn.	4, 500
Moorhead, Minn.	4, 500
Red Wing, Minn.	6, 870
Rochester, Minn.	5, 500
Saint Cloud, Minn.	6, 000
Waseca, Minn.	3, 008
Winona, Minn.	16, 000
Brownsville, Mo.	1, 200
Hannibal, Mo.	12, 878
Kansas City, Mo.	56, 000
Marysville, Mo.	5, 009
Springfield, Mo.	12, 000

TABLE 4 cont.

City	Population 1885
Bismark, N. D.	2, 500†
Newport, N. H.	2, 612
New Brunswick, N. J.	17, 166
Paterson, N. J.	60, 000
Passaic, N. J.	9, 000
Perth Amboy, N. J.	4, 808
Rahway, N. J.	6, 840
Trenton, N. J.	29, 910
Binghamton, N. Y.	17, 317
Dunkirk, N. Y.	9, 700
Flushing, N. Y.	6, 683
Ithaca, N. Y.	9, 105
Lockport, N. Y.	13, 522
Port Jervis, N. Y.	8, 678
Rome, N. Y.	12, 194
Sing Sing, N. Y.	5, 009
Syracuse, N. Y.	64, 586
Wilmington, N. C.	17, 350
Coshocton, O.	3, 500
Elmore, Ohio	1, 144
Lima, Ohio	7, 800
Massillon, O.	9, 011
Pataskala, O.	700
Tiffin, O.	7, 879
Waverly, O.	1, 800
Portland, Oregon	29, 000
Beaver Falls, Pa.	8, 000
Bradford, Pa.	10, 000
Chambersburg, Pa.	6, 900†
Chester, Pa.	14, 996
Danville, Pa.	8, 346
Frackville, Pa.	2, 500
Hazleton, Pa.	10, 000
Lock Haven, Pa.	8, 000
New Castle, Pa.	10, 000
Phoenixville, Pa.	7, 000
Pottsville, Pa.	13, 381
Towanda, Pa.	3, 814
Westerly, R. I.	6, 000

TABLE 4 cont.

City	Population 1885
Spartanburg, S. C.	3, 253
Sioux Falls, S. D.	6, 400
Clarksville, Tenn.	7, 326
Knoxville, Tenn.	24, 850
Memphis, Tenn.	33, 593
Union City, Tenn.	4, 300
El Paso, Texas	4, 500
Gainesville, Texas	8, 500
Hartford, Vt.	820
Woodstock, Vt.	2, 700†
Tacoma, Wash.	6, 972
Wall Walla, Wash.	3, 500
Palatine, W. Va.	800
Appleton, Wis.	10, 496
Beloit, Wis.	5, 500
Hudson, Wis.	3, 000
Kenosha, Wis.	5, 043
Racine, Wis.	16, 031
River Falls, Wis.	2, 500

Legend:
      †Estimated

The 133 cities represented in Table 4 were divided into ten divisions, each qualifying the method employed in teaching music reading. They were:

No Cities.

50 Places in which music is taught by rote, or without system.
14 On the basis of "Fixed Do" as a system.
52 On the basis of "Movable Do" as a system.
 2 On the basis of "Tonic sol-fa" system for said instruction.
 4 Using both "Fixed Do" and "Movable Do. "
 2 Using "Fixed Do" and "Tonic Sol-fa. "
 4 Using "Movable Do" and "Tonic sol-fa. "
 1 Using "Tonic Sol-fa" and "Numerical style. "
 3 Using "Different systems, " but not specifying. 18

The fact that 52 of the 132 (Sic 133) were using the <u>movable do</u> does not necessarily mean that more cities were using that method. More questionnaires could have been sent to schools employing such a device for teaching vocal music.   The factor of chance selection may have influenced the findings.

Table 5 indicates that nineteen of the 343 (sic 344) cities said that they employed a special teacher of music who alone was doing the teaching.   The methods of instruction employed by these teachers were six.   (Appended to Table 5).   During the early history of public school music most of the special music teachers were working in conjunction with the regular classroom instructor. In the larger cities, where finances permitted the employment of one or two special music instructors, their services were so much in demand that it was impossible for them to adequately meet the needs of each schoolroom under their supervision.   This necessitated supervisor and regular classroom teacher cooperation in the teach-ing of the daily music lesson.   Before 1850 the idea of having the teacher of the regular classroom conduct the music lesson was in vogue in some places.

TABLE 5

Places Where Musical Instruction Was Given By
Special Teachers of Singing Only (1885)[19]

City	Reported Population 1885
Morrilton, Ark.	1, 200
South Evanston, Ill.	2, 080
Franklin, Ind.	3, 500
Greencastle, Ind.	5, 000
Kokomo, Ind.	5, 000
Wichita, Kan.	13, 000
Concord, Mass.	3, 922
Battle Creek, Mich.	10, 061
Calumet, Mich.	8, 500
Hillsdale, Mich.	5, 000
Lake Linden, Mich.	3, 000

TABLE 5 cont.

City	Reported Population 1885
Saint Johns, Mich.	2,613
Stillwater, Minn.	15,608
Poughkeepsie, N.Y.	20,207
Newark, O.	10,000
Xenia, O.	8,000
McKinney, Tex.	12,000
Brattleborough, Vt.	5,880
Black River Falls, Wis.	1,800

The special teacher (Table 5) employed the following methods of teaching music:

No. Cities	
2	Used "Fixed do."
13	Used "Movable do."
1	Used "Movable do" and "Tonic sol-fa."
1	Used "Round-note system."
1	Used "Staff-system."
1	Used "Combination" of methods.

Table 6 reveals that a very common procedure among the 344 cities in question was to employ a special music teacher who was aided in his work by the regular instructional personnel. This plan was in use from coast to coast.

TABLE 6

Places Where Music Was Taught By Both Special
and Ordinary Teaching Force in 1885[20]

City	Reported Population 1885
Oakland, Cal.	43,109
Hartford, Conn.	42,553
Naugatuck, Conn.	5,000†
New Haven, Conn.	61,388
Norwich (Center), Conn.	7,565† (††)
Washington, D.C.	177,625

TABLE 6 cont.

City	Reported Population 1885
Chicago, Ill.	629, 985
Clinton, Ill.	2, 700†
Rock Island, Ill.	11, 868
Evansville, Ind.	38, 000
Fort Wayne, Ind.	26, 880
La Fayette, Ind.	14, 860
Logansport, Ind.	11, 198
Princeton, Ind.	2, 700
Richmond, Ind.	12, 742
Terre Haute, Ind.	26, 042
Union City, Ind.	2, 600
Winchester, Ind.	2, 000
Keokuk, Ia.	14, 000
Oscaloosa, Ia.	4, 598
Ottumwa, Ia.	11, 000
Baltimore, Md.	332, 315
Brookline, Mass.	8, 074
Cambridge, Mass.	52, 740
Chelsea, Mass.	25, 000
Easton, Mass.	3, 901
Fitchburg, Mass.	13, 500
Gloucester, Mass.	19, 329
Lawrence, Mass.	39, 178
Lynn, Mass.	50, 000†
Malden, Mass.	13, 464
Marlborough, Mass.	10, 126
North Adams, Mass.	10, 192
Northampton, Mass.	13, 248
Peabody, Mass.	9, 033
Pittsfield, Mass.	13, 364
Somerville, Mass.	25, 725
Taunton, Mass.	21, 145
Waltham, Mass.	14, 445
Winchester, Mass.	4, 500
Woburn, Mass.	12, 000
Worcester, Mass.	70, 000
Ann Arbor, Mich.	9, 400
Grand Haven, Mich.	6, 000
Grand Rapids, Mich.	42, 000
Hastings, Mich.	2, 700
Ionia, Mich.	5, 000
Saginaw, Mich.	14, 000
Ypsilanti, Mich.	4, 984

TABLE 6 cont.

City	Reported Population 1885
Minneapolis, Minn.	115, 000
St. Paul, Minn.	100, 000
St. Peter, Minn.	4, 000
St. Joseph, Mo.	32, 431
Dover, N. H.	11, 687
Jersey City, N. J.	187, 950
Orange, N. J.	13, 206
Brooklyn, N. Y.	650, 000†
Buffalo, N. Y.	154, 375
Elmira, N. Y.	20, 541
Hudson, N. Y.	8, 670
Jamestown, N. Y.	18, 000
Kingston, N. Y.	22, 000
Utica, N. Y.	39, 536
Yonkers, N. Y.	18, 892
Akron, O.	16, 467
Canton, O.	12, 258
Cincinnati, O.	255, 000
Circleville, O.	6, 250
Cleveland, O.	227, 760
Columbus, O.	66, 669
Galion, O.	6, 000
Garrettsville, O.	969
Hamilton, O.	12, 122
Lebanon, O.	2, 707
London, O.	3, 100
Martin's Ferry, O.	5, 100
Painesville, O.	3, 987
Ravenna, O.	4, 000
Toledo, O.	50, 143
Washington, C. H., O.	4, 200
Willoughby, O.	1, 001
Wilmington, O.	3, 000†
Erie, Pa.	27, 730
Norristown, Pa.	13, 234
Philadelphia, Pa.	847, 170
Pittsburg, Pa.	180, 000
Shenandoah, Pa.	14, 000
Titusville, Pa.	9, 046
Cranston, R. I.	6, 000
Pawtucket, R. I.	19, 030
Providence, R. I.	104, 857

TABLE 6 cont.

City	Reported Population 1885
Yankton, S. D.	3, 591
Huntington, W. Va.	5, 000
La Crosse, Wis.	22, 000
Madison, Wis.	10, 324
Milwaukee, Wis.	115, 571

Legend:

    † Estimated
    (††) District
    Note: Information taken directly from study.

The cities represented in Table 6 employed the following methods of teaching music reading:

Cities	
65	Used "Movable do. "
6	Used "Fixed do. "
3	Used "Tonic sol-fa. "
9	Used "Movable do" with "Tonic sol-fa. "
2	Used "Fixed do and Movable do. "
11	Used Unique or exceptional methods.

By 1890 public school music had become an established profession. During the period 1830-1890 there were 351 cities in twenty-five states and the District of Columbia offering music instruction. Horace Mann as Secretary of the Massachusetts State Board of Education reported in 1844 that 117 towns and cities in his state were offering vocal music instruction. Of the 117, five cities were included among those to be found, leaving a net of 112. The two sources mentioned above permit us to state that prior to 1890, at least 463 towns and cities were offering public school music in America.

School music introductions were more numerous in Massachusetts New York, Pennsylvania, and Ohio. In secondary institutions whether private or public, schools for boys, girls, and boys and girls were receiving vocal and some instrumental (piano, guitar, etc.) music instruction. It was found that the fixed- do, movable-do, tonic-sol-fa, and the numerical style were the favorite methods

employed in teaching music reading. There were many schools
not having music. It was found that the reasons for the lack of
music instruction were expense, music misunderstood by professional and lay groups, failure in attempts to inaugurate a
definite music program, lack of time, and inability of teaching
force to teach it. Those schools which did not employ a special
music teacher left its instruction to chance or did not even
encourage it. The statistical picture presented in this chapter
was the fruition of sixty years of sustained growth in the field
of American public school music.

Notes

1. Report of the United States Commissioner of Education,
    1874. 550-553.

2. Report of the United States Commissioner of Education,
    1870. 312.

3. Report of the United States Commissioner of Education,
    1872. 55.

4. Report of the United States Commissioner of Education,
    1874. 550-553.

5. Report of the United States Commissioner of Education,
    1876. 532-537.

6. Report of the United States Commissioner of Education,
    1877. 338-342.

7. Report of the United States Commissioner of Education,
    1878. 336-341.

8. Report of the United States Commissioner of Education,
    1879. 338-342.

9. Report of the United States Commissioner of Education,
    1874. 1-1v.

10. Ibid., 1-1v.

11. The Study of Music in Public Schools. Bureau of Education,
     Circular of Information. No. 1. 1886. 41-78.

12. _Ibid._, 51-52.

13. _Ibid._, 52-53.

14. _Ibid._, 53.

15. _Ibid._, 55-59.

16. _Ibid._, 55-59.

17. _Ibid._, 60-65.

18. _Ibid._, 60-65.

19. _Ibid._, 66-67.

20. _Ibid._, 68-72.

BIBLIOGRAPHY

1. New York University Henry Barnard Manuscripts Letters

   N. Y. U. No. 207.   Theodore Dwight, to Henry Barnard, December 11, 1838.

   N. Y. U. No. 359.   George L. Foote to Henry Barnard, January 28? 1840.

   N. Y. U. No. 433.   Alexander Dallas Bache to Henry Barnard, July 21, 1840.

2. Reports of the United States Commissioner of Education (music teaching is mentioned in the following reports on the pages indicated).

   1870.   pages 98, 100, 118, 127, 142, 163, 168, 169, 171, 174-175, 215, 217-218, 251, 296, 312, 406, 407, 535.

   1871.   pages 91-92, 165-168, 304-305, 320-321, 329-330, 536-537.

   1872.   (Music in common schools) pages 39, 52, 55, 121, 151, 206-208, 273, 275, 536, 579.

   1873.   pages 5, 23, 31, 40, 41, 71, 161-162, 190-191, 249, 267, 280, 281, 303, 316, 317, 318, 374, 409, 432, 436.

   1874.   pages 20-21, 24, 43-44, 103-104, 170, 207-208, 220-221, 268, 281, 297, 298, 311, 328, 331, 358, 362, 399, 471, 550.

   1875.   pages lxvii, lxx, lxxi-lxxii, 18, 50, 51, 62, 83, 84, 86, 88, 89, 96, 106, 107, 118, 121, 123, 129, 132, 187-188, 195, 213, 216, 228-229, 280, 293, 296, 297, 322, 325, 332, 337, 351, 364, 379, 399, 401, 411, 418, 427.

   1876.   pages ccvi, 14, 20, 67, 71, 171, 266, 280, 395, 396, 403, 404, 532-537.

   1877.   pages lxx-lxxi, lxxviii-lxxix, xxv, 16, 22, 26-27, 47, 55, 197, 338-343.

   1878.   xxxviii, xl, xliii-xlv, lxxviii-lxxix, cxl, cxli-cxliii, clxxv, 10, 17, 28-29, 44-45, 62, 70-71, 72, 77, 83, 85, 90, 93, 100, 105, 108-110, 116-117, 123, 124, 143, 167-168, 175-177, 193-

1878 cont. 194, 207, 228, 231, 249, 336-341, 361-365, 446-482, 584-593, 597-598, 601, 608-609, 614-617, 720-721.

1879. pages 177, 216, 338-344, 368-375, 388-412, 459-496, 600-611, 615-617, 632-633, 638-641, 675-684, 687, 693-694.

1880. pages 231, 255, 279, 288, cxc.

3. State or Territorial Superintendent of Instruction Reports.

(Note: Hundreds of other reports were examined, but those that are cited contained pertinent information)

Alabama 1854, 1869, 1871, 1872, 1873-76, 1879, 1886, 1887, 1894.

Arizona 1889-1890, 1895-1896, 1897-1898, 1898-1906.

Arkansas 1883-1886, 1889-1890. (Biennial Reports ending 1872, 1882.)

California 1851-1854, 1856, 1858, 1878-79.

Colorado Biennial reports, ending 1881.

Connecticut 1842, 1848, 1857, 1862, 1868/1869, 1871/1872.

Georgia 1885-86, 1893.

Illinois Biennial reports, ending 1858, 1860, 1868, 1872, 1876, 1880, 1882, 1884, 1888.

Indiana Biennial reports, ending 1878, 1882, 1892.

Iowa Biennial reports, ending 1852, 1861, 1866, 1869, 1872, 1885.

Kansas 1861, 1863, 1864, 1865, 1866, 1867, 1868, 1869, 1870, 1871, 1872, 1873, 1874, 1875, 1876, 1878, 1880, (Biennial reports, ending 1882, 1884, 1886.)

Kentucky 1854, 1855, 1859-1860, 1864, 1865, 1866, 1867, 1869, 1876, 1880-1881, 1884-1886.

Louisiana 1860, 1864, 1865, 1866, 1867-68, 1870, 1871, 1872, 1873, 1874, 1875, 1877, 1879, 1880, 1883, 1892, 1893.

Maine 1873, 1875.

Maryland 1866, 1867, 1872, 1873, 1874.

Massachusetts 1839, 1844, 1845, 1846, 1847, 1873, 1874.

Michigan   1853, 1859, 1875, 1880.

Minnesota   1897, 1891/1892.

Mississippi   1871.

Missouri   1872.

Nevada   1865, 1868-72, 1879-82, 1885-86.

New Hampshire   1877, 1880, 1889.

New Jersey   1864, 1871, 1873, 1874, 1879.

New York   1828, 1829, 1830, 1832, 1833, 1834, 1835, 1836, 1838,
       1840, 1843, 1844, 1845, 1852, 1853, 1854, 1855, 1856,
       1858, 1859, 1860, 1861, 1862, 1863, 1864, 1865, 1867,
       1868, 1869, 1870, 1871, 1872, 1873, 1874, 1875, 1876,
       1877, 1878, 1880, 1881, 1883, 1884, 1886, 1889.

North Carolina   1877, 1880.   (Biennial reports, ending 1882, 1884,
       1886, 1888, 1890)

Ohio   1854, 1855, 1856, 1881, 1886.

Oregon   1887, 1889.   (Biennial reports, ending 1891, 1900.)

Pennsylvania   1833, 1834, 1836, 1837, 1839, 1840, 1841, 1843,
       1848, 1849, 1850, 1853, 1854, 1881, 1884.

Rhode Island   1848, 1856, 1864, 1868, 1874, 1875, 1876, 1877,
       1881, 1882, 1883.

South Carolina   1869, 1870, 1871, 1872, 1873.

South Dakota   Biennial reports, ending 1894, 1896, 1898.

Tennessee   1872, 1875, 1877, 1880.

Texas   Biennial reports, ending 1882, 1884, 1886, 1888.

Utah   1864, 1865, 1867, 1869, 1871.   (Biennial reports, ending
       1879, 1881, 1883.)

Vermont   1847, 1848, 1857, 1858, 1859, 1860, 1861, 1863, 1864,
       1867, 1869, 1872, 1874, 1880, 1882, 1886, 1888.

Virginia   1871, 1872, 1873, 1874, 1875, 1876, 1877, 1878, 1879,
       1880, 1881, 1882, 1883, 1884, 1885, 1888.

Washington   1890 (Biennial reports, ending 1873, 1881, 1885, 1887,
       1889.)

West Virginia Biennial reports, ending 1878, 1880, 1884, 1896.

Wisconsin 1850, 1852, 1854, 1855, 1857, 1859, 1860, 1861, 1863,
     1865, 1869, 1870, 1871, 1872, 1873, 1875, 1878, 1879,
     1880, 1884, 1886.

Wyoming Biennial reports, ending 1892, 1920, 1924.

4. City Superintendent or School Board Reports

Alabama   Selma, 1908.
                     Talledega, 1910.

Illinois   Chicago, 1858, 1859, 1860, 1861, 1866, 1869,
                         1870, 1871, 1872, 1873, 1874, 1878,
                         1879, 1881, 1883.
                     Cook County School, 1862.
                     Springfield, 1870.

Indiana   Greencastle, 1883, 1884.
                     Indianapolis, 1879.
                     Terre Haute, 1875.

Iowa   Oskaloosa, 1889-1890, 1890-1891.
                     Sioux City, 1890-1891.

Kansas   Lawrence, 1871.

Kentucky   Lexington, 1898-1899.
                     Louisville, 1866-1867.

Maryland   Baltimore, 1846.

Massachusetts   Beverly, 1861, 1862, 1866.
                     Boston, 1826, 1848, 1850, 1851, 1852, 1853,
                         1854, 1856, 1858, 1863, 1864, 1865,
                         1877.
                     Cambridge, 1843.
                     Charlestown, 1856.
                     Dorchester, 1850, 1852, 1856, 1857, 1865,
                         1866, 1867, 1869.
                     Lawrence, 1856.
                     Lowell, 1842, 1851.
                     Newbury, 1861.
                     Newburyport, 1847, 1868, 1869, 1870.
                     Salem, 1856.
                     Shrewsbury, 1851.
                     Somerville, 1849.
                     Springfield, 1858.
                     West Roxbury, 1852, 1856.
                     Worchester, 1871.

Michigan   Detroit, 1886.
                      Grand Rapids, 1886.

Minnesota   Minneapolis, 1871, 1888.

Mississippi   Greenville, 1898.

Missouri   St. Louis, 1858, 1868, 1869, 1870, 1871, 1872,
                          1873, 1877, 1881, 1886.

New Jersey   Jersey City, 1868, 1869, 1883.
                      Trenton, 1889.

New York   Albany, 1870, 1873, 1877, 1878.
                      Brooklyn, 1856, 1856-1860, 1861, 1862, 1863,
                          1864, 1865, 1866, 1877, 1878.
                      New York City, 1849, 1851, 1852, 1853, 1854,
                          1855, 1857, 1869, 1870, 1874, 1875,
                          1877, 1878, 1879, 1880, 1881, 1882,
                          1883, 1884, 1885, 1889, 1895, 1899, 1900.
                      Oswego, 1866-1877 (13th-24th inclusive)
                      Syracuse, 1852, 1855, 1859, 1860, 1861, 1872,
                          1875, 1880, 1883, 1884, 1887, 1893.
                      Troy, 1866, 1884.
                      Utica, 1869, 1873, 1876, 1878.
                      Warsaw, 1879-1860.

Ohio   Cleveland, 1869, 1870.
                      Cincinnati, 1870, 1871, 1875, 1876, 1878,
                          1879, 1882, 1883, 1885.
                      Columbus, 1886, 1890.
                      Dayton, 1882.
                      Toledo, 1889, 1890.

Pennsylvania   Allegheny, 1874.
                      Philadelphia, 1819, 1820, 1821, 1823, 1833,
                          1834, 1835, 1836, 1837, 1838-46, 1847-
                          1852, 1860, 1861, 1864.
                      Pittsburgh, 1870.

Rhode Island   Newport, 1866, 1868, 1870, 1873, 1877, 1883,
                          1884, 1885, 1886.

                      Providence, 1846, 1854, 1858, 1860, 1863,
                          1866, 1867, 1870, 1872, 1873, 1874,
                          1875, 1876, 1877, 1878, 1879, 1881,
                          1882, 1883, 1884, 1885.
                      Richmond, 1863.
                      Warwick, 1887.

South Carolina   Charleston, 1881, 1882.
                      Darlington, 1891.

South Carolina cont. Greenwood, 1905.
                     Spartanburg, 1902.

South Dakota   Yankton, 1896.

Tennessee   Knoxville, 1876.
                     Memphis, 1859, 1860, 1867.
                     Nashville, 1871, 1878.

Utah   Salt Lake City, 1895.

Virginia   Alexandria, 1889.
                     Richmond, 1889.

Vermont   Brandon, 1870.
                     Hardwick, 1862.
                     Newbury, 1856, 1861, 1875.
                     Pittsford, 1875, 1879.

Washington   Seattle, 1885.

West Virginia   Wheeling, 1900, 1901.

Wisconsin   Janesville, 1888.
                     Milwaukee, 1848, 1849, 1863, 1864, 1867,
                                1868, 1872, 1878, 1880, 1881, 1882,
                                1883, 1884.

Washington, D. C.   1845, 1866, 1870, 1871, 1875, 1878, 1887,
                     1888.

5.   Music Books and Collections

The Boston Academy's Collection of Church Music: Consisting of
        the Most Popular Psalm and Hymn Tunes, Anthems, Sentences,
        Chants, Etc., Old and New. (Boston: J. H. Wilkins and R. B.
        Carter, 1843). 357.

Curwen, John. The Teacher's Manual of the "Tonic Sol-Fa Method,"
        Dealing with the Art of Teaching of Music. Third Edition.
        (London: J. Curwen and Sons) 392.

Hullah, John. Time and Tune in the Elementary School A New
        Method of Teaching Vocal Music. (London: 1877). 188.

Mason, Lowell. Juvenile Lyre. (Hartford: Richardson, Lord and
        Holbrook, 1832).

Mason, Lowell. The Song-Garden. (The Song-Garden-Second Book).
        (Boston: Oliver Ditson and Company, 1864). 206.

Mason, Luther W.   The National Music Course, The New First
        Music Reader.   Preparatory to Sight-singing.   Based
        Largely upon C. H. Hohmann.   (New York: Ginn and Company,
        1886).   120.

Mueller, C. E. R. , and Blackman, O.   School Songs.   Book Two.
        Edition with Piano Accompaniment, and School Edition.
        (Chicago: Geo. Sherwood and Company).   96.

Root, Geo. F.   The Glory: A Collection of New Music for Singing
        Classes, Musical Conventions and Choirs.   (Cincinnati: John
        Church and Co.).   400.

Root, Geo. F.   The New Coronet.   A Collection of Music for Sing-
        ing Schools, Musical Conventions and Choirs; Consisting of a
        Course for Elementary Instruction and Training.   A Large
        Number of Part Songs, Solos, Duets, Quartets, Glees and
        Choruses, and a Smaller Number of Tunes, Anthems and
        Chants.   (Chicago: Root and Cady, 1865).   303.

Suffern, J. W.   The Galaxy: A New and Brilliant Collection of
        Music for Choirs, Conventions, Singing Classes and Musical
        Societies.   (Cleveland: S. Brainard's Sons, 1877).   304.

Tucker, Henry.   Nine O'Clock in the Morning.   A Choice Collection
        of Popular Songs, Duets, Trios, Sacred Pieces, etc.   De-
        signed for the Use of Schools, Seminaries, Classes, and the
        Home Circle, with Suitable Rudimentary Exercises and
        Lessons.   (New York: William A. Pond and Co. , 1867).
        224.

Tufts, John W. and Holt, H. E.   The Aoelean Collection: Part-
        Songs for Female Voices.   Third Reader Supplement, of the
        Normal Music Course.   (Chicago: Silver, Burdett and Co. ,
        1888).   208.

Woodbury, I. B.   The Liber Musicus: Or New York Anthem Book,
        and Choirs' Miscellany, Comprising Anthems, Choruses,
        Quartette, Trios, Duets, Songs, Etc. , (New York: F. Hunting-
        ton, 1851).   224.

Zuchtmann, Frederick.   Teachers' Manual of the American Music
        System.   (New York: Richardson, Smith and Co. , 1902).
        113.

6.   Pamphlets

Brooks, Edward.   Special Report of the Teaching of Music in the
        Elementary Schools.   (Philadelphia: Burk and McFetridge Co. ,
        1895).   20.

Education in Charleston, South Carolina. The Disabilities of the
    Unaided South in Public School Facilities. (Charleston,
    S. C.: The News and Courier Book Presses, 1881).   32.

Frazier, Benjamin W. Education of Teachers. Office of Education,
    Department of Interior, Pamphlet No. 60. (Washington:
    Government Printing Office, 1935).   42.

Gray, Ruth A. Doctors' Theses in Education. Office of Education,
    Department of Interior, Pamphlet No. 60. (Washington:
    Government Printing Office, 1935).   69.

Lapp, John A. ed. , Music as a Career. (Chicago: Published by
    Institute of Research, 1937).

Martin, George H. Report on the Teaching of Music in the Public
    Schools of Massachusetts. (Boston: Wright and Potter Print-
    ing Co. , 1906).   25.

Report of the Special Committee on Reduction of Studies in Public
    Schools of the First School District of Pennsylvania.
    (Philadelphia, Pa.: Crissy and Markley, 1861).   16.

Schools and Classes for the Blind, 1917-18. Office of Education,
    Department of Interior, Bulletin No. 78. (Washington:
    Government Printing Office, 1920).   20.

7.   Bulletins

American Education as Described by the French Commission to the
    International Exhibition of 1876. Bureau of Education,
    Circular of Information, No. 5, 1879. (Government Printing
    Office, Washington 1879).   37.

Bush, George G. History of Education in New Hamsphire. Bureau
    of Education, Circular of Information, No. 3, 1898.
    (Government Printing Office, Washington. 1898).   170.

Earhart, Will. Music in the Public Schools. Bureau of Education,
    Bulletin, No. 33, 1914. (Government Printing Office,
    Washington, 1914).   81.

Earhart, Will and Boyd, Charles N. Recent Advances in
    Instruction in Music. Bureau of Education, Bulletin, No.
    20, 1923. (Government Printing Office, Washington, 1923).
    21.

Easton, John. Education in Music at Home and Abroad. The Study
    of Music in Public Schools. Bureau of Education, Circulars
    of Information, No. 1, 1886. (Government Printing Office,
    Washington, 1886).   41-78.

Hayes, Cecil B.   The American Lyceum, Its History and Contri-
        bution to Education.   Office of Education, Bulletin, No. 12.
        (Government Printing Office, Washington, 1932).   72.

Hood, William R., Weeks, Stephen B., and Ford, Sidney.   Digest
        of State Laws Relating to Public Education in Force January
        1, 1915.   Bureau of Education, Bulletin, No. 47, 1915.
        (Government Printing Office, Washington.   1916).   987.

List of Publications by Members of Certain College Faculties and
        Learned Societies in the United States, 1867-1872.   Bureau
        of Education, Circular of Information, No. 4, 1873.
        (Washington: Government Printing Office, 1873).   155.

Manchester, Arthur L.   Music Education in the United States
        Schools and Departments of Music.   Bureau of Education,
        Bulletin, No. 4, 1908.   (Washington: Government Printing
        Office, 1908).   85.

Mayes, Edward.   History of Education in Mississippi.   Bureau of
        Education, Circular of Information, No. 2, 1899.   (Washing-
        ton: Government Printing Office, 1899).   290.

Mayo, A. D.   Industrial Education in the South.   Bureau of
        Education, Circular of Information, No. 5, 1888.   (Washing-
        ton: Government Printing Office, 1888).   ix.

McConathy, Osbourne.   Music Education.   Office of Education,
        Bulletin, No. 20, 1931.   Volume I.   (Washington: Govern-
        ment Printing Office, 1932).   323-352.

Philbrick, John D.   City School Systems in the United States.
        Bureau of Education, Circular of Information, No. 1, 1885.
        (Washington: Government Printing Office, 1885).   207.

Selected List of Works in the New York Public Library.   Bulletin
        of the New York Public Library, 12:32-67.   January to
        December, 1908.

Shinn, Josiah H.   History of Education in Arkansas.   Bureau of
        Education, Circular of Information, No. 1, 1900.   (Washing-
        ton: Government Printing Office, 1900).   121.

Teachers' Institutes.   Bureau of Education, Circulars of Information,
        No. 2, 1885.   (Washington, D. C.: Government Printing
        Office, 1885).   206.

The Study of Music in Public Schools.   Bureau of Education,
        Circular of Information, No. 1, 1886.   (Washington: Govern-
        ment Printing Office, 1886).   78.

The Training of Teachers in Germany. Bureau of Education,
        Circulars of Information, No. 1, 1878. (Washington:
        Government Printing Office, 1878). 36.

Thorpe, Francis N. Benjamin Franklin and the University of
        Pennsylvania. Bureau of Education, Circular of Information,
        No. 2, 1892. (Washington: Government Printing Office,
        1893). 450.

Whitehill, A. R. History of Education in West Virginia. Bureau
        of Education, Circular of Information, No. 30, 1902.
        (Washington: Government Printing Office, 1902). 165.

Wright, Edith and Gray, Ruth A. Bibliography of Research Studies
        in Education. 1930-1931. Office of Education, (Washington:
        Government Printing Office, 1932). 459.

8.   Books

Allan, James A. The Old Model School, Its History and Romance
        1852-1904. "Si monumentum requiris, circumspece."
        (Melbourne: Melbourne University Press, 1934). 225.

Bardon, Fred B. A Historical Recapitulation of the Public Schools
        of Madison, N. J. 1910. 64.

Barnard, Henry. American Pedagogy. Education, the School and
        the Teacher, in American Literature. (Hartford: Brown and
        Gross, 1876). 539.

Barnard, Henry. German Educational Reformers. (Hartford: Brown
        and Gross. Revised Edition, 1878). 724.

Barnard, Henry. Life, Educational Principles, and Methods of John
        Henry Pestalozzi; with Biographical Sketches of Several of
        His Assistants and Disciples. (New York: F. C. Brownell,
        1859). 230-238.

Barnard, Henry. National Education in Europe. (Hartford: Case,
        Tiffany and Company, 1854). 890.

Barnard, Henry. National Education Systems, Instructions and
        Statistics of Public Instruction. (New York: E. Steiger,
        1872). 902.

Barnard, Henry. Reports and Documents Relating to the Public
        Schools of Rhode Island, for 1848. Order of the General
        Assembly, Providence. 1849. 560.

Barnard, Henry. Reports of the Condition and Improvement of the
        Public Schools of Rhode Island, 1845. (Providence: B.
        Cranston and Co., 1846). 255.

Barnard, Henry. True Student Life. Letters, Essays, and
     Thoughts on Studies and Conduct. (Hartford: 1873). 552.

Birchenough, C. History of Elementary Education in England and
     Wales from 1800 to the Present Day. (London: W. B. Olive,
     1914). 394.

Birge, Edward B. History of Public School Music in the United
     States. (Philadelphia: Oliver Ditson Company, 1937). 323.

Boese, Thomas. Public Education in the City of New York: Its
     History, Condition, and Statistics. (New York: Harper and
     Brothers, 1869). 228.

Bourne, Wm. C. History of the Public School Society of the City
     of New York. (New York: Wm. Wood and Co. , 1870). 768.

Bourne, Wm. C. History of the Public School Society of the City
     of New York. (New York: Geo. P. Putnam's Sons, 1873).
     757.

Bradbury, William F. History of the Handel and Haydn Society,
     1890-1897. 76.

Bradbury, William F. The Cambridge High School History and
     Catalogue. (Cambridge, Mass: Moses King, Publisher,
     1882). 93.

Brissot de Warville, J. P. New Travels in the United States of
     America Performed in 1788. (London: 1792).

Brown, Elmer E. The Making of Our Middle Schools. (New York:
     Longmans, Green, and Co. , 1914). 547.

Brubacher, John S. Henry Barnard on Education. (New York:
     McGraw-Hill Book Company, Inc. , 1931). 298.

Cady, Calvin B. Music-Education an Outline. Second Edition.
     (Chicago: Clayton F. Summy Co. , 1904). 80.

Caldwell, Otis W. and Courtis, Stuart A. Then and Now in
     Education 1845-1923. (New York: World Book Company,
     1924). 400.

Chambers, Rev. T. W. Proceedings at the Centennial Anniversary
     of the Dedication of the North Dutch Church, (New York,
     N. Y. , 1869).

Clark, Kenneth S. Municipal Aid to Music in America. (New York:
     National Bureau for the Advancment of Music). 297.

Cubberley, Ellwood P.   Public Education in the United States.
    (Boston: Houghton Mifflin Company, 1919).   517.

Darwin, Erasmus.   A Plan for the Conduct of Female Education in
    Boarding Schools.   (London: J. Drewry, 1797).   128.

Descoeudres, Alice.   The Education of Mentally Defective.
    (New York: Heath and Company).   312.

Edwards, George T.   Music and Musicians of Maine.   (Portland,
    Maine: The Southworth Press, 1928).   542.

Elson, Louis C.   The History of American Music.   (New York:
    The Macmillan Company, 1904).

Elson, Louis C.   The National Music of America.   (Boston: L. C.
    Page and Company, 1899).   326.

Elson, Louis C.   The National Music of America.   (Boston: L. C.
    Page and Company, 1924).   367.

Fisher, W. A.   Notes on Music in Old Boston.   (Boston: Oliver
    Ditson Co., 1918).   96.

Goepp, Philip H.   Annals of Music in Philadelphia and History of
    the Musical Fund Society from its Organization in 1820 to
    the year 1858.   (J. P. Lippincott Company, 1896).   202.

Griffin, M. I. J.   American Catholic Historical Researches.
    (Philadelphia, 1887).   167.

Grizzell, Emit D.   Origin and Development of the High School in
    New England before 1865.   (New York: The Macmillan
    Company, 1923).   428.

Hall, G. S. and Mansfield, John M.   Hints Toward a Select and
    Descriptive Bibliography of Education.   (Boston: D. C. Heath
    and Company, 1886).

Henderson, W. J.   Early History of Singing.   (New York: Longmans,
    Green and Co., 1921).   201.

Hood, George.   A History of Music in New England: With Bio-
    graphical Sketches of Reformers and Psalmists.   (Boston:
    Wilkins, Carter and Co., 1846).   252.

Hubbell, Mark S.   The Charter of the City of Buffalo.   (Buffalo,
    New York: 1896).   425.

Jones, F. O.   Handbook of American Music and Musicians.
    (Canaseraga, New York, N. Y., 1886).

Koos, Leonard V. The American Secondary Schools. (Boston:
    Ginn and Company, 1927). 755.

Lahee, Henry C. Annals of Music in America. (Boston: Marshall
    Jones Company, 1922). 298.

Lippincott, H. M. Early Philadelphia, Its People, Life and Progress.
    (Philadelphia, 1917).

Lutkin, Peter Christian. The Hale Lectures, 1908-9; Music in the
    Church. (Milwaukee: The Young Churchman Company, 1910).
    274.

Macatamney, Hugh. Cradle Days of New York. (1609-1825).
    (New York: Drew and Louis, 1909). 230.

Mann, Horace. Annual Reports of the Secretary of the Board of
    Education of Massachusetts for the Years 1839-1844).
    (Boston: Lee and Shephard, 1891). 466.

Martin, George H. The Evolution of the Massachusetts Public
    School System. (New York: D. Appleton and Company, 1902).
    284.

Mason, Lowell. How Shall I Teach Music? (Boston: Oliver
    Ditson Co., 1875). 32.

Mason, Lowell. Manual of the Boston Academy of Music, for
    Instruction in the Elements of Vocal Music, on the System
    of Pestalozzi. (Fifth Edition). (Boston: Wilkins, Carter,
    and Co., 1847). 252.

Mason, Lowell and Seward, Theodore F. The Pestalozzian Music
    Teacher. (Boston: Oliver Ditson and Co., 1871). 314.

Mason, William. Memories of a Musical Life. (New York: The
    Century Company, 1901). 306.

Mathews, W. S. B. A Hundred Years of Music in America.
    (Chicago: G. L. Howe, 1889). 715.

Monroe, Will S. Bibliography of Education. (New York: D. Apple-
    ton and Company, 1897). 202.

Monroe, Will S. History of Pestalozzian Movement in the United
    States. (New York: C. W. Bardeen, 1907).

Moore, Rev. W. H. History of St. Georges Church, Hempstead, L. I.
    (New York, N. Y., 1881).

Morrison, Alfred J. The Beginnings of Public Education in Virginia.
    1776-1860. (Richmond: Davis Bottom, 1917). 195.

Mursell, James L. Human Values in Music Education. (New York:
    Silver, Burdett, and Company, 1934). 388.

Noffsinger, John S. Correspondence Schools, Lyceums,
    Chautauquas. (New York: The Macmillan Co., 1926). 145.

O'Callaghan, E. B. The Documentary History of the State of New
    York. Vol. I. (Albany, New York: Weed, Parsons and Co.,
    1849). 786.

O'Callaghan, E. B. The Documentary History of the State of New
    York. Vol. II. (Albany, New York: Weed, Parsons and
    Co., 1849). 1211.

O'Callaghan, E. B. The Documentary History of the State of New
    York. Vol. III. (Albany, New York: Weed, Parsons and
    Co., 1850). 1215.

O'Callaghan, E. B. The Documentary History of the State of New
    York. Vol. IV. (Albany, New York: Charles Van Benthuy-
    sen, 1851). 1144.

Painter, T. V. H. A History of Education. (New York: D. Appleton
    and Company, 1899).

Palmer, A. E. The New York Public School Being a History of
    Free Education in the City of New York. (New York: The
    Macmillan Company, 1905). 440.

Parker, Edwin P. History of the Second Church in Hartford.
    (Hartford, Conn., 1892).

Pease, Lewis F. Finding List for the Music Library. (Princeton. :
    The University Library, 1909). 93.

Perkins, Charles C. and Dwight, John S. History of the Handel
    and Haydn Society of Boston, Massachusetts. 1815-1890.
    (Boston: Alfred Mudge and Sons, 1883-1893). 558-123.

Potter, Alonzo and Emerson, George B. The School and the
    School-master. (New York: Harper and Brothers, 1848).
    552.

Pratt, Daniel J. Annals of Public Education in the State of New
    York, from 1626 to 1746. (Albany. The Argus Company,
    1872). 152.

Pratt, W. S. The Music of the Pilgrims. (Boston. Oliver Ditson
    Co., 1921). 80.

Putnam, Daniel. The Development of Primary and Secondary Public
    Education in Michigan. (Ann Arbor, Michigan: George Wahr).
    273.

Reddy, Rev. Wm. and Smyth, W. C.   First Fifty Years of
    Cazenovia Seminary 1825-1875.   (New York: Nelson and
    Phillips, 1877).   832.

Reichel, William C.   A History of the Rise, Progress, and Present
    Condition of the Moravian Seminary for Young Ladies, at
    Bethlehem, Pa.   (Philadelphia: J. B. Lippincott and Co.,
    1870).   570.

Ritter, F. L.   Music in America.   (New York: Charles Scribner's
    Sons, 1900).   521.

Ryan, Thomas.   Recollections of an Old Musician.   (New York:
    E. P. Dutton and Company, 1899).   274.

Schlesinger, Arthur M.   Political and Social Growth of the United
    States (1852-1933).   (New York: MacMillan Company, 1936).
    564.

Scholes, Percy A.   The Puritans and Music in England and New
    England.   (London: Oxford University Press, 1934).   428.

Seybolt, Robert F.   The Private Schools of Colonial Boston.
    (Cambridge, Mass: Harvard University Press, 1935).   106.

Shotwell, John B.   A History of the Schools of Cincinnati.   The
    School Life Company, 1902.   608-15.

Silver, Edgar O.   Condition of Music Instruction in the Public
    Schools of the U. S.   (Boston: New England Publishing Co.,
    1890).   17.

Smith, Edward.   A History of the Schools of Syracuse for Its Early
    Settlement to January 1, 1893.   (Syracuse, New York: C. W.
    Bardeen, 1893).   347.

Sonneck, O. G.   Bibliography of Early Secular American Music.
    (Washington, D. C.: H. L. McQueen, 1905).   194.

Sonneck, O. G.   Early Concert-Life in America.   (Leipzig: Breitkopf
    and Härtel, 1907).   338.

Sonneck, O. G.   Suum Cuique.   Essays in Music.   (New York: G.
    Schirmer, Inc., 1916).   271.

Steele, William L.   Galesburg Public Schools, Their History and
    Work.   (Galesburg, Illinois: Board of Education, 1911).   454.

Stockwell, Thomas B.   A History of the Public Education in Rhode
    Island.   (Providence: Providence Press Company, 1876).
    458.

Swett, John. American Public Schools. History and Pedagogics.
    (New York: The American Book Co. , 1900). 320.

Upton, William Treat. Art-Song in America. (Boston: Oliver
    Ditson Company, 1930). 279.

Walter, Thomas. Grounds and Rules of Music Explained: Or, an
    Introduction to the Art of Singing by Note Fitted to the
    Meanest Capacities Recommended by Several Ministers.
    (Boston. 1746).

Walters, Raymond. The Bethlehem Bach Choir. (New York:
    Houghton Mifflin Co. , 1918). 343.

Warner, Fred M. The General School Laws of Michigan. (Lansing,
    Michigan: Robert Smith Printing Co. , 1903). 152.

Wheelock, Charles F. The University of the State of New York the
    State Department of Education. Secondary Education Report
    for the School Year Ending July 31, 1917. (Albany: The
    University of the State of New York, 1920). 599.

Wightman, Joseph M. Annals of the Boston Primary School
    Committee from its First Establishment in 1818, to its
    Dissolution in 1855. (Boston: George C. Rand and Avery,
    1860). 305.

Woods, G. H. School Bands and Orchestras. (Boston: Oliver
    Ditson Co. , 1920). 198.

Woody, Thomas. Quaker Education in the Colony and State of
    New Jersey. (Philadelphia: University of Pennsylvania,
    1923). 408.

Zimmern, Alice. Methods of Education in the United States.
    (New York: MacMillan And Co. , 1894). 178.

9. Articles.

Adams, T. D. "The Philosophy of Music in the Schools. " New
    England Journal of Education, 9: (April 3, 1879), 211-212.

"Aids to Science. Music. " The New York Teacher, 9: (July,
    1860), 442-445.

Aiken, Walter H. "Music in the Cincinnati Schools. " Journal of
    Proceedings of the Seventh Annual Meeting of the Music
    Supervisors' National Conference. Board of Education,
    Tulsa. 1924. 46-55.

Alcott, W. A.   "William Channing Woodbridge." The American
        Journal of Education, 5: (June, 1858), 51-64.

"Allen, Anna M."   School Music, 9: (March-April, 1909), 30-32.

Allis, John M.   "Music in Our Public Schools." The Michigan
        Teacher, 9: (November, 1874), 391-399.

Andrews, E. A.   "Letter of Communication." American Annals of
        Education and Instruction, 4: (July, 1834), 330-331.

"Annual Report of the Superintendent of Common Schools for 1846."
        Journal of the Rhode Island Institute of Instruction, 1:
        (March, 1846), 99.

"Annual Reports of the Boston Academy of Music from 1833 to
        1840 Inclusive." The North American Review, 52: (April,
        1841), 320-338.

Ansorge, Charles.   "Singing in Schools." The Illinois Teacher, 10:
        (March, 1864), 115-119.

Bache, A. D.   "Elementary Schools." The American Journal of
        Education, 8: (June, 1860), 444.

Bache, A. D.   "Public Schools of Lancaster." The Connecticut
        Common School Journal, 3: (June, 1841), 162-5.

Bache, A. D.   "Report on the Organization of a High School for
        Girls, and Seminary for Female Teachers." The Connecticut
        Common School Journal, 3: (November, 1840), 162.

Baldwin, Ralph L.   "From the Civil War to 1900-Settling the
        Problem of Reading." Papers and Proceedings of the Music
        Teachers' National Association, Forty-Fourth Annual Meeting,
        New York City, December 27-29, 1922. (Hartford News
        Printing Co., 1923). 165-178.

Barnard, Henry.   "Plan of Operation for 1867-68." Report of the
        United States Commissioner of Education, (Washington:
        Government Printing Office, 1867). xii-xiii.

Barnes, Edwin N.   "Emory Poole Russell." School Music, 18:
        (November-December, 1917), 26-27.

Beach, Frank A.   "Music in the Normal School." School Music,
        17: (September-October, 1916), 21-27.

Beck, Herbert H.   "Lititz as an Early Musical Centre." Papers
        Read Before the Lancaster County Historical Society, 19:
        March 5, 1915). 71-84.

"Benjamin Jepson;" School Music, 16: (September, 1915), 40, 42, 44.

Birchard, Clarence C. "The Passing of a Friend." Music Supervisors' Journal, 7: (September, 1920), 5-7.

Birge, Edward B. "Edward Birge." School Music, 22: (January-February, 1921), 36-38.

Birge, Edward B. "One Hundred Years of School Music." Music Educators' Journal, 22: (September, 1935), 19.

Birge, Edward B. "Public School Music's Contribution to Musical Education." Papers and Proceedings of the Music Teachers' National Association at its Fiftieth Annual Meeting, Rochester, New York. December 28-30, 1926. (Hartford: New Printing Co., 1927). 187-203.

Bloomfield, Daniel. "Important Events in Musical History." The Etude, 26: (February, 1908), 85.

Bloomfield, Daniel. "Important Events in Musical History." The Etude, 26: (March, 1908), 161.

"Boston Academy of Music." American Annals of Education and Instruction, 4: (July, 1834), 327.

"Boston Academy of Music." American Annals of Education and Instruction, 5: (July, 1835), 329-330.

"Boston Academy of Music." American Annals of Education and Instruction, 8: (January, 1838), 44.

Boucher, Helen C. "The Training of the Grade Teacher in Music." Journal of Proceedings of the Seventeenth Annual Meeting of the Music Supervisors' National Conference, (Tulsa: Board of Education, 1924). 296-298.

Bourgard, Caroline B. "Early Music in the Louisville Public Schools." School Music, 15: (November-December, 1914), 32, 34.

Bowen, T. H. "On Teaching Music." The New York Teacher, 1: (October, 1852), 205-206.

Bowen, T. H. "On Teaching Music." The New York Teacher, 1: (October, 1852), 266-269.

Brainard, E. C. "Charms of Music." The New York Teacher, 5: (October, 1855-September, 1856), 256-257.

Brand, M. E.   "Some Helpful Things I have Learned From My
    Experience in Teaching Music." Journal of Proceedings
    and Addresses of the National Educational Association,
    Topeka: Kansas Publishing House, 1888).   643-648.

Brown, Gladys A.   "Instrumental Music in Our Public Schools."
    Music Supervisors' Journal, 3: (November, 1916), 12, 14,
    16, 18.

Brown, Gladys A.   "Instrumental Music in Our Schools."   Music
    Supervisors' Journal, 3: (January, 1917), 28, 30.

Cady, C. M.   "Music."   The Illinois Teacher, 3: (1857), 146-151.

"Carlisle Schools---Music."   The Pennsylvania School Journal,
    7: (August, 1858), 37-38.

"A Century of Music in Buffalo Schools."   Music Educators'
    Journal, 23: (March, 1937), 26-27, 78-83.

Chamberlin, Professor.   "Singing in Common Schools."   Michigan
    Journal of Education, 7: (May, 1860), 183-185.

"Chicago Notes."   The Schoolmaster, 3: (June 1, 1883), 173.

Clapp, Henry L.   "Music in Elementary Schools."   Education, 24:
    (May, 1904), 548-555.

"Claronian School."   American Annals of Education and Instruction,
    7: (March, 1837), 186.

Coburn, E. L.   "Music in the United States for the Last Twenty-
    Five Years."   Journal of Proceedings of the Third Annual
    Meeting of the Music Supervisors' National Conference,
    16-19.   Published by the Association, 1910.

Coffman, Lotus D.   "The New Education."   Journal of Proceedings
    of the Seventeenth Annual Meeting of the Music Supervisors'
    National Conference, 81-88.   (Tulsa: Board of Education,
    1924).

"Common School Convention, at Marietta."   American Annals of
    Education, 6: (1838), 41.

"Common Schools in Cincinnati."   Journal of the Rhode Island
    Institute of Instruction, 1: (April, 1846), 133-134.

Condon, Randall J.   "Address of Welcome."   Journal of Proceedings
    of the Music Supervisors' National Conference, 33-35.
    Seventeenth Annual Meeting, (Tulsa Board of Education,
    1924).

"Convention of Teachers of Vocal Music." American Annals of Education and Instruction, 5: (June, 1835), 281-282.

"Convention of Teachers of Vocal Music." American Annals of Education and Instruction, 6: (October, 1836), 473-474.

Cooke, James F. "The Advent of Endowed Institutions in American Musical Education." The Etude, 24: (February, 1906), 57-58.

Crafts, George E. "Music in Home and School." Education, 24: (March, 1904), 407-410.

Curtis, George H. "Music a Necessity." The American Journal of Education and College Reveiw, 2: (July, 1856), 44-50.

Damon, Inez. "The Present Status of Public School Music." Journal of Proceedings of the Seventeenth Annual Meeting of the Music Supervisors' National Conference, (Tulsa: Board of Education, 1924), 88-95.

Damrosch, Frank. "Public School Music Leads to Higher Citizenship." The Etude, 26: (March, 1968). 193.

DeFellenberg, William. "Pestalozzi, De Fellenberg and Vehrli." The American Journal of Education, 10: (March, 1861). 81-92.

Dickey, Frances M. "The Early History of Public School Music in the United States." School Music, 15: (May, 1914). 5, 16, 19, 23.

Dickinson, Edward. "Music in America Fifty Years Ago and Its Significance in the Light of the Present." Proceedings of the Music Teachers' National Association, Fifty-Second Year, 9-26. Published by the Association, Hartford. 1929.

Earhart, Will. "The Evolution of Public School Music in the United States." Music Supervisors' Journal, 10: (1924). 6, 8, 10.

Earhart, Will. "Music Credits for Outside Study Discussed and and Reports Submitted." School Music, 18: (May-June, 1917). 5-9.

"Eclectic Academy of Music in Cincinnati." American Annals of Education and Instruction, 4: (June, 1834). 289.

"Educational Items." The Ohio Journal of Education, 6: (January, 1857). 25.

"Educational Labors of Lowell Mason." The American Journal of Education, 4: (September, 1857). 141-147.

"The Elements of Music." The Connecticut Common School, 1:
    (March 15, 1839). 108-109.

Elson, Louis C. "Our Public Education in Music." The Atlantic
    Monthly, 92: (August, 1903). 252-255.

Elson, Louis C. "Our Uplift in Music." The World's Work, 8:
    (July, 1904). 4992-4995.

Elson, Louis C. "Singing." Musical Herald, 3: (May, 1882). 188.

Farnsworth, Charles H. "School Music in Berlin, Paris, and
    London." Papers and Proceedings of the Music Teachers'
    National Association at its Thirtieth Annual Meeting,
    Washington, D. C. December, 28-31, 1908. (Hartford:
    Case, Lockwood, and Brainard Company, 1909). 128-147.

"The Fellenberg Institution at Hofwyl." The American Journal of
    Education and Monthly Lyceum, 1: (June, 1830), 255-261.

"Fifty Years a Supervisor." School Music, 14: (November-December,
    1913).

Finck, Henry T. "What the Musical World Needs Most." The
    Etude, 26: (February, 1908). 83-84.

Flueckiger, Samuel. "Why Lowell Mason Left the Boston Schools."
    Music Supervisors' Journal, 22: (February, 1936), 20-23.

Fowle, William B. "Vocal Music." American Annals of Education
    and Instruction, 5: (May, 1835), 225-229.

Fyke, C. A. "Music." Indiana School Journal, 26: (September,
    1881), 432-434.

Gammell, Professor. "First Annual Report of the Executive
    Committee." Journal of the Rhode Island Institute of
    Instruction, 1: (February, 1846), 58-59.

Gartlan, George H. "Some Early Supervisory Experiences."
    Music Supervisors' Journal, 13: (October, 1926), 29, 31.

Gebhart, D. R. "Music in the South." Music Supervisors' Journal,
    8: (October, 1921), 14-16.

Gehrkens, Karl W. "Entrance Credits to College and Credits in
    Music for the College Degree." School Music, (November-
    December, 1920), 25-29.

Gehrkens, Karl W. "The Evolution of Public School Music in the
    United States." Music Supervisors' Journal, 10: (February,
    1924), 8, 10, 12.

Gehrkens, Karl W. "The Twentieth Century -- A Singing Revival."
Papers and Proceedings of the Music Teachers' National
Association at its Forty-Fourth Annual Meeting, New York
City, December 27-29, 1922. (Hartford: News Printing Co.,
1923), 178-188.

"German Music." The Common School Journal, 9: (January 15,
1847), 31.

Giddings, T. P. "A B C Methods Applied to the Teaching of
Music." School Music. 11: (September-October, 1910),
6-14.

Giddings, T. P. "Early Events in the Professional Life of One
T. P. Giddings." Music Supervisors' Journal, 14: (February,
1927), 13, 15, 67.

Giddings, T. P. "Pedagogy." School Music, 15: (January-February,
1914), 5-7.

Gilman, Lawrence. "The New American Music." The North
American Review, 79: (December, 1904), 868-872.

"Girls and Music." The Indiana School Journal, 23: (1878), 29-30.

Glynn, Maude E. "Music and Americanization." Music Supervisors' Journal, 7: (September, 1920), 14, 16, 18, 20.

Gordon, George W. "Boston Academy of Music First Annual Report." American Annals of Education and Instruction, 3:
(August, 1833), 373-377.

Griggs, Herbert. "Content and Extent of Music in Public Schools."
Journal of Proceedings and Addresses of the Thirty-Eighth
Annual Meeting of the National Educational Association,
(Chicago: University of Chicago, 1899). 977-981.

"A Group of Native American Musicians." The American Monthly,
19: (January-June, 1899), 435-436.

Hadden, Cuthbert J. "Lowell Mason American Educator and
Musical Pioneer." The Etude, 28: (March, 1910), 165.

"Hamlin E. Cogswell." School Music, 5: (September, 1905), 43.

Hanford, F. "Vocal Music in Our Public Schools." The Illinois
Teacher, 16: (September, 1870), 283-285.

"Hans Georg Nägeli." The American Journal of Education, 7:
(September, 1859), 300.

Hawn, Abraham D.   "Music in Schools."   The Pennsylvania School
    Journal, 5: (December, 1856), 204.

Hayden, P. C.   "The Ultimate Object of Music Study in the Schools."
    Journal of Proceedings and Addresses of the Thirty-Eighth
    Annual Meeting of the National Educational Association,
    (Chicago: The University of Chicago Press, 1899).   972-977.

Heath, W. F.   "Aids in Elementary Music Teaching."   Journal of
    Proceedings and Addresses of the National Educational
    Association, 1888.   (Topeka: Kansas Publishing House, 1888).
    637-643.

Heath, W. F.   "Practical Lessons in Music."   Journal of Education,
    New England and National, 23: (February, 25, 1886), 117-118.

Heath, W. F.   "Practical Lessons in Music."   Journal of Education,
    New England and National, 23: (March 18, 1886), 165.

Hentschel, E.   "Instruction in Singing."   The American Journal of
    Education, 8: (June, 1860), 633-660.

Hill, Thomas.   "The Ear and the Voice."   The Ohio Educational
    Monthly, (April, 1862), 97-104.

Hillbrand, E. K.   "How Music Found its Way into American Public
    Schools."   The Etude, 42: (March, 1924), 163-164.

Holman, F. S.   "Music in Schools."   Journal of Education, New
    England and National, 22: (November 5, 1885), 300.

Holt, H. E.   "Better Teaching or a New Notation, Which?"   Journal
    of Proceedings and Addresses of the National Educational
    Association for the Year, 1886.   (Massachusetts:
    Observer Book and Job Print, 1887).   590-605.

Holt, H. E.   "Methods in Teaching Music."   Journal of Proceedings
    of the National Education Association.   Session of the Year
    1884.   (Massachusetts: J. E. Farwell and Co., 1885).
    213-216.

Holt, H. E.   "Music in Schools."   Journal of Education, New England
    and National, 22: (September 10, 1885), 175.

Howe, N.   "On Music."   The Pennsylvania School Journal, 2:
    (February, 1854), 239.

"Importance of Vocal Music in Popular Education."   The English
    Journal of Education, 1: (1843), 64.

"Instruction in the City of New York."   American Annals of
    Education and Instruction, 2: (July, 1832).   411-412.

"Intelligence from Ohio." American Annals of Education, 8: (1838), 181.

Jennings, Miss. "Singing in Our Schools." Journal of Education, New England and National, 22: (December 24, 1885), 419.

Jepson, Benjamin. "Forty-Six Years' Experience as a Supervisor of Public School Music." School Music, 11: (May, 1910).

Jepson, Benjamin. "Reminiscences of Early Days in School Music." School Music, 8: (March, 1908).

"John Bailey." School Music, 18: (March-April, 1917), 19-20.

"Juvenile Music." American Annals of Education and Instruction, 5: (January, 1835), 42-43.

Kinkeldey, Otto. "Music Education and Public Libraries." School Music, 17: (November-December, 1916), 13-17.

Lawrence, Clara E. "Early School Music Methods." Music Educators Journal, 25: (December, 1938), 20-23.

"Letters." American Annals of Education and Instruction, 4: (July, 1834), 330-331.

"Life of Dr. William Mason 1829-1908." The Etude, 26: (September, 1908), 555.

"List of Publications by Lowell Mason." The American Journal of Education, 4: (September, 1857), 148.

Little, Vivian G. "Music in Schools and Colleges." Music Supervisors Journal, 3: (November, 1916), 7-11.

Loomis, George B. "Music in Normal Schools." Journal of Proceedings of the American Normal School, and the National Teachers' Association at Cleveland, Ohio. 1870. (Washington: James H. Holmes, 1871). 66-72.

"Louisville's Tribute to a Veteran Musician." School Music, 12: (November, 1911), 5-7.

Lutkin, Peter C. "Music in its Relation to the University." Report of Illinois Music Teachers Association, Twenty-First Annual Convention, Decatur, Illinois. May 11-14, 1909. (Lincoln, Illinois: Daily New Herald, 1910), 5-17.

Maddy, J. E. "National Orchestra Summer Camp. Music Supervisors' Journal, 14: (October, 1927), 65-67.

Mann, Horace. "Music. " The Pennsylvania School Journal, 15:
        (June, 1867), 308.

Marcy, L. J. "On Vocal Music in Schools. " The Journal of
        Education and Teachers' Magazine, 1: (1854), 191-192.

Mason, Daniel G. "An Unpublished Journal of Dr. Lowell Mason. "
        The New Music Review and Church Music Review, 10:
        (December, 1910), 16-18.

Mason, Daniel G. "An Unpublished Journal of Dr. Lowell Mason. "
        The New Music Review and Church Music Review, 10:
        (January, 1911), 62-67.

Mason, Daniel G. "How Young Lowell Mason Travelled To
        Savannah. " New England Magazine, 26: (April), 236-240.

Mason, Daniel G. "Music in the Colleges. " The Outlook, 76:
        (April, 1904), 982-987.

Mason, Daniel G. "Our Public School Music. " The Outlook,
        76: (March 19, 1904), 701-706.

Mason, Lowell. "Church Music. " The North American Review,
        N. S.   15: (1827), 244-246.

Mason, Luther W. "Music in Schools. " The American Institute of
        Instruction, (Boston, Massachusetts: A Mudge and Son, 1870).
        50-60.

Mathews, W. S. B. "John S. Dwight, Editor, Critic and Man. "
        Music, 15: (November, 1898, to April, 1899), 523-540.

M'Burney, S. "The Tonic Sol-Fa System. " Journal of Proceedings
        and Addresses of the National Educational Association,
        (Topeka: Kansas Publishing House, 1888), 633-637.

McConathy, Osbourne. "From Lowell Mason to the Civil War --
        A Period of Pioneers. " Papers and Proceedings of the Music
        Teachers' National Association at its Forty-Fourth Annual
        Meeting, New York City, December 27-29, 1922. (Hartford:
        News Printing Co. , 1923), 158-166.

McConathy, Osbourne. "Music in Our Public School in 1876 and
        Since. " Proceedings of the Music Teachers' National
        Association. Annual Meeting of the Fifty-Second Year,
        (Hartford, 1929), 186-197.

M'Naught, W. G. "School Music Abroad. " School Music, 13:
        (November-December, 1912), 20-22, 32, 34, 36, 38.

Miessner, Otto.   "Credit for Music Granted High School Students. "
    Twenty-Fifth Annual Convention of the Illinois Music Teachers'
    Association, Bloomington, Illinois.   May 13-16, 1913.
    102-109.

Miessner, Otto W.   "What The Conference Does for You. "   Music
    Supervisors' Journal, 10: (October, 1923), 20-22.

Moore, Earl B.   "The Growth and Changing Status of Independent
    Schools of Music Since 1876. "   Proceedings of the Music
    Teachers' National Association, Annual Meeting of the Fifty-
    Second Year.   (Hartford: Published by the Association, 1929).
    234-243.

Moszkowski, Moritz.   "The Paris Conservatory of Music. "   The
    Etude, 28: (January, 1910), 9-10.

Moszkowski, Moritz.   "The Paris Conservatory of Music. "   The
    Etude, 28: (February, 1910), 81.

"Mr. Barnard's Labors in Connecticut. "   Barnard's American
    Journal of Education, 1: (1856), 669, 685-686, 695, 697.

Mudge, G. O.   "Horace Mann and His Educational Ideas. "   The High
    School Journal, 20: (May, 1937), 166.

"Music. "   The Illinois Teacher, 2: (April, 1856), 92.

"Music a Prime Factor in Education. "   Musical Herald, 4:
    (February, 1883), 40.

"Music and Misery. "   New England Journal of Education, 4: (July
    15, 1876), 152.

"Music and Morals. "   Journal of Proceedings of the National
    Educational Association, (Peoria, Illinois: N. C. Nason, 1873),
    21-22.

"Music for Schools. "   The Ohio Journal of Education, 4: (December,
    1855), 357-358.

"Music in Common Schools. "   American Annals of Education and
    Instruction, 1: (July, 1831), 330.

"Music in Jacksonville. "   The Illinois Teacher, 5: (1859), 243.

"Music in School. "   The Ohio Journal of Education, 7: (June, 1858),
    310.

"Music in Schools. "   American Annals of Education, 8: (1838),
    32-34.

"Music in Schools." The Common School Journal, 4: (September, 1842), 258-260.

"Music in Schools." The Connecticut Common School Journal, 1: (January, 1840), 90.

"Music in Schools." The Illinois Teacher, 5: (1859), 265-267.

"Music in Schools." The Illinois Teacher, 11: (March, 1865), 78-80.

"Music in Schools." The Michigan Teacher, 9: (February, 1874), 68.

"Music in Schools." The New York Teacher, 6: (1857), 270.

"Music in the Chelsea School." (1906-1907) School Music, 7: (November, 1906), 9-12.

"Music in the French Public Schools." Common School Advocate, 1: (September, 1839), 262.

"Musical Convention at the South, A" The Musical Pioneer, 12: (December, 1867), 2.

"Musical Culture." New England Journal of Education, 4: (July 15, 1876), 42-43.

"Musical Instruments in School." The Illinois Teacher, 5: (1859), 273-274.

Myers, S. S. "Some Reasons Why Music Should Be Taught in All Public Schools." Music Supervisors' National Conference Yearbook, (Published by the Association. 1917). 138-144.

"New Orleans, Louisiana." Journal of the Rhode Island Institute of Instruction, 1: (1846), 236-237.

Nixon, Professor. "On the Influence of Music." American Annals of Education and Instruction, 5: (November, 1835), 507-510.

"Normal Academy of Music." The Musical Pioneer, 12: (May, 1867), 6.

"The Normal Musical Institute at North-Reading." New York Musical Review and Gazette, 11: (April 14, 1860), 115, 120, 137.

"Normal Schools in Massachusetts." The Connecticut Common School Journal, 1: (March, 1839), 97.

"Notices." American Annals of Education and Instruction, 2: (July, 1832), 398-400.

"Notices of Colleges, Schools, Etc." The Ohio Journal of Education, 3: (March, 1854), 94-95.

"On Simplifying Instruction in Vocal Music." The English Journal of Education, 4: (1846), 360-363.

"On Teaching Vocal Music in Schools." The English Journal of Education, 2: (1844), 232-236.

Otis, Philo A. "The Development of Music in Chicago." Papers and Proceedings of the Music Teachers' National Association at its Forty-Second Annual Meeting, Chicago, (December 29-31, 1920. (Hartford: Published by the Association, 1921), 109-127.

Owen, Herman E. "Report of Public School Commission for the Year Ending, June, 1905." Papers and Proceedings of the Music Teachers' National Association at its Twenty-Eighth Annual Meeting Oberlin, Ohio, June 26-29, 1906. (Hartford: Case Lockwood and Brainard Company, 1906), 85-88.

Pearson, William. "On Teaching Vocal Music in Schools." The English Journal of Education, 2: (1844), 257-266.

Perkins, H. S. "Reminiscences of Early Days in School Music." School Music, 8: (May, 1908).

Perrot, Augustus. "On Vocal Music." The Pennsylvania School Journal, 2: (March, 1854), 292-295.

"A Plea for Vocal Music in Public Schools." A Journal of Proceedings of the American Normal School, and the National Teachers' Associations at Cleveland, Ohio. Sessions of 1870. (Washington: James H. Holmes, 1871). 133-141.

Powell, William B. "Methods of Teaching Music." Journal of Proceedings and Addresses of the Thirty-Eighth Annual Meeting of the National Educational Association, (Chicago: University of Chicago Press, 1899). 987-988.

"Primary Schools of Germany." The Indiana School Journal, 1: (May, 1856), 140.

Prime, Nathaniel S. "The Duty of Cultivating Music as a Part of General Education." The American Journal of Education and College Review, 2: (October, 1856), 339-345.

"Proceedings of the American Lyceum." American Annals of Education and Instruction, 3: (August, 1833), 345-356.

"Public Instruction in Northampton." American Annals of Education and Instruction, 7: (June, 1837), 254-255.

"Public Singing in Schools." The Common School Journal, 2:
    (March, 1840), 82-83.

Purchas, Arthur G. "What is the Best Method of Teaching Vocal
    Music?" The English Journal of Education, 2: (1844),
    173-176.

Raub, A. N. "Vocal Culture." The Pennsylvania School Journal,
    14: (January, 1866), 163.

Raumer, von Karl. "Music." The American Journal of Education,
    4: (December, 1857), 448-449.

Raumer, von Karl. "The Life and Educational System of Pestalozzi."
    The American Journal of Education, 3: (June, 1857), 401-416.

"Report of the Executive Committee of the State Normal School."
    Journal of the Rhode Island Institute of Instruction, 1:
    (March 16, 1846), 108.

"Resolution." American Institute of Instruction, (Springfield,
    Massachusetts: Clark W. Bryan and Co., 1873). 24-29.

Ripley, F. H. "Musical Intelligence in Children." Journal of
    Education. New England and National, 23: (April 22, 1886),
    251.

Russell, William. "Moral Education." The American Journal of
    Education, 9: (September, 1860), 25-26.

Russell, William. "Music as an Imitative Art." The American
    Journal of Education, 3: (March, 1857), 55.

Scholes, Percy A. "Musical Education in the British Isles."
    Papers and Proceedings of the Music Teachers' National
    Association, Thirty-Sixth Annual Meeting, Pittsburg, Pa.,
    December 29-30, 1914. (Hartford: Published by the
    Association, 1914), 30-40.

Seidl, Anton. "The Development of Music in America." The Forum,
    13: (May, 1892), 388-393.

Sharland, J. B. "Vocal Music as a Branch of Common School
    Instruction." American Institute of Instruction, (Boston,
    Massachusetts, 1888), 199-203.

Shaw, Elsie M. "Standardization of Sight-Reading." Journal of
    Proceedings of the Third Annual Meeting of the Music
    Supervisors' National Conference, (1910), 37-52.

Silver, Edgar O. "The Growth of Music Among the People."
    Journal of Proceedings and Addresses, National Educational

Association, Toronto, Canada. (New York: Published by the Association, 1891). 813-815.

"Singing." The Connecticut Common School Journal, 2: (March 1, 1840), 161.

"Singing in Common Schools." The Common School Journal, 3: (June 15, 1841), 189-190.

"Singing in School." The Ohio Journal of Education, 4: (April, 1855), 117-118.

"The Singing Master." New York Musical Pioneer and Chorister's Budget, 1: (October, 1855), 4.

Slayton, J. H. L. "Music in the Schools." The Illinois Teacher, 1: (July, 1855), 167-168.

Smith, Herman F. "Conference Marks Twenty-Nine Years of Growth." Musical America, 56: (March 25, 1936), 3.

Spencer, C. C. "Various Methods of Teaching Vocal Music in Schools." The English Journal of Education, 2: (1844), 197-206.

"State Education Convention." American Annals of Education and Instruction, 7: (July, 1837), 329.

Stewart, N. Coe. "President's Address." Journal of Proceedings and Addresses of the National Educational Association. (Topeka: Kansas Publishing House, 1888), 629-633.

Stovall, Anna M. "Music in the Kindergarten." Journal of Proceedings and Addresses of the Thirty-Eighth Annual Meeting of the National Educational Association, (Chicago: University of Chicago Press, 1899), 559-563.

Stowe, Calvin E. "Course of Instruction in the Primary Schools of Germany." The American Journal of Education, 8: (June, 1860), 371-379.

Stowe, Calvin E. "Professor Stowe's Report on the Course of Instruction in the Common Schools of Prussia." The Connecticut Common School Journal, 1: (May, 1839), 137-138.

"Subjects and Methods of Instruction in the Primary Schools of Prussia." The American Journal of Education, 8: (June, 1860), 413-415.

Suliot, T. E. "On the Teaching of Vocal Music to Large Numbers." The Ohio Educational Monthly, 13: (January, 1864), 1-5.

Suliot, T. E. "On the Teaching of Vocal Music to Large Numbers."
The Ohio Educational Monthly, 12: (February, 1864), 50-51.

Suliot, T. E. "On the Teaching of Vocal Music to Large Numbers."
The Ohio Educational Monthly, 13: (March, 1864), 68-72.

Suliot, T. E. "On the Teaching of Vocal Music to Large Numbers."
The Pennsylvania School Journal, 12: (April, 1864), 311-314.

Tapper, Thomas. "What Power Does the Child Gain Thru Music
Study." Journal of Proceedings and Addresses of the Thirty-
Eighth Annual Meeting of the National Educational Association,
(Chicago: The University of Chicago Press, 1899), 981-986.

"Tenth Annual Report of the Boston Academy of Music." The
Common School Journal, 4: (September, 1842), 257-260.

"Third Annual Report of the Secretary of the Board of Commissioners
of Common Schools." The Connecticut Common School
Journal, 3: (May, 1841), 240, 250, 254.

"Thirty-Nine Years Supervisor in the Public Schools." School
Music, 12: (November, 1911), 5-7.

Tindall, Glenn M. "Music Appreciation in the High School."
School Music, 21: (May-June, 1920), 38, 40, 43, 45, 46.

Tourjee, Eben F. "Musical Education in Common Schools."
Reports of the United States Commissioner of Education,
1871. (Washington: Government Printing Office, 1871),
536-537.

Tourjee, Eben F. "A Plea for Vocal Music in Public Schools,"
Addresses and Journal of Proceedings of the American
Normal School, and the National Teachers' Associations,
1870. James W. Holmes, 1871), 133-141.

Upham, J. Baxter. "Vocal Music as a Branch of Education in
Our Common Schools." American Institute of Instruction,
(Springfield, Mass.: Clark W. Bryan and Co., 1873),
161-185.

"Vocal Music." The Connecticut Common School Journal, 4:
(March 1, 1842), 59-60.

"Vocal Music in Schools." The Pennsylvania School Journal, 9:
(August, 1860), 59.

"Vocal Music, or Singing." The Connecticut Common School
Journal, 4: (April 15, 1842), 116.

Webster, W. F. "Music and the Sacred Seven," Music Supervisors'
Journal, 14: (May, 1927).

"Western Literary Institute. " American Annals of Education and Instruction, 7: (January, 1837), 40.

Westhoff, F. W. "Music in the Public Schools. " Twenty-Fifth Annual Convention of the Illinois Music Teachers' Association, Bloomington, Illinois. (May 13-16, 1913), 45-54.

"What is the Best System of Teaching Vocal Music in Schools?" The English Journal of Education, (1844), 173-176.

"William Bentley Fowle. " American Journal of Education, 10: (June, 1861), 597-608.

Wood, Joseph. "Musical Education. " The Pennsylvania School Journal, 7: (August, 1858), 53-56.

Woodbridge, William C. "On Vocal Music as a Branch of Common Education. " American Annals of Education and Instruction, 3: (May, 1833), 193-212.

Woodbridge, William C. "On Vocal Music as a Branch of Common Education. " The American Institute of Instruction, (Boston: Hilliard, Gray, Little and Wilkins, 1831), 231-255.

10. Theses and Dissertations

Baldwin, Sister Mary F. Lowell Mason's Philosophy of Music Education. Unpublished Master's Thesis. Catholic University of America. Washington, D. C. 1937. 34.

Boogher, Elbert W. G. Secondary Education in Georgia, 1732-1858. University of Pennsylvania, Philadelphia, (1933), 452.

Butler, Vera M. Education as Revealed by New England Newspapers Prior to 1850. Doctorate Dissertation. Temple University. Philadelphia, (1935), 503.

Cummins, Clyde M. Music in the Public Schools of the United States. Unpublished Master's Thesis, University of Chicago, (1917), 79.

De Revere, Mary L. Public Interest in Music on the Eve of the American Revolution. Unpublished Master's Thesis, Columbia University, (1925), 34.

Fox, Otto L. The Present Status of Music Teaching in the High Schools of California. Unpublished Master's Thesis, University of California, (1928).

Guinn, John A. The Public School Music Situation in the United States. Unpublished Master's Thesis, University of Texas, (1929).

Harney, Julia C.   The Evolution of Public Education in Jersey
      City.   Unpublished Doctorate Dissertation, New York
      University, (1931),   254.

Lamek, John E.   Music Instruction in Catholic Elementary Schools.
      Unpublished Doctorate Dissertation, Catholic University of
      America, (1933),   91.

Monroe, Samuel F.   The Development of Instrumental Music in
      the Public Schools of United States.   Unpublished Master's
      Thesis, New York University, (1930),   105.

Mulhern, James.   A History of Secondary Education in Pennsylvania.
      Doctorate Dissertation, University of Pennsylvania.
      Philadelphia, (1933),   714.

Raison, Mary M.   A Study of the Status of Public School Music
      in Ohio,   Unpublished Master's Thesis, Ohio Wesleyan
      University.   (1930),   96.

Smith, Samuel.   Music Supervision in Connecticut Public Schools.
      (Case Studies, Methods, Recommendations, Principles).
      Unpublished Doctorate Dissertation.   New York University,
      (1933),   772.

Williams, Antoinette McLean.   Education in Greenville County,
      S. C. Prior to 1860.   Unpublished Master's Thesis,
      University of South Carolina.   (1930),   49.

Yont, Rose.   Status and Value of Music in Education.   (Lincoln
      Nebraska: The Woodruff Press, 1916),   355.

Young, Clarence R.   The Status of Music in Indiana High Schools.
      Unpublished Master's Thesis, University of Indiana, (1931),
      73.

11.   Miscellaneous

Annual Report of the Secretary of State of New York, as Superin-
      tendent of Common Schools.   Albany, New York.   (July,
      1852),   159.

Bache, A. D.   Report on the Organization of a High School for
      Girls, and Seminary for Female Teachers, 1840.   38.

Catalogue of the Exhibition.   Horticultural Hall.   Boston, January 11,
      to 26, 1902.   (Boston: Chickering and Sons, (1902), 78.

Educational Documents.   Wisconsin, January, 1850.   I.   Inauguration
      of the Chancellor of the University, II.   Report of the Board
      of Regents, III.   Report of the Superintendent of Public

Instruction, Sentinel and Gazette Power Press Print.
(Milwaukee: 1850), 199.

Fifth Annual Report of the Inspector of State High Schools State
of Minnesota for the School Year Ending July 31, 1898.
Submitted to the State High School Board, (Minneapolis:
1898), 36.

First Annual Report of the Williams Secular School. (Edinburgh:
(McLachlan and Stewart, MDCCCL), 20.

Grove's Dictionary of Music and Musicians, Pratt, Waldo, Seldon
Editor. Volume 6. (American Supplement). Theodore
Presser Company, (Philadelphia, Pennsylvania: 1920), 412.

The Hawes School Memorial Containing an Account of Five Reunions
of the Old Hawes School Boys' Association, One Reunion of
the Hawes Girls' Association, and a Series of Biographical
Sketches of the Old Masters: Together With a List of the
Members of the Two Associations, and a Reproduction of the
Programmes at Some of the Exhibitions. (Boston: David
Clapp and Son, 1889), 227.

A History of Education in the State of Ohio. A Centennial Volume.
Published by Authority of the General Assembly. (Columbia,
Ohio, 1876), 449.

Hubbell, Mark S. The Charter of the City of Buffalo. Buffalo.
(1896), 425.

Inauguration of Hon. John H. Lathrop, LL. D. Chancellor of The
University of Wisconsin, at the Capitol, Madison, January
16, 1850. (Milwaukee: Sentinel and Gazette Power Press Print,
1850), 199.

Laws and By-Laws Relative to Public Instruction in the City of
New York. January, 1870. (New York: The New York
Printing Co., 1870), 410.

Letter to the Speaker of the House of Representatives. Secretary's
Office, Harrisburg, Pa., February 19, 1838. 62.

Letters From Hofwyl by a Parent, on the Educational Institutions of
De Fellenberg. With an Appendix, Containing Woodbridge's
Sketches of Hofwyl, Reprinted From the Annals of Education.
(London: Longman, Brown, Green, and Longmans, 1842), 372.

McCarty, H. D. Classification and Course of Study Recommended
for the District Schools of Kansas. (Topeka, Kansas: State
Printing Works, 1873), 24.

A Manual for the Use of the State High Schools of North Dakota
        Published by the (State) High School Board.   August, 1909.

Manual of the Board of Education of the City and County of New
        York.   (New York: Cushing and Bardua's Steam Presses,
        1876),   337.

Manual of the Board of Education of the City and County of New
        York.   (New York: Hall of the Board of Education, 1883),
        401.

The Musical Fund Society of Philadelphia.   Act of Incorporation
        Approved February 22, 1823.   Amendment Thereof Approved
        April 28,   1857, And By-Laws as Revised and Amended May
        7, 1912.   Together With a List of Officers and Members,
        Historical Data, and List of Portraits.   September, 1930.
        67.

Pestalozzi and His Times.   A Pictorial Record Edited for the
        Centenary of His Death by the Pestalozzianum and the
        Zentralbibliothek.   (Zurich: Buchdruckerei Berichthaus:
        (New York: G. E.   Stechert and Co. ,   1928), 80+165 plates.

Proceedings of the California State Teachers' Institute, Held at
        Mercantile Library Hall, San Francisco, September 13-16,
        1870.   (Sacramento, California: D. W. Gelwicks, 1871), 78.

Rejoinder to the "Reply" of the Hon. Horace Mann, Secretary of
        the Massachusetts Board of Education, to the "Remarks"
        of the Association of Boston Masters, Upon His Seventh
        Annual Report.   (Boston: Charles C. Little and James
        Brown, 1856), 55+56+40+64.

Remarks on the Seventh Annual Report of the Hon. Horace Mann,
        Secretary of the Massachusetts Board of Education. (Boston:
        Charles C. Little and James Brown, 1844), 144.

Report of the Committee of the State of Ohio Appointed to Collect
        Information, Prepare and Report a System of Common
        Schools, Friday, January 14, 1825.   (Columbus, Ohio:
        P. B. Olmsted, 1825).

Report of the Education Commission of the City of Chicago.
        (Chicago: The Lakeside Press, 1899), 248.

Report of the Secretary of the Interior; Being Part of the Message
        and Documents Communicated to the Two Houses of Congress
        at the Beginning of the Second Session of the Forty-Second
        Congress.   Volume II.   (Washington: Government Printing
        Office, 1872), 715.

Report to the City Council of Providence, Presented June 1, 1846,
     By Their Committee, Appointed September 3d, 1838, To
     Superintend The Erection of School Houses, on the Re-
     organization of the Public Schools.   (Providence: Knowles and
     Vose, 1846), 22.

Second Annual Report of the Inspector of State Graded Schools,
     State of Minnesota, July 31, 1897.   (Minneapolis, 1897),
     59.

A Survey.   The Giving of High School Credits for Private Music
     Study.   C. M. Tremaine, Director National Bureau for the
     Advancement of Music.   (New York: National Bureau for the
     Advancement of Music, 105 West 40th Street), 105.

NAME INDEX

Ackley, W. N. 133
Adams, Samuel 22
Aiken, Charles 99, 101, 102, 103, 219, 220.
Aiken, Walter H. 101, 102, 124.
Alcott, W. A. 44
Allen, Anna H. 363
Allen, David 363
Allen, David P. 233, 240
Allen, George N. 237
Alling, F. C. Mrs. 231, 246
Allis, John M. 207, 210
Andrews, Abraham 73
Andrews, E. A. 67, 209
Andrews, Joseph P. 145
Ansorge, Charles 109, 175, 183, 189
Arnold, Willet H. 132

Bache, Alexander D. 93, 98-100, 123, 194, 206, 210
Bailey, E. H. 186
Bailey, John E. 244
Baker, Benjamin F. 20, 52, 182, 368
Baker, Everett L. 99, 113, 141
Baker, H. S. 160
Baker, James N. 237, 247
Baldwin, Sister Mary F. 59
Ballard, Levi W. 363
Ballou, E. F. 135, 141, 363
Bancroft, S. C., Miss 134, 141
Barnard, Henry 42, 96, 98, 182, 207, 210, 251, 254
Barr, Colonel 76
Barry, John 16
Barth, Hans 272
Bartlett, J. E. 241
Bates, Marianne 232, 246
Beckwith, Eliza C., Mrs. 237
Beecher, Lyman 57
Belding, John B. 232, 247
Biard, Peter, Rev. 9

Billings, William 16, 20, 22, 27, 365
Bimboni, Alberto 311
Bing, Rudolph 317
Bingham, Silas 99, 104
Birge, Edward Bailey 30, 53, 56, 58, 189, 229
Blackman, Orlando 108, 109, 155, 157, 175, 212
Boice, John 15
Botefuhr, W. D. 239
Bourgard, Caroline B. 118, 127
Bourne, William O. 97
Bowen, Daniel 113
Bradbury, William B. 20, 186, 226
Braille, Louis M. 251, 368
Breil, Joseph 311
Bristow, George F. 166, 384
Britton, Allen P. 96
Brooks, Charles, Rev. 52
Brown, Elmer Ellsworth 30
Brown, S. L. 207
Brownell, George 14
Brownlee, James H. 238, 245
Bucknam, Jacob 15
Buisson, M. Ferdinand 165
Bush, George C. 172
Butler, Henry M. 233, 241, 363
Butler, Vera M. 86
Butterfield, F. H. 221

Cady, C. M. 186, 241
Caldwell, S. 117
Carillo, Julian 272
Barth, Hans 272
Carter, Frank 148
Carter, Henry 117, 363
Chamberlin, Prof. 210
Chandler, Eliza 141
Channing, W. E. 39
Chauncery, Rev. 18
Cheney, Moses 20

439

Clark, Anna S. Miss 235
Clark, E. S. 154
Clark, Frances E. , Mrs. 265
Clark, J. H. 104
Clark, J. L. 99
Clarke, Charles M. 99, 116, 363
Clarke, Hugh A. 243
Clemmer, J. N. 147
Coburn, E. L. 201
Coe, H. B. 120
Coerne, Louis 311
Coggeshall, J. 132
Cogswell, Hamlin E. 363
Colburn, William F. 99, 101-103, 363
Cole, Samuel W. 363
Coleman, Benjamin, Dr. 19, 365
Coley, Jane 112, 141
Collister, Samuel 186
Comstock, John L. , Dr. 42
Conant, Levi 74
Condon, Randall J. 37
Cook, T. J. 186
Cooke, M. D. , Mrs. 111, 363
Cookinham, Solon U. 141
Coolidge, President Calvin 339
Cooper, Oscar H. 150
Crane, Julia Ettie 368
Crooks, Richard 269
Crosby, W. E. 159
Crouch, Ralph 9
Cubberley, Ellwood P. 37, 124, 170, 172, 250

Dailey, Darley 20
Damrosch, Walter 311
Daniel, J. H. 221, 363
Daniell, W. H. 232
Danks, Jarvis H. 103
Davenport, Josiah 19
Davis, Benjamin 27
Davis, Mary 231, 247
Davis, Warren 154, 363
Dean, Philotus 145
De Fellenberg, M. 33
Dekoven, Reginald 311
Dennis, Charles M. 357
De Revere, Mary L. 31
Deshon, Moses 15, 16

Dickey, Frances 122, 128
Dickinson, Edward 249
Dickstein, Samuel 266
Divoll, Ira 120
Douglass, O. S. , Mrs. 231, 246
Doyle, Charlotte O. 116, 363
Drake, A. J. 53
Drake, M. Auzolette 232
Dunster, Henry, Rev. 10
Durfee, B. W. 114
Dutton, Robert H. 231, 246
Duxbury, Mary F. 146
Dwight, John Sullivan 30, 40, 182, 189
Dykema, Peter W. 358

Earhart, Will 256
Eastman, George E. 256
Eaton, John 166, 378, 384, 389
Eddy, Nelson 269
Edwards, George T. 28, 30
Eichberg, Julius 363
Eliot, Samuel A. 50, 59
Elson, Louis C. 30, 57, 97
Emerson, Irving 363
Emerson, Luther O. 20
Emerson, Samuel 23
Engelhardt, Zephrim 28
Engles, George 258, 277
Enstone, Edward 14
Esputa, John 144, 217, 363
Eveleth, John 23
Everett, Dr. 184

Fallen, William 119, 363
Farmer, Henry 146
Farnham, George L. 115
Fitz, A. 182
Fitz, William 132
Flueckiger, Samuel L. 53, 57-59
Fonda, Alexander 112
Foote, E. M. 186
Foote, George L. 207
Fowle, William B. 66, 98
Fraley, J. L. , Mrs. 232, 247
Frank, J. L. 131
Franzen, Bengt 338, 357
French, Jacob 20

Fruit, J. J.   160
Fyke, C. A.   208, 210

Gallaudet, Rev.   41
Galloway, Tod B. , Judge   277
Gammell, Professor   182
Gardner, D. E   235
Gatti Casazza, Guilio   272
Gavian, Ruth Wood   358
Gilbert, N.   99, 105, 175, 363
Ginn, Edwin   226
Gleeson, W.   28
Glover, Nathan L.   363, 366, 368
Godfrey, Charles   99, 119, 363
Goodrich, W. M.   47
Gordan, George William   65
Gould, Anna L. , Mrs.   154, 363
Gould, Nathaniel D.   20, 62, 363
Grant, Henry F.   144, 187, 363
Grant, S. B.   143
Gravel, Victor   256
Green, Herbert   135, 141
Greene, Charles H.   186
Greene, George F.   142
Grosvenor, C. P.   143
Guy, T. J.   141

Hadden, J. Cuthbert   60
Hadley, Henry   311
Hahn, J. H.   368
Haight, John T.   256
Halbert, E. P. , Mrs.   232, 247
Hallowell, Benjamin   16
Hamilton, Edward   368
Hamm, William A.   358
Hammond, Laurens   271
Hanks, J. F.   99, 104, 363
Hanson, Howard   263, 357
Harney, Julia C.   127
Harrington, Jr. , Joseph   99
Harris, John   26
Harrison, James L.   145
Hastings, Thomas   20
Hathorne, Frank E.   231
Hawley, Giles P.   231, 247
Haynes, Phebe, M.   231, 247
Hazelton, F.   90, 141
Hesselius, Gustavus   26

Hewitt, J. H.   117
Highly, Warren   213
Hillbrand, E. K.   58, 84
Hodgdon, William A.   363
Hoffsinger, John F.   188
Hohmann, Christian Heinrich   226
Holbrook, Daniel   114
Holbrook, Josiah   179
Holcomb, Julia   231, 246
Holden, Oliver   20
Holmes, D. C.   145
Holt, H. E. ,   166, 197, 200, 214, 226, 232, 234, 363, 368, 369, 384
Holyoke, Samuel A.   20-21
Hood, George   28, 30
Hopkinson, Frances   20, 22
Howard, Francis E.   363
Howe, Horace Mrs.   136, 142, 231, 247
Howe, S. Jubal   47
Hubzman, Dr.   237
Hunnicut, C. W.   335
Hunt, Herold C.   323
Huntington, Charles W.   363

Ilsley, F. I.   230
Ivers, James   14
Ives, Elam   36, 44, 63, 65, 83, 92, 93, 96, 180, 190, 195, 197, 199, 226, 336, 363, 367

Jackson, Dr.   47
Jantz, A.   132, 133, 363
Jardine, John Alexander Mrs.   263
Jepson, Banjamin   137, 218, 219, 225, 363
Joan, James   16
Johnson, A. N.   53, 182
Johnson, Edward   272
Johnson, J. A.   53
Johnson, James C.   60
Jones, Archie N.   291, 298, 304
Jones, Darius E.   89, 141, 363
Jones, Joseph C.   164
Johnston, C. F.   150
Junkermann, G. F.   101, 102, 363

Killip, Lizzie 232, 246
Killip, W. W. 186
Kimbal, Jacob 20
Kimball, Kittie M. 231
Kingsley, E. D. 104
Kingsley, George 363
Kinnear, William B. 60
Knapp, E. M. , Mrs. 235

La Croix, Vaillant 234
Lamek, John E. 28
Landon, Charles W. 384
Laudon, Charles W. 166
Law, Andrew 20-21
Lawler, Vanett 339, 357, 358
Lawrence, Clara E. 201
Leach, Daniel 117
Leach, Ebenezer 89, 141
Leonard, P. J. 234
Lester, Ordelia A. 231, 247
Lincoln, L. P. 363
Lloyd, Thomas Spencer 135, 141
Loche, Elisha 102, 363
Lombard, Frank 75, 99, 106, 107, 363
Loomis, George B. 154, 186, 363
Lothrop, Thomas 136
Lutkin, Peter C. 31
Lyon, James Rev. 19, 20, 22
Lyon, Richard 10

Mach, I. F. 114
Maddy, Joseph E. 256
Mann, Horace 39, 46, 47, 53, 75, 76, 204, 205, 206, 399
Marsh, John B. 232, 247
Marsh, Mary 231
Martin, George H. 54, 59
Marvin, E. 186
Mason, Daniel Gregory 30, 57
Mason, Lowell, 20, 36, 39, 44, 48, 49, 50-58, 60, 62-63, 65, 66, 83, 88, 96, 99, 101, 103, 158, 180-182, 186, 190-192, 194-195, 197, 199, 200, 203, 204, 208-210, 224, 226, 233, 237, 336, 363, 366-367
Mason, Luther Whiting 82, 84, 99, 102, 119, 165-166, 197, 200, 363, 368, 384

McAllister, A. R. 256
McCarty, H. D. 158
MacDonald, Jeanette 269
McFadon, O. E. 160
McIntosh, R. M. 184
McLean, Levi 21
McLean, John B. 134, 231, 246
McVicar, P. 158
Mason, T. B. 92, 99, 363
Mather, Dr. Cotton 12
Mathews, W. S. B. 60
Meade, Walter S. 117, 363
Mellen, Prentiss 23
Merrick, John 23
Mershon, W. H. 239
Metcalf, Frank J. 60
Miller, L. B. 186
Mischka, Joseph 232, 233, 247
Moddie, H. A. 256
Monteith, John 216
Moore, Grace 269
Mower, Nathaniel L. 363
Mowery, William A. 60
Mulhern, James 94
Murray, James 114
Myers, Amelia B. 231, 247

Naef, Joseph N. 36
Nägeli, Hans 35, 50, 64, 191, 226
Newhall, Colonel 47
Nichols, Mamie E. 234
Nixon, Professor 91, 97, 182, 188
North, W. B. 251
Northern, P. W. , Mrs. 239
Norton, Alida 232, 247

Ogolevets, A. S. 271
Oliver, H. K. 363

Paige, W. H. 363
Paine, John Knowles 237
Palmer, A. Emerson 126
Palmer, A. S. 141
Parish, Ariel 218
Parker, Horatio 311
Parkhurst, John C. 231, 247
Parks, Mary E. 232, 247

Parson, D. 104
Patchin, Ira 112
Patterson, Samuel F. 145
Peabody, George 368
Pease, E. 102, 163
Peck, J. Bidwell 186
Pelham, Peter 15
Perkins, Charles C. 30
Perkins, H. S. 226, 363
Perkins, Theodore E. 187
Perkins, W. O. 186
Pestalozzi, 32, 44, 51, 62, 83, 93, 192, 195
Petrillo, James C. 314, 323, 334
Pfeiffer, M. T. 35, 50, 64, 191, 207
Phillips, P. 225-226
Pitts, Lilla Belle 359
Plagge, Chrisopher 99, 107, 175, 363
Platt, J. Evarts 237
Plowe, E. H. 238, 242
Powell, Joseph P. 102, 363
Pratt, Waldo Seldon 28
Presser, Theodore 166, 384
Propert, David 16

Raison, Melissa 124
Rale, Father Sebastian 9, 365
Ranger, Dr. 47
Raumer, Carl 36
Read, Jacob 20
Redington, J. C. O. 246
Rhoads, Joshua 253
Rice, John 15
Richard, Gabriel Father 366
Richardson, Merrill 183
Richman, Luther C. 323
Richmond, Elizabeth, 231, 246
Richmond, Libbie S. 231
Rickoff, Andrew J. 161-162, 212-213
Ritter, Frederick Louis 241
Roberts, Timothy L. 232, 247
Rolfing, R. C. 270
Roosevelt, President Franklin 339
Root, George F. 20, 53, 163, 186
Ross, James H. 60

Rote, W. C. 158
Russell, Skiner 15
Ryan, Thomas 57

Saba, Alois 272
Sather, John 19
Schang, F. C. 268
Schneider, Father 365
Scholastica, Sister 360
Schuman, William 327-331, 335
Seeger, Charles 340
Sewall, Dr. Samuel 20
Seybolt, Robert F. 29
Sharland, John B. 363
Sherwin, W. F. 187
Shotwell, John B. 30, 124
Sill, J. M. B. 233
Slayton, J. L. 99, 107, 175, 363
Smith, Edward 126
Smith, James F. O. 131, 217
Smith, Margaret 208
Smith, Samuel Francis 49, 60, 367
Snyder, D. D. 187
Sokoloff, Nikolai 263, 278
Soldan, Charles F. Rev. 135
Sousa, John Phillip 255
Southgate, Horatio 23
Steele, O. G. 90
Steele, William L. 125, 175
Stewart, N. Coe 166, 212-213, 363, 384
Stickney, John 19
Stock, Frederick 263
Stockwell, Thomas B. 127
Stowe, Rev. Calvin E. 36, 38, 45, 92, 103, 363
Studebaker, John W. 265, 278
Study, J. N. 154
Suffern, J. William 163
Sumner, Seth 99, 116, 363
Sunderman, Lloyd F. 28, 44, 56-57, 84, 96, 200, 209, 227, 248, 298, 304, 358
Swan, Timothy 20
Swan, William D. 73
Swarthout, Gladys 269
Sweet, S. N. 89, 182
Swift, E. Hargrove 277

Sykes, Charles M.   232, 246
Symmes, Thomas Rev.   13, 18,
  19

Tarbill, H. S.   154
Taylor, Deems   311
Thayer, A. W.   60
Thomas, Theodore   368
Thurston, Samuel   363
Tibbett, Lawrence   268
Tice, John H.   120
Thomas, G. A.   132
Tillinghast, William   99, 107,
  175, 187, 363
Tilton, Frederick W.   131
Tinker, M. S.   154, 363
Tomlins, William L.   351
Tower, David B.   74
Tremaine, C. M.   280, 283, 295
Trousdale, Leon   149
Trowbridge, Edward   124, 141,
  363
Tuckey, William   19
Tufts, John W.   226, 232, 368
Tufts, Rev.   12
Turpin, James   104

Umstattd, J. G.   304
Underwood, iii
Upham, J. Baxter   81, 87, 214

Van De Wall, William   273, 278
Van Meter, W. C.   99, 119, 363
Vining, G. V.   99, 113, 141, 363

Waghorne, John   14
Wainright, J. W.   256
Walker, W. K. Mrs.   232, 247
Walter, Rev. Thomas   12, 365
Warner, S. P.   107, 175
Warren, S. W.   187
Watson, John   23
Webb, George J.   20, 44, 50,
  56, 62-63, 65, 83, 96, 99,
  181, 190, 203, 208, 336, 363
Webster, C.   141
Webster, William C.   99, 363
Wells, W. H.   107, 108
Westhoff, F. H.   209-210
Whipple, M.   99

White, Jason   99, 116, 363
Whiting, M. Antoinette   232,
  247
Whitman, Mr.   106, 175
Whitman, Paul   263
Whitney, Clara S.   232, 246-
  247
Whittemore, Edward E.   109,
  155, 157, 175, 198, 363
Wightman, Joseph M.   86
Wilkie, Wendell   341
Wilkinson, Abbie, Mrs.   238
Willard, Emma, Mrs.   41
Williams, A. C.   187
Williams, Frankwood E.   272
Williams, Henry Jr.   74
Willis, Benjamin C.   347-348,
  358
Wilsey, Alvin   363
Wilson, J. Ormond   144
Winchester, President   48
Witherspoon, Herbert   272
Wood, Benjamin W.   117, 363
Woodbridge, William C.   36,
  39-40, 42-43, 50, 62, 64,
  88, 96, 99, 175, 180, 188,
  190, 200, 203, 207, 210,
  363, 367
Woodbury, Isaac   20

Yon, Pietro   271
Yont, Rose   249

Zinker, M. Z.   363
Zook, George F.   279, 283,
  304

SUBJECT INDEX

Academic Perspectives, 298
  Teacher qualifications, 298
After Civil War and school music, 150
After World War II, 305
  Concepts in the 1940's, 305
  Planning objectives, 305
  Problems, 306
American composers, 311
American Federation of Musicians, 315, 355
American opera, 310
  Composers, 311
  Life commission, 356
America's musical culture, 308
Attitude of Community music, 301

Bache, Dr. Alexander and music, 100
Bands, 256
Basic concepts in music education, 357
Bay Psalm Book, 10, 11
Beginnings of school music, 49, 88
  Henry Barnard and vocal music, 96
  In Pennsylvania, 93, 94
  Ives and Pennsylvania, 92
  Music refining man, 91
  Musical academies, 91
  Objections to music teaching, 89
  Opening speech, "On Vocal Music, " 88
  Singing in America, 7
  Spread of vocal music, 88
  State affiliations, 1933, 353
  T. B. Mason and Music, 92
  Teaching music in Pennsylvania, 93
  Teachers' Conventions, 96
  Western Literary Institute, 91
  Woodbridge champions music, 88

Bill of Rights, 344
Boston Academy of Music, 63
Boston and school music, 64
  Academy purposes, 64
  Annual music festivals, 78
  Early adoption, 65
  Encouraging beginnings, 72, 75
  Horace Mann, 75
  Instruction begins, 71
  Magna Charta, 62, 72
  Massachusetts a pioneer, 75, 76, 82
  Monitorial School, 65
  Mount Vernon School, 67
  Need for teachers, 68
  Objections against music, 70
  Pestalozzian principles, 65
  Resolutions advocating music, 70
  Secondary vocal music, 75
  Systematic instruction, 80, 81
  Training music teachers, 83
  Vocal classes, 62
  Woodbridge's speech, 62
Braille, Louis, 251
Brussels Conference on music education, 337, 338
Buisson, M. Ferdinand on music, 166
  Music in schools, 166
  Significance of study, 167

California-Western Conference, 353
"Canned Music" 260
Catholic elementary music, 9
  Early music education, 8
Chicago and early music, 105
  Achievements, 155
  1871 music report, 156
  Gilbert, N. , 105
  In-service training, 108
  Inspectors consider music, 105
  Lack of teachers, 108

Music spreads in Illinois, 105
Music teachers employed, 107
Primary and grammar music,
    108
Salaried music teacher, 106
Whitman and music, 106
Child's Bill of Rights, 355
Church music, 309
Cincinnati music, 102
    Affiliates with NFMC, 351
    1910 convention, 351
    School trustees, 102
    Vocal teachers, 102
Classroom teacher teaches
    music, 212
    Chicago examination, 220
    Chicago plan, 213, 214
    Early experiments, 213
    Evaluating instruction, 221
    Examination, 217, 218, 223
    Examinations for certification,
        222
    Instructional obstacles, 215
    Length of instructional period,
        216
    Textbooks and adoptions, 224-
        227
Cleveland meeting in 1908, 351
    Conjunction with NEA, 351
Code of Ethics, 323
College and Directors National
    Association, 342
College Band Directors, 355
    Constitution, 355
Collegiate status of music, 237
    Collegiate music spreads, 239
    First institution to give, 237
    Graduates, 301
    Growth in Normal Schools, 239
    Harvard University, 237
    Illinois Normal Schools and
        Universities, 239
    Music instruction, 239
    Sacred music study, 237
    Teacher placements, 301
    Use of books, 237
    Vocal and instrumental music,
        237
Colonial Music, 12
    Part singing, 12
    Private school music, 17

Singing by note, 18, 21
Singing lessons, 17
Uncultivated singing, 13
Committee on Instrumental
    Affairs, 257
    Music contests, 352
    Vocal Affairs, 257, 352
Community music, 276
Concert perfection, 298
Congregational singing, 7, 11
Connecticut and vocal music,
    118
    After the Civil War, 143
    Before the Civil War, 118
Contest movements, 257
Convention of Vocal Teachers,
    96, 180
Coolidge Administration and
    music, 339
Council of In-and About Clubs,
    343
    Past-Presidents, 342
    State Editors, 342
    State Supervisors of Music,
        342
Credit for Music, 257
Curriculum for the music
    teacher, 356
Curtailment of school services,
    283

Dark Ages of American music,
    22
Demobilization and music, 308
    G. I. Bill, 308
    Provisions of Bill, 308
Depression and music, 279
    Achievements, 299
    Commission on music study,
        280, 281
    Curtailments, 285
    Economic crises and music,
        279
    Economic-social values of
        music, 280
    "Frill" subject, 279
    Philosophy of era, 299
    Professional music, 299
Detroit National Meeting, 351
    High School Music Committee,
        351

Dickstein Bill, 266
Division of Music, Pan American Union, 340
Dual supervision, 211

Early adoptions of vocal music, 65
  Conventions in Ohio, 182
  Leaders, 361, 363
  Leaders in Normal Schools, 246
  Musical conventions, 26
  Music education, 27
  Protagonists, 99
  Singing books, 190
Early singing teachers, 20
  New Psalm Singer, 22
  Singing society, 21-23
Early singing societies, 23
  Choral organizations, 24
  Handel and Haydn Society, 24
  Importance of, 25
Economic crises and music, 279
  Influence on music, 202
Editorial Board of MENC, 342
Educational Conventions, 179
  Beginnings, 179
  First meetings, 180
  Singing-school convention, 179
  Vocal teachers, 180
Education of professional musicians, 337
Electric organs, 271
Examinations, 217-218, 223
Expansion of vocal music, 144
  In large cities, 144
  In white and colored schools, 144

Finals for state competitions, 354
First mass in New England, 9, 10
First National High School Chorus, 353
  Band contest, 352
  Supervisors orchestra, 352
Federal Government and music, 265
  U. S. Office of Education, 265
Federal Music Project, 262
  Achievements, 263

WPA cultural thrusts, 262
Foundations of Music, 1830-1840, 122
Franciscan music, 8, 10
"Frill" subject, 279
"Fuguing Tunes," 22

G. I. Bill, 308
Golden Anniversary, 350
  Commission, 356
  Observance, 356
"Good Neighbor" program, 354
Growth of music education, 361, 377
  Cities using special music teacher, 379
  Horace Mann and education, 399
  How music was being taught, 385
  Music taught by regular teachers, 390
  Music Teachers' National Association Survey, 384
  Secondary music in 1874, 383
  Science, of music, 377
  Taught by special and regular teachers, 395
  Taught by special teachers, 395
  U. S. Commissioner reports, 378
  Where music is not taught, 386
Growth of Music Educators National Conference, 342
  Interscholastic music activities, 342

Hammond organ, 271
Handel and Haydn Society, 24
Harvard University, 237
Higher education and music, 230
  Early instructors in New York State, 231
  Normal Schools, 230
  Normal School music spreads, 233
Hoeppel Bill, 267
Hofwyl Institute, 33

Illinois music, 110
    Jacksonville and Galesburg, 110
Illinois Survey of High Schools,
    293, 295
    Curtailments, 296
    1934 report, 295
    Social values of, 295
Indianapolis meeting, 351
Indians and music, 8, 9
Industrial fatigue, 275
    Music's roll in, 275
Institute movement and music,
    182
    Rhode Island Institute, 182
Inter-American music, 339
International Society for Music,
    337, 338, 343

Journal of Research, 342, 356

Kentucky and early music, 118
    Luther Whiting Mason, 119
    Secondary school music, 119
Keokuk, Iowa meeting, 350
    First meeting, 337
Keyboard business, 269
    Growth, 270

Latin American musicians, 340
Lay participation, 274
    Chicagoland Festival, 274
Legislation and music, 266
    American Guild of Musical
        Artists, 268
    California takes steps, 266
    Dickstein Bill, 266
    Hoeppel Bill, 267
Library of Congress, Music
    Division, 354
Lincoln, Nebraska, National
    Meeting, 351
    Membership, 351
    Violin class teaching, 351
"Lining Out" method, 17
Lowest ebb for membership,
    MENC 353

Magna Charta of Music, 72
Mann and vocal music, 75
    Massachusetts Board of
        Education, 399

Maryland, early music, 117
Mason, Lowell, 46
    Achievements, 46
    Biography, 46
    Boston Academy of Music, 50
    Contributions, 54
    Dismissed, 53
    First Supervisor of Music,
        46
    Gratuitous teaching, 51
    Handel and Haydn Society, 47
    Mason and Webb, 50
    Mason and Woodbridge, 50
    Problems as supervisor, 52
    Publications, 55
    Visits Europe, 51
Mason, Luther Whiting, 103
    Comes to California, 165
    In Boston, 103
    In Cleveland, 103
    Primary music, 103
Mechanical instrument inno-
    vations, 260, 271
    "Canned Music," 260
    Effects of depression, 260
    Hammond organ, 271
    Quarter toned piano, 272
Method in music education, 190
    Boston Academy, 190
    Chicago and school music, 198
    Early achievements, 199
    Early singing books, 190
    European influence, 190, 191
    Exercise plan, 197
    Mason on teaching, 194
    Mason's Manual, 191, 192, 193
    Pestalozzian influences, 191
    Rudimentists and combination-
        ists, 195
    Woodbridge, Ives, and Lowell
        Mason, 190
Minneapolis National, 1914, 351
    Journal authorized, 351
    Members, 351
    Report on Community Songs,
        351
Music Education Exhibitors
    Association, 356
    "Wartime" period, 354
Music education in Normal
    Schools and Colleges, 240

For the blind, 253
For physically handicapped,
  251
Henry Barnard, 251
Louis Braille, 251
Music Education's Cultural
  Contributions, 344
Bill of Rights, 343, 344
Intellectual, 346
Social, 346
Spiritual, 347
Music Educator's Journal, 342
Music Educators National
  Conference, 323, 336
Code of Ethics, 323
Declaration of Faith, 350
Division Boards, 354
Moves Chicago office, 355
Professional musician, 323
Research Council, 342
State affiliation, 353
Student membership, 342
Music for every child, 352
Music in American cultural Life,
  261
Art museums, 310
Higher education, 261
The Home, 309
Illinois High Schools, 294
Municipal music, 308
New Orleans, 119
Status of Musical Growth, 311,
  312, 318
Summer camps, 310
Music in American Education,
  355
American Life Commissions,
  343
American Unity, 354
Advancement Program, 355
During Civil War, 154
Educator musician, 320
Educators in U. S. 336
For elementary grades, 352
For exceptional children, 343
Growth in the south, 147
In industry, 316
Industry council, 342
Instruction in Indiana, 154
International relations, 343

Massachusetts, 75
Monitorial School, 65
New Jersey, 118
Normal Schools, 239, 246
Pennsylvania, 93
Prior to Civil War, 100
School and community, 337
Music Supervisors' National
  Conference, 336
First Chorus, 351
1917 meeting, 351
Organized, 350
Violin class demonstration,
  351
World War I effort, 351
Music taught by special and
  and ordinary teachers, 396
By special teachers, 395
Usual teaching force, 390
Music taught in Missouri, 120
In St. Louis, 120
In Wisconsin, 120
Music teacher qualifications,
  288
Depression era, 288, 289, 298
Music teaching in Normal Schools,
  236
In Tennessee, 120
Music Therapy, 272
Early beginnings, 272
Experiments and conclusions,
  273
Williams and Van De Wall,
  272, 273

National Association of College
  Wind and Percussion instruct-
  ors, 342
National, Divisional, and State
  Units, 337
National Association of Secondary
  School Principals, 355
National Bureau for the advance-
  ment of music, 352
National Education Association,
  354
Invites, 354
National Education Council, 1918,
  352
  Eastern Music Supervisors
  Conference, 352

National High School Orchestra,
352
National Interscholastic Music
Activities, 356
National Music Education Society,
313
Major concerns, 313
Music Convention of Boston,
53
Orchestra contest, 257
National School music contest,
257, 258
National Teachers' convention,
183
NSBOVA and school compe-
titions, 354
Piano manufacturers, 270
School Vocal Association, 353
New era for choral music, 353
New York State School Music,
134
Buffalo music makes strides,
134, 136
Early agitation, 111
Early champions, 141
Early music education, 139
Evidences of deemphasis, 112
Music in 1843, 111
Normal schools offer music,
134
Primary music, 114
Rochester exerts leadership,
114
Schenectady County, 112
Steady development of school
music, 135
Vocal music on the increase,
135
Nordic music teachers, 339
Normal Musical Institute, 185
Impact on early music, 186
Institute conductors, 186
Their contributions, 188
Triumvirate of Institute
conductors, 186
North Central Conference first
meeting, 352

Objections against vocal music,
70
Official adoption of school music,
60

Ohio and school music:
160
Charles Aiken, 101, 103
Cincinnati music teaching, 102
Cleveland teaching staff, 161
Lowell Mason in Cleveland,
103
Regular teacher as music
teacher, 161
Successes, 162
Teachers in Cincinnati, 102
Triad magazine, 353
Old Style Singing, 18
Old world musical culture, 7
Opposition to singing, 13
Optional instruction, 215
Organ instruction in schools,
343

Pan American Union, 340
Pestalozzianism, 32
Effects on American music,
44
Hofwyl Institute, 32
On vocal music, 34
Pfeiffer and Nägeli, 35
Principles of teaching, 65
Theory of instruction, 35
Pfeiffer and Nägeli, 35
Philadelphia and early music,
100
Piano instruction in schools, 343
Pioneers in music education,
361, 371
Pittsburgh National meeting,
1915, 351
Community music, 351
"Lobby sings" 351
Places where music is not
taught, 386
Post-Civil War and vocal music,
159
Eastern cities increase music,
129
Embryonic developments in
south, 129
Expansion, 129
Music in Maryland, 133
Music in Providence, 130
Music in Rhode Island, 131
Music suffers setback, 129

Primary music makes progress, 134
Post-World War I, 275
    Achievements, 276
    Credit for music, 257
    Early bands, 256
    Music during twentieth century, 255
    Music education, 255
Pre-Civil War vocal music, 32
Primary music, 103, 116
Professional Antipathy, 333
    Honesty, 297
    Musicians, 299, 323
Professional Musician, 314, 324
    Artist musician, 317
    Challenge to music educator, 324
    Critical point of view, 326
    Music critic, 331
    Place in society, 314
    Plight of Professionals, 315
    Post-World War II status, 315
    School music performance, 328
    William Schuman and music educator, 326
Professional organization of music educators, 336
    Brussels Conference on music education, 338
    Brussels and music education, 337
    Coolidge administration, 339
    Educators in the U. S. 336
    Inter-American and Inter-Hemisphere, 339
    International society for, 337
    Latin America, 340
    Meeting at Keokuk, 337
    MENC, 336
    Music Supervisors' National Conference, 336
    National and divisional units, 337
    Psalm singing, 17
    Psalterium Americanum, 12
    UNESCO, 337

Radio broadcasting, 271
    School of the Air, 271
Radio in education, 352

Rhode Island and Music Education, 116
    Primary and grammar music, 116
Rhode Island Institute of Instruction, 182
Rochester, New York, National Meeting, 1913, 351
    Community Singing Committee, 351
    High School orchestras, 351
Roosevelt, President and cultural relations, 339

Salary reductions, 286, 290
    North Dakota, 286
    Results, 292
    Salary studies, 291
    South Dakota, 287
Scandinavian union for music education, 338
School of the Air, 271
School music educator, 319
    Code of Ethics, 321
    Plight of Professional, 323
    Professional musician, 319
School Music in Washington, D. C., 117
Secondary school vocal and instrumental music, 383
    In 1874, 383
Secularization of church service, 18
"Service Version," National Anthem, 352
Significant developments, 27
    Early music education, 27
    Events, 1603-1895, 361, 365, 374
    Music Supervisors' National Conference, 350
Singing by note, 18, 21
Singing school, 19
Singing school convention, 179
Social and Economic Reconstruction, 150
"Song of Democracy," 357
Southern Conference for Music Education, 352
Special music teacher prior to 1880, 379
Southeast Asia Regional meeting, 338

State Advisory Committees
established, 1920, 352
State Music Education Periodicals
and Editors, 343

States offering school music:
Alabama, 149
California, 164, 165
Drafts Bill on Educational
Organization, 122
Delaware, 146
Florida, 149
Georgia, 149
Illinois, 158
Indiana, 122
Iowa, 122
Kansas, 158
Louisiana, 148
Michigan, 121
Ann Arbor, Battle Creek,
Flint, Kalamazoo, Lansing,
Monroe, 121, 163
Missouri, St. Louis, 120
Nevada, 164
New Hampshire, 146
New Jersey, Perth Amboy, 146
Pennsylvania, 144
South Carolina, 148
Tennessee, Nashville, 149
Texas, 150
Territory of Washington, 165
Vermont, 146
Wisconsin, 159
State Presidents National
Assembly, 342, 355
State Supervisors of Music, 343
String Instruction, 343
Student membership plan, 355
Superstition and music, 26
Supervision and instruction of
music, 211
Experiments in Cleveland, 212
Experiments with dual super-
vision, 211
Hosea Holt reports on, 214
Problems, 211
Symphonic Band instrumentation,
353
Symphony orchestra movement,
259
Growth, 259

Teacher Institutes in Rhode
Island, 182
Movement spreads, 182, 183
Teachers' Conventions, 96, 181
Early Conventions in Ohio,
182
In the U. S. 184
The Lyceum, 181
Support, singing, 185
Vermont Convention, 181
Western Literary Institute,
182
Teachers of School Music, 330
"These Things We Believe," 349
Twenty-fifth Anniversary
Convention, 1932, 353

UNESCO and Music Education,
337
U. S. Commissioner Reports,
378

Values of Music Education, 202
Arguments against, 202
Arguments for, 209
Association for the Advance-
ment of Education, 206
Church and school music, 208
Dr. Bache on European
music, 206
Early advocates of, 203
Horace Mann on, 204
Woodbridge on vocal music,
207
Various methods of teaching
music reading, 399

W. P. A. Cultural Thrusts, 262
Wendell Wilkie, 341
Western Literary Institute, 91
Widespread Development of
Music, 123
Willis and music education, 347
Woodbridge, William C. and 36
American Annals of Education,
44
Boston Academy of Music, 36
Contributions, 43
Elam Ives, Jr., 36
First Champion, 39
Meets Pestalozzi, 42

European tour, 39
World War II, 276
   Pre World War II, 276
   Community music, 276